About the Authors

James R. Lewis is a world recognized authority on nontraditional religious movements, and is the editor of the only academic journal dedicated to alternative religions. He is currently chairman of the Department of Religious Studies at the World University of America.

Professor Lewis is the author of *The Astrology Encyclopedia, The Encyclopedia of Afterlife Beliefs and Phenomena* and *The Dream Encyclopedia*. He has also contributed to the *New Age Almanac, Religious Leaders of America,* and *The Churches Speak* series.

Evelyn Dorothy Oliver is founder and executive director of the Association of World Academics for Religious Education (AWARE), a religious amnesty organization that works to overcome religious and cultural prejudices. She holds a doctorate in divinity and is internationally known for her more than twenty years work as a business and personal relationships counselor.

ANGELS
A to Z

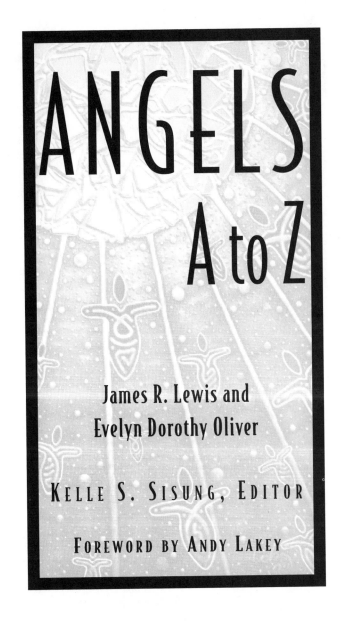

ANGELS
A to Z

James R. Lewis and
Evelyn Dorothy Oliver

KELLE S. SISUNG, EDITOR

FOREWORD BY ANDY LAKEY

VISIBLE
INK
PRESS

DETROIT   NEW YORK   TORONTO   WASHINGTON, D.C.

ANGELS
A to Z

Copyright © 1996 by Visible Ink Press™

Library of Congress Cataloging-in-Publication Data

Lewis, James R.
      Angels A to Z/James R. Lewis, Evelyn Dorothy Oliver; Kelle Sisung, ed.
         p. cm.
      Includes bibliographical references and index.
      ISBN 0-7876-0652-9 (soft)—-ISBN 0-7876-0489-5 (hard)
      1. Angels—-Dictionaries. I. Oliver, Evelyn Dorothy. II. Sisung, Kelle. III. Title.
BL477.l45 1996
291.2'15'03—-dc20

                               95-35403
                                   CIP

Front cover illustration: #840 by Andy Lakey, 1994; original work 6 x 5. Appears courtesy of the artist.

Published by Visible Ink Press™
a division of Gale Research Inc.
835 Penobscot Building
Detroit, MI 48226-4094

Visible Ink Press is a trademark of Gale Research Inc.

Most Visible Ink Press™ books are available at special quantity discounts when purchased in bulk by corporations, organizations, or groups. Customized printings, special imprints, messages, and excerpts can be produced to meet your needs. For more information, contact Special Markets Manager, Visible Ink Press, 835 Penobscot Bldg., Detroit, MI 48226. Or call 1-800-776-6265.

Art Director: Mary Krzewinski
Developmental Editor: Kelle Sisung

Jim and I lovingly dedicate this book to my three daughters:

Nicole Suzanne Ruskell (Nikki), truly an angel embodied. Your soulful beauty expresses a depth of love, wisdom, and healing far beyond your earthly years.

Doreen Elyse Berman (Doey), impeccable beauty, insightful wit, and creative genius. May your achievements as a producer fulfill your dreams of bringing love and peace into the world.

Melenie Anne Llorin (Sunshine), the beauty of a movie star. Your brilliant language skills and creativity make heads turn wherever you go. May you, too, fulfill your dreams of writing books.

I thank each of you for choosing me to be your mother and accepting Jim as a "dad."

Also to Jim's parents, Bea and Jim Lewis, for always being there for us and loving me as a daughter. By your example, you have taught each of us how to be loving supportive parents. God bless you Mom and Dad.

To my Mom and Dad, Mae and Robert Oliver, who are with the angels—I love you and miss you.

Lastly, to the children of the world and their families, Jim and I dedicate this book. The power to change this fearful, painful world into a loving protective place where everyone's hopes and dreams can be realized lies in the hands of the children. Angels provide the inspiration.

—EDO

ALSO FROM VISIBLE INK PRESS

Encyclopedia of Afterlife Beliefs and Phenomena

What lies beyond? Is communication with the dead possible? This compelling guide addresses questions that have endured since the dawn of humankind, and reports on such recent trends as the increase in near-death experiences due to the use of defibrillators. Nearly 250 entries, presented in A-to-Z order, discuss ancient and modern theories, various cultural and religious belief systems, terms such as channeling and *déjà vu*, and prominent figures and associations. Foreword by Dr. Raymond Moody. By James R. Lewis, 7.25" x 9.25" paperback, 444 pages, 75 illustrations, ISBN 0-7876-0288-4.

The Dream Encyclopedia

Are our dreams significant? Do they, as some believe, hold healing powers? Can they spark creative inspiration? Warn us of things to come? This fascinating guide explores 250 dream-related topics, from astral projection to vision quests, clearly illustrating how dreams influence culture, religion, history, art, literature, and our personal lives. By James R. Lewis, 7.25" x 9.25" paperback, 438 pages, 60 illustrations, ISBN 0-7876-0156-X.

New Age Almanac

An expert's look at the personalities and significant events that have shaped and are shaping our future, from alternative medicine to "green" consumerism. By J. Gordon Melton, 6" x 9" paperback, 495 pages, illustrations, ISBN 0-8103-9402-2.

The Vampire Book:
The Encyclopedia of the Undead

This definitive vampire guide will satisfy your thirst for vampire lore and legends from around the world with unprecedented coverage of the historical, literary, mythological, biographical, and popular aspects of one of the world's most mesmerizing subjects. Foreword by Martin V. Riccardo, founder of the Vampire Studies Network. By J. Gordon Melton, 7.25" x 9.25" paperback, 792 pages, 110 illustrations, ISBN 0-8103-2295-1.

The Astrology Encyclopedia

To meet the needs of the curious, the committed, and the casual reader, this A-to-Z compilation of more than 750 essays and articles covers technical, historical, and popular aspects of astrology. By James R. Lewis, 7.25" x 9.25" paperback, 630 pages, 75 illustrations, ISBN 0-8103-9460-X.

Contents

A 1

Abaddon Abdiel Abraham Abraxas
Acts of the Holy Angels Adam Adramelechk Aeon
Africa Ahriman (Angra Mainyu) Ancient of Days
Anderson, Joan Wester Angel Clothed in a Cloud
Angel of Death Angel of Fire Angel of the Furnace
Angel of the Lord Angel of Peace Angel of the Presence
Angel Stores Angel Times Angelica Angelico, Fra
Angelolatry Angelology Angelophany Angelos Angels
Angels of Mons Angels of Punishment
Angels of the Seven Churches Angel's Trumpet
AngelWatch Newsletter Apocalypse
Apocrypha and Pseudepigrapha Appolion Apsara
Archangels Architecture, Angels in Archon Ariel
Art, Angels in Asmodeus Astaroth
Astrology, Rulership, and Angels Asura Azazel

B 65

Balaam Battlefield, Angels on the Beelzebub Beliar
Beliel Belphegor The Bible, Angels in Birds Blake,
William Bodhisattva Bodies of Angels Bogey-Man
Book of Jubilees Brownies Buddhism Burnham,
Sophy

C 87

Camael Channeling Cherubim
Cherubim and Seraphim Society Choirs Christianity
Clarence Oddbody Collective Unconscious
Color, Angels and Communication with Angels
Constellations Contemporary Angel Artists
Cottingley Fairies Cupid

D 115

Daemon (Daimon) Dante Alighieri Day, Leonard C.

Days of the Week (Angels and the) Dead Sea Scrolls
Deathbed Visions Demiurge Devas Devidasi
Devils, Demons, and Fallen Angels Dionysius the Areopagite
Directions (Angels of the) Djibril Dominions (Domina-
tions) Dragons Dubbiel Dwarfs

E 141

Egypt Elementals Elijah Elohim Elves
Enoch, Book of Eros Eschatology Ethnarchs
Evangelical Authors Evolution of Angels Ezekiel

F 155

Fairies The Fall of the Angels Familiars Final Judgment
Findhorn First Church of Angels Fravashi
Freeman, Eileen Elias Fylgir

G 169

Gabriel Gandharvas Gender of Angels Ghosts and Angels
Giotto Gnomes Gnosticism Goblins Graham, Billy
Greece (Ancient) Gremlins Guardian Angels
Guardian Spirit (Shaman; Spirit Guide; Tutelary Spirit)

H 195

Hadraniel Hafaza Halo (Nimbus; Aureole)
Harps and the Music of Heaven Harut and Marut
Hayyoth Healing, Angelic Heaven and Hell Hermes
Hierarchy of Angels Hinduism Hocus Pocus
Holidays, Angel Holy Immortals (Amesha Spentas)
Holy Spirit (Holy Ghost) Houri Hours (Angels of the)
Hypnos

Foreword

Angels have always been an important part of my life, constantly providing me with a steady stream of faith, hope, knowledge, light, and love. Ever since I was a child, I was haunted by the sense that something or someone was always with me—an invisible guardian that followed and protected me.

I was four years old when my beloved grandfather tragically committed suicide. The devastation I felt was unbearable. In the midst of this time of great sadness, I realized Grandpa was in a better place and that he was with the angels.

Angels gave me a sense of comfort that put my heart at peace. As I progressed through different stages of my life, I felt Grandpa with me. His energy was especially strong during four different near-death experiences, the last occurring in 1986 when I was twenty-six.

I overdosed on cocaine and knew I was dying. I stumbled through the front door of my home, and made it to the shower where I thought I could halt the dying process. In this impossible state of consciousness, I recall a sense of sobriety as I pleaded for God to forgive my sins and take me to heaven. I desperately vowed commitment to serve humankind if he would restore my health.

With time running out, I begged repeatedly to live, to stay in this world. I began to feel a response. A movement started at my feet. Seven beings swirled up and enveloped me, subtly recreating me. My body dematerialized as it was lifted to another place. The images I paint now are echoes of this experience.

I awoke in the hospital; I.V.'s were in my arms and my throat was sore from having my stomach pumped. How did I get there? A friend of mine who never comes to see me had felt the need to drop in on me at home unannounced. Finding the door open, he walked through the living room, down the hall, directly to the shower where my experience had just started to enter a stage of weightlessness. In his reality, I was motionless and lying on the floor, the shower water still running. In my art, I keep recalling this period of infinite existence—this window into a timeless dimension.

This was the turning point of my life. The angels were so powerful and touched me so profoundly that the impact of the experience completely changed all aspects of my existence. I deeply felt and appreciated my opportunity to be alive. The angels also helped me look away from myself and toward the needs of humankind. I developed a burning desire to give to others—a strong urge to channel this new-found celestial love. I knew I had to create through the medium of painting.

At first, however, I experienced frustration and confusion. I didn't know what to do with this angelic information, so I sketched angels as I remembered seeing them. I realized that just because I had been fortunate enough to encounter angels didn't mean I had instant clarification. But the deeply instilled need to create the angels I had seen persisted. By constantly sketching them, I discovered a deeper magnification and connection with the original experience. Unfortunately, I still didn't know what direction I should follow.

My second experience with angels occurred in 1990. This time I gained the focus that was missing from my earlier encounters. In this experience, a ball of light was projected at my forehead. Three messengers then appeared and outlined the preliminary schedule according to which I was to paint two thousand angels between then and the year 2000. This vision of what I must do was clear and precise. I took action and began creating the first of two thousand angel paintings.

Angels encourage us by guiding us onto a path that will lead to happiness and hope. The key to utilizing the angelic energy is to take action in one's life. Angels work best and most effectively when faith and action are applied as a form of following through on inspiration. There is indeed something bigger out there. The following pages of *Angels A to Z* provide guidance and information for all. Remember to follow the lead of angels, and be kind and good to everyone.

—Andy Lakey

Introduction

> Not since the Middle Ages, when angels were thought to oversee all things material, have these winged beings loomed so large in the popular imagination.
>
> —*New Age Journal,* April 1994

A ngel books, angel jewelry, angel newsletters, specialized angel stores, and even an angel cover story in *Time* magazine (December 1993)— clearly we are in the midst of a national phenomenon, a steadily rising interest in celestial beings that is not just confined to the New Age movement. As a statistical indication of increasing interest, a 1992 Gallup Youth poll found that 76% of American teenagers believed in angels—up from 64% in 1978. And the interest in angels is not confined to New Age enthusiasts; Frank E. Peretti, an evangelical author with a marked anti-New Age message, has written two runaway best-sellers, *This Present Darkness* and *Piercing the Darkness,* which feature battles between celestial angels and fallen angels. (His upcoming novel, *The Oath,* is expected to be equally well received.) These works reflect the increasing fascination with angels among traditional Christians.

The appeal of angels is easy to understand. In an age of uncertainty and upheaval, it is extremely comforting to believe in the existence of spiritual beings whose principal employment is the protection and encouragement of human beings. In the words of Ps. 91:10–11:

> He will give his angels charge of you,
> To guard you in all your ways.
> On their hands they will bear you up,
> Lest you dash you foot against a stone.

In point of fact, far and away the great majority of contemporary angel books focus on stories in which people are helped by angels in some way. Typical of this literature is the kind of encounter reported in Eileen Elias Freeman's book, *Angelic Healing*. Freeman relates that she had an encounter with an angel in the guise of a hospital nurse. On the night before Eileen's cancer surgery, she was unable to sleep. She prayed and received the sacraments of the church, but she was still crying into her pillow and shaking with fear. Suddenly, a voice next to her said, "Can I help?" She felt a warm hand on her shoulder. She turned over to see a nurse sitting by her bed. Eileen told him she was scared, that she would never get through her illness, that she would die, and that the cancer had already spread too far.

"Get a hold of yourself," the man said quietly. "None of what you say is true. There's a purpose in everything that happens. You just have to get through this and learn from it. Whatever happens, God won't abandon you. Don't give in to the fear."

Eileen looked at the man in amazement, as this was the same message she had been receiving in response to her prayers. She asked him if he was an angel. His response was, "I suppose I am. After all, we nurses are sometimes called 'angels of mercy,' aren't we? You'd better try to get some sleep or your real angel will be put out." Eileen closed her eyes for an instant, and when she reopened them the nurse was gone. In his place was a luminous glow, which she perceived only for a moment before it faded away. If the bulging shelves of angel books that one can find in almost any bookstore are an accurate indication, there is a significant portion of the population that cannot get enough of these miracle stories.

Angels are the traditional intermediary spiritual beings between god and humanity. They are defined by their function of message-bearer, although this role does not exhaust their activities. Originating in Zoroastrianism, they are particularly (though not exclusively) found in the Western family of religions—Judaism, Christianity, and Islam—where God is conceived as being so elevated he does not intervene directly in the world. Angels are often pictured delivering messages to mortals or in other ways carrying out God's will. Many religions contain notions of guardian angels, who are angels assigned to watch over and protect individuals.

Angels are traditionally pictured cohabiting heaven with deceased human beings, and in the contemporary period it is not uncommon to find confusion between angels and ghosts. Thus, for example, people often equate guardian angels with the spirits of departed human individuals. Popular movies even portray the deceased with wings—an attribute formerly reserved for angels. These portrayals fly in the face of the traditional understanding of angels as a separate order of creation. They were never (with a few legendary exceptions) incarnated in human bodies. Another contrast between traditional and contemporary angelology is that the focus of most traditional angel lore was on the activity of God through his angels, whereas in the contemporary period God almost seems to have been eclipsed by his angels. Let us, by way of contrast, examine a more traditional miracle story, the apostle Peter's rescue by an angel in the Book of Acts.

The setting for this tale is the persecution of the early Christian Church in Palestine. Herod the king (grandson of Herod the Great), appointed to his position by Rome, executed James, the brother of John, and imprisoned Peter with the intent of executing him as soon as the Feast of Unleavened Bread had passed. Aware of Peter's impending fate, the community prayed for his deliverance:

> Peter was kept in prison; but earnest prayer for him was made to God by the church. The very night when Herod was about to bring him out, Peter was sleeping between two soldiers, bound with two chains, and sentries before the door were guarding the prison; and behold an angel of the Lord appeared, and a light shone in the cell; and he struck Peter on the side and woke him, saying, "Get up quickly." (Acts 12:5–7)

The first point to note is that the Christian God is one who responds to prayer. In this case, he sends an angel to answer the prayers of the Christian community. This is consistent with the traditional Hebrew understanding of a regal divinity who sends angels out from the court of heaven to deliver his messages to his people. The angel directs Peter to dress and follow him out of prison. Peter, half asleep, thinks he is in a dream.

> When they had passed the second guard, they came to the iron gate leading into the city. It opened to them of its own accord, and they went out and passed on through one street; and immediately the angel left him. (Acts 12:10)

The larger theme—God intervening in human affairs to rescue a captive—is entirely consistent with tradition, an echo of God's rescue of his people from their captivity in Egypt and Babylon. It is also significant to note that the angel appears rather abruptly, accomplishes the task at hand, and then departs as soon as the task is complete. This mode of action tends to deemphasize the importance of the angel and gives the glory to God. In this instance, when relating the story of his rescue to other believers, Peter "described to them how the Lord had brought him out of the prison" (Acts 12:17), thus focusing attention—and particularly praise—on God rather than on his agent.

As messengers of God (the Greek word *angelos* means "messenger"), angels are particularly characteristic of the great monotheistic faiths of the West. This is the case because in polytheistic systems, gods and goddesses often arrive in person to deliver messages. Religious authorities in the monotheistic traditions, fearing a return to polytheism, have often expressed concern over excessive focus on angels. The historical example of Zoroastrianism is instructive in this regard.

Angels in the proper sense first emerged in Zoroastrianism, the first true monotheism. In the history of religions, Zoroastrianism, founded in Persia by the prophet Zoroaster in about 1000 B.C., has been an unusually fruitful faith, exercising an influence on the doctrines of other religions disproportionate to its size. Angels are but one part of Zoroastrianism's legacy to its sister/brother religions, Judaism, Christianity, and Islam.

While it is difficult to reconstruct the details of Zoroaster's original message, it appears that his intention was to reform the preexisting religion of the area rather than to create a new religion. It is also clear that Zoroaster preached the centrality of one god, Ahura Mazda. The other divinities of the earlier pantheon were reduced to the status of mere agents of the supreme deity—i.e., to the status of angels. Also, some of the gods of the original pantheon were transformed into demons, although this transformation may have been due to factors completely independent of the reforming activities of Zoroaster. As Zoroastrianism developed, the number of celestial beings multiplied, leading some observers to remark that the old polytheistic system had unwittingly been revived in the later stages of this religious tradition.

Judaism was similarly threatened by an overemphasis on angels. The Jewish religion is a complex tradition that has experienced a number of important transformations over the millennia. While most accounts of angel history attribute Zoroastrianism as the first religion to have true angels, attendant spiritual beings served Yahweh from the very first biblical narratives, long before Persian religious ideas began to exercise an influence on Judaism.

The biblical God sends out his angels to carry messages, to protect, and to destroy. They also have the function of constantly offering praise to Yahweh. Only in the latter books of Hebrew Scriptures (the Christian Old Testament) do angels begin to do more than simply worship God and carry out his orders, as when the angel of the Lord in the book of Zechariah intercedes with God on behalf of Israel (1:12–13). The latter books of the Hebrew Bible, particularly the book of Daniel, reflect the distinct influence of Persian angelology. As a result of several centuries of Persian control of the Middle East, Jews were brought into contact with Zoroastrian religious ideas. Of decisive significance in view of later developments in Judaism's sister/brother religions, Christianity and Islam, was Zoroaster's doctrine of the ongoing struggle between good and evil—a dualistic world view that included war between good and evil angels. Earlier Hebrews had not postulated an evil counter-divinity or devil opposed to Yahweh. In the book of Job, for example, Satan is a member of the heavenly court whose role appears to be that of a prosecuting attorney rather than that of an enemy of God.

In order to explain the origin of a devil in the traditionally non-dualistic faith of Judaism, new stories were developed, though they were never incorporated into Scripture. These extra-biblical writings explained evil in terms of the revolt and/or disobedience of God's angels. In one story, Satan declared himself as great as God and led a rebellion of angels against the celestial order. Defeated, he and his followers were tossed out of heaven, and subsequently have continued to war against God by attempting to ruin the Earth, God's creation. A less well-known, alternative narrative, which is best preserved in the apocryphal Book of Enoch, is that a group of angels lusted after mortal females, and Fell after leaving their heavenly abode and copulating with them.

In addition to the notion of an ongoing spiritual warfare between good and evil, Judaism also adopted the idea of a final judgment and resurrection of the dead at the end of time—a time when righteousness would finally triumph. This happy ending would be preceded by an all out war in which the angels of God would defeat Satan and his fallen angels once and for all. These notions particularly characterized the thought world of the Essenes, a small Jewish sect whose surviving writings, the Dead Sea Scrolls, are characterized by an apocalyptic, endtime emphasis that pictured a supernatural redemption at the hand of God and his angels.

Beyond the Hebrew Bible, a number of important bodies of Jewish religious literature further developed notions about angels. The most important of these are the Talmud. While attempting to tone down what they viewed as an unhealthy overemphasis on angels, the talmudic rabbis simultaneously recognized such post-biblical innovations as the division between angels of peace and evil angels. The talmudic literature also adds much detailed speculation on the nature of angels without changing the fundamental notions that had been developed earlier. Much the same can be said about Jewish mystical speculations, such as those contained in the Zohar.

Christianity inherited its angels from Judaism. Angels eventually came to be so important that some of the early Church councils worried that devotion to angels was eclipsing devotion to God. Medieval Christian angelology moved in two directions. The first is characterized by a fascination with the personalities of specific angelic figures. Such writings as the Books of Enoch, the Testament of Abraham, and the Apocalypse of Elijah describe the functions of angels named Uriel, Raguel, Sariel, Jeremiel, and others who serve alongside Gabriel, Michael, and Raphael. Christian non-canonical writings, especially the Nag Hammadi texts, continue and elaborate upon this trend. The second tradition of Medieval angelology is primarily a philosophical one, focusing on such issues as the corporeality or non-corporeality of angels, and the precise ordering of the hierarchy of angels.

Many of the conventions of angelic representation were established in the Medieval period. In other words, certain artistic conventions allow one to immediately recognize pictures of angels—e.g., human figures with wings, white robes, halos, and sometimes harps. Wings signify that angels are celestial beings, white robes and halos symbolize purity and holiness, and harps indicate that angels sing God's praises.

The last major monotheistic tradition is Islam, a religion founded in Arabia by the Prophet Muhammad in the year 622 A.D. *Mala'ika* is the Islamic term for angel and like the Greek word *angelos,* means *messenger.*

Angels are regularly mentioned in the Islamic holy book, the Koran. Some, such as Djibril (Gabriel) and Mikhail (Michael), are also found in Judaism and Christianity. Djibril and Mikhail are two of four important Muslim archangels. The other two are Izra'il and Israfil. Djibril (often spelled Jibril) is of especial importance in Islam. It was Djibril who originally contacted The Prophet and who dictated the Koran to him. Djibril was also the angel who conducted Muhammad to heaven during the Night Journey. In some areas of the world, angels, many with unusual names, play an important role in popular Islam. These practices may be rooted in the pre-Islamic religions of those areas.

As messengers of god, angels are most properly denizens of the monotheistic faiths. Nevertheless, it is not necessarily absurd to seek angel-like beings in non-monotheistic religions. As part of their efforts to discover parallel beings in other religions, contemporary authors often mention certain Hindu/Buddhist spirits/demi-gods, such as devas, apsaras, and gandharvas, as well as such messenger divinities of the classical Greek and Roman pantheon as Eros, Hermes, and Nike. These latter deities are particularly appropriate for comparison as they contributed iconographically to Christian angels.

Another class of beings that invites comparison with angels are fairies. Fairies are a kind of nature spirit that, under different names and guises, are found in every part of the world. Often pictured as small humanoid beings with wings, they present the appearance of mini-angels. Unlike angels, however, fairies have always had a mixed relationship with humanity. As nature spirits concerned with natural processes, they do not normally seek out human contact, but, when they take a liking to someone, they will help her or him in various ways. On the other hand, they have also been pictured as mischievous beings who enjoy playing pranks on people. Because the Church did not have room in its world view for morally neutral spiritual beings who were neither good nor evil, fairies were rejected as agents of Satan. Traditional religious authorities were thus responsible for driving a wedge between fairies and angels, and the rather obvious family resemblance between them has been obscured ever since.

In the West, angels began a gradual decline in importance in the wake of the rise of modern science in the early modern period. The physical sciences undermined belief in the concrete reality of heaven, hell, angels, and devils. The only important countervailing tendency was the emergence of depth psychology, which gave these entities new plausibility as mental phenomena. Carl Jung, for instance, postulated the existence of a collective unconscious and discussed mythology and religion in terms of the "primordial images," or "archetypes," in the collective unconscious that every human being inherits. Using this approach, it is possible to acknowledge demons, spirits, and angels as the personifications of the unconscious, rather than as literal spiritual beings existing independently of our perceiving minds.

The notion of angels as actual, literal beings came back into fashion within two distinct subcultures, modern Evangelical Protestantism and the contemporary metaphysical/New Age subculture. Within evangelicalism, renewed interest was stimulated by Billy Graham's popular 1975 book, *Angels*. This book as well as other works that were composed in the wake of *Angels*'s success investigated the nature and the purpose of angels. These books provide thoroughly biblical guides to the world of angels, and are filled with stories of personal experiences that fit the scheme of biblical angelology.

Evangelical authors generally agree with the theory that the Christian God created the angels—countless thousands of them—some time before he created the physical universe. A war in heaven resulted in the expulsion of Satan and his angels. Human beings were created later, in God's image, a little lower than the angels. Regarded as messengers of the word of God, the good angels serve him as well as his people, whereas evil angels serve Satan and his purposes. God has provided assistance for men in their spiritual conflicts, through the actions of countless angels at his command, who provide unseen aid on our behalf.

More recently, evangelical interest in angels was stimulated by Christian novelist Frank E. Peretti whose works feature "spiritual warfare" between Christian angels and fallen angels. The action in these novels moves back and forth between two interacting levels: while angels and devils cross swords in the spiritual realm, Peretti's human heroes and heroines do battle with New Agers, witches, psychologists, secular education advocates, and other groups viewed by conservative Christians as being under demonic influence. The Christians' concentrated prayers provide power and protection for warrior angels, who are then empowered to win their battles against supernatural demons. A decisive defeat of Satan's legions in the spiritual realm leads more or less directly to the defeat of Satan's earthly minions.

The story of the metaphysical/New Age interest in angels begins with a nineteenth-century occult movement, Theosophy. While the term *Theosophy* has more than one meaning, in contemporary usage it refers to the particular synthesis of ideas that manifested in the Theosophical Society that was founded in New York in 1875. Theosophy postulates a complex view of the universe within which humanity's origins, evolution, and ultimate destiny are delineated in some detail. Like the ancient Gnostics, who they view as one of their predecessors, Theosophists populate the cosmos with innumerable spiritual entities. A significant class of these entities are what Theosophists call *devas,* which is a Sanskrit term for the demi-gods of Hinduism and Buddhism. Within Theosophy, devas are the rough equivalents of angels, although devas have many more functions than do Christian angels. In particular, devas oversee natural forces, and are responsible for building up forms on inner planes as well as on the physical plane.

Devas became part of the more general metaphysical subculture in the early 1970s when a movement known as Findhorn was being featured in New Age periodicals. The early Findhorn community focused around a highly successful vegetable garden in which community members were engaged in a unique cooperative arrangement with agricultural devas (understood in Theosophical terms). Dorothy Maclean, a member of the Findhorn community, communicated directly with devas during the first several years after the Findhorn Garden was started in Scotland. After establishing communication with these nature spirits and determining that she and the other two people at Findhorn, Peter and Eileen Caddy, were to build their garden in cooperation with the devas, Maclean posed specific gardening questions to the devas and received answers from them. Putting these answers into action, the Findhorn Garden, renowned for its inexplicably abundant produce, was created.

Thus the devas, who had long been identified with the angels of Western religious traditions, entered the consciousness of the New Age, though it was more than two decades before they occupied center stage. How long angels will ride their current crest of popularity is difficult to predict. One anomalous indicator is that the New Age shares its present angel craze with the conservative Christian subculture—an unprecedented parallelism that indicates the interest in angels may be more durable than earlier New Age pursuits. A more historically informed glance at angelic matters indicates a high correlation between an interest in angels and millennial expectancy. If this correlation holds true in the present case, angels should be with us until at least the end of the millennium.

Angels A to Z is the one resource that will enable you to fully embrace the angel phenomenon. In a single source, we have attempted to provide an overview that is not limited to a list of angels or a historical overview. Rather, it has been our goal to provide a unique blend of entries that truly embodies everything to do with angels.

In *Angels A to Z* you will encounter angels from myriad religious traditions, from the Hindu asura and the Zoroastrian fravashi to Christian principalities. We introduce you to good angels and fallen angels; angel herbs; angels in legend and lore; and angel theosophists such as Rudolf Steiner and Emanuel Swedenbörg. We delve into the contemporary scene, investigating angels in the occult, metaphysics, and New Age traditions. You can explore angels across the ages through the works of traditional artists (like Giotto and Rembrandt) and the very contemporary artwork of artists such as Glenda Green and Karyn Martin-Kuri. We even answer the etymological question: Where do the terms *angel* and *demon* come from? From halos to wings, *Angels A to Z* gives you the big picture.

The alphabetical form of *Angels* lets you quickly locate your entry of interest, and bold-face terms direct you to related entries in the text. If *Angels* makes a devotee out of you, we have included three appendices: an angel bibliography to help you locate additional sources; an angel filmography, complete with synopses and cast lists, for your favorite movies; and an angel resource appendix to guide you to retail and mail order merchandise, music and video services, organizations, periodicals, and World Wide Web home pages.

Acknowledgments

In an enterprise of this scope, authors incur many more debts than it is possible to acknowledge in a short space. At the risk of missing some important people, we would like to acknowledge the following:

Above anyone else, we would like to express our deepest, heartfelt gratitude to our editor, Kelle Sisung, who for all intents and purposes became the author in the final stages of the composition of this volume. Without the dedication and creative input of this editorial "angel," the present encyclopedia might never have been completed. More generally, we would like to thank Peg Bessette, Chris Nasso, and the other folks at Gale Research/Visible Ink Press who have been our friends as well as our business partners, and without whose support this encyclopedia might never have gotten off the ground.

Many of the entries in this volume were composed by outside authors, whose expertise proved unparalleled. A sincere thank you to Michela Zonta, Robert Griffin, Kathryn Sampson, Kenneth Estell, Lee and Kay Holzinger, Jennifer Robinson, Lori Sender, Peter O'Hara, Ann Sheridan, and Matthew Merta.

One of the perks of working on this title has been the wonderful opportunity to work with people in the angel community who gave so freely of their time and advice. At the risk of inadvertently failing to mention some of these folks, we would like to acknowledge the assistance and/or inspiration of Eileen Freeman, Zannah, Linda Wephula, Patricia Rust, Anita and Larry Gershman, and Denny Dahlmann. A special word of thanks to Andy Lakey who generously contributed the cover art and the foreword to the present volume. Andy also took a special interest in the project, and was a never-failing source of encouragement.

Acknowledgments

An extra special word of thanks goes to the book's guardian angel, Leonard Day, whose dedication and support were unflagging.

We would like to acknowledge the efforts of Michael Flanagin of the Archive for Research in Archetypal Symbolism (ARAS) of the C. G. Jung Institute of San Francisco; J. Gordon Melton of the American Religions Collection (ARC) in Santa Barbara, California; and Leonard Day, all of whom provided illustrations for our volume. Unless noted otherwise, photos appear courtesy of ARAS, ARC, or Dover publications.

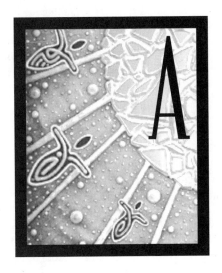

Abaddon

Abaddon (Destroyer) is the Hebrew name for the Greek Apollyon, known as the Angel of the Bottomless Pit (Revelation 10), who ties up the Devil for a millennium (Revelation 20).

Several sources speak of Abaddon, including *The Thanksgiving Hymns* (a **Dead Sea Scroll**), which mentions the "Sheol of Abaddon" and the "torrents of Belial that burst into Abaddon," as well as the first-century *Biblical Antiquities of Philo.* Abaddon is also referred to as a place—the pit—in **Milton**'s *Paradise Regained.*

Abaddon is further identified as a **demon,** or the Devil himself, in the third-century *Acts of Thomas,* as well as in John Bunyan's Puritan classic, *Pilgrim's Progress.*

Elsewhere, Abaddon is invoked by Moses to bring down the rain over Egypt, as reported by Mathers in *The Greater Key of Solomon.* There is also a reference to Abaddon as the sixth lodge of the seven lodges of hell in the work of the Cabalist Joseph ben Abraham Gikatilla. In various sources, Abaddon is identified as an angel of death and destruction, demon of the abyss, and chief of demons of the underworld.

Sources:

Bunyan, John. *Pilgrim's Progress.* Reprint. New York: Dutton, 1954.

Davidson, Gustav. *A Dictionary of Angels: Including the Fallen Angels.* 1967. Reprint. New York: Free Press, 1971.

The Key of Solomon the King. Translated and edited from manuscripts in the British Museum by S. Liddell MacGregor Mathers. Reprint. York Beach, Maine: Samuel Weiser, 1989.

Strayer, Joseph R. *Dictionary of the Middle Ages.* Vol. 1. New York: Charles Scribner's Sons, 1982.

Abdiel

The name Abdiel is first mentioned in the Bible (First Chronicles), where Abdiel is a mortal and a resident of Gilead. However, thereafter in history and literature, Abdiel (meaning "servant of God") is an angel.

The first traceable reference to Abdiel as an angel occurs in *The Book of the Angel Raziel,* a work written in rabbinic Hebrew during the Middle Ages. The most complete account of Abdiel, however, appears in *Paradise Lost,* the epic poem by **John Milton,** which recounts the tale of **Satan**'s rebellion against God. During the uprising, Abdiel is the only angel who remains faithful to God and refuses to rebel. Satan insists that he and his followers were really meant to rule Heaven, but Abdiel argues that Satan must be less powerful than God because God created him. Satan responds that this is just one more lie from the Father of Lies. Abdiel does not believe this, forces out other rebel angels, and attacks Satan himself with a "mighty sword stroke."

Abdiel is also mentioned in *The Revolt of the Angels,* by Anatole France, although there he is known by the name Arcade.

Sources:

Davidson, Gustav. *A Dictionary of Angels: Including the Fallen Angels.* 1967. Reprint. New York: Free Press, 1971.

France, Anatole. *The Revolt of the Angels.* 1914. Reprint. New York: Heritage Press, 1953.

Ronner, John. *Know Your Angels: The Angel Almanac with Biographies of 100 Prominent Angels in Legend and Folklore, and Much More.* Murfreesboro, Tenn.: Mamre Press, 1993.

Abraham

Two accounts appear in the Old Testament that involve Abraham, the first patriarch of the people of Israel, and angels. The first recounts Abraham's visitation by three angels at Mamre, the second is the angel who prevents Abraham from sacrificing his son Isaac.

Chapter 18 of Genesis constitutes one of the most dramatic theophanies reported in the Bible, in which God, in the accompaniment of angels comes unexpected as the dinner guest of Abraham at Mamre.

It is reported that while he was sitting at the entrance of his tent, "Abraham looked up and saw three men standing nearby. When he saw them, he hurried from the entrance of his tent to meet them and bowed low to the ground." Then, he offered them some water to refresh themselves, and something to eat, and while they were eating under a tree, they asked him where was his wife Sarah, and said, "I will surely return to you about this time nest year, and Sarah your wife will have a son."

Abraham does not recognize God by the oaks of Mamre until the promise of a son is made. Only at that point does Abraham suspect that his visitors are heaven sent.

The relationship that exists among the three men and God is confusing, because although it is God who appears, it is reported in the first verse that Abraham sees three men. Also, in some verses all three men speak, whereas in others only God speaks.

Tradition is divided regarding this point. The three angels appear as a triple manifestation of God, and are thus identified by Christians as the Old Testament trinity. Other interpretations consider God to be only one of the three men.

The prediction of the birth of Sarah's son in nine months represents the object of the visit, and this incident incorporates the affirmation of God's omnipotence.

In chapter 22 of Genesis, it is reported that when the Lord tempted Abraham by ordering him to sacrifice his son, it was an angel who came to hold his hand:

> When they reached the place God had told him about, Abraham built an altar there and arranged the wood on it. He bound his son Isaac and laid him on the altar, on top of the wood. Then he reached out his hand and took the knife to slay his son. But the angel of the Lord called out to him from heaven, "Abraham! Abraham!" "Here I am," he replied. "Do

not lay a hand on the boy," he said. "Do not do anything to him. Now I know that you fear God, because you have not withheld from me your son, your only son."

Then, after Abraham sacrificed a ram instead of his son, the angel of the Lord spoke to him again, and said, "I swear by myself, declares the Lord, that because you have done this and have not withheld your son, your only son, I will surely bless you and make your descendants as numerous as the stars in the sky and as the sand on the seashore. Your descendants will take possession of the cities of their enemies, and through your offspring all nations on earth will be blessed, because you have obeyed me."

The story of the brutal trial of Abraham's faith has been depicted as a literary masterpiece, and it marks the Abraham cycle of stories. It has aroused the theological interests of authors such as Kierkegaard, who considered it a classic parable on the radical meaning of faith.

Abraham, who had to cut himself off from his past when he left his homeland, is now tested and summoned to give up his entire future, by giving up the child of his old age. As a matter of fact, the fulfillment of God's promise depends on Isaac's life. Abraham's fear of God is revealed in his obedience, although this could result in his son's death.

Sources:

Laymon, Charles M., ed. *The Interpreters's One-Volume Commentary on the Bible*. New York: Abingdon Press, 1971.

West, James King. *Introduction to the Old Testament*. New York: Macmillan, 1981.

Abraxas

Abraxas was an ancient religious movement prominent during the first few centuries of the common era that was associated with **Gnosticism** and which affected **Judaism, Christianity,** and contemporaneous paganism. Its central teaching was that this world is the creation of an evil deity who traps human spirits in the physical realm; our true home is the absolute spirit (the *pleroma*), to which we should seek to return by rejecting the pleasures of the flesh.

Two distinct types of entities, **aeons** and **archons,** are associated with Gnosticism. The aeons are higher spiritual beings who reside in the pleroma. The archons are created by the evil demiurge (a subordinate deity and creator of the material world); they are the rulers who govern this world and act as guardians, preventing the sparks of light (i.e., the divine essence of individual human beings) from returning to the pleroma.

Abraxas appears to have originally referred to the Great Unknown, out of which the aeons and the pleroma itself emerged. In later Cabalistic thought, however, Abraxas became the designation of the chief aeon. Some ancient writers portrayed Abraxas as a demon or archon who ruled other archons. Abraxas was also associated with magic and is said to be the source of the familiar term *abracadabra.*

Sources:

Davidson, Gustav. *A Dictionary of Angels: Including the Fallen Angels.* 1967. Reprint. New York: Free Press, 1971.

Robinson, James M. *The Nag Hammadi Library.* 1977. Reprint. New York: Harper & Row, 1981.

Acts of the Holy Angels

A traditional theme for Catholic artists is a series of eleven biblical incidents collectively referred to as the Acts of the Holy Angels. These eleven acts are as follows:

1. *The Fall of Lucifer.* No detailed account is given in the Bible concerning the fall of **Lucifer,** however the Revelation of John (Rev. 12:3–4) alludes to Lucifer taking with him one-third of the stars of heaven: "And there appeared another wonder in heaven; and behold a great red dragon, having seven heads and ten horns, and seven crowns upon his heads. And his tail drew the third part of the stars of heaven, and did cast them to the earth."

2. *Adam and Eve's Ejection from the Garden.* After **Adam** ate from the Tree of Knowledge, "the Lord God banished him from the Garden of Eden to work the ground from which he had been taken. After he drove the man out, he placed on the east side of the Garden of Eden **cherubim** and a flaming sword flashing back and forth to guard the way to the tree of life" (Gen. 3:23, 24).

3. *Abraham's Visitation by Three Angels.* In chapter 18 of Genesis, **Abraham** is visited by three angels who announce that his barren, elderly wife Sarah will conceive and bear a son called Isaac.

4. *The Angel Who Prevents Abraham from Sacrificing Isaac.* Chapter 22 of Genesis tells the story of the Lord ordering Abraham to sacrifice his son, Isaac. An angel intervenes.

5. *Jacob Wrestling with an Angel.* "And Jacob was left alone; and a man [an angel] wrestled with him until the breaking of the day. When the man [angel] saw that he did not prevail against Jacob, he touched the hollow of his thigh; and Jacob's thigh was put out of joint as he wrestled with him" (Gen. 32:25).

THE EXPULSION FROM THE GARDEN OF EDEN BY JACOPO DELLA QUERCIA (MAIN
PORTAL, SAN PETRONIO, BOLOGNA, CA. 1430). (COURTESY ARAS)

6. *Angels Moving Up and Down "Jacob's Ladder."* "And he
dreamed, and behold a ladder set up on the earth, and the top of it
reached to heaven; and behold the angels of God ascending and descending on it" (Gen. 28:12).

7. *The Three Princes Delivered from a Fiery Furnace.* Three young
men who refuse to bow down to King Nebuchadnezzar are cast into the
fiery furnace and saved by the hand of God. Nebuchadnezzar responds in
Daniel 3:24–28, "Blessed be the Lord God of Shadrach, Meshach, and
Abednego who hath sent his angel and delivered his servants that trusted
him, and have changed the king's word, and yielded their bodies, that
they might not serve nor worship any god except their own God."

8. *The Army of Sennacherib Slain by an Angel.* As reported in chapter 19 of Kings, after King Sennacherib of Assyria threatened Hezekiah, King of Judah, Hezeziah prayed to Yahweh:

> "O Lord, God of Israel, enthroned between the Cherubim, you alone are God over all the kingdoms of the earth. You have made heaven and earth. Give ear, O Lord, and hear; open your eyes, O Lord, and see; listen to the words of Sennacherib has sent to insult the living God. It is true, O Lord, that the Assyrian kings have laid waste these nations and their lands. They have thrown their gods into the fire but only wood and stone, fashioned by men's hands. Now, O Lord our God, deliver us from his hand, so that all kingdoms on earth may know that you alone, O Lord, are God!"

The Lord, who listened to Hezekiah's prayer, sent him a message through Isaiah, who prophesied Sennacherib's fall:

> That night the angel of the Lord went out and put to death a hundred and eighty-five thousand men in the Assyrian camp. When the people got up the next morning, there were all the dead bodies! So Sennacherib king of Assyria broke camp and withdrew. He returned to Nineveh and stayed there. (Kings 19:35–36)

JACOB WRESTLING WITH THE ANGEL BY GUSTAVE DORÉ.

9. *Raphael Protecting Tobias.* About to embark upon a dangerous journey into unknown lands, "Tobias went out in search of one who knew the road so that he might accompany him into the land of the Medes. He went out and saw before him the Angel Raphael, without in the least suspecting that this was an angel of God" (Tobias 5:4).

10. *The Punishment of Heliodorus.* The story of Heliodorus is found in 2 Maccabees 3. Heliodorus was an official of the Seleucid court, and was sent by Seleucus IV Philopater to confiscate funds from the Temple in Jerusalem. Seleucus was convinced to seek funds deposited in the Temple by Simon, the administrator of the Temple, who conspired with Apollonius, the Seleucid governor of Coele Syria and Phoenicia.

Once in the Temple, Heliodorus encountered an apparition: a rider wearing golden armor on a horse, and two youths, who stroke Heliodorus

ANNUNCIATION BY PIERO DELLA FRANCESCO (FRESCO, SAN FRANCESCO AREZZO, CA. 1455). (COURTESY ARAS)

repeatedly. Heliodorus was then saved by the prayers of the high priest Onias III.

11. *The Annunciation.* According to Luke (1:26–38), "In the sixth month, God sent the angel Gabriel to Nazareth, a town in Galilee, to a virgin pledged to be married to a man named Joseph, a descendant of David. The virgin's name was **Mary.** The angel went to her and said, "Greetings, you who are highly favored! The Lord is with you." Mary was greatly troubled at his words and wondered what kind of greeting this might be. But the angel said to her, "Do not be afraid, Mary, you have found favor with God. You will be with child and give birth to a son, and you are to give him the name Jesus. He will be great and will be called the Son of the Most High. The Lord God will give him the throne of his father David, and he will reign over the house of Jacob forever; his kingdom will never end."

Sources:
New Catholic Encyclopedia. Vol. 1 Washington, D.C.: Catholic University of America, 1981.
Giovetti, Paola. *Angels: The Role of Celestial Guardians and Beings of Light.* Translated by Toby McCormick. York Beach, Maine: Samuel Weiser, 1993.
Richardson, Alan, and John Bowden, eds. *The Westminster Dictionary of Christian Theology.* Rev. ed. Philadelphia: Westminster Press, 1983.

Adam

Adam, the first human being according to the Judeo-Christian-Islamic family of religions, is associated with angel lore in several accounts. His most significant interaction surrounds the Ejection from the Garden, as reported in Genesis (3:23–24).

In this chapter of Genesis, the overriding struggle is internal when man must choose between his relationship and obedience to God, who has established the limits of man's destiny, and his own free will.

Temptation occurs through the medium of a serpent (often identified as **Satan**), representing cleverness and magical power, who awakens Eve's desire for the forbidden Tree of Knowledge, the fruit of which has been prohibited by God. The serpent suggests that God has deceived her by saying that the fruit will bring death. Eve accepts the fruit, and then offers it to Adam, who by eating it accepts to exchange "life" for knowledge. It has been suggested that the eating of the fruit represents man's attempt to take what he does not rightfully possess, what belongs to God alone, and what only he can control.

The first thing that Adam and Eve realize after eating the fruit is that they are naked; along with this realization comes shame. Their instinctive reaction is to hide, to exculpate. But the consequences of their action is inescapable, and suffering and misery enter the world, while the serpent becomes a symbol of evil. Paradise is irretrievably lost.

"The Lord God banished him from the Garden of Eden to work the ground from which he had been taken. After he drove the man out, he placed on the east side of the Garden of Eden **cherubim** and a flaming sword flashing back and forth to guard the way to the tree of life."

The cherubim mentioned in this episode are known from ancient Near Eastern lore as mythological winged animals, usually with human faces. This episode belongs to the **Acts of the Holy Angels,** a series of eleven biblical incidents that have constituted a traditional theme for Catholic artists.

ADAM AND EVE BY ALBRECHT DÜRER (1504).

Beyond the Genesis narrative, of particular importance is the tale that involves the angel **Lucifer,** whose jealousy of Adam ultimately led to his fall from heaven and the beginning of his career as the master of evil. In the Cabala, Adam is Tipereth (Beauty), the sixth sephira. In the **apocryphal** work the Apocalypse of Moses, Adam is taken bodily into heaven in a fiery chariot driven by **Michael,** a tale clearly reminiscent of **Elijah**'s ascension. There is also a story, recorded in the Revelation of Moses, that the four **archangels** buried Adam.

Sources:

Davidson, Gustav. *A Dictionary of Angels: Including the Fallen Angels.* 1967. Reprint. New York: Free Press, 1971.

Laymon, Charles M., ed. *The Interpreter's One-Volume Commentary on the Bible.* New York: Abingdon Press, 1971.

West, James King. *Introduction to the Old Testament.* New York: Macmillan, 1981.

Adramelechk

Adramelechk (King of Fire) is one of two **throne** angels generally linked with the angel Asmadai, one of the two potent thrones mentioned in **Milton**'s *Paradise Lost.* He is mentioned in demonography as the eighth of the ten archdemons and as a great minister and chancellor of the Order of the Fly, an infernal order founded by **Beelzebub.** In rabbinic literature, it is said that when conjured Adramelechk manifests in the form of a mule or a peacock.

Adramelechk, who has also been equated with the Babylonian Anu and with the Ammonite Moloch, is mentioned in various sources, such as *The History of Magic,* where he is pictured as a horse; 2 Kings, where he is regarded as a god to whom children of the Sepharvite colony in Samaria were sacrificed; and **Milton**'s *Paradise Lost,* where he is referred to as both an idol of the Assyrians and a fallen angel overthrown by **Uriel** and **Raphael** in combat.

Sources:

Davidson, Gustav. *A Dictionary of Angels: Including the Fallen Angels.* 1967. Reprint. New York: Free Press, 1971.

Seligmann, Kurt. *The History of Magic.* New York: Pantheon, 1948.

Aeon

The aeons are superior spiritual beings in the ancient religious system known as **Gnosticism.** According to the Gnostics, the aeons were the first beings to emerge from the *pleroma*, "the absolute spirit," which is the true home of the human spirit.

The precise number of aeons varied. In one common schema—discussed by the Christian anti-Gnostic Irenaeus—there were thirty aeons, arranged in fifteen pairs, from Depth and Silence to Theletos (Desire) and **Sophia** (Wisdom). According to the Gnostic Basilides, there were 365 aeons. Yet other sources specify eight, twelve, or twenty-four.

Prior to the general acceptance of the **Dionysian** schema of the **hierarchy** of angels, some Christian writers used the term *aeon* to refer to one of the angelic orders.

Sources:

Davidson, Gustav. *A Dictionary of Angels Including the Fallen Angels.* 1967. Reprint. New York: Free Press, 1971.
Robinson, James M. *The Nag Hammadi Library.* 1977. Reprint. New York: Harper & Row, 1981.

Africa

There are several examples of God's servants, messengers, and agents in African religious beliefs. The many divinities of the Ashanti, for instance, are thought to be God's servants and mouthpieces, acting between him and his creatures. The Ewe consider the divinity of the cowries to be God's servant, and the Igbo divinities are said to be God's agents.

The Chagga believe that God has a minister or servant who carries out his instructions and it was he who found out that humanity had broken God's commandment by eating the forbidden fruit. God sent his servant to punish the people of the world, and on two other occasions to warn them against living wickedly. It is believed that this demigod also causes sickness, famine, smallpox, and war, mocks the wicked, kills people, and demands cattle, sheep, and goats as sacrifices to God.

The Swazi say that God has a "one-legged" messenger, while the Songhay believe that there are "angels" who survey the world and humanity from God's seventh heaven. The Lozi assign two councillors to God, one of whom is his messenger; both are intermediaries between God and human beings. It is reported that the Gumuz have **guardian angels** who act as intermediaries between men and God and refer human prayers to him.

According to the Vugusu, God has servants who are the spirits of people that died long ago and who now act as guardians of families and individuals. The spirits of the first two men on earth are considered nearest to God in rank and act as messengers and executors of the divine will.

An evil divinity is also said to have servants that are the spirits of wicked humans like witches and sorcerers and who are similarly evil-minded, bringing sickness and death to men. The Yao see God as having many servants. The Igbira think that all departed are God's humble agents or servants.

Some societies personify natural objects or describe them mythologically as God's servants or agents. The Ashanti hold that God once sent the rivers and sea, who were his children, to receive honor from men, and in turn to confer benefits on mankind. The religious leader of the Meru is referred to as the messenger of God, whom God selects and who stands as his representative. The Nuer believe that God uses a variety of things—such as natural circumstances, spirits, spears, and beasts—as agents through which he takes human life.

The Bambuti consider lightning and rainbows to be servants of God. They also hold that he has spirit servants in charge of game. Rain is considered by the Suk to be God's servant whose duty is to carry water; when this water spills, men experience or see it as rain. The Didinga do not eat fish, believing that fish came down to earth in lightning as God's messengers.

A number of peoples consider their kings and chiefs to be God's special agents through whom he carries out his rulership of the world. Such societies include the Bavenda, Sangama, Shilluk, and Shona.

Although the basic Yoruba worldview is ultimately monotheistic, the Yoruba are simultaneously polytheistic, postulating a pantheon of some four hundred demigods called **orishas.** In the syncretistic religious systems of the Western Hemisphere—systems such as Santeria (Cuba) and Candomblé (Brazil) that mix the Yoruba tradition with Catholicism and other religious elements—orisha are retained as important demigods. In these later religions, the comparison between orishas and angels is particularly appropriate, given that Catholic saints and angels supplied important models for the role orishas play in these new religions. For example, among the Candomblé it is believed that each person receives two orishas (one male, one female) at birth, who play the role of "guardian angels."

Among some African peoples there is a sort of angelic rite in which angels are specifically evoked and called down, either to give and receive messages or to enter into the body of the ritualist. In its simplest manifestation this results in the phenomenon of "possession," which in some religions is the chief rite. Whether the beings who possess are called gods or spirits, they may certainly be seen as angels, since they come down from and return to heaven and form a link between humanity and God.

—*Michela Zonta*

Sources:

Field, M. J. *Angels and Ministers of Grace: An Ethno-Psychiatrist's Contribution to Biblical Criticism.* New York: Hill and Wang, 1971.

Mbiti, John S. *Concepts of God in Africa.* New York: Praeger, 1970.

Parisien, Maria. *Angels & Mortals: Their Co-Creative Power.* Wheaton, Ill.: Quest, 1990.

Ray, Benjamin C. *African Religions: Symbol, Ritual, and Community.* Englewood Cliffs, N.J.: Prentice-Hall, 1976.

Wilson, Peter Lamborn. *Angels.* New York: Pantheon Books, 1980.

Ahriman (Angra Mainyu)

Ahriman (or Angra Mainyu) is the Zoroastrian **Satan** and the prototype of Satan for the Judeo-Christian-Islamic family of religions. The central theme of Zoroaster's religious vision is the cosmic struggle between the god of light, Ahura Mazda (Wise Lord), and his angels and the god of darkness, Ahriman (Evil Spirit), and his demons. Unlike **Zoroastrianism**'s related religious traditions, in which the outcome of the war between God and the Devil has already been decided, Zoroastrianism portrays the struggle as more or less evenly matched (although many strands of the tradition would assert that Ahura Mazda's triumph is inevitable). Individuals are urged to align themselves with the forces of light and will be judged according to whether their good or evil deeds predominate. Eventually there will be a final battle (a Zoroastrian Armageddon) between good and evil in which it is anticipated that Ahriman and his hosts will be defeated. The earth will then be renewed, evil people destroyed, and the righteous resurrected.

Zoroastrianism differs from other monotheisms in its conceptualization of the genesis of Satan. Mainstream **Judaism, Christianity,** and **Islam** all view Satan as a **fallen angel** who was cast out of heaven, either for disobeying God or for rebelling against God. By way of contrast, early Zoroastrians believed Ahriman to be very much on par with Ahura Mazda, and that they even created the world together, which explains why the world is such a mixture of good and bad. Later thinkers speculated that the two beings were twins, both fathered by Zurvan (Boundless Time). Ahriman is not very creative, however, in that his evil creations are always responses to his brother's good creations. For example, when Ahura Mazda created life, Ahriman responded by creating death. Ahriman also formed an infernal host as an inverted mirror image of the celestial host. For instance, in opposition to Asha, the Archangel of Truth, he created the archdemon Druj, "the Lie."

Sources:

Davidson, Gustav. *A Dictionary of Angels: Including the Fallen Angels.* 1967. Reprint. New York: Free Press, 1971.

Eliade, Mircea, ed. *A History of Religious Ideas.* Vol. 1. Chicago: University of Chicago Press, 1978.

Noss, John B. *Man's Religions.* 4th ed. New York: Macmillan, 1969.

Ronner, John. *Know Your Angels: The Angel Almanac with Biographies of 100 Prominent Angels in Legend and Folklore, and Much More.* Murfreesboro, Tenn.: Mamre Press, 1993.

Ancient of Days

The name Ancient of Days is used in the Cabala to denote Kether, first of the sefiroth, as well as Macrosopus (God as He Is in Himself). It also denotes the "holy ones of the highest," and in Daniel (7:9) it is used to refer to God. In *The Divine Names,* Ancient of Days, which has also been used to refer to Israel, is defined by **Dionysius the Areopagite** as "both the Eternity and the Time of all things prior to days and eternity and time." **William Blake** refers to the Ancient of Days as Urizen, the figure of Jehovah. The *Ancient of Days* is also the title of one of Blake's most famous illustrations.

Sources:
Davidson, Gustav. *A Dictionary of Angels: Including the Fallen Angels.* 1967. Reprint. New York: Free Press, 1971.

Margolies, Morris B. *A Gathering of Angels: Angels in Jewish Life and Literature.* New York: Ballantine, 1994.

Anderson, Joan Wester

Author, lecturer, and teacher Joan Wester Anderson was born in Evanston, Illinois. She began her writing career in 1973 with a series of family humor articles for local newspapers and parenting magazines. Since that time her work, totaling ten books and more than one thousand articles and short stories, has been published nationally in magazines and newspapers such as *Woman's Day, Modern Bride, Virtue, Modern Maturity, Chicago Parent,* and the *New York Times.*

Anderson's first brush with guardian angels came in 1983, when a good samaritan appeared during a Christmas Eve snowstorm to help her son Tim get home for the holidays. The stranger towed Tim and his college friend to safety and mysteriously disappeared, leaving no tire tracks behind. This strange encounter provoked Anderson to find out if others had similar experiences. She posed her question in several national magazines and the response was overwhelming. These experiences led to the publication of her 1992 book, *Where Angels Walk, True Stories of Heavenly Visitors.*

THE ANCIENT OF DAYS BY
WILLIAM BLAKE (1794).

Where Angels Walk has recently completed its fifty-sixth week on
the *New York Times* best-seller list and has been translated into eleven
languages. With domestic sales totaling more than 1.2 million copies, it is

considered today's best-selling angel book, and the only one to appear on the national religion best-seller list for two consecutive years. A sequel to *Angels*, titled *Where Miracles Happen, True Stories of Heavenly Encounters,* was published in 1994, as was *An Angel to Watch Over Me, True Stories of Children's Encounters with Angels* (1994). Both books were written in response to suggestions from readers.

Anderson has appeared on several national television programs, including *Good Morning America, Geraldo, Mother Angelica Live, NBC Nightly News,* and *Sightings,* and was featured in the recent television documentaries *Angels: Beyond the Light* (NBC) and *Angel Stories* (The Learning Channel). She has been interviewed on more than two hundred local, national, and international radio shows. She and her husband live in Arlington Heights, Illinois, and are the parents of five grown children.

Sources:

Anderson, Joan Wester. *An Angel to Watch Over Me, True Stories of Children's Encounters with Angels.* New York: Ballantine, 1994.

————. *Where Angels Walk, True Stories of Heavenly Visitors.* New York: Ballantine, 1992.

————. *Where Miracles Happen, True Stories of Heavenly Encounters.* Brooklyn, N.Y.: Brett Books, 1994.

JOAN ANDERSON (PHOTO BY STEVE KAGAN, COURTESY JOAN ANDERSON)

Angel Clothed in a Cloud

An angel clothed in a cloud appears to St. John the Divine in his vision of the end of the world as reported in Rev. 10:1–10:

> Then I saw another mighty angel coming down from heaven. He was wrapped in a cloud, with the rainbow round his head; his face shone like the sun and his legs were like pillars of fire. In his hand he held a little scroll unrolled. His right foot he planted on the sea, and his left on the land. Then he gave a great shout, like the roar of a lion; and when he shouted, the seven thunders spoke. I was about to write down what the seven thunders had said; but I heard a voice from heaven saying, "Seal up what the seven thunders have said; do not write it down." Then the angel that I saw standing on the sea and

the land raised his right hand to heaven and swore by him who lives for ever and ever, who created heaven and earth and the sea and everything in them: "There shall be no more delay; but when the time comes for the seventh angel to sound his trumpet, the hidden purpose of God will have been fulfilled, as he promised to his servants the prophets."

Then the voice which I heard from heaven was speaking to me again, and it said, "Go and take the open scroll in the hand of the angel that stands on the sea and the land." So I went to the angel and asked him to give me the little scroll. He said to me, "Take it, and eat it. It will turn your stomach sour, although in your mouth it will taste sweet as honey." So, I took the little scroll from the angel's hand and ate it, and in my mouth it did taste sweet as honey; but when I swallowed it my stomach turned sour.

Chapter 10 of Revelation is part of a longer interruption in the discussion of the seven trumpets signaling the end time. The sixth trumpet has already been sounded, but the seventh angel with the seventh trumpet, signaling the advent of the anti-Christ, has yet to appear. There was also a delay before the opening of the seventh seal in chapter 5. Some commentators have suggested this signifies that God is for some reason delaying final judgment.

This interlude begins with a description of "another mighty angel" coming down from heaven. The purpose of the angel seems to be to announce the "seven thunders" (the number seven probably derived its sacred character from the seven visible planets). After the seven thunders utter their prophecies, John is about to record their message when he is commanded by a loud voice from heaven to "seal up what the seven thunders have said; do not write it down."

The specific identification of the seven thunders and why John was directed not to record their message are highly debated. According to James M. Efird, the best conjecture seems to be that the thunders represent another cycle of judgment. He states that all numbers in Revelation are cycles of judgment and that had these thunders been enumerated they would have been essentially the same as the seven seals and the seven trumpets. Efird believes they are not recorded because "in **apocalyptic** literature there is almost always found the teaching that God shortens the time of suffering for the sake of the elect" (See Mark 13:20). Describing yet another cycle of judgment would thus have indicated a longer period before the end of Christian persecution. If the thunders were not recorded, they would not come to pass and the day would draw nearer when the seventh angel blows his trumpet and God's hidden purpose is fulfilled.

John is next told to take the scroll from the angel arrayed with a cloud and eat it in a scene reminiscent of one in the book of Ezekiel (2:3–8). This passage perhaps symbolizes the need for John to thoroughly digest the scroll's contents before revealing the predictions. God's message is sweet in his mouth as one of the elect, but the message he must deliver to those who refuse God is bitter.

—*Robert Griffin*

Sources:

Alexander, David, and Pat Alexander, eds. *Eerdman's Handbook to the Bible.* Grand Rapids, Mich.: William B. Eerdman's, 1973.

Asimov, Issac. *Asimov's Guide to the Bible: The Old and New Testament.* Reprint. New York: Avenel Books, 1969.

Efird, James M. *Revelation for Today: An Apocalyptic Approach.* Nashville: Abingdon, 1989.

Henry, Matthew. *Commentary on the Whole Bible.* Grand Rapids, Mich.: Zondervan, 1960.

Angel of Death

The notion of an angel who extracts the soul from the body at death seems to have developed from earlier ideas about divinities of death. Such figures are widespread in world culture. In **Hinduism,** for example, Yama is the god of the dead. In the earliest Vedic texts, Yama ruled an afterlife realm not unlike the Norse Valhalla in which the deceased enjoyed carnal pleasures. As Hinduism was transformed in the post-Vedic period, Yama became a rather grim demigod who snared the souls of the departed and conducted them to the otherworld.

The angel of death concept was most fully developed in rabbinical **Judaism.** As did Yama, the Jewish angel of death (*malakh ha-mavet*) metamorphosed across time. At first these biblical emissaries of death were clearly under the direct command of God, as for example in Second Samuel:

> Then the angel stretched out his arm towards Jerusalem to destroy it; but the Lord repented of the evil and said to the angel who was destroying the people, "Enough! Stay your hand." (2 Sam. 24:16)

Although no biblical reference identifies a particular angel or group of angels as having the specialized task of meting out death, many references do make allusions to "destroying angels" (Exod. 12:23, 2 Sam.

24:16, and Isa. 37:36); a fatal "reaper" (Jer. 9:20), and "messengers of death" (Prov. 16:14).

Only in postbiblical literature does the idea of the angel of death as such emerge. This "angel" gradually develops into a demonic figure acting on his own initiative. According to the **Talmud,** the angel of death was identified with **Satan,** and the notion of the angel of death as evil was reflected in many folktales and in many folk practices associated with death, burial, and mourning. For instance, one commonly known bit of folklore is that it is impossible to die in the midst of studying the Torah.

The many folktales associated with the angel of death fall into roughly three categories. In the first group, which may be called tales of horror and magic, the stubborn and cruel angel of death is a kind of antihero, somewhat like Dracula in many vampire stories. In the second category the angel of death can be defeated, especially by human deception. In these tales he is portrayed as being rather stupid. In the final group the angel of death is moved by compassion to spare someone's life or otherwise act benevolently. In many of these narratives the confrontation with the angel of death occurs on a wedding night, during which one of the two betrothed is fated to die.

THE ANGEL OF DEATH BY ALBERT STERNER (CA. 1915). (COURTESY ARC)

Sources:

Encyclopaedia Judaica. Vol. 2. New York: Macmillan, 1971.

Masello, Robert. *Fallen Angels . . . and Spirits of the Dark.* New York: Perigree, 1994.

Sykes, Egerton. *Who's Who: Non-Classical Mythology.* New York: Oxford University Press, 1993.

Wigoder, Geoffrey. *The Encyclopedia of Judaism.* New York: Macmillan, 1989.

Angel of Fire

Angel of Fire is a term that has been used to describe many distinct angels. They include:

Agni is the Vedic god of fire and mediator between gods and men.

Ardarel is the angel of fire in occult lore.

Arel is an angel invoked in ritual **magic** using a sun symbol. The name Arel is inscribed on the seventh pentacle of the sun.

Atar is the Zoroastrian angel of fire and chief of the rank of angels known as **yazatas.**

Atuniel, whose name means "furnace," is an angel of fire in rabbinic angelology.

Gabriel, according to the **Zohar,** attacked Moses for neglecting to observe the covenantal rite of circumcision with regard to his son Gershom. Gabriel came down in a flame of fire, in the form of a burning serpent with the purpose of destroying Moses for this sin.

Jehoel or Jehuel is the principal angel over fire according to *Berith Menucha,* a seventeenth-century cabalistic text.

Madiel is the chief character of Sergei Prokofiev's opera *L'Ange de Feu.* He is the angel of fire and appears before a sixteenth-century visionary in the form of a German knight.

Nathaniel (Nathanel), who, according to Jewish lore, is lord over the element of fire. According to *The Biblical Antiquities of Philo,* King Jair of Israel, a worshipper of the false god Baal, ordered seven men faithful to God to be burned. The angel Nathaniel extinguished the flames and allowed the seven men to escape. Then Nathaniel burned King Jair and one thousand of his servants.

Seraph, whose name means "fiery serpent," is one of the angels who has dominion over the element of fire. He is the angel who touched Isaiah's lips with a live coal so that Isaiah might be clean and fit to speak to God:

> Then one of the seraphim flew to me carrying in his hand a glowing coal which he had taken from the altar with a pair of tongs. He touched my mouth with it and said, "See, this has touched your lips; your iniquity is removed, and your sin is wiped away." (Isa. 6:6–7)

Uriel, whose name means "Fire of God," is an angel of noncanonical lore who was known as the regent of the sun and flame of God. In Catholic tradition Uriel is thought to be the angel who stood at the gate of the lost Eden with a fiery sword.

Sources:

Margolies, Morris B. *A Gathering of Angels: Angels in Jewish Life and Literature.* New York: Ballantine, 1994.

New Catholic Encyclopedia. Vol. 1. Washington, D.C.: Catholic University of America, 1981.

Richardson, Alan, and John Bowden, eds. *The Westminster Dictionary of
Christian Theology.* Rev. ed. Philadelphia: Westminster Press, 1983.

Angel of the Furnace

The legend of the Angel of the Furnace (or Fiery Furnace) is
described in the book of Daniel in the Hebrew Scriptures (the Old Testament). Three Jewish princes were confined in Babylon around 500 B.C.
Sidrach (or Shadrach), Misach (or Meshach), and Abednego refused to
comply with King Nebuchadnezzar's orders to worship a golden idol,
which they believed to be a false god. Nebuchadnezzar ordered them cast
into a blazing furnace that was so hot the men who threw the princes into
the fire were themselves consumed by the flames.

The princes, however, were not only unharmed but were also seen
walking in the fire with a fourth being, who was described by Nebuchadnezzar as having a form like that of "the son of God." This unnamed
angel of the Lord delivered the three princes from death. King Nebuchadnezzar, so affected by this astonishing feat, commanded that anyone who
said anything disrespectful of the Hebrew God Yahweh be destroyed.

Sources:

Davidson, Gustav. *A Dictionary of Angels: Including the Fallen Angels.* 1967.
    Reprint. New York: Free Press, 1971.
Gaster, Theodore. *Myth, Legend, and Custom in the Old Testament.* New York:
    Harper & Row, 1969.

Angel of the Lord

The Judeo-Christian Scriptures often mention the angel of the
Lord. In the earliest passages in the Bible, this is often simply a phrase
referring to the presence of God. At other times, the angel of the Lord is a
specific angel, such as **Michael, Metatron,** or **Gabriel.**

In the Old Testament the term angel of the Lord or angel of God
appears in such accounts as Genesis 22, the sacrifice of Isaac; Exodus 3
when Moses is faced with the burning bush; and Numbers 22, the story of
Balaam. In the New Testament, Herod is struck down by the angel of the
Lord in Acts 12:23, where, in this case, the angel could be construed as
an **angel of death.**

Sources:

Davidson, Gustav. *A Dictionary of Angels: Including the Fallen Angels.* 1967.
    Reprint. New York: Free Press, 1971.

Ronner, John. *Know Your Angels: The Angel Almanac with Biographies of 100 Prominent Angels in Legend and Folklore, and Much More.* Murfreesboro, Tenn.: Mamre Press, 1993.

Angel of Peace

The angel of peace is an unnamed angel in Jewish legend. Among other things, he leads **Enoch** in his tour of heaven in 1 Enoch. According to the Testament of Benjamin, the angel of peace plays the role of **psychopomp** to the souls of righteous people when they die. Other bits of folklore include the story that the angel of peace opposed the creation of humanity and was burned by God as punishment (although apparently subsequently resurrected). Finally, the angel of peace is sometimes pluralized, as when it is said that angels of peace are present whenever the Sabbath is being ushered in.

Sources:
Margolies, Morris B. *A Gathering of Angels: Angels in Jewish Life and Literature.* New York: Ballantine, 1994.
Sparks, H. F. D., ed. *The Apocryphal Old Testament.* Oxford: Clarendon Press, 1984.

Angel of the Presence

The angel of the presence has played a diverse and not particularly consistent series of roles. In the **Book of Jubilees,** for example, the angel of the presence is the angel who relates the revelation to Moses. Although the number varies somewhat, there are customarily twelve angels of the presence, also known as angels of the face. **William Blake,** for example, mentions seven angels of the presence in his poem "Milton," and rabbinic lore sometimes refers to the seventy tutelary (national) angels as angels of the presence.

Sources:
Davidson, Gustav. *A Dictionary of Angels: Including the Fallen Angels.* 1967. Reprint. New York: Free Press, 1971.
Ronner, John. *Know Your Angels: The Angel Almanac with Biographies of 100 Prominent Angels in Legend and Folklore, and Much More.* Murfreesboro, Tenn.: Mamre Press, 1993.

Angel Stores

New topics of interest invariably generate specialized merchandise.. It should thus surprise no one that whole lines of new products have emerged in the wake of the current angel fad—products that fill the shelves of both Christian and New Age bookstores and boutiques. What *is* surprising is that the angel fad should have expanded to the point where it can comfortably support specialized angel stores.

The emergence of such stores is facilitated by the supportive nature of what might be called an "angel community," namely a diverse group of people who together constitute an informal network of individuals with a special interest in angelic matters. There is also at least one organization that has been developed with the express purpose of helping individuals set up angel outlets. This organization is HALOS, an acronym for Helping Angel Lovers Own Stores.

HALOS was founded by Denny Dahlmann, who, in 1993, started his own store, *Angel Treasures,* in Royal Oak, Michigan. The store was a runaway success, eventually grossing over four hundred dollars per square foot of store space, which places it in the top 5 percent of United States retail stores. When a newspaper reporter asked him about his phenomenal success, Dahlmann responded that he felt customers were "buying good feelings"—customers generally believed that angels can "be counted on to help them with their lives." Dahlmann's HALOS literature, which offers to assist new angel businesses, states that *Angel Treasures* has over two thousand angel-related items from over two hundred vendors with products from some twenty different countries.

Sources:

Dahlmann, Denny. *HALOS* (flyer). Farmington Hills, Mich.: Angel Treasures, Inc., 1994.

Funke, Doug. "Angels spell success at gift boutique." *The Eccentric.* June 16, 1994, pp. 1F–2F.

Angel Times

Angel Times is the first slick, full-color magazine devoted exclusively to angels. Published bimonthly, the first edition was the November/December 1994 issue. The brainchild of Linda Whitmon Wephula of Atlanta, Georgia—who had no previous experience in magazine publishing—*Angel Times* went from idea to product in less than six months and was an instant success. By its second issue it was already being distributed nationally.

Angel Times features articles by some of the nation's most popular angel authors, reports of angel encounters, celebrity interviews, angel art, children's stories, poetry, and a resource guide. Although the magazine is not affiliated with any particular religious denomination, staff members nevertheless say they feel they are working with angels to spiritually uplift their readers. *Angel Times* is available at bookstores and magazine

ANGEL TREASURES BOUTIQUE, ANN ARBOR, MICHIGAN.
(COURTESY DENNY DAHLMANN)

DENNY DAHLMANN, FOUNDER OF ANGEL TREASURES.
(COURTESY DENNY DAHLMANN)

COVER OF FIRST ISSUE, *ANGEL TIMES*. (REPRODUCED COURTESY *ANGEL TIMES*)

stands or may be ordered from Suite 400, 4360 Chamblee-Dunwoody Rd., Atlanta, GA 30341.

Sources:
Angel Times 1 Nov./Dec. 1994): 1.

Angelica

Angelica, *Angelica archangelica,* is the herb of the angels. A member of the parsley family, it grows to six feet and has greenish white flowers that grow in large umbrellalike clusters. It is a biennial, a type of plant that completes its life cycle in two years, but its life can be prolonged by cutting the flowers before the buds open. Angelica is native to northern Europe and Asia. Some say it got its name because it blooms in the spring, in time for Michaelmas (the festival in honor of the archangel **Michael**), which was originally held on May 8. Others say it was named after the Russian port of Archangel by botanist John Tradescant.

One legend regarding angelica says that in 1665, a community of monks, whose members were dying of the plague, was saved when one of the monks had a dream in which an angel told them to eat angelica. As soon as they chewed the plant they were cured.

Historically angelica had many uses as an herbal remedy. In rural parts of northern Europe the locals chewed angelica seeds to ward off disease. Angelica was also taken to treat rabies, pleurisy, coughs, and gastritis. The juice was even poured into the ear as a cure for deafness. Some herbalists still use angelica for stomach and intestinal disturbances.

Today angelica seeds are essential ingredients in Benedictine, a French liqueur originally made by Benedictine monks, and chartreuse, an aromatic liqueur made by the Carthusian monks in Grenoble, France and Tarragona, Spain.

In times past, angelica was used to ward off evil. The juice from angelica roots was taken to ensure a long life and to protect against witches. According to *Gerard's Herbal,* published in England in 1597, angelica was used to counter evil spells and charms, and was in demand as an amulet.

Angelica candy was also popular and can still be found in some gourmet shops. It is made by peeling angelica stalks and cutting them into short lengths, then simmering them until tender. Finally, the pieces are simmered in a rich sugar or honey syrup until crystallized.

Sources:
Freeman, Eileen Elias. "Angelica—the Herb of the Angels." *AngelWatch,* January–February 1993.

Angelico, Fra

The Italian Renaissance painter Giovanni da Fiesole, better known as Fra Angelico, was born in 1387 as Guido di Pietro near the castle of Vicchio in the upper valley of the Mugello, not far from Florence. In 1407 he and his brother presented themselves at the Dominican convent of the Observance at Fiesole, and after a year's novitiate at Cortona he took the cowl under the name of Fra Giovanni. Angelico was the name bestowed on Fra Giovanni by his fellow monks.

Because they remained loyal to the Roman Pope Gregory XII in a period of schism and dissension during which Florence shifted its allegiance to the antipope Alexander V, the Dominican monks were expelled from Fiesole by the Florentine government. They took refuge at Foligno and Cortona, but eventually returned to their monastery at Fiesole in 1418, after the Council of Constance. During the years of exile, Fra Giovanni served his apprenticeship as an illuminator and fresco painter, although his contacts with Florentine artistic life did not begin until 1418.

In 1436 the Observant monks left Fiesole for the convent of San Marco at Florence, where Fra Giovanni was asked to paint two pictures for the convent church and to decorate the chapter house, refectory, hospice, cloisters, and cells with frescoes. He was later called to Rome to decorate the chapel of Nicholas V at the Vatican, which kept him busy until 1449, when he was appointed prior of the convent of San Marco, which office he held for three years. He died in Rome in 1455 at the age of sixty-eight.

Fra Angelico portrayed angels as unearthly beings, creatures unlike any human. While wonderfully celestial, Angelico's angels are also decidedly feminine. He adhered to this mode of representation in spite of the strongly held contemporaneous belief that angels were sexless. Two exquisite examples can be found in his depiction of angels in the Linainuoli Altarpiece, in Florence, and in the *Angel of the Annunciation.*

The eponymous *St. Michael,* an exquisite small picture now in the Academy at Florence, is brilliantly celestial. The lance and shield and the lambent flame above Michael's brow are the only emblems, the flame symbolizing spiritual fervor. The rainbow-tinted wings are raised and fully spread, meeting above and behind the head. The armor is of a rich dark red and gold. The pose and the countenance indicate the reserved power and the godlike tranquility of the heavenly warrior and mark him as the patron of the Church Militant.

Fra Angelico's *Annunciation* conveys reverence and simplicity. This fresco on the wall of the corridor in the convent of San Marco is considered one of the most beautiful and spiritual Annunciations in existence. Its sweetness and charm have given it a universal appeal, which is reminiscent of its creator. Mary is innocence incarnate sitting in a portico flanked by a flower-carpeted garden, which is symbolic of her virginity. Fra Angelico has pictured Mary (who slightly leans toward her heavenly visitor) and Gabriel in such a way that the two seem equal in purity and goodness, giving the impression that Gabriel is superior only in her knowledge of the impending birth. The angel is decidedly feminine with

ANNUNCIATION BY FRA ANGELICO (FRESCO, SAN MARCO, FLORENCE, CA. 1440–45). (COURTESY ARAS)

rainbow-tinted wings and gently crossed hands sans the often depicted lily or scepter.

In the *Annunciation* in the Museo del Gesù, Cortona, the two main figures are framed. Mary's mantle, as it flows down her back, echoes the foreshortened arches, while the angel, who is a bundle of curves, echoes the frontal arches. The result is that the angel, glimpsed at the very moment of alighting, betrays no movement at all, while every line in the Virgin's figure is galvanized as she starts from her absorption in the prayer book on her knee.

Adoring angels abound in Fra Angelico's *Last Judgment*. The trumpet angels are placed below the Judge, indicating that they can be heard in all the earth, whereas the angels who announce the fate of all who are judged direct the blessed and the damned to their respective places.

Fra Angelico's *Coronation,* in the Louvre, shows the Virgin kneeling to be crowned, accompanied by a group of musical angels on each side. The painting is characterized by a deliberate trick of perspective: the divergent angles from which the scene is viewed are calculated to heighten the illusion of distance between the choir of angels and saints, on the one hand, and Christ and the Virgin, on the other.

Never have angels been more angelic than the ones portrayed in Fra Angelico's *St. Dominic,* also in the Louvre, in which a group of the saint's brethren are seated at table in the white habit and black mantilla of their order. They are served by two, winged angels magnificently robed in rich blue and gold and adorned with little gold halos, who gently bring food to the friars' table with simple dignity, as if in imitation of the humility of Christ.

Sources:

Argan, Giulio Carlo. *Fra Angelico and His Times.* Lausanne, Switzerland: Imprimeries Réunies, 1955.

de la Croix, Horst, and Richard G. Tansey. *Art Through the Ages.* 6th ed. New York: Harcourt Brace Jovanovich, 1975.

MacGregor, Geddes. *Angels: Ministers of Grace.* New York: Paragon House, 1988.

Pope-Hennessy, John. *Fra Angelico.* London: Phaidon Press, 1952.

Angelolatry

"Angelolatry" is the veneration or worship of angels. Historically, because in the great missionary faiths of **Islam** and **Christianity,** there has been a tendency for the older polytheistic deities to reemerge as angels, angelolatry has often been rejected as a form of idolatry. Throughout the ages this has led to great debate.

Within traditional Christianity, the Council of Nicaea in A.D. 325 declared belief in angels a part of dogma, which apparently caused an explosive renewal of angel veneration. As a consequence, in 343 the Synod of Laodicaea condemned the worship of angels as idolatry. Later, in 787, the Seventh Ecumenical Synod reinstated a carefully defined and limited cult of the **archangels.**

The earliest devotions, both in the East and the West, centered primarily on the archangel **Michael,** with liturgical feasts and prayers to Michael mentioned as early as the fourth century. Belief in the angelic cult of faith grew throughout the following centuries, and claimed among its proponents theologians including St. Bernard of Clairvaux (d. 1153), Pierre Caton (d. 1626), Johannes Tauler, and Ludolph of Saxony. Associations and confraternities were formed to honor angels and angelic devotion blossomed.

By the nineteenth century and into the twentieth, angelic devotion took several forms: associations and societies such as the Archconfraternity of St. Michael Archangel (erected in 1878 by Leo XIII), and the Philangeli "Friends of Angels," founded in England in 1950 by Mary Angela Jeeves; patronages; publications, such as *L'Ange gardien,* put out by the Clerics of St. Viator, France; liturgical and nonliturgical rites or practices (e.g., masses that honor specific archangels); and prayers, invocations, and novenas (namely the Litany of All Saints, the prayer in the Communion of the Sick, and the blessing of homes).

Sources:
New Catholic Encyclopedia. Vol. 1. Washington, D.C.: Catholic University of America, 1981.
Richardson, Alan, and John Bowden, eds. *The Westminster Dictionary of Christian Theology.* Rev. ed. Philadelphia: Westminster Press, 1983.
Ronner, John. *Know Your Angels: The Angel Almanac with Biographies of 100 Prominent Angels in Legend and Folklore, and Much More.* Murfreesboro, Tenn.: Mamre Press, 1993.
Wilson, Peter Lamborn. *Angels.* New York: Pantheon, 1980.

Angelophany

Abraham Lincoln frequently mentioned that he was visited by angels at the White House.

Angelology

Angelology—the study or science of angels—is a term usually reserved for more elaborate theories or theologies of angels. It would be appropriate for example, to refer to **Thomas Aquinas**'s systematic speculations on angels as an angelology.

With foundations in biblical angel narratives, two Western Christian angelological traditions developed during the Medieval period. Drawing upon the extensive angel lore in the **pseudepigraphal** writings (e.g., the **Book of Enoch**), one tradition was characterized by a focus on the traits of specific named angels, both good and evil. The other tradition was marked by philosophical reflections on such issues as whether or not angels have bodies and the functions of the various **choirs** of the angelic hierarchy as laid out by **Dionysius.** The systematic treatment of angels in Aquinas's *Summa Theologiae* is representative of this latter tradition.

Sources:

Ronner, John. *Know Your Angels: The Angel Almanac with Biographies of 100 Prominent Angels in Legend and Folklore, and Much More.* Murfreesboro, Tenn.: Mamre Press, 1993.

Strayer, Joseph R., ed. *A Dictionary of the Middle Ages.* Vol. 1. New York: Charles Scribner's Sons, 1982.

Angelophany

"Angelophany" is the visible or otherwise tangible manifestation of angels to human beings. The concept is similar to theophany, the visible manifestation of a diety. In traditional angel lore, angels often visit human beings, but are usually invisible to them. The promptings that one supposedly receives from a **guardian angel,** conveyed in the form of vague feelings or intuitions, are not tangible enough to be considered angelophanies. Paradigmatic angelophanies are the visible manifestations of angels that occurred to traditional religious figures, such as the appearance of **Gabriel** to **Mary,** the mother of Jesus.

Sources:

Ronner, John. *Know Your Angels: The Angel Almanac with Biographies of 100 Prominent Angels in Legend and Folklore, and Much More.* Murfreesboro, Tenn.: Mamre Press, 1993.

Wilson, Peter Lamborn. *Angels.* New York: Pantheon, 1980.

Angelos

The word *angelos,* from which we derive angel, is a Greek word meaning "messenger." Because many communities of Jews were scattered outside the holy land around the second century B.C., it was decided to translate Hebrew Scriptures into the universal language of the day, which—primarily as a result of Alexander the Great's conquest of the eastern Mediterranean some centuries before—was Greek. The Hebrew word for angel is *malakh,* meaning "heavenly messenger" (basically the same as *mala'ika,* the **Islamic** term for angel). Translators seem to have considered both *angelos,* which refers to rather ordinary messengers, and *daimon,* which refers to a peculiarly Greek guardian spirit that could influence the individual for good or for bad. Because of the complexity

of the notion of *daimon,* translators chose to use *angelos,* and the name stuck. The word *daimon,* however, lost its positive connotations and became the root of the English term *demon.*

Sources:

Giovetti, Paola. *Angels: The Role of Celestial Guardians and Beings of Light.* Translated by Toby McCormick. York Beach, Maine: Samuel Weiser, 1993.

Ronner, John. *Know Your Angels: The Angel Almanac with Biographies of 100 Prominent Angels in Legend and Folklore, and Much More.* Murfreesboro, Tenn.: Mamre Press, 1993.

Wilson, Peter Lamborn. *Angels.* New York: Pantheon, 1980.

Angels

In **Dionysius the Areopagite**'s hierarchical scheme the term *angels* is reserved for the lowest **choir,** which works directly with human beings. The word *angel* derives from the Greek *angelos,* meaning "messenger," and bearing messages is the primary defining function of angels. Originating in **Zoroastrianism,** they are found particularly in the Western family of religions—**Judaism, Christianity,** and **Islam**—where God is conceived of as so elevated that he does not intervene directly in the world.

In the Western religions, angels are exclusively good beings. They are opposed by evil spirits (devils or demons), who are sometimes "fallen angels," angels who revolted against God and were tossed out of heaven. By the **Middle Ages,** according to Cabalistic count, the number of angels hovering close to the earthly realm peaked at 301,655,722. From this choir emerge the beings known as **guardian angels** who are assigned to watch over and protect individuals. According to the Talmud every Jew is assigned eleven thousand guardian angels at birth. In Christian lore, it is suggested that each individual receives two at birth: "one for the right hand, which inspires him to good, and one on the left, which nudges him toward evil" (Godwin, p. 69).

Sources:

Eliade, Mircea, ed. *Encyclopedia of Religion.* 16 vols. New York: Macmillan, 1987.

Godwin, Malcolm. *Angels: An Endangered Species.* New York: Simon and Schuster, 1990.

Guiley, Rosemary Ellen. *The Encyclopedia of Ghosts and Spirits.* New York: Facts on File, 1992.

Angels of Mons

At the beginning of the first World War, a battle occurred near the town of Mons, Belgium, in which German troops were able to defeat the allied British, French, and Belgian forces. Between August 23 and 28, 1914, a number of apparitions appeared to these soldiers on the battlefield.

The German attack was so heavy and the British so outnumbered that complete annihilation was expected. The battle took a turn, however, when a vision appeared between the lines of the two fighting factions. According to an account by two British officers, while the British were retreating, the German army suddenly ceased fire and stood in amazement as "a troop of angels" stood in their way.

Another account during the same battle from Captain Cecil Hayward of the British Army states that while the British were retreating through Mons under heavy fire, the shelling from both sides stopped dead and amazed British soldiers witnessed four or five large white-robed beings appear between the lines, arms outstretched. At that point, the German army began to retreat. Captain Hayward also recounted another vision that, just as the British forces were about to be surrounded, the sky opened and luminous figures floated between the two warring armies.

Toward the end of the retreat from Mons, there were a number of other mysterious sightings. A letter from a British lieutenant-colonel appearing in the *London Evening News* gives his account of August 27, at which time he and a number of other officers witnessed a large amount of cavalry on either side of the road at a distance, trotting at the same pace. One officer took a small party out to reconnoitre, but did not see the horsemen when they approached the point at which the mysterious cavalrymen had appeared. While all of the officers and men were over-fatigued, all agreed to witnessing the apparition.

Another related account occurred on August 28. A British non-commissioned officer related to the *Evening News* that during the British retreat from Mons, as he was standing guard with a number of other soldiers, an excited officer approached him inquiring if they had witnessed anything peculiar. The officer and soldiers then observed in the sky a strange light above the German line from which three robed figures appeared, the center one larger and with outspread wings. The figure remained for about 45 minutes.

On September 29, the *Evening News* published a story written by celebrated author Arthur Machen entitled "The Bowmen." The story tells of British soldiers saved from total defeat by spirits of English bowmen from centuries before, called upon by the spirit of St. George. Machen stated that the story was fictional, and that he had written it to raise the spirits of the British citizens in light of the defeat at Mons. However, as reports of the apparitions began to appear at the same time, Machen's fictional bowmen soon became known as "The Angels of Mons." (See also **Battlefield, Angels on the**)

—*Matthew F. Merta*

Sources:
Price, Hope. *Angels*. New York: Avon Books, 1993.
Stokesbury, James L. *A Short History of World War I*. New York: William Morrow and Company, 1981.
Thompson, C. J. S. *The Mystery and Lore of Apparitions*. London: Harold Shaylor, 1930.

Angels of Punishment

According to certain Jewish commentaries on the Scriptures the angels of punishment are Kushiel, Lahatiel, Shoftiel, Makatiel, Hutriel, Pusiel or Puriel, Rogziel, and Amaliel. **Ariel** is the angel in charge of punishments in hell. According to other sources, Moses encountered five angels of punishment in heaven: Af, angel of anger; Kezef, angel of wrath; Hemah, angel of fury; Hasmed, angel of annihilation; and Mashit, angel of destruction.

Sources:
Davidson, Gustav. *A Dictionary of Angels: Including the Fallen Angels*. New York: Free Press, 1971.
Sparks, H. F. D., ed. *The Apocryphal Old Testament*. Oxford: Clarendon Press, 1984.

Angels of the Seven Churches

The Book of Revelation is composed of letters that were reputedly dictations from an angel to John of Patmos. Seven churches, each represented by its own angel, were the center of the seven Christian communities in the province of Asia (at that time in history—the eastern Mediterranean was referred to as Asia). St. Jerome and many of the Greek fathers (i.e., early leaders of the Church in the eastern Mediterranean world), as well as other commentators, believed that the seven angels (the **guardian angels** or heavenly archetypes of the seven churches) were the designated recipients of the letters, which either praised, reprimanded, or warned each church and its respective angel.

John describes the beings as seven stars, which follows the Semitic correlation between stars and angels. Also interesting is that in the Book of Revelation, and throughout the New Testament, the term *angel* denotes a *superterrestrial* being. An ambiguity as to the meaning of the term angel arises in this story, however. Many Latin fathers (early leaders of the Church in the eastern Mediterranean), along with many modern commentators, think that perhaps John meant *bishop* or *leader,* rather than *angel,* as the designated recipient of the letter to each church, for only human beings—not angels—could be held responsible for the merits or sins of an

organization. Either interpretation is problematic, in that in the genre of apocalyptic literature, the association of angels with churches or with particular human beings is virtually unknown.

Sources:

Davidson, Gustav. *A Dictionary of Angels: Including the Fallen Angels.* 1967. Reprint. New York: Free Press, 1971.

Freedman, David Noel. *The Anchor Bible Dictionary.* Vol. 1. New York: Doubleday, 1992.

New Catholic Encyclopedia. Vol. 1. Washington, D.C.: Catholic University of America, 1981.

Angel's Trumpet

Angel's trumpet is the common name for *Datura stramonium,* or jimsonweed. The name is attributed to the tubular shape of the flower, said to resemble **Gabriel**'s trumpet, which the archangel will blow on the Day of Judgment according to the Book of Revelation. Others say the plant was so named because it is poisonous and anyone who eats the plant is likely to hear Gabriel's horn prematurely!

Angel's trumpet grows three to six feet and bears large, showy flowers similar to morning glories. The plant was discovered in ancient times and has been used by religious groups to induce visions. Native Americans of what is now the southwestern United States used it in spiritual ceremonies. South American Indians used the plant as an anesthetic while performing surgeries. Drugs that have been isolated from angel's trumpet include atropine (used to relieve spasms and dilate the pupil of the eye), hyoscyamine (used as a sedative and hypnotic) and scopolamine (used in producing twilight sleep).

Sources:

Freeman, Eileen Elias. "Angel's Trumpet." *AngelWatch,* March–April 1993.

AngelWatch Newsletter

AngelWatch is a bimonthly newsletter and resource guide about angels. Originated by **Eileen Freeman,** best-selling author of *Touched by Angels, Angelic Healing,* and *The Angels' Little Instruction Book,* the newsletter is published by the AngelWatch Foundation, of which Free-

THE APOCALYPTIC *DAMNED CAST INTO HELL* BY LUCA SIGNORELLI (FRESCO FROM THE SAN BRIZIO CHAPEL OF THE CATHEDRAL IN ORVIETO (1500–1504). (COURTESY ARAS)

man is founder and director. Perhaps the most broad-ranging of current angel periodicals, *AngelWatch* includes scholarly articles on relevant topics along with accounts of personal experiences with angels. New publications are also reviewed and angel conferences are announced. Of particular value is the resource guide, which is updated in each issue. Contact *AngelWatch,* P.O. Box 1362, Mountainside, NJ 07092.

Sources:

Hauch, Rex, ed. *Angels: The Mysterious Messengers*. New York: Ballantine, 1994.

Apocalypse

In popular usage, *apocalypse* is sometimes used to refer to non-supernatural mass destruction, such as the annihilation that often accompanies warfare, as graphically depicted in the popular 1979 film, *Apocalypse Now.*

Derived from an ancient Greek word for "revelation," *apocalypse* originally referred to a literary genre in which mysterious revelations were given or explained by a supernatural figure such as an angel. For example, the Book of Revelation, perhaps the most familiar example of this class of literature, begins with the assertion that the source of the revelation about to be related is an angel: "The revelation of Jesus Christ, which God gave him to show to his servants what must soon take place; and he made it known by sending his angel to his servant John" (Rev. 1:1). Apocalyptic literature generally paints an **eschatological** (endtime) scenario that includes wars—sometimes between legions of angels and legions of **demons**—plagues, and other acts of destructive violence, which is why it acquired its destructive connotations. The genre began with Jewish apocalyptic literature around the third century B.C.

In the contemporary period, the approach of the year 2000 on the Western calendar has led to heightened interest in popular belief about the end of the world, with most portrayals of the endtime picturing an apocalyptic scenario. There has been a steady flow of predictions that the world is coming to an end, and, as the end of the second Christian millennium approaches, the number has slowly increased.

Interest in angels has traditionally been associated with **millennialism,** especially when the millennium is viewed as emerging in the wake of a God-directed apocalypse. This is largely because of the importance of angels in relevant Scripture; if a work like the Book of Revelation is taken as a literal scenario of the endtime, then angels become significant as the central actors in the drama of the final days.

Sources:

Cohn, Norman. *The Pursuit of the Millennium.* London: Oxford University Press, 1957.

Eliade, Mircea, ed. *Encyclopedia of Religion.* 16 vols. New York: Macmillan, 1987.

Lanternari, Vittorio. *The Religions of the Oppressed: A Study of Modern Messianic Cults.* New York: Mentor, 1956.

Morris, Henry M. *The Revelation Record: A Scientific and Devotional Commentary on the Book of Revelation.* Wheaton, Ill.: Tyndale House, 1983.

Mounce, Robert H. *Book of Revelation: The New International Commentary on the New Testament.* Grand Rapids, Mich.: Wm. B. Eerdmans, 1977.

Apocrypha and Pseudepigrapha

Between approximately 200 B.C. and A.D. 100, numerous religious writings were circulating in the Jewish world that, although they had the flavor of Scripture, were eventually rejected from the Jewish canon. These books of dubious authenticity are referred to as the Apocrypha (from Greek *apokryptein,* to hide away; *apocryphal* later acquired the connotation of "spurious") and the Pseudepigrapha (anonymous or pseudonymous writings, the latter often attributed to a famous biblical personage, like **Elijah** or **Enoch**). These writings were characterized by an apocalyptic emphasis that often pictured supernatural redemption at the hands of God and his angels, a trait they share with the **Dead Sea Scrolls** and with the Book of Revelation.

One reason these writings were rejected from the canon was that they populated the cosmos with so many angels that the rabbis feared new forms of idolatry focused on angelic beings would emerge. In the Book of Enoch (40:1), for instance, the author observes that he "beheld thousands of thousands, and myriads and myriads, and an infinite number standing before the Lord of spirits," a description that seems to have inspired the author of the Book of Revelation (5:11).

Many of the writings rejected from the Jewish canon by the rabbis were retained in the Catholic canon. With respect to angel lore, the most important of these apocryphal compositions is **Tobit,** a book that contains the tale of the angel **Raphael** aiding Tobias, son of Tobit. During the Reformation, the Protestants decided to eject all of the apocryphal books from their Bible and adopt the Jewish canon as the Protestant Old Testament. This action was taken primarily because certain books of the Apocrypha seemed to support the notion of **purgatory** (an idea rejected by Protestants) or the belief that the living could somehow "buy" salvation for the dead (as, for example, in 2 Macc. 12:43–46).

Sources:
Laurence, Richard, trans. *The Book of Enoch.* Thousand Oaks, Calif.: Artisan Sales, 1980. (Originally published 1882.)
Margolies, Morris B. *A Gathering of Angels: Angels in Jewish Life and Literature.* New York: Ballantine, 1994.
Metzger, Bruce M. *The Apochrypha.* New York: Oxford University Press, 1977.

Appolion

The name Appolion (also Appolyon or Apollyon) means "destroyer" and refers to the angel of hell's bottomless pit. As described in Rev. 9:1–11 and 20:1–8, Appolion opens the shaft of this pit and lets out upon the earth a swarm of locusts with humanlike faces. The locusts proceed to torture those of mankind who "have not the seal of God upon their forehead." The locust "king," Appolion later takes on an even greater challenge than managing his brood, which is to seize **Satan,** bind him, and then throw him in the bottomless pit for a thousand years. Appolion locks Satan away, so that he "should deceive the nations no more, till the thousand years were ended"(after which Satan comes out again for a short while to try to entrap mankind once again).

In most biblical references, Appolion is a good angel who serves God, but in other writings he has fallen and succumbed to evil. In John Bunyan's *Pilgrim's Progress,* for example, Appolion is the Devil himself, with fire and smoke coming out of his belly. In Hebrew, Appolion is known as **Abaddon,** and in Greek lore he is the fallen sun god Apollo, living in hell as a serpent angel. The name Appolion has also been used to mean hell itself.

Sources:

Davidson, Gustav. *A Dictionary of Angels: Including the Fallen Angels.* 1967. Reprint. New York: Free Press, 1971.

Godwin, Malcolm. *Angels: An Endangered Species.* New York: Simon and Schuster, 1990.

Ronner, John. *Know Your Angels: The Angel Almanac with Biographies of 100 Prominent Angels in Legend and Folklore, and Much More.* Murfreesboro, Tenn.: Mamre Press, 1993.

Apsara

In many ways, apsaras (the word is derived from *ap,* "water") differ from the traditional Western conception of angels. For instance, as the nymphs of southern Asia, they are best known for their inordinate interest in sex. The mistresses of the **gandharvas,** (said to reside in the sky or in trees), they are shape-shifters and are fond of bathing. The apsaras are also the singers and dancing girls of the heavenly paradise. Perhaps their role as celestial singers is what ultimately associated them with angels.

In the Vedas, the most ancient religious texts of Hinduism, the apsaras performed the role of **valkyries,** escorting the valiant warriors slain in battle to heaven, which may also have influenced observers to perceive them as angelic. Unlike the valkyries, however, the apsaras would—true to their nature—seduce the heroes as they were flown to heaven.

Finally, in Hindu mythology, the apsaras were often sent to earth to seduce ascetics who seemed on the verge of attaining a divine state, and thus posed a threat to the status of the gods. Therefore they were angel-like in the sense that they performed duties at the behest of the gods, although these duties were decidedly nonangelic.

Sources:
Garg, Ganga Ram, ed. *Encyclopedia of the Hindu World.* Vol. 2. New Delhi: Concept Publishing, 1992.
Stutley, Margaret, and James Stutley. *Harper's Dictionary of Hinduism: Its Mythology, Folklore, Philosophy, Literature, and History.* New York: Harper & Row, 1977.

Archangels

The prefix "arch," meaning principal or preeminent, when attached to the word angel, literally translates as chief-angel. Depending on the reference souirce this high-ranking choir may be composed of four, six, seven, or nine angels. For instance, according to the Book of Revelation, there are seven archangels who stand in the presence of God. While **Michael, Gabriel,** and **Raphael** are generally agreed to be three of the seven archangels, the identity of the other four is subject to debate. Possible candidates are **Uriel, Raguel, Zadkiel,** Saraqael, Remiel, Anael, Orifiel, Uzziel, **Raziel,** and **Metatron.** The Koran only recognizes four and actually names only two, **Djibril** (Gabriel) and Michael.

According to **Dionysius** the archangels are "messengers which carry Divine Decrees." They carry God's messages to humans and are ultimately in command of God's armies of angels who constantly battle the Sons of Darkness, with Michael at the helm.

In art archangels are usually depicted with larger wings and many eyes. Of the archangels, the most often represented are Raphael, Gabriel, and Michael.

Sources:
Davidson, Gustav. *A Dictionary of Angels: Including the Fallen Angels.* New York: Free Press, 1971.
Ronner, John. *Know Your Angels: The Angel Almanac With Biographies of 100 Prominent Angels in Legend and Folklore, and Much More.* Murfreesboro, Tenn.: Mamre, 1993.

Architecture, Angels in

Angels are an essential feature in religious art and architecture; in sacred structures angels are depicted in frescoes, mosaics, sculpture, or as ornaments for liturgical accoutrements. In secular architecture angels often appear as painted or sculpted details on such items as corbels or brackets, or accompanied by arabesques (flowing, fancifully intertwined

DETAIL OF FRIEZE FROM THE VILLA OF MYSTERIES, POMPEII, CA. 50 B.C. (COURTESY ARAS)

branches of flowers and leaves) or scrolling on plasterwork, or incorporated into other architectural elements.

Angels in Classical Architecture

In ancient Greece and Rome the winged motif symbolized victory.
Winged figures frequently were used in classical vase paintings, wall
paintings, and sculpture. The most notable example of this motif is the
winged goddess of victory, *Nike of Samothrace,* circa 190 B.C., which
currently stands in the Louvre in Paris. Several such winged figures are
featured on the marble frieze from the Alter of Zeus and Athena erected
in about 180 B.C. (now in the Staatliche Museen in Berlin), which dra-
matically illustrates *The Battle of Gods and Giants* in seven-foot-high
panels.

The excavations at the site of the ancient cities of Herculaneum in 1738 and Pompeii in 1748 in what is now Italy uncovered numerous well-preserved frescoes and mosaics, some of which depict winged figures.

In A.D. 79 the cities were covered with ash from the eruption of Mount Vesuvius, however, the interiors of a large number of structures remained preserved. Excavations reveal that public and private structures featured large, brilliantly colored murals; because of the small number of doors and windows in these structures, a considerable amount of wall space remained that was suitable for decoration. Walls in a structure excavated at Pompeii, now known as the Villa dei Misteri, display scenes of winged figures and humans carrying out what is believed to be some mysterious rite; the room itself is thought to have been used as a banquet room or possibly a place for the celebration of a Dionysian cult. The winged figures along the frieze are painted in the relief style set against a red background. Similar wall painting exists at other sites in Pompeii and Herculaneum.

Angels in Early Christian Architecture

Prior to the middle of the fourth century, Christian angels were portrayed as wingless beings. Some art historians claim that the winged Roman goddess of victory was first transformed into a winged Christian angel in Assyria and that the concept then spread via Asia Minor to western Europe. However, there is no conclusive evidence to support this claim.

Nevertheless, the architecture of the Christian church utilizes an abundance of Biblical scenes that portray angels; in particular artists worked from theologian's concept of angels. The old church represented angels as wingless harbingers, as wanderers with a staff, or as young men clothed in simple tunics, as evident in the Priscilla catacomb of Rome. The catacombs, a vast network of chambers running beneath the city of Rome, contain many small rooms called *cubicula,* which were decorated with brightly painted frescoes. It is believed that during the period of Christian persecution these cubicula were used as chapels.

In A.D. 325 Constantine established Christianity as the official religion of the Roman empire and the churches built during his reign feature brilliantly colored mosaics portraying angels.

In addition to mosaics, angels and other figures were carved into the capitals of columns as architects of this period departed from the classical Doric, Ionic, and Corinthian orders. Winged figures known as *genii,* often appeared on Christian sarcophagi and on other relics as symbols of the victory of good over evil. Other themes featuring Christian angels included the Visitation of Mary, the mother of Christ, by angels; angels announcing the incarnation of Christ; Christ's Ascension accompanied by angels; Christ enthroned in glory surrounded by angels; angels singing praises; and the angel whose sword protects the church against evildoers.

Charlemagne, like Constantine, desired to create a unified Christendom and produced an environment in which the depiction of angels flourished; the Holy Roman empire existed as a central force in Europe for over one thousand years. The *Imperial Diptych,* an ivory carving from Constantinople dating to around A.D. 500 and believed to have come from the so-called "Place of Charlemagne," features two winged figures typical of the time.

Ottonian architecture of the tenth century followed the course set by its Carolingian predecessors. Several examples of Ottonian architecture exist, including the abbey church of Saint Michael in Hildesheim, Germany. The nave at Saint Michael's features a painted ceiling illustrating several biblical scenes containing angels.

The Byzantine style, which first appeared in the fourth century, was a synthesis of Hellenistic and Eastern influences. The exterior wall surfaces of Byzantine structures were often ornamented with relief carvings. Church interiors featured brightly painted colored mosaics, marble veneering, or frescoes depicting episodes in the life of Christ, the apostles, saints, and martyrs, other narratives from the Bible, or ceremonial scenes of the time. Early in the sixth century the Italian city of Ravenna was made the western seat of the Byzantine empire. Examples of Byzantine depictions of angels can be found in the apse mosaics of San Vitale, built between 527 and 547. One mosaic features Christ seated between angels and saints.

The apse mosaic of the Cathedral of Torcello shows an angel high above the Virgin Mary and the infant Christ. In 726 an edict of Leo III banned religious imagery in the Byzantine empire. The iconoclastic debate was influenced in part by the rise of **Islam** and its nonrepresentational art. The ban was lifted in 843.

Angels in the Architecture of the Eastern Church

Angels of the Eastern Church were depicted as dignified protectors, never as female or children. **Seraphim** were portrayed as having six wings covering their body so that only the head was visible; **cherubim** were portrayed as having four wings; ordinary angels had only two wings. In Asia Minor the adoration of angels was customary, and churches built in honor of angels were known throughout. (The archangel **Michael** was the first to be adored by a cult.) Depictions of Michael and **Gabriel,** in particular, became fixtures at church entrances.

Angels in Romanesque Architecture

Architecture during the late eleventh and early twelfth centuries represented a revived interest in the architecture and construction principles of ancient Rome; the style developed as a direct response to the liturgical needs of the church. The carvings at Saint Pierre Cathedral in Angoulême, built between 1115 and 1135, serve as an excellent example of the illustrative style of the period. The tympanum of the south portal illustrates the Second Coming of Christ, with Christ enthroned and flanked by Matthew, Mark, Luke, and John, and an attendant angel holding a record of the deeds of humankind. Angels are similarly treated in a portal at Saint Lazare, which dates to ca. 1130, in Autun, France.

THIS SIXTH-CENTURY MOSAIC FROM THE BASILICA DE SAN VITALI IN RAVENNA FEATURES CHRIST FLANKED BY SAINTS AND ANGELS. (COURTESY ARAS)

Angels in Gothic Architecture

The style first referred to as Gothic flourished from about 1150 to 1420 in Italy, and to 1500 in Northern Europe. The Gothic style originated in the church architecture of the Burgundy and Normandy regions of what is now France. Such architectural innovations as the development of the rib vault and the flying buttress led to the building of higher, lighter structures. The system of flying buttresses further developed into a system of semi-arches adorned with pinnacles and statues. The use of stained glass further added to the lightness of Gothic structures. The period also witnessed the increased adoration of the Virgin Mary, the Mother of Heaven, who was often depicted in the company of angels. The three west portals of Chartres Cathedral (built between 1194–1220) show Christ in majesty with the Virgin Mary, Christ's Ascension into heaven, and his Second Coming. Angels are prominently featured. The north portal of the west façade illustrates Christ's Ascension—Christ is pictured in the tympanum's center supported by angels, above a portal filled with flying angels addressing the seated apostles.

Angels in Renaissance Architecture

The period known as the Renaissance actually consists of three eras: the early Renaissance (1420 to 1500), the High Renaissance (1500 to 1550), and the Late Renaissance, or Age of Mannerism (1530 to 1600). The period was a time of revived interest in classical ideas; buildings during this period reflected a fascination with ancient Greece and Rome. Included among the period's most significant developments in the area of the arts and architecture were the exercises in perspective and in classical proportions.

The repertoire of Renaissance motifs included garlands, scroll-work, nymphs, and winged forms. Angel-like forms, reminiscent of those of ancient Rome, were included among the carved figures that crown the porches and pediments of the Villa Rotunda (built between 1550 and 1553) near Vicenza, Italy and the San Giorgo Maggiore (built in 1656) designed by Venetian architect Andrea Palladio. The work of Palladio served as inspiration for architects of the much later Georgian period (1714 to 1830). Similar motifs appear in the work of the English architect and furniture maker Robert Adams.

The depiction of little angels with robes and long trains of garland became popular during the Renaissance, as well as the use of *putti,* or children's heads with wings. Feminine angels were first represented during this period; from this point onward the concept of angels as female beings became increasingly frequent. Cherubs in the company of the Madonna and Child was another recurrent image. The marble tomb of Leonardo Bruni sculpted by Bernardo Rossellino features on its side two winged figures supporting an inscribed tablet and is crowned with two winged *genii* holding an escutcheon atop the great arch surrounding the tomb. The tympanum shows the Madonna and Child with two cherubim, and the base of the tomb features a rank of cherubim bearing garland.

Angels in Baroque and Rococo Architecture

The Baroque style flourished from about 1600 to about 1770; the later phase of the Baroque is often referred to as the Rococo and lasted from about 1720 to the period's close. The Baroque was an outgrowth of the aesthetic concepts developed during the Renaissance. Ornamentation abounds in Baroque and Rococo architecture and the decorative arts, often in the form of three-dimensional elements emanating from the

THE ORNATE SCROLLWORK, WINGED FIGURES, AND CHILDREN'S HEADS WITH WINGS ARE TYPICAL OF THE RENAISSANCE STYLE. DETAIL OF WROUGHT-IRON SPANISH GATES IN CHESTER CATHEDRAL, GUADALAJARA, 1558. (COURTESY CONWAY LIBRARY, COURTAULD INSTITUTE OF ART)

structure's surfaces. Extensive use of frescoes for walls and ceiling and elaborate molding were typical during the period.

Representative of the Baroque, two massive marble female angels wielding trumpets crown the arched entry to Scala Regina, the monumental stairway leading to the papal apartments in the Vatican, designed by Gianlorenzo Bernini and built between 1663 and 1666. The *baldacchino,* the massive canopy above the altar of Saint Peter's, also designed by Bernini and built between 1624 and 1633, is supported by four spiral columns topped by four colossal angels standing guard.

The Rococo was essentially an interior style carried out in furniture and the decorative arts. Delicate, undulating lines and sinuous curves were characteristic of the style; gilded moldings, ormolu (gold-colored furniture mounts), and relief sculpture were also typical. The ceiling fresco at the Villa Pisani in Stra, Italy, titled *The Apotheosis of the Pisani Family* is an exceptional example of the Rococo treatment of angels. Painted by Giambattiota Tiepolo in 1761, the fresco depicts angels of all types fluttering through sunlit skies and resting on clouds.

Angels in Romantic Classical Architecture

The nineteenth century was a period of romantic nationalism inspired by the past and the influences of ancient Rome is evident in much of the architecture and decorative arts of the period; many of the symbols of the French Revolution were borrowed from ancient Rome. Frequently used motifs included military insignia, crossed swords, arrows, and winged figures.

Arc de Triomphe built between 1806 and 1836 and designed by Jean François Thérèse Chalgrin, features four massive high-relief and several smaller bas-reliefs illustrating scenes from the Republic's history.

One of the large reliefs by artist François Rude, *The Departure of the Volunteers* or *La Marseillaise,* shows French volunteers (dressed in classical attire) being led by the winged goddess of liberty to defend the new Republic from foreign enemies. Winged figures also crown the richly ornamented façade of the Paris Opéra (Académie Nationale de Musique), another treasure of French romanticism built between 1861 and 1874 by Charles Garnier.

Angels in Victorian Architecture

The Victorians displayed considerable originality in ornamentation and it may even be said that they made the greatest contribution to architectural ornamentation and the decorative arts. Revived interest in the

"LA MARSEILLAISE," ARC DE TRIOMPHE, PARIS, 1833–36, FRANCOIS RUDE.
(COURTESY ARAS)

Architecture, Angels in

Gothic, Rococo, and classical styles encouraged the use of ornamental grotesques, monsters, and even angels. Large parts of façades of Victorian structures were used to illustrate mythological scenes and other stories. Buildings often were clad with carved terra cotta panels, terra cotta and brick sculpture, mosaic, or ceramic tile. Scenes of cherubs with garland trailing discretely over their bodies were typical, for Victorians regarded such ornamentation charming.

In addition to the architecture inspired by the revival movements of the Victorian age, angel-like figures were well suited to the Art Nouveau, a style that flourished from about 1890 to World War I. The Art Nouveau as an ornamental style was based on organic forms, especially those suggesting movement. Flowing, organic winged forms were typical not only in exterior architecture details but in furniture, textiles, wallcovering, glass, ceramics, and jewelry. Works by architects such as Victor Horta and Antonio Gaudí serve as excellent examples of the Art Nouveau style.

THE USE OF WINGS IS TYPICAL OF THE ART DECO STYLE. DETAIL OF A 30TH-FLOOR FRIEZE, CHRYSLER BUILDING, NEW YORK. DESIGNER, WILLIAM VAN ALEN.

Angel in Modern Architecture

The architecture and decorative arts of the twentieth century is more eclectic (as seen in the Art Deco style), more organic (as seen in the prairie and revival styles), and yet more functional (as seen in the international style) than that of prior periods. The Art Deco style, in particular, seemed to best lend itself to the treatment of angels. The style, which reached its peak between the two world wars, featured winged figures in murals, gold-lacquered angel-like beings, and similar figures in wood inlay, bent chrome, or blown glass. The most extravagant examples of Art Deco can be found in theaters, hotels, and department stores.

Architectural ornamentation following World War II has tended to be less of an extraneous embellishment and more a part of the overall architectural statement. Architects of the late twentieth century have worked closely with artists. For instance, the Metropolitan Opera House at the Lincoln Center for the Performing Arts features murals by painter Marc Chagall. The murals *Triumph of Music* and *Source of Music,* both painted in 1966, show angels and other winged figures dancing and performing. An even more spectacular display of angels can be seen in Saint Patrick's Church in Oklahoma City, which features ten-foot sculptured angels in relief.

—*Kenneth Estell*

Sources:

Barnard, Julian. *The Decorative Tradition.* London: The Architectural Press, 1973.

Berefelt, Gunnar. *A Study on the Winged Angel: The Origin of a Motif.* Stockholm: Almquist and Wiksell, 1968.

Brigidi, Stephen. *Angels of Pompeii.* New York: Ballantine Books, 1992.

Harling, Robert, ed. *Dictionary of Design and Decoration.* New York: The Viking Press, 1973.

Redstone, Louis G. *Art in Architecture.* New York: McGraw-Hill, 1968.

Short, Ernest. *The House of God: A History of Religious Architecture.* London: Eyre and Spottswoode, 1955.

Watkin, David. *A History of Western Architecture.* London: Berrie and Jenkins, 1986.

Archon

Archon, a Greek term meaning "ruler," is the name of a class of entities who played an important role in **Gnostic** thought and who are roughly comparable to evil **archangels.**

According to the Gnostic myth of creation, **Sophia,** one of the spiritual beings (**aeons**) residing in the *pleroma* (human kind's true home, "the absolute spirit") inadvertently creates another entity—often called

Yaldabaoth—who creates our familiar world (Robinson, p. 9f). This creation involves the emanation of the seven levels of the classical cosmos, corresponding to seven planetary spheres of the Ptolemaic astronomical scheme. The archons are the rulers who govern each of these levels and act as guardians, preventing the sparks of light (i.e., the divine essence of individual human beings) from returning to the pleroma. Part of the knowledge imparted to the Gnostics is information on how to bypass these archons on their journey back to the pleroma (Robinson, p. 33f).

One result of conceptualizing the cosmos as the creation of an evil divinity is that the angelic beings in the heavenly spheres surrounding the earth—the archons—are also evil. Familiarity with Gnosticism allows us to understand certain otherwise unintelligible passages in the writings of certain early Christians, who were clearly influenced by the Gnostic perspective, for example, the oft-quoted passage about spiritual warfare from the book of Ephesians (6:12):

> [W]e are not contending against flesh and blood, but against the principalities, against the powers, against the world rulers of this present darkness, against the spiritual hosts of wickedness in the heavenly places.

What, one might well ask, is the meaning of "the spiritual hosts of wickedness in the heavenly places?" Isn't the locus of evil spiritual forces in hell, which is traditionally conceptualized as being below rather than above the earth? In this passage and others that might be cited, "heavenly wickedness" refers to the archons. Even the word "rulers" here is a translation of the Greek *archon,* so that the original passage reads, "archons of this present darkness."

Sources:
Layton, Bentley. *The Gnostic Scriptures*. Garden City, N.Y.: Doubleday, 1987.
Robinson, James M. *The Nag Hammadi Library.* 1977. Reprint. New York: Harper & Row, 1981.
Turner, Alice K. *The History of Hell*. New York: Harcourt Brace, 1993.

Ariel

Ariel, meaning "lion of God," is referred to as an angel in the pseudepigraphal Ezra, as well as in *The Key of Solomon the King*. He is represented as lion-headed in various tracts on magic, and in Thomas Heywood's *The Hierarchy of the Blessed Angels* (1635), he is among the seven princes who rule the waters and is called "Earth's great Lord." According to Cornelius Agrippa, Ariel is also the name of a city, called Ariopolis. In addition, for Jewish mystics, Ariel was a poetic name for Jerusalem.

The Bible mentions Ariel as the name of a man, as another name for Jerusalem (Isa. 29), and as the name of an altar, whereas other sources refer to Ariel as an angel who assists **Raphael** in the cure of disease. The *Testament of Solomon* says he controls demons. In some occult writings, Ariel is the third **archon** (ruler) of the winds. He is also a ruler of winds in **Gnostic** lore, which says Ariel is an older name for Ialdabaoth (the Gnostic creator). According to the Coptic *Pistis Sophia,* Ariel is in charge of punishment in the lower world, whereas practical Cabala says he was originally of the order of **virtues.**

Ariel has also often been mentioned in popular works. **Shakespeare** speaks of Ariel in *The Tempest,* casting him as a sprite (a **fairy**), and **Milton** refers to him as a rebel angel, overcome by the seraph **Abdiel** in the first day of fighting in heaven. The life of the poet Shelley, who referred to himself as Ariel, is the subject of André Maurois's *Ariel.*

Finally, according to Archibald Sayce ("Athenaeum," October 1886), a connection can be made between Ariel and the *arelim,* or *erelim,* mentioned in Isaiah (33:7) as an order of angels equated with the order of **thrones.**

Sources:

Davidson, Gustav. *A Dictionary of Angels: Including the Fallen Angels.* New York: Free Press, 1967.

Heywood, Thomas. *The Hierarchy of the Blessed Angels.* London: Adam Islip, 1635.

The Key of Solomon the King. Translated and edited from manuscripts in the British museum by S. Liddell MacGregor. 1889. Reprint. York Beach, Maine: Samuel Weiser, 1989.

Art, Angels in

Angels and **archangels** and **cherubim** and **seraphim** have always been fruitful sources of inspiration for painters and sculptors. Early images of angels emerged from a creative interplay between the artist's personal vision and traditional canons, usually based upon Scripture.

It has often been assumed that only Christianity and Judaism express belief in angels, and that only Christian artists have depicted them, because Jewish law forbids all such representations. However, angels or angel-like beings also exist in classical mythology, shamanism, **Zoroastrianism, Hinduism, Buddhism,** Taoism, and **Islam.** In fact, and contrary to popular opinion, Islam does not prohibit such images, and its artists, particularly Sufi mystics, have derived a rich iconography of angels from all sources that nourish the Islamic "mythos," from the Jewish and Christian traditions, to **Gnosticism,** and Manichaeanism.

THE SIREN BIRD OF HEAVEN FROM THE *RUSSIAN LUBOK*. THIS WINGED CREATURE IS A DEPICTION OF THE HINDU APSARA. (EIGHTEENTH CENTURY, HISTORICAL MUSEUM, MOSCOW)

In both monotheistic and polytheistic traditions, angels represent messengers of God, or gods and goddesses. They are viewed as the inhabitants of an intermediate world and, according to **Muhammad,** are sent by God to earth to search out those places where individuals or groups are engaged in remembering or invoking the Deity.

Evolution of Christian Beliefs Concerning Angels

The Council of Nicaea in A.D. 325 declared belief in angels a part of dogma. In 343 the Synod of Laodicaea condemned the worship of angels as "idolatry." Finally, in 787 the Seventh Ecumenical Synod reinstated a carefully defined and limited cult of the archangels, which took root in the Eastern church; in the West, however, distrust of angels remained.

The Hebrew Scriptures (the Old Testament) represent the angels as an innumerable host, discerning good and evil by reason of superior intelligence, and doing the will of God. Not until the Babylonian captivity do we read about evil angels who wreak havoc among men, according to an angelological theory that draws from the religion of ancient **Mesopotamia** and the teachings of Zoroaster. The angels of the New Testament have sympathy for human sorrow, attend prayerful souls, and conduct the spirits of the just to heaven.

By the end of the fourth century, the Christian church developed a profound belief in the existence of both good angels, inciting human beings to pursue good, and evil angels, tempting them to sin. The church fathers maintained this faith in their writings, which teach that angelic help may be invoked in time of need.

The theologians of the **Middle Ages** originated a systematic classification of the Orders of the Heavenly Host, based on the classification of St. Paul, and assigned to each rank its distinctive office. The angelic host was divided into three **hierarchies,** and these again into nine **choirs.** The first hierarchy includes **seraphim, cherubim,** and **thrones.** The second hierarchy includes the **dominations, virtues,** and **powers;** the third, **princedoms, archangels,** and **angels.**

From the third hierarchy come the ministers, or governors, and messengers, or councillors, of God. The choristers of heaven are also angels, whose title, signifying messengers, is given to men bearing important tidings. The Evangelists are usually represented with wings, John the Baptist is often depicted as angel, and the Greeks sometimes even represented Christ with wings, calling him the great angel of the will of God.

Depiction of Angels in Christian Art

The lack of Jewish religious art, and the paucity of New Testament descriptions, presented no barrier to the art of Christianity. As far as the representation of angels is concerned, the aureole or nimbus is never omitted from the head of an angel and is always, wherever used, the symbol of sanctity.

Wings, the distinctive angelic symbol, are emblematic of spirit, power, and swiftness. This theme is very common throughout the entire Middle Ages and constitutes the first portrayal of the accepted Christian idea of angels as winged beings. The figure of the winged angel evolved during the fourth century, soon crystallized into a formula and remained common until the sixth century, after which it came into its own again in Carolingian art and the Romanesque art of Italy and southern France. It was foreign to Gothic art, although it became common again in Italy during the thirteenth through fifteenth centuries.

The Glory of Angels, the representation of great numbers of angels surrounding the Deity, the Trinity, or the glorified Virgin, is generally composed of the hierarchies of angels in circles, each hierarchy in its proper order. Complete versions of the Glory of Angels, with nine circles, are rare. Most artists contented themselves with two or three and sometimes merely a single circle. The nine circles of angels are represented in various ways and are frequently seen in ancient frescoes, mosaics, and sculptures. The princedom and power orders are represented by rows and groups of angels, all wearing the same dress and the same tiara.

The use of color constituted one of the most important elements in the proper painting of seraphs and cherubs, whereas greater freedom was permitted in the portrayal of other angelic orders. For instance, the inner circle in a Glory should be glowing red, the symbol of love; the second should be blue, the emblem of light, which symbolizes knowledge.

The colors of the oldest pictures, the illuminated manuscripts, the stained glass, and the painted sculptures were most carefully considered, although gradually the color scheme was less faithfully observed. By the beginning of the sixteenth century, it was not unusual to see the wings of cherubim in various colors, and cherub bursts with no apparent wings floating in clouds. **Raphael**'s famous *Madonna di San Sisto* and Perugino's *Coronation of the Virgin* illustrate this change.

The five angelic choirs that follow the seraphim and cherubim were not very common in art, although they were painted with great accuracy in the works of the medieval theologians. Archangels represented merely as part of their order are usually in complete armor and bear swords with

GIOTTO'S *FLIGHT INTO EGYPT* (FRESCO, SCROVEGNI CHAPEL, PADUA, 1304–1306).
(COURTESY ARAS)

the points upward and sometimes hold a trumpet. Angels are robed and wield wands, although the wand is frequently omitted, as when the hands are folded in prayer or musical instruments are in use.

All angels are supposedly masculine and are represented as having young and beautiful human forms and faces. They are never old, and infant angels symbolize the souls of regenerated men, or the spirits of those who die in infancy. Also, because angels are changeless, time does not exist for them and they enjoy perpetual youth.

The earliest pictures of angels depict ample drapery, usually white, although delicate shades of blue, red, and green were frequently employed. The Venetians used a pale salmon color in the drapery of their angels, while the early German painters affected angelic draperies of vast expanse and weighty coloring, embroidery, and jewels.

In many old churches, angels carved in marble, stone, or wood or painted on glass, frescoes, or other surfaces fill all spaces. When the stricter theological observances prevailed, however, angels were not permitted as mere decorations, but were supposed to illustrate some solemn and significant teaching of the Church. During the first three centuries of Christianity, it was not permitted to represent angels, who were pictured in a crude manner.

Until the tenth century, angels in art were curiously formed, and more curiously draped. **Giotto** was the first artist to approach the ideal representation of angels, and his pupils excelled him in their concept of what these celestial beings could be. It was **Fra Angelico,** however, who first succeeded in portraying absolutely unearthly angels. No angel of Fra Angelico's resembles any human creature, whereas the angels of other masters often resemble a beautiful boy or a happy child. Also, Fra Angelico's angels are feminine, almost without exception.

The angels of Giotto and Benozzo Gozzoli are also quite feminine, whereas **Michelangelo,** whose angels are not winged, fail to represent such celestial beings. Leonardo da Vinci's angels almost smile, while Correggio reproduced lovely children who served as models for his angels. In paintings by Francesco Albani and Guido Reni, angels are often attractive and elegant boys, as may be seen in the illustration of the child Jesus with angels, by Albani.

Raphael's angels, especially in his later works, are sexless, spiritual, graceful, and, at the same time, the personification of intelligence and power, as may be seen in the illustration of the archangel **Michael,** as well as in the *Expulsion of Heliodorus from the Temple,* in the Stanza della Signatura in the Vatican, in which angels are without wings. **Rembrandt,** too, painted wonderful angels that are poetical, unearthly apparitions. Botticelli's Neoplatonism inspired him with a vision of angels as human and classical as Raphael's, but somehow more genuinely mystical and supernatural, as can be seen in his *Mystic Nativity.*

Among **contemporary artists,** there are significant representations of angels by Auguste Rodin, Max Ernst, Paul Klee, and, especially, Marc Chagall. Chagall was a Russian painter who was obsessed by angels, as evidenced in his *The Fall of the Angel,* which is characterized by a violent red color in which the angel burns while falling.

—*Michela Zonta*

Sources:
de la Croix, Horst, and Richard G. Tansey. *Art Through the Ages.* 6th ed. New York: Harcourt Brace Jovanovich, 1975.

Jiménez, José. *El àngel caìdo. La imagen artìstica del àngel en el mundo con-temporàneo*. Barcelona: Editorial Anagrama, 1982.

Serres, Michel. *La Legende des Anges*. Paris: Flammarion, 1993.

Wilson, Peter Lamborn. *Angels*. New York: Pantheon, 1980.

Asmodeus

The name Asmodeus means "creature [or being] of judgment." Originally a Persian demon, he was later incorporated into Jewish lore, where he was known as "a raging fiend." The Book of **Tobit** tells a story about how Asmodeus killed the seven previous bridegrooms of Sarah and then planned to strike once more against the eighth—a young man named Tobias. But this time Asmodeus was not successful, as the archangel **Raphael** was protecting Tobias. Raphael exiled Asmodeus to upper Egypt, where he was kept under restraint by another angel until he finally moved on to hell.

Asmodeus shows up in other writings, such as *The Devil on Two Sticks,* by Alain R. Le Sage, in which he is the central character. In *The Devil's Own Dear Son,* by James Branch Cabell, Asmodeus is the son of **Sammael** and **Lilith** (who is Adam's first wife). In the legends of Solomon, Asmodeus (also known as Saturn and Marcolf or Morolf) is held responsible for creating carousels, music, dancing, and drama.

In Jewish legend, Asmodeus is said to be the father-in-law of the Bar Shalmon, who is a demon. In demonology, it is said that one should invoke Asmodeus only when bareheaded; otherwise, he will trick the supplicant. Asmodeus is also in charge of gaming houses.

Sources:

Cabell, James Branch. *The Devil's Own Dear Son, a Comedy of the Fatted Calf*. New York: Farrar, Straus, 1949.

Davidson, Gustav. *A Dictionary of Angels: Including the Fallen Angels*. 1967. Reprint. New York: Free Press, 1971.

Godwin, Malcolm. *Angels: An Endangered Species*. New York: Simon and Schuster, 1990.

Le Sage, Alain R. *The Devil on Two Sticks*. London, printed privately for the Navarre Society, 1927.

Ronner, John. *Know Your Angels: The Angel Almanac with Biographies of 100 Prominent Angels in Legend and Folklore, and Much More*. Murfreesboro, Tenn.: Mamre Press, 1993.

Astaroth

Astaroth is mentioned in a variety of sources, each offering contradictory identification. In Arthur Waite's *The Book of Black Magic and of*

Pacts, before Astaroth fell he was a prince of the order of **thrones.** In Spence's *An Encyclopedia of Occultism,* Astaroth belonged to the order of **seraphim.** The *Grimorium Verum* maintains that Astaroth has set up residence in America.

In *The Lemegeton,* Waite refers to Astaroth as a great duke in the infernal regions, whereas according to Barrett in *The Magus,* he is called Diabolus in the Greek language. It is said that when he is invoked Astaroth manifests as a beautiful angel astride a dragon carrying a viper in his right hand. According to Voltaire, Astaroth was an ancient god of Syria, whereas De Plancy argues that he was one of the seven princes of hell who visited Faust.

Sources:

Barrett, Francis. *The Magus.* New Hyde Park, N.Y.: University Books, 1967.
Davidson, Gustav. *A Dictionary of Angels:Including the Fallen Angels.* 1967. Reprint. New York: Free Press, 1971.
Spence, Lewis. *An Encyclopedia of Occultism.* Rev. ed. New Hyde Park, N.Y.: New York University Books, 1974.
Waite, Arthur Edward. *The Book of Black Magic and Ceremonial Magic: The Secret Tradition in Goetia including the rites and mysteries of Goetic theurgy, sorcery and infernal necromancy.* New York: Causeway Books, 1973.

Astrology, Rulership, and Angels

In the language of **astrology** (the study or science of the stars) rulership refers to an association of the planets with the signs of the **zodiac** and other phenomena whereby each planet is said to "rule" certain sets of objects and activities. This relationship is one of kinship based on recognized traits and associations. Thus, Mars rules war and iron, the sign Aries, pioneering activities, the planet Venus rules love, the sign Taurus, possessions, marriage, etc. If one were to translate this older notion of "rulership" into modern language, one would likely use another expression, *association.* However, centuries ago the relationship of ruler and ruled must have seemed a natural one to people who lived under systems of royal government, and thus this "ruler" relationship was chosen to serve as a metaphor in other realms of thought.

Because angels and planets are both inhabitants of the celestial spheres, it is natural that cultures have historically associated angels with astrology. In traditional, Western angelology, this connection is typified in the mystical system known as the Cabala. The Cabala provides a system of correspondences that was later picked up by ceremonial magicians, who utilized a knowledge of astrology in their magical practices. It was even said that the angels taught the Cabala to mortals to give them a path back to God.

As angels proliferated in the European **Middle Ages,** they further came to be viewed as serving specialized functions. From this specialization, it was almost inevitable that they would come to be associated with various phenomena, much like traditional planetary associations. It was therefore natural that angels should be described as governing or *ruling* various things and activities. Thus there are angels that rule the wind, the various **planets,** and even love.

Sources:

Davidson, Gustav. *A Dictionary of Angels: Including the Fallen Angels.* 1967. Reprint. New York: Free Press, 1971.

Lewis, James R. *Astrology Encyclopedia.* Detroit, Mich.: Gale Research, 1994.

THE ASTRONOMY BY
CHARLES-NICOLAS COCHIN
THE YOUNGER (CA. 1715–90).

Asura

Asura is a southern Asian term for "demon," the closest thing that **Hinduism** has to a **fallen angel.** In the Vedas, India's earliest recoverable religious texts, the term *asura* is used interchangeably with the word *deva,* both of which refer to the gods and goddesses of the Vedic pantheon. By the time of the epics—the Ramayana and the Mahabharata— *asura* had come to mean "demon," and *deva* had come to mean "divine." In the new pantheon of classical Hinduism, the old Vedic gods were demoted to the status of demigods (the devas) and occasionally perform functions that Westerners often view as angel-like.

In classical Hindu mythology as embodied in the Puranas, the devas and the asuras are locked in ongoing conflict. Whereas the legions of the Judeo-Christian **Satan** failed to take over heaven in their original rebellion and were cast into hell, in southern Asian mythology the asuras often storm out of the underworld, succeed in taking over heaven, and drive the devas out. The devas then appeal to the high god (usually Vishnu, though occasionally Shiva or the Goddess), who appears and defeats the asuras, driving them back into the hell worlds, and reestablishing the deva/asura balance of power.

One element of Hinduism that distinguishes it from Western religions is the notion of reincarnation. As this notion was brought to bear on southern Asian mythology, devas became capable of ignoble actions that could result in their punishment (their "fall") by being reborn as asuras. Similarly, and unlike Western demons, asuras developed the capacity to perform noble actions, which could result in the reward of being reborn as devas.

Sources:

de Bary, William Theodore, ed. *Sources of Indian Tradition.* Vol. 1. New York: Columbia University Press, 1958.
Garg, Ganga Ram, ed. *Encyclopaedia of the Hindu World.* Vol. 30. New Delhi: Concept Publishing, 1992.
Stutley, Margaret, and James Stutley. *Harper's Dictionary of Hinduism: Its Mythology, Folklore, Philosophy, Literature, and History.* New York: Harper & Row, 1977.

Azazel

Azazel was one of the chieftains of the two hundred fallen angels who, according to the **Book of Enoch,** came to earth to mate with mortal women (Gen. 6:2–4). Azazel, it is said, taught men how to fashion weapons and introduced women to such things as cosmetics (thus encouraging vanity). He is mentioned by name in the book of Leviticus

(16:8–10), where he appears to have been some sort of a desert creature to whom the ancient Israelites dedicated their scapegoats containing the sins of the nation:

> Aaron shall cast lots upon the two goats, one lot for the Lord and the other lot for Azazel. And Aaron shall present the goat on which the lot fell for the Lord, and offer it as a sin offering; but the goat on which the lot fell for Azazel shall be presented alive before the Lord to make atonement over it, that it may be sent away into the wilderness to Azazel.

The early Israelites had no totally evil demonic beings. It was only later, after the Hebrews encountered the **Zoroastrian** religion, that they developed an evil anti-god opposed to Yahweh. Interpreting Lev. 16:8–10 from the perspective of a later time, the rabbis seem to have identified Azazel as the **Devil,** or as one of the Devil's infernal chieftans.

Sources:

Davidson, Gustav. *A Dictionary of Angels: Including the Fallen Angels.* 1967. New York: Free Press, 1971.

Prophet, Elizabeth Clare. *Forbidden Mysteries of Enoch: Fallen Angels and the Origins of Evil.* Livingston, Mont.: Summit University Press, 1983.

Ronner, John. *Know Your Angels: The Angel Almanac with Biographies of 100 Prominent Angels in Legend and Folklore, and Much More.* Murfreesboro, Tenn.: Mamre Press, 1993.

Four angels standing on the four corners of the earth, holding the four winds of the earth.

—The Bible, Rev. 7:1

Balaam

The story of Balaam constitutes one of the favorite subjects of famous painters, such as **Rembrandt,** whose most remarkable representation of angelic scenes is *The Angel and The Prophet Balaam* (Musée Cognacq-Jay, Paris). According to the story reported in Numbers 22, Balak, king of the Moabites, summons the prophet Balaam from the land of Amaw. At first God forbids, then later allows Balaam to follow the summons. God's angel is opposed to Balaam going, and after the show-down between man and angel, Balaam is again allowed to proceed on his voyage. It is reported that,

> Balaam got up in the morning, saddled his donkey and went with the princes of Moab. But God was very angry when he went, and the angel of the Lord stood in the road to oppose him. Balaam was riding on his donkey, and his two servants were with him. When the donkey saw the angel of the Lord standing in the road with a drawn sword in his hand, she turned off the road into a field. Balaam beat her to get her back on the road. Then the angel of the Lord stood in a narrow path between two vineyards, with walls on both sides.

When the donkey saw the angel of the Lord, she pressed close to the wall, crushing Balaam's foot against it. So he beat her again. Then the angel of the Lord moved on ahead and stood in a narrow place where there was no room to turn, either to the right or to the left. When the donkey saw the angel of the Lord, she lay down under Balaam, and he was angry and beat her with his staff.

Balaam, who did not initially recognize the angel as such, was finally illuminated.

Then the Lord opened Balaam's eyes, and he saw the angel of the Lord standing in the road with his sword drawn. So he bowed low and fell facedown. Then Balaam said, "I have sinned. I did not realize you were standing in the road to oppose me. Now if you are displeased, I will go back." But the angel let him go, and Balaam went with the princes of Balak.

This story constitutes a delightful interlude in the Numbers narrative, although it does not add considerable substance to the history of Israel's fortunes in Transjordan. There is some uncertainty about the original beginning of the episode, since verse 18 reports that Balaam refused the offer of Balak's messengers, and has declared that he must obey God's command.

The talking ass represents a note of intentional humor. Although speaking animals are not too uncommon in the literature of antiquity, the only other parallel in the Old Testament is the serpent in the Garden of Eden.

Sources:

Laymon, Charles M. *The Interpreter's One-Volume Commentary on the Bible.* New York: Abingdon Press, 1971.

MacGregor, Geddes. *Angels: Ministers of Grace.* New York: Paragon House, 1988.

West, James King. *Introduction to the Old Testament.* New York: Macmillan, 1981.

Battlefield, Angels on the

In times of war, soldiers often embrace a stronger bond with religion and the supreme being, which may be due to the closeness and possibility of death in battle. It is not unusual, therefore, for soldiers to witness apparitions of holy figures that can be interpreted as needed guidance. While most of these visions are witnessed by one person, and can be regarded as either hoaxes or products of an overactive imagina-

REMBRANDT'S *THE STORY OF BALAAM'S ASS* (MUSÉE COGNACQ-JAY PARIS, 1626).

tion, there are a number of cases where apparitions of angels, saints, and other religious figures during battles have been documented by a large number of people.

Many warring nations, especially those with Christian populations, often call upon patron saints to guide their forces during battle. For example, England calls upon St. George, while Spain enlists the guidance of St. Leo the Elder, and St. Michael and Joan of Arc are driving forces in France. Moreover, there have also been a number of angelic appearances. Both the Old and New Testament contain such stories. However, many more such cases have occurred since the writings of these books and are documented in other historical records.

During the fifth century A.D., Attila and his tribe of Huns battled Romans and other European civilizations. When he and his forces were threatening Rome, he was approached by Pope Leo who pleaded for the safety of the city. Attila immediately removed his army from the vicinity, claiming that as the Pope was speaking, he witnessed "two shining beings not of this earth" standing beside him. The figures had flaming swords, and threatened Attila with death if he proceeded further. The Church later was convinced that the two figures were **Saint Peter** and Saint Paul.

When the Goths invaded Gaul in A.D. 433, St. Albin (who was then archbishop of the city of Embrun) called upon and prayed to St. Marcellinus for the protection of the city. The Goths had laid siege to the city, and eventually reached the immediate fortifications. During the battle, a vision of St. Marcellinus appeared with a legion of angels, which threw the assailants from the walls and turned the Goth's weapons against them. The Goths were slaughtered, and the survivors fled in panic.

In A.D. 624, at the battle of Bedr, Mohamet and his army of about three hundred soldiers defeated the Koreishites, which numbered in the thousands. According to reports, leading Mohamet's army on a white horse was the archangel **Gabriel.**

In the middle part of the sixteenth century, the Asian tribe of Badagars were intent on killing a local missionary named Francis Xavier and wiping out all Christians in the nearby settlements of Trauancor and Comorinum. When Xavier learned of their plan, he went alone to confront them. As he appeared before the army of Badagars, the army's officers claimed that a large figure stood beside Xavier, with lightning coming from his eyes. At that point, the army was ordered to retreat.

On October 7, 1571, the navy of Selim II, sultan of the Turks, was defeated at the battle of Lepanto. The battle is always ascribed to Pope Pius V, who, during a Rosary procession on that date, suddenly opened a window and announced to participants, "It is now time to give thanks to God for the great victory He has granted to our arms." Official records state that at the same time the Pope made his announcement, the Turkish navy received its defeat. Turkish sailors taken prisoner avowed that they witnessed Jesus Christ, Saint Peter, Saint Paul, and an army of angels with swords in hand fighting against the Turks. The angels blinded the Turks with the smoke of their own cannons. This incident helped confirm Pius for canonization in 1712.

The twentieth century is not without its share of appearances by angelic figures during battles. One of the most famous sightings occurred during the First World War at the Battle of Mons in 1914 (see **Angels of Mons**). Another account occurred in July of 1918, in a battle near Béthune, France. British soldiers watched in amazement as German artillery began shelling some open ground between the front lines of the two armies. When the shelling stopped, the German infantry rose up from their trenches and began marching toward the field in mass formation. Suddenly, they halted, then retreated in confusion. Accounts from German prisoners state that they witnessed a brigade of cavalry approaching the German lines across the open field. The Germans thought that they were colonial militia, as they were all dressed in white and were mounted on white horses. As they got into range, the cavaliers were then attacked with machine gun fire. However, not one mounted soldier nor horse fell from the onslaught. When the troops were within clear view of the Germans, it was noted that the whole cavalry brigade was being led by a golden-haired rider carrying a sword at his side. The Germans fled in panic.

During the end of World War II, the Russian army was advancing through Danzig, East Prussia (now Gdansk, Poland). Children were temporarily living in a makeshift schoolhouse, which although in peril of being bombarded by Russian artillery, survived and was known as "the island of peace." One evening, during a prayer service at the schoolhouse, a young boy who had no religious upbringing began verbally pressing upon one of the nurses, saying, "It came up to here on them" as he tapped his breastbone. When the nurse asked what he meant, the boy explained he had seen men ablaze with light in every corner of the building, and that they were so tall the gutters on the roof came up to their chests.

The continent of Africa has seen a lot of violence within the past few decades due to political and social turmoil. In one instance during the Jeunesse Rebellion in the Congo, a rebel army advanced upon a school where approximately two hundred children of missionaries lived, with the intent of killing everyone at the residence. The school was only protected by a fence and a few soldiers, while the rebels numbered in the

Battlefield, Angels on the

George Washington often credited his guardian angel for his success at Valley Forge.

hundreds. For three days, the rebels attempted to storm the school, but each time they approached, they would suddenly stop and retreat. One wounded and captured rebel, when asked why his army did not attack, stated that each time they approached the school, they witnessed hundreds of soldiers dressed in white surrounding the compound.

—*Matthew F. Merta*

Sources:

Anderson, Joan Wester. *Where Angels Walk*. New York: Ballantine Books, 1992.

Brewer, E. Cobham. *A Dictionary of Miracles*. 1884. Reprint. Detroit, Mich.: Gale Research, 1966.

Price, Hope. *Angels*. New York: Avon Books, 1993.

Thompson, C. J. S. *The Mystery and Lore of Apparitions*. London: Harold Shaylor, 1930.

Beelzebub

Beelzebub appears several times in the New Testament, only once in the Old Testament, and never in apocalyptic literature. While the origin of his name is uncertain, Beelzebub shared the destiny of many heathen gods who lived in the land of Canaan and were turned into demons when the Jews began to filter in and develop what came to be monotheistic **Judaism.** He was mocked by the Jews as "Baalzebub, lord of flies," who created and controlled flies in the Philistine city of Ekron. He was originally known as "Baal the prince," the chief god in the Canaanite pantheon. Baalzebub appeared in 2 Kings 1:2 as the god called upon by Ahaziah, King of Israel (ca. 853–51 B.C.) to cast out demons.

In the New Testament his name is transformed into Beelzebub, and is used to refer to the Devil. He was called the prince of devils by the Pharisees, and as such he appears in Luke 11:19 when Jesus is accused of casting out demons through Beelzebub. In contemporary usage, Beelzebub is another name for **Satan.**

Sources:

Eliade, Mircea, ed. *Encyclopedia of Religion*. 16 vols. New York: MacMillan, 1987.

Encyclopedia Judaica. New York: MacMillan, 1971.

Masello, Robert. *Fallen Angels . . . and Spirits of the Dark*. New York: Perigee, 1994.

Beliar

Beliar, meaning "worthless," is mentioned as the personification or symbol of evil in various sources, including Deuteronomy, Judges, and 1

Samuel, as well as in the work of two modern writers, Thomas Mann and Aldous Huxley. He is the angel of lawlessness in the apocryphal the *Martyrdom of Isaiah* and **Satan** in the Gospel of Bartholomew. **Milton** refers to Beliar as a "false-titled son of God," whereas the medieval Schoolmen (philosophers) assert that he was once part of the order of angels and part of the order of **virtues.** In Francis Glasson's *Greek Influence in Jewish Eschatology,* however, Beliar is not regarded as an angel, rather he is compared with Ahriman, chief devil in Persian mythology.

Sources:
Davidson, Gustav. *A Dictionary of Angels: Including the Fallen Angels.* 1967. Reprint. New York: Free Press, 1971.
Glasson, T. Francis. *Greek Influence in Jewish Eschatology.* London: Society for Promoting Christian Knowledge, 1961.

Beliel

Beliel was a fallen angel who presented himself to and danced before King Solomon in *Das Buch Beliel,* by Jacobus de Teramo. In 2 Corinthians, Beliel is cast in the role of **Satan** when Paul of Tarsus asks how Christ and Beliel can agree. Victor Hugo, deriving his description of Beliel from **occult** mythology, refers to Beliel as hell's ambassador to Turkey.

A fuller account of Beliel occurs in **John Milton**'s *Paradise Lost.* When Beliel first appears, Milton declares, "A fairer person lost not Heav'n: For dignity compos'd and high exploit." But later the truth is seen that "all was false and hollow," and that "a spirit more lewd/ Fell not from Heav'n," and that Beliel was indeed "vice itself."

Sources:
Davidson, Gustav. *A Dictionary of Angels: Including the Fallen Angels.* 1967. Reprint. New York: Free Press, 1971.
Ronner, John. *Know Your Angels: The Angel Almanac with Biographies of 100 Prominent Angels in Legend and Folklore, and Much More.* Murfreesboro, Tenn.: Mamre Press, 1993.

Belphegor

Belphegor (Lord of the Opening) was once an angel of the order of **principalities,** the third-lowest order in the traditional **hierarchy** of nine orders of angels. He later became a god of licentiousness in ancient Moab. In hell, Belphegor is the demon of inventiveness, and when called upon, appears in the likeness of a young woman.

According to the *Dictionnaire Infernal,* by De Plancy, Belphegor was hell's ambassador to France. Victor Hugo concurs in *The Toilers of the Sea,* placing Belphegor in Paris. In *Paradise Lost,* by **John Milton,** Belphegor is a variant for Nisroc, whom he says is of the "Principalities of the Prime."

One story describes how the devils of hell were upset to hear about the existence of couples on earth who were apparently happily married. Belphegor was sent out on a mission to investigate, but soon discovered in his searches that the rumor was groundless.

Sources:

Davidson, Gustav. *A Dictionary of Angels: Including the Fallen Angels.* 1967. Reprint. New York: Free Press, 1971.
De Plancy, Collin. *Dictionnaire Infernal.* 4th ed. Bruxelles: Chez Tous Les Libraires, 1845.
Hugo, Victor. *Toilers of the Sea.* 1888. Reprint. New York: T. Y. Crowell, 1961.
Ronner, John. *Know Your Angels: The Angel Almanac with Biographies of 100 Prominent Angels in Legend and Folklore, and Much More.* Murfreesboro, Tenn.: Mamre Press, 1993.

The Bible, Angels in

In Christian tradition angels have generally been presumed to be a higher order of beings than humans. The Bible, moreover, by failing to enunciate any clear view of the status of angels, is open to an interpretation that would accord better with modern evolutionary theories of the universe. If humanity is rooted in lower forms of life, it would be difficult to dismiss the notion that there might be higher forms of life toward which humanity is slowly rising.

That the angels have a nature similar to humans, different only in the degree of their perfection, is suggested by Jesus in his application of Ps. 82:6 in John 10:34–37. He seems to suggest that angels are beings such as men and women might become if they were to rise above their present condition and realize their spiritual nature to its fullest. The notion that angels are beings whose nature we share, though in an undeveloped way, runs counter to the medieval scholastic tradition, in which even the beatified saints in heaven are of a different order of being than the angels.

Angels have an obvious role in monotheistic religions such as **Judaism, Christianity,** and **Islam,** in that they are needed as a means of communication from God to man. The English word *angel* is derived from the Greek word *angelos* (messenger), which in turn stems from the

Hebrew *mal'ak,* also meaning "messenger." Nevertheless, angels in the Bible are more than messengers. They constitute the court of heaven and surround the throne of God. The notion of an entourage of adoring angels is one that would come naturally to a people who had adopted the symbolism of God as king and supreme potentate.

In Hebrew the word *mal'ak* is sometimes used in conjunction with Yahweh or **Elohim,** signifying "the angel of the Lord" or "the angel of God." In some later books angels appear as God's retinue. They are even called *bene elohim,* "God's sons," and in Greek, *hoi hagioi,* "the holy ones." It is important to remember that the Hebrews had a polytheistic background, so even when they became strictly monotheistic, they may have had a residual need to do something with the old pantheon. By displacing the gods of the past and replacing them with angels, they could preserve the central concept of God as One. Later on, in the development of Christianity, the saints were to function similarly.

The creation of angels is referred to in the Book of Psalms, and the New Testament alludes to it also (Col. 1:16). In Gen. 6:1–4, there is an interesting allusion that explains the origin of heroes: as the human race multiplied, certain angels, "the sons of God," were attracted to "the daughters of men" and had sexual union with them. This reflects a notion found in Greek and other cultures' folklore in which mortal women are seduced by immortal gods.

In the Hebrew Scriptures, angels often appear in human form and are not always recognized by the recipients of the divine message. In Gen. 22:11 "the angel of the Lord," who has a special mission to protect Israel, stays the hand of **Abraham** to prevent him from slaying his beloved son Isaac as a sacrificial offering to God. In Exod. 3:2 Moses sees an angel "in the shape of a flame of fire" in a burning bush. In Gen. 19 two visitors who come to Lot to warn him and his family of the approaching destruction of Sodom and Gomorrah are designated angels. Gen. 28:12 reports **Jacob**'s dream in which he saw a ladder from heaven to earth on which angels were climbing up and down. "The angel of the Lord" in some way helps the Israelites through the Red Sea (Exod. 14:19), and an angel also appears to **Balaam,** Joshua, Gideon, and the parents of Samson.

Beginning with the book of Daniel, in which they have the function as **watchers,** angels acquire specific names and personalities, possibly as a result of Persian influence. **Gabriel** (in human form, 8:16; 9:21) explains the meaning of Daniel's visions, and **Michael** ("the prince of angels," 10:13; 10:21; 12:1) appears as the captain of a heavenly host fighting "the angel of Persia." In Isaiah's vision (Isa. 6) angels are

Bible

The Christian Bible offers some 300 references to angels.

described in poetic detail, some with six wings, each pair with a function of its own.

Angels are everywhere in the New Testament. Gabriel prophesies and explains the births of **John the Baptist** (Luke 1:11–20) and Jesus (Luke 1:26–38). Michael is the champion against the legions of the fallen angel **Satan** (Jude 9, Rev. 12:7). Unnamed angels comfort Jesus in the wilderness (Matt. 4:11), minister to him during his agony in Gethsemane, and testify to the Resurrection (Matt. 28:2–7; John 20:12).

They are reported watching over Christ's "little ones" (Matt. 18:10), rejoicing over a contrite sinner (Luke 15:10), being present when Christians worship together (1 Cor. 11:10), and bringing prayer before God (Rev. 8:3). They are even associated with the Last Judgment, during which they are in charge of the seven bowls, trumpets, and seals of the **Apocalypse.** As a matter of fact, the Apocalypse, or Book of Revelation, is so permeated with references to angels that the casual reader might almost suppose it to consist of a treatise on their activities.

Angels also appear several times in the Acts of the Apostles, notably to the centurion Cornelius (10:3–7, 10:22), to the apostles **Peter** and John, whom an angel releases from prison (5:19; 12:7–10), and to Philip, whom an angel directs to Gaza. The writer of Acts reminds his readers that the Saduccees do not believe in angels, while the Pharisees do (23:6–7). Paul, in a dream, is visited by an angel who assures him that all on the ship will be saved (27:23–24). In the apocryphal book of **Tobit** (5:4–11:8), the angel **Raphael** guides the quest of Tobias, helping him to conquer a demon that had slain the previous husbands of his bride, Sarah, and to restore the sight of his father, Tobit.

Sources:

Capps, Charles. *Angels.* Tulsa, Okla.: Harrison House, 1984.

Encyclopedia of Early Christianity. Vol. 846 of the Garland Reference Library of the Humanities. New York: Garland Publishing, 1990.

Godwin, Malcolm. *Angels: An Endangered Species.* New York: Simon and Schuster, 1990.

Kinnaman, Gary. *Angels: Dark and Light.* Ann Arbor, Mich.: Servant Publications, 1994.

MacGregor, Geddes. *Angels: Ministers of Grace.* New York: Paragon House, 1988.

Mounce, Robert H. *Book of Revelation: The New International Commentary on the New Testament.* Grand Rapids, Mich.: Wm. B. Eerdmans, 1977.

Birds

In world mythology, birds are often symbols of the spirit. In particular, they are portrayed as messengers to the gods and as bearers of the

JESUS COMFORTED BY AN
ANGEL IN THE GARDEN OF
GETHSEMANE.

souls of the dead to the otherworld. From these associations with birds,
angels ultimately derived their **wings.** The connection of birds with
angels springs from two distinct experiences of the sacred.

First, in all world religions, but particularly in Western religions, there is a tendency to view the sacred as especially associated with celestial phenomena (e.g., "Our Father Who art in Heaven . . ."). Because the heavens seem to be the peculiar "residence" of divinity, it is a natural step to regard birds as closer to the sacred, even as potential emissaries of the gods. By the same token, it is natural to assume that celestial beings have wings, either literally or symbolically.

Second, to the ancients the air itself was a spiritual substance—a medium that could be felt but not seen. In many cultures, even the word for soul is the same as the word for breath: one's breath is the invisible yet tangible part of the person that seems to leave the body and escape into the atmosphere upon death. To members of many traditional societies, birds were marvelous creatures who could shake themselves loose from the earth and float aloft in the spiritual medium of the air. It is but a short step from seeing birds as travelers of the spirit realm to attributing wings to spirit beings.

THE EAGLE BY GUSTAVE DORÉ. ILLUSTRATION FOR DANTE'S *DIVINE COMEDY.*

Sources:

Cirlot, J. E. *A Dictionary of Symbols.* New York: Philosophical Library, 1971.
Jung, Carl G., ed. *Man and His Symbols.* Rev. ed. New York: Anchor Press/Doubleday, 1988.
Leach, Maria, and Jerome Fried, eds. *Funk & Wagnalls Standard Dictionary of Folklore, Mythology, and Legend.* San Francisco: Harper & Row, 1979.

Blake, William

The work of the English mystical poet and artist William Blake (1757–1827) is full of visions of angels. Blake, who is known to many for his poem "Tiger! Tiger! Burning Bright," was born in London. He attended Henry Pars's drawing school in the Strand, and at the age of fifteen he was apprenticed to the engraver James Basire. After ending apprenticeship in 1779, he went to the Royal Academy, where he first exhibited a picture in 1780.

In 1783 his friends paid for the printing of *Poetical Sketches,* and in 1784 Blake married Catherine Boucher, who was destined to be very important for his work. In 1789 Blake issued *Songs of Innocence,* the first considerable work to be executed by his novel method of "illuminated printing," combining text and decorations on a simple etched plate.

By 1795 Blake had lived through the American and French revolutions, which left a deep impression. His *Songs of Experience* (1794) are permeated by undertones of indignation and pity for the human state. These poems also show the strong influence of mystical writers such as Paracelsus, Jakob Böhme, and **Emanuel Swedenbörg.**

Among Blake's illuminated books are *The Marriage of Heaven and Hell* (1793), a work mixing satires on Swedenbörg with metaphysical and religious discussions; *The Book of Thel* (1789), a delicate allegory of the descent of the soul from eternity into mortal life; *Visions of the Daughters of Albion* (1793), in which free love is defended; *The First Book of Urizen* (1794), containing an account of the creation of the material world and of mankind burdened with the problem of evil; *Europe: A Prophecy* (1794); *The Book of Los* (1795); *The Book of Ahania* (1795); and *The Song of Los* (1795).

Two later and longer poems are the symbolic *Milton* (1808) and *Jerusalem* (1804–20). In *Milton,* the whole problem of an evil world is correlated with Blake's own psychological struggles. It is in this poem that Blake asks whether Jerusalem could have been built amid England's "dark, satanic mills." In the epic *Jerusalem,* man awakes from error and is finally redeemed by union with God. His last major poem, *The Everlasting Gospel* (ca. 1810), is a series of fragments expressing his unorthodox view of Christianity and the life of Christ.

Blake painted and produced occasional engravings for booksellers. On the suggestion of the painter John Linnell, Blake engraved his own designs for *Inventions to the Book of Job* (1826). For the astrologer John Varley, Blake drew many "visionary heads," portraits of imaginary visitors, usually historical characters. Among these was the celebrated "Ghost of a Flea." He also worked on one hundred illustrations for **Dante**'s *Divine Comedy.* The **Bible** was always his favorite source for subjects, and when illustrating the poets, such as Milton or Bunyan, he chose semireligious themes.

Blake's works, both his writings and his drawings, are full of angels, and much of his imagery and symbolism are adopted from Böhme and Swedenbörg, both of whom deviated from prevailing theological opinion. Böhme was a mystical and theosophical writer, whereas Swedenbörg was a scientist who devoted himself to studies arising out of what he claimed to be persistent communications from angels and other agencies in a spiritual world. Blake was influenced by Böhme's idea that there are three principles—heaven, hell, and our own world—and that

ONE OF WILLIAM BLAKE'S PROPHETIC VISIONS FROM HIS ILLUSTRATIONS OF THE
BOOK OF JOB (1825). (COURTESY ARAS)

every spirit is confined in its own principle, the evil angels in hell and the good in heaven.

In the frontispiece to *The Marriage of Heaven and Hell,* Blake shows each kind of spirit in its own dwelling, one of either fire or light. In the drawing entitled *Good and Evil Angels,* he represents the Devil as blind and thus unable to see the Good Angel, whom he is trying to approach but cannot, since neither can perceive the other, one bathed in the light of God and the other covered by blackness and encompassed by burning fire.

Blake was a Platonist and was also knowledgeable about reincarnation and the karmic principle. He saw angels, good and evil, as the real forces behind the weaknesses and the triumphs of mortal men and women. Blake insisted that eternity is complete harmony, and therefore angels and spirits are androgynous, with no separate principles of male and female, but only the one of humanity.

—*Michela Zonta*

Sources:

Blier, John. *Blake's Visionary Universe.* Manchester, England: Manchester University Press, 1969.

MacGregor, Geddes. *Angels: Ministers of Grace.* New York: Paragon House, 1988.

Morton, A. L. *The Everlasting Gospel: A Study in the Sources of William Blake.* London: Lawrence & Wishart, 1958.

Schorer, Mark. *William Blake: The Politics of Vision.* New York: Henry Holt, 1946.

Bodhisattva

Buddhism, one of the major eastern religions, teaches that the ultimate goal of the religious life is to escape the cycle of death and rebirth (*samsara*) and achieve *nirvana,* an ineffable state of supreme enlightenment and bliss. The founder of Buddhism, Gautama Buddha (ca. 600 B.C.), was a former ascetic who became a highly practical spiritual teacher. The Buddha taught that human beings must depend on their own efforts to escape the cycle of death and rebirth. His early teachings did not include angels or angelic beings, but consisted of a three-fold path of morality, meditation, and wisdom.

While the Buddha himself was profoundly antispeculative and antimetaphysical, many of his later followers were not. Particularly after Buddhism split into Theravada (the Teachings of the Elders, found today in Sri Lanka and Southeast Asia) and Mahayana (the Greater Vehicle, found today in Korea, Japan, and Taiwan), metaphysical speculation flowered in Mahayana Buddhism and resulted in the introduction of angel-like helper beings. Mahayana Buddhists differentiated themselves from the Theravada Buddhists primarily through the introduction of the bodhisattva concept. The bodhisattva (Being of Wisdom), is a being who has reached the final stage on the path to nirvana, but having incredible compassion for the suffering masses of humanity, chooses to postpone entry into the final blissful state and remain on earth to help others achieve salvation. The bodhisattva inhabits a self-created realm existing somewhere between the earthly and the purely spiritual, no longer subject to the limitations of materiality. He or she could help others less spiritually advanced by bringing them into this realm by means of his or her personal spiritual power.

According to the religious writings of the Mahayana Buddhists, each bodhisattva resolves to assist all beings in every way:

> Whatever all beings should obtain, I will help them to obtain . . . The virtue of generosity is not my helper—I am the helper of generosity. Nor do the virtues of morality, patience, courage, meditation and wisdom help me—it is I who help them. The perfections of the bodhisattva do not support me—it is I who support them. . . .

The ten paramitas ("perfections") of the bodhisattva include the six mentioned in the passage above, plus an additional four mentioned in other sources. These further perfections are: skill in knowing the right means to take in leading individuals to salvation according to their diverse personalities and life situations, determination, strength and knowledge.

In addition to the ten perfections, the following virtues are attributed to the bodhisattva. Most of these are analogous to those traditionally attributed to Western angels.

> There are ten (sic) ways by which a bodhisattva gains . . . strength: . . .

> He will give up his body and his life . . . but he will not give up the Law of Righteousness.

> He bows humbly in pride to all beings, and does not increase in pride.

> He has compassion on the weak and does not dislike them.

> He gives the best food to those who are hungry.

> He protects those who are afraid.

> He strives for the healing of those who are sick.

He delights the poor with his riches.

He repairs the shrines of the Buddha with plaster.

He speaks to all beings pleasingly.

He shares his riches with those afflicted by poverty.

He bears the burdens of those who are tired and weary.

Similar to angels, bodhisattvas were many in number and each was known by his or her own name, i.e., Avalokiteshwara (He Who Looks Down in Mercy), Amitabha (Boundless Light), and Manjushri (Beautiful Lord). Devotion to a particular bodhisattva was believed to be a path to salvation for the lay Buddhists.

Sources:
Conze, Edward. *Buddhist Thought in India*. Reprint. Ann Arbor: University of Michigan Press, 1967.

De Bary, Wm. Theodore, ed. *Sources of Indian Tradition*. Vol. 1. New York: Columbia University Press, 1958.

MacGregor, Geddes. *Angels: Ministers of Grace*. New York: Paragon House, 1988.

Parrinder, Geoffrey, ed. *World Religions From Ancient History to the Present* New York: Facts on File, 1983.

Ronner, John. *Know Your Angels: The Angel Almanac with Biographies of 100 Prominent Angels in Legend and Folklore, and Much More*. Murfreesboro, Tenn.: Mamre Press, 1993.

Zimmer, Heinrich. *Philosophies of India*. Reprint. New York: Macmillan, 1987.

Bodies of Angels

Medieval Christian theologians frequently pondered the question of whether angels are purely spiritual or also have subtle, ethereal bodies. This question in not immediately answered by Scripture. In some passages (e.g., Heb. 1:14) angels are called "spirits," suggesting the incorporeal nature that the great thirteenth-century thinker **Thomas Aquinas** later assigned to them; in other passages they seem to have some kind of embodiment.

In Luke 20:36, however, Jesus is reported as saying that we, after our resurrection, are to be "like the angels." Because we are to have an embodiment of some kind in the resurrected state, however transfigured it may be, Jesus' statement seems to imply that angels have an embodiment. In his application of Ps. 82:6 in John 10:34–37, Jesus suggests that the angels have a nature similar to ours and that it is different from his only in the degree of perfection.

Origen (ca. 185–ca. 254), considered by many to be both the greatest biblical scholar and the most original mind of the patristic period, attributed to angels a subtle or ethereal body. This opinion was also held by such later scholastic philosophers as Duns Scotus (ca. 1266–1308). The opposite point of view, however, was argued by Thomas Aquinas, who asserted that since intellect is above sense, there must be some creatures who are incorporeal and therefore comprehensible by the intellect alone. These incorporeal creatures are angels; hence, angels are purely spiritual and do not have bodies, although they can, when visiting the earthly realm, sometimes assume bodies, as in the scriptural account of **Abraham**'s entertaining angels (Gen. 18).

Sources:

Edward, Paul, ed. *The Encyclopedia of Philosophy.* New York: Macmillan, 1967.

MacGregor, Geddes. *Angels: Ministers of Grace.* New York: Paragon House, 1988.

Magill, Frank N., ed. *Masterpieces of World Philosophy.* New York: Harper-Collins, 1990.

Bogey-Man

The word *bogey-man* derives from the term *boggart* or *bogy,* a type of **fairy** related to **brownies.** Some accounts portray the bogey-man as a kind of **goblin,** an unpleasant but not necessarily evil creature. However, whereas a brownie would adopt a house in order to help the inhabitants, a boggart would adopt a home in order to torment and generally make mischief with the residents. They are said to delight in tormenting small children by stealing their food and by almost suffocating them at night, hence the foundation for the caution "the Bogey-Man will get you if you don't watch out."

Sources:

Briggs, Katharine. *An Encyclopedia of Fairies.* New York: Pantheon, 1976.

McCoy, Edwin. *A Witch's Guide to Faery Folk.* St. Paul, Minn.: Llewellyn, 1994.

Book of Jubilees

The Book of Jubilees is an apocryphal work composed during the intertestamental period. According to this book, the angels were created on the first day of Creation:

On the first day He created the heavens which are above and the earth and the waters and all the spirits which serve before

Him—the angels of the presence, and the angels of sanctification, and the angels of the spirits of the winds, and the angels of the spirit of clouds, and of darkness. . . . (Giovetti, p. 19)

The Book of Jubilees also recounts the central angel tale of the **Book of Enoch,** in which a group of angels mate with mortal females, fall from grace and become devils after leaving their heavenly abode. The Book adds that God sent the Flood to destroy the race of sinful giants who were the offspring of these unnatural unions.

Sources:

Giovetti, Paola. *Angels: The Role of Celestial Guardians and Beings of Light.* Translated by Toby McCormick. York Beach, Maine: Samuel Weiser, 1993.

Metzger, Bruce M. *The Apochrypha.* New York: Oxford University Press, 1977.

Prophet, Elizabeth Clare. *Forbidden Mysteries of Enoch: Fallen Angels and the Origins of Evil.* Rev. ed. Livingston, Mont.: Summit University Press, 1992.

Brownies

Brownies are a type of **fairy,** residing, according to tradition, in Scotland, both the Highlands and the Lowlands, as well as the northern, eastern, and midlands of England. They are also known as *bwca* (booka), *bodach, fenodoree,* and house brownies. One modern writer asserts that they are found worldwide—in Denmark (where they are called *nis*), Russia (*domovoi*), North Africa (*yumboes*), and China (*choa phum phi*). They are said to be short (about three feet tall), ragged, with pointed ears, brown of complexion, and wear brown clothes.

For the most part they are extremely beneficent beings, taking care of the house or farm in which they live and the humans they adopt. Brownies are traditionally portrayed as intelligent beings who seek out deserving people to serve. They are also supposed to be nocturnal beings—one piece of folklore is that the cock crows not in order to awaken humans but to tell brownies that it is time to retire.

As helpful spirits, it was traditional to set out milk and cakes for the house brownies. This had to be done carefully, because, according to brownie folklore, this fairy being would be offended by the offer of payment. This peculiar trait was explained in diverse ways, such as that brownies were divinely appointed to ease the curse of **Adam.** Another theory is that this part of brownie lore derived from a stage in British history when the aboriginal inhabitants would work for the dominant Celts in exchange for food and clothing. Being proud as well as not wishing to feel bound to their benefactors, the aborigines would accept payment only if it was offered in a way that did not seem to transform them into paid servants.

Sources:

Briggs, Katharine. *An Encyclopedia of Fairies.* New York: Pantheon, 1976.
McCoy, Edwin. *A Witch's Guide to Faery Folk.* St. Paul, Minn.: Llewellyn, 1994.

Buddhism

Buddhism is a major world religion with a long and ancient history. Buddhism was founded by Siddhartha Gautama Buddha in northern India in the 6th century B.C. The Buddha spent several years of his life in extreme fasting and meditation with a group of religious ascetics, but did not find the enlightenment he sought. Legend has it that after he left the monks to continue his quest on his own, he sat down under a bo-tree and resolved to remain in meditation there until he achieved enlightenment. After a night of spiritual struggle with the forces of **Mara,** the evil one, he became the Awakened, the Buddha and entered a blissful, eternal, spiritual realm of being (nirvana). Out of compassion for the suffering of humanity, the Buddha forestalled entering nirvana. He chose instead to remain in his physical body and live out his lifespan in order to proclaim the Dharma, the eternal truth to which he had awakened.

The Buddha was a religious reformer teaching "the Middle Way" between extreme asceticism and materialism. The goal of the religious life of the Buddhists is to escape the cycle of rebirth (samsara) and achieve nirvana. The Buddha taught his disciples a three-fold path of meditation, morality, and wisdom toward this goal. His disciples were originally wandering shramanas (ascetic monks) who eventually settled into permanent communities.

Buddhism flourished for a time in India, but in the twelfth century A.D was supplanted through Islamic invasion. The Buddhist communities now extant are primarily in China, Tibet, Korea, Japan, and southeast Asia. It was not until the schism between Theravada Buddhism and Mahayana Buddhism occurred (first century A.D.) that the Buddhists embraced the idea of the **bodhisattva** or Being of Wisdom, somewhat akin to Western angels. In Theravada Buddhism, the older school of Buddhist thought, nirvana could only be achieved by those who, like the Buddha, lived the life of the ascetic monk. Mahayana Buddhism "the Greater Vehicle (to salvation)," offered salvation to all, by additional means. The practice of devotional Buddhism was introduced, allowing lay Buddhists to achieve eternal bliss through the intercessions of the bodhisattvas.

Sources:

De Bary, Wm. Theodore, ed. *Sources of Indian Tradition.* Vol. 1. New York: Columbia University Press, 1958.

Conze, Edward. *Buddhist Thought in India.* 1962. Reprint. Ann Arbor: University of Michigan Press, 1967.

MacGregor, Geddes. *Angels: Ministers of Grace.* New York: Paragon House, 1988.

Parrinder, Geoffrey, ed. *World Religions From Ancient History to the Present* New York: Facts on File, 1983.

Ronner, John. *Know Your Angels: The Angel Almanac with Biographies of 100 Prominent Angels in Legend and Folklore, and Much More.* Murfreesboro, Tenn.: Mamre Press, 1993.

Burnham, Sophy

Sophy Burnham is the best-selling author of the nonfiction books *A Book of Angels* (1990) and *Angel Letters* (1991) and the novels *Revelations* (1992) and *The President's Angel* (1993).

Burnham did not set out to publish *A Book of Angels.* Its genesis began much earlier in her life, when at the age of twenty-eight, according to Burnham, an angel saved her life. In her book, she describes this incident when, as she was about to tumble off a cliff while skiing, a skier dressed in black positioned himself in front her to interrupt her fall. He then disappeared. Burnham kept this encounter a secret for almost twenty years, and then began to collect all the mysterious and inexplicable things that had happened to her in her life and to people who were very close to her.

In the late 1980s an equally remarkable incident took place that led to the writing of *The President's Angel.* Burnham had read a biography of **Padre Pio,** which said that the Italian priest, who died in 1964, would answer prayers addressed to him. Through Padre Pio, Burnham asked God to show her what she could do to help promote peace on earth. Immediately, a sentence popped into her head, and then another sentence: "It was on the 695th day of his reign that the President saw the angel. He awoke from a light and fitful sleep to see the form balancing on the end of his bed." She immediately started writing the sentences down and in this way, she wrote the first chapter. Burnham completed the novel and it was published in 1992.

Burnham stands out among angel writers. Her appeal can, in part, be contributed to a distinctly objective style. Her approach is scholarly and focused and she illuminates her readers without lapsing into doggeral sentimentality. *A Book of Angels,* for example, recounts not only present-

SOPHY BURNHAM (PHOTO BY MICHAEL DAVIS, COURTESY SOPHY BURNHAM)

day angel encounters, but also explores angels throughout history and among various cultures.

Burnham was born in Baltimore, Maryland in 1936 and graduated cum laude from Smith College in 1958. She has also written juvenile fiction and numerous plays. Ms. Burnham is currently serving as the manager of the Fund for New American Plays in Washington, D.C.

Sources:

Freeman, Eileen Elias. "Sophy Burnham: the Woman Behind *Angel Letters*." *AngelWatch*. September–October 1992.

Freeman, Eileen Elias. "An Interview with Sophy Burnham: Part 2." *AngelWatch*. October 1993.

Hauck, Rex, ed. *Angels: The Mysterious Messengers*. New York: Ballantine Books, 1994.

Who's Who In America 1995. New Providence, N.J.: Reed Reference, 1995.

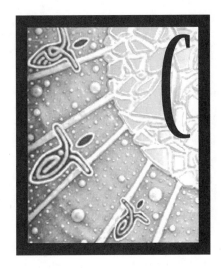

We shall find peace. We shall hear the angels, we shall see the sky sparkling with diamonds.

—Anton Pavlovich Chekhov, *Uncle Vanya*

Camael

Camael (He Who Sees God) is traditionally regarded as chief of the order of **powers** and one of the **sefiroth.** In magic lore, he is said to appear in the guise of a leopard crouched on a rock when invoked. Among occultists, he ranks as a count of the nether regions and is frequently referred to as the ruler of the planet Mars, as well as one of the governing angels of the seven planets. Within Cabalistic lore, on the other hand, he is considered one of the ten **archangels.**

Some researchers claim Camael was originally the god of war in Druid mythology. Eliphas Levi, in *The History of Magic* (1963), says he personifies divine justice. Other sources cite him as one of the "seven angels which stand in the presence of God." Clara Clement, in her 1898 book *Angels in Art,* regards him as the angel who wrestled with **Jacob,** and also as the angel who appeared to Jesus during his agony in the Garden of Gethsemane.

Sources:
Clement, Clara Erskine. *Angels in Art*. Boston: L. C. Page, 1898.
Levi, Eliphas. *The History of Magic*. London: Rider, 1963.

Margolies, Morris B. *A Gathering of Angels: Angels in Jewish Life and Literature*. New York: Ballantine, 1994.

Channeling

Channeling is a more recent term for what spiritualists traditionally termed mediumship—an event or process in which an individual "channel" is able to transmit information from a non-ordinary source, most often from a non-embodied spirit. While some channels retain full consciousness during their transmissions, most of the prominent **New Age** channels are what spiritualists refer to as trance mediums—mediums who lose consciousness while a disembodied spirit takes over the channel's body and communicates through it. These spirits frequently claim to be spiritually advanced souls whose communications consist of metaphysical teachings.

As vehicles for communication, channels are merely the most recent manifestations of a phenomenon that can be traced back at least as far as archaic shamanism. Ancient shamans mediated the relationship between their communities and the other world, often transmitting messages from the deceased. Modern channels also sometimes view themselves as being in the tradition of ancient prophets, transmitting messages from more elevated sources. With respect to this teaching function, contemporary channels can be placed in the tradition of Western Theosophy.

A number of popular New Age books have been produced by automatic or inspired writing, including those authored by Ken Carey and Ruth Shick Montgomery. Other than Montgomery's books, the most well-known "channeled" book is probably *A Course in Miracles,* which claims to be the New Age teachings of the historical Jesus. Some channelers are primarily psychics who give private readings to individual clients. Others conduct workshops and lectures for large groups, and have become quite well-known in New Age circles.

As a movement without a set doctrine or without religious authorities to determine what new ideas should be admitted or excluded in the New Age belief system, the New Age subculture has shown a remarkable permeability with respect to new notions. This relative fluidity has been reflected in the channeling phenomena, so that channeled entities tend to speak about whatever is the current hot topic of interest within the subculture. With respect to angels, however, the tendency has been for New Age mediums to start channeling angels, rather than for them simply to speak about them.

While the present explosion in angel channeling reflects a new fad, it should also be noted that angel channeling has a number of important precedents upon which the current rage builds. In particular, in certain strands of the theosophical tradition a number of people claimed to have received messages from the **devas** (the theosophical term for angelic beings) even before the New Age came into being as a distinct movement (which has been dated as emerging in the early 1970s). For example, Mark Prophet, the founder of Summit Lighthouse (the predecessor organization to **Elizabeth Clare Prophet**'s Church Universal and Triumphant), was receiving dictations from the **archangels** over two decades ago. It should also be noted that **Findhorn,** the well-known (in New Age circles) community in Scotland, claimed that its remarkable vegetable garden was built on a cooperation between devas and community members, and some people in the community channeled information from the devas (though the term *channeling* was not in vogue at the time).

Perhaps unsurprisingly, contemporary channeled angels (in contrast to the earlier angelic messengers of Findhorn and the Prophets) who are riding the crest of the new angel fad have relatively little to say that has not already been said by earlier channeled entities. The core theme of new age philosophy is the dictum, derived ultimately from new thought, that we create our own reality and hence are responsible for everything that we experience. If we are unhappy with our lives, we need only change our mind and the world we experience will change accordingly.

An example of a contemporary channeler is Elaine Regis out of Beverly Hills, Michigan. Regis is a painter who, during an average two-hour session, opens herself up to an individual's **guardian angel,** and through a kind of automatic painting, is capable of capturing on canvas what the guardian looks like. Regis claims that spiritual guides offer comfort and direction to the individual, but stresses that they are not there to dictate specific action. "Everyone has a free will," according to Regis. The picture of your spiritual guide is meant as a source of meditation, for an individual to explore their inner consciousness.

Cherubim

It is said that the cherubim are formed by the archangel Michael's tears shed over the sins of the faithful.

Sources:
Klimo, Jon. *Channeling*. Los Angeles: Jeremy P. Tarcher, 1987.
Kowalski, Greg. "Artist takes flight with angels," *The Birmingham-Bloomfield Eccentric,* 9 March 1995, p. 9A.

Cherub See: Cherubim

Cherubim

Cherubim rate second in the **hierarchy** according to the **Dionysian** schema of angels. The word is taken from the Akkadian language and

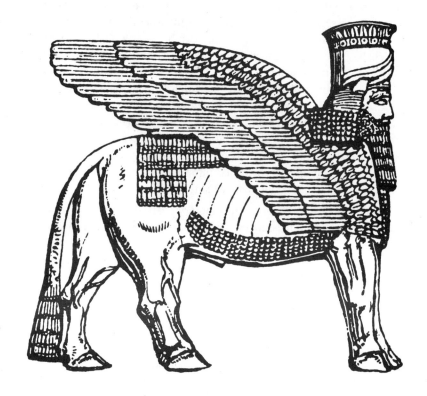

ASSYRIAN GUARD—THE ORIGINAL CHERUBIM.

means "one who prays" or "one who intercedes." Ancient Assyrian art depicts cherubim as having large, winged bodies of sphinxes, eagles, and other animals, with faces of lions or human beings. They were positioned at the entrance to temples and palaces as threshold guardians and were regarded as spirits of protection.

The cherubim are the first angels mentioned in the Bible, when they are placed by God at the gates of Eden to prevent **Adam** and Eve from returning to the Garden: "He drove out the man; and at the east of the garden of Eden he placed the cherubim, and a flaming sword which turned every way, to guard the way to the tree of life" (Gen. 3:24). In this passage and others (e.g., the cherubim carved on the Ark of the Covenant in Exod. 25:18–22) these angels are clearly performing the guardian function they served in ancient Assyria.

In the Dionysian tradition, **Gabriel** is said to be the chief of the order of cherubim. The **Talmud** equates the cherubim with the Order of Ophanim (the wheels or chariots) or the Order of Hayoth (holy beasts). The cherubim are also known as the record keepers who express their love of knowledge and wisdom by helping to carry out the will of God. A fascinating process of evolution has transformed these monstrous beasts that guarded the buildings of ancient times to the modern chubby little cherubs seen on holiday cards at Christmas and Valentine's Day.

Sources:

Davidson, Gustav. *A Dictionary of Angels: Including the Fallen Angels.* 1967. Reprint. New York: Free Press, 1971.

Mansfield, Richard. *Angels: An Introduction to the Angelic Hierarchy.* Encinitas, Calif.: Estuary Publications, 1994.

THREE PUTTI WITH SHIELD AND HELMET BY ALBRECHT DÜRER (CA. 1500).

Cherubim and Seraphim Society

The Cherubim and Seraphim Society is an independent African church founded in Nigeria in 1925 by Christianah Abiodun Akinsowon as a result of angelic visions. The church is organized according to angelic hierarchies, and members assume such titles as mother cherub and mother seraph. The founder's visions involved flights to heaven, in which an angel escorted her from her bed to the celestial regions and showed her many sights, including hosts of singing angels.

After several visions, Akinsowon met Moses Orimolade Tumolase, an itinerant missionary. Together they prayed for guidance and became the center of an emergent prayer group. Receiving guidance for a new association, they established the Cherubim and Seraphim Society, attributing God as the founder and the archangel **Michael** as captain.

Church members believe that through the inspiration of the **Holy Spirit,** the society has learned precisely how God wishes his people to serve and worship him—in the same manner as the angels serve and worship God in heaven. Members are quick to point out that they worship God in the *manner* of angels; they do not worship the angels themselves. Among other doctrines, the church believes that every individual has a personal **guardian angel.** Members wear to their worship robes decorated with a variety of symbols. They also stress the singing of hymns (a primary function of angels), and celebrate the traditional angel holidays.

Sources:

Freeman, Eileen. "The Cherubim and Seraphim Society: Portrait of an African National Church." *AngelWatch* 2, no. 3 (June 1993): 1, 10–11.

Omoyajowo, J. Akinyele. *The Cherubim and Seraphim Society: The History of an African Independent Church.* New York: Nok Publishers, 1982.

Choirs

In the ancient Western world, particularly medieval Europe, it was believed that angels were arranged in hierarchical order. Perhaps because the angels were believed to continually sing the praises of God, the levels of the angelic hierarchy came to be referred to as choirs.

In the schema of the early sixth-century theologian **Dionysius the Areopagite**—a highly influential outline that was later adopted by **Thomas Aquinas**—the angels are arranged into nine choirs, which are grouped into three hierarchies (perhaps reflecting the Trinity). In descending order of closeness to God they are:

First Hierarchy	*Second Hierarchy*	*Third Hierarchy*
Seraphim	**Dominions**	**Principalities**
Cherubim	**Virtues**	**Archangels**
Thrones	**Powers**	**Angels**

Sources:

MacGregor, Geddes. *Angels: Ministers of Grace.* New York: Paragon House, 1988.

Strayer, Joseph R., ed. *Dictionary of the Middle Ages.* 13 vols. New York: Scribner, 1982–89.

Christianity

Though only partially indoctrinated into the Christian faith, a belief in angels has been an element of Christianity since its beginning. Long before Christ (1000–600 B.C.), the prophet Zoroaster, or Zarathustra, transformed the ancient Babylonian and Assyrian winged messengers into **archangels.** Zoroaster developed a monotheistic religion based on concepts of good and evil, the foundation of which was a supreme God who radiated seven holy archangels representing seven fundamental moral ideas. When the Jews were exiled from Babylon they took with them **Zoroastrianism,** the official religion of King Darius I of Persia, who helped them rebuild their temple in 519 B.C. Thus the Zarathustrian lore on angels was incorporated into **Judaism.**

Centuries later, when members of the Jewish faith professed their belief in Jesus Christ as the Messiah and Savior, they brought with them to the new Christianity the Zarathustrian-influenced angelology of early Judaic writings from the books of Daniel, **Enoch,** and **Tobit.** (Angels are also mentioned many times in the biblical Old Testament, but no **hierarchy** or philosophy regarding their nature is laid down.) In the new faith angels were considered servants of Christ and the Church, supplementing their former role as guardians of Israel.

In Christianity angels were appointed to preside over baptism and repentance. The archangel **Michael**—who, in the Book of Enoch, leads the angelic troops that defeat the rebellious archangel **Lucifer** and his followers and cast them into hell—was given charge over prayers and supplications. The angels were also believed to be capable of bringing humans to salvation by serving as models of the pure and unending worship of God and Christ. As Christians turned from involvement with earthly values, they hoped to move ever toward the angelic life, claiming a promise to become as the angels in heaven after the Resurrection (Luke 20:36; Matt. 22:30; Mark 12:25). St. Augustine of Hippo wrote (ca. A.D. 400): "The angels have care of us poor pilgrims; they have compassion on us and at God's command they hasten to our aid, so that we, too, may eventually arrive at our common fatherland."

Early Christians further believed that angels joined them in taking part in the Divine Service; that they helped celebrate feasts of Christendom on earth; that they carried men's prayers before God and watched over Christians from heaven; and that they would lead the souls of men to the next world at death. Indeed, angels were believed to serve man at God's request: "For he shall give his angels charge over thee, to keep thee in all thy ways. They shall bear thee up in their hands, lest thou dash thy foot against a stone" (Ps. 91:11–12). Martin Luther, in *Table Talk* (ca. 1510), affirms, "An angel is a spiritual creature created by God without a body, for the service of Christendom and the church."

Angelic Cult

Early church fathers struggled with the question of whether, and to what degree, angels should be a part of Christian doctrine. St. Paul did not favor the veneration of angels, yet in A.D. 325 the Council of Nicea decreed that faith in angels was part of Church dogma. Just eighteen years later, at the Synod of Laodicea, the cult (veneration, devotion, honor) of angels was declared idolatrous. Four and a half centuries later,

Christianity

Unofficially two guardian angels are assigned to each Christian, one for the right hand, which inspires him to good, and one for the left, which urges him toward evil.

in 787, the Seventh Ecumenical Synod reestablished the cult of angels, with certain limitations.

Angelic cult was most widespread during the **Middle Ages,** beginning in the West with St. Benedict (543) and moving into the time of Pope Gregory the Great (ca. 590). Current concepts of angels blossomed with St. Bernard of Clairvaux (d. 1153). In 1259 St. **Thomas Aquinas,** known as the "Angelic Doctor," gave a series of lectures on angels at the University of Paris. Those fifteen discourses over a period of a week were written down and formed the foundation of Christian ideas about angels for the next eight hundred years. Throughout the Scholastic period (thirteenth through seventeenth centuries) theologians studied the nature of angels, and angelic devotion continued to grow—especially among Dominican, Franciscan, and Jesuit orders.

By the end of the Renaissance, interest in angels was waning as science moved into the forefront of thought. Martin Luther (1483–1546) still relied on angels as his guides, but the Protestant John Calvin (1509–64) considered speculation about angels a waste of time. It was around this time, however, that **Emanuel Swedenbörg** (1688–1772) developed his monumental works on angels, supposedly received clairvoyantly from the heavenly beings themselves. Among them are *Heaven and Hell* and *Angelic Wisdom: Concerning Divine Love and Wisdom.* Swedenbörg greatly influenced the poet **William Blake,** Johann Wolfgang von Goethe, and the nineteenth-century philosopher **Rudolph Steiner,** among others.

The Catholic Church now teaches as part of its dogma that before he created the earth God created a kingdom of invisible spirits—the angels—who are personal beings and not more powers, and that, while many angels have been named through the centuries, the only names that may be used in angelic cult are the two occurring in the **Bible,** Michael and **Gabriel,** and **Raphael,** who appears in the apocryphal Book of Tobit. (A fourth angel, **Uriel,** "God is my light," is named in the apocryphal book *2 Esdras*.) Masses and prayers in honor of the three archangels have become an integral part of the Catholic Church; suppliants invoke the angels in the prayer in the Communion of the Sick, in the burial service of adults, in the blessing of homes; and in the Litany of All Saints and novenas. Among the Orthodox churches, the three archangels are honored in Liturgy (Mass and Divine Office) and in observance of special feasts.

There is never a question, though, that Jesus Christ is superior to angels; while angels are revered as God's messengers and helpers, as those who are allowed to be ever in his presence, they are not to be worshipped by Christians. St. Augustine is credited with putting the veneration of angels in its proper perspective: ". . . we honor them out of charity, not out of servitude" (*De vera religione* 55.110; PL 34:170).

The Archangels

Central to Christianity are the biblical appearances of the archangel Gabriel (whose name means "strength of God") to the Virgin **Mary** to tell her she will conceive and give birth to Jesus (Luke 1:26–32). (The Blessed Virgin herself is now considered to be one of the highest angels, sitting at the throne of God and accompanied by the baby angels, or cherubs.) Gabriel's words to Mary, "Hail Mary, full of grace, the Lord is with thee, blessed art thou among women," became one of the most prominent prayers in Catholicism. Gabriel also appears to Zacharias to announce that his son will be called **John the Baptist** (Luke 1:11–19). An angel believed to be Gabriel tells the shepherds by night of the Savior's birth at Bethlehem (Luke 2:8–11). He is also considered by the Catholic Church to be the angel who comforted Christ in the Garden of Gethsemane. Catholics celebrate the Feast of St. Gabriel on March 24.

The archangel Raphael's guidance of young Tobias on his long and dangerous journey in the Book of Tobit plants the seed for the concept of **guardian angels.** Raphael is said to be one of the seven angels that stand before the throne of God. He is also known as the angelic physician—his name means "medicine of God"—since he restored health to Tobias and gave his aged father back his sight by instructing Tobias in using the entrails of fish as medicine. Raphael is called upon today to protect travelers and to heal the sick. Many claim that he makes hospital visits. The Feast of St. Raphael is celebrated by Catholics on May 18.

It is the archangel Michael (known as St. Michael in the Catholic Church), however, who has received the most attention by Christians. Michael, whose name means "like God," is considered the leader of the angels, and is generally thought to be the angel who appeared to Moses in the burning bush on Mount Sinai. St. Thomas Aquinas said Michael defeated Satan in the Battle of Heaven, and will defeat the Antichrist at the **Apocalypse.** Michael and other angels have appeared to the saints for many centuries. **Joan of Arc** declared that Michael was the young warlike angel who appeared to her and announced her mission to save France. He was the only individual angel honored in liturgical feasts before the ninth century, and devotion to this powerful angel was evidenced by the fourth century in the churches in and near Constantinople. The Feast of St. Michael and the Angels was celebrated as early as the fifth century near Rome. Michael is said to have appeared at Monte

Gargano (near Foggia, Italy) around the year 490, and at Mont-Saint-Michel (Manche, France) in the year 708. St. Michael is still honored at those sanctuaries today. The Archonfraternity of St. Michael Archangel was erected by Pope Leo XIII in 1878. In modern times, Michael has been considered the patron saint of Germany, as well as of grocers, sailors, soldiers, and policemen. He is honored on Michaelmas, September 29 in the Roman Catholic and Anglican churches, and November 8 in the Greek, Armenian, and Coptic churches.

The Evil Angels

As fervently as God's good angels are revered in Christianity, so the evil angels are feared and despised. Catholicism teaches that the devil (Satan) and the demons were angels who were created virtuous by God but fell from grace by their own will, though the church does not say how they so grievously sinned. In the summer of 1986, however, Pope John Paul II said, "The fall consists in the free choice of those spirits who were created, and who radically and irrevocably denied God and His kingdom, usurping His sovereign rights and attempting to subvert the economy of salvation and the very ordering of the entire creation. . . . Thus the evil spirit tried to plant in human beings the seed of rivalry, insubordination, and opposition to God. . . ."

Other accounts of the fall of Satan and his followers say it was Satan's pride in his own greatness and jealousy of God's new creation, man, that brought about the Battle of Heaven and the evil angels' fall from grace into eternal damnation. Most Christian churches today teach that Satan is a very real presence in the word, ever seeking to turn man from God through endless temptation to sin. His threat is as great to the Christian as the guardian angel's protection is a comfort. In fact, says modern evangelist **Billy Graham,** people today are far more obsessed with evil, especially with the occult and devil worship, than they are with good. He wrote his book *Angels: God's Secret Agents* in 1975 to try and counter the fascination with evil and to offer hope, comfort, and guidance to world-weary modern man.

The Order and Nature of Angels

Various theories about the way the angels are ordered in heaven, their numbers, their appearance, and so forth have been postulated throughout history. **Dionysius** the Pseudo-Areopagite, a Syrian who lived about A.D. 500 and was for centuries erroneously believed to be the same Dionysius converted by St. Paul at Athens (Acts 17:34), developed the best-known hierarchy of angels in his book *The Celestial Hierarchy*. His hierarchy consists of nine **choirs** of angels divided into three triads. In descending order they are: **seraphim, cherubim, thrones; dominions, virtues,** and **powers;** and **principalities,** archangels, and angels. Others to develop angelic orders were Pope Gregory the Great, the poet **Dante,** Saint Ambrose (fourth-century bishop), and Clement of Alexandria. Judaic and apocryphal writings, including the *Sibylline Oracles* and the "Shepherd of Hermes," also contain theories about the orders of angels. Modern writer **Sophy Burnham,** in *A Book of Angels,* says all of this speculation shows "only that we know nothing whatsoever about angels and cannot hope to." She further adds, "We do not know what angels are or whether they stand in hierarchies in the skies. Nor whether they are assigned their duties according to seniority. We know nothing of this other realm, except that we are given brief, fleeting glimpses in our hearts."

What about the nature of angels? Most Christian sources say they beings of pure spirit and light, emanating a love that is far beyond human experience. In his 1986 speech Pope John Paul II said angels are "free and rational purely spiritual beings" and "the truth about angels is inseparable from the central revelation, which is the existence, majesty and glory of God that shines over the whole visible and invisible creation." Further, the pope said angels are "creatures of a spiritual nature, gifted with intellect and free will, superior to man."

The Catholic Saint Bridget (ca. 1303–73), who experienced many heavenly visions, said if a person should see an angel in all his beauty the mortal would be so ravished with delight that he would die of love.

Sources:

Burnham, Sophy. *A Book of Angels: Reflections on Angels Past and Present and True Stories of How They Touch Our Lives.* New York: Ballantine: 1990.

Encyclopedia of Early Christianity. Vol. 846 of the Garland Reference Library of the Humanities. New York: Garland, 1990.

Georgian, Linda. *Your Guardian Angels: Use the Power of Angelic Messengers to Enrich and Empower Your Life.* New York: Simon & Schuster, 1994.

Giovetti, Paola. *Angels: The Role of Celestial Guardians and Beings of Light.* Translated by Toby McCormick. York Beach, Maine: Samuel Weiser, 1989.

Graham, Billy. *Angels: God's Secret Agents.* Reprint. 1975. Dallas: Word Publishing, 1994.

New Catholic Encyclopedia. Vol. 1. Reprint. Washington, D.C.: Catholic University of America, 1981.

Saint Michael and the Angels. Compiled from Approved Sources. Rockford, Ill.: TAN Books, 1983.

Clarence Oddbody

Clarence, possibly the most recognized angel in cinematic lore, is the affable, bumbling character who appears to George Bailey in the 1946 Frank Capra classic, *It's a Wonderful Life*.

The story takes place on Christmas Eve in the tiny hamlet of Bedford Falls. Our hero, George (played by Jimmy Stewart), so despondent by the misplacement of savings and loan funds, muses that he is better off dead than alive. Enter his celestial guide in the form of Clarence Oddbody A-S 2 (angel second-class).

Capra's opening sequence actually takes place in heaven—a decidedly celestial sphere composed of swirling planets and shooting stars. This is not a typical cinematic residence of the angels, but it is in holding with the prevailing notion that angels reside somewhere in the sky. We get the sense that these angelic beings are quite far removed from Earth, and that their primary function is to act as overseers to mankind. They are creatures of light that radiate when they converse.

In this instance, it is decided that Clarence, the 200-year-old clockmaker is to go to Earth to aid George, the latest misguided soul. It is interesting to note that Capra employs a heaven that is composed of a distinct hierarchy, and further that within this hierarchy angels communicate according to a theory postulated by St. **Thomas Aquinas**: higher angels can enlighten lower angels, however the lower orders cannot reciprocate this enlightenment to their superiors.

Therefore, Clarence, as a mere angel second-class doesn't have his wings, and because of this deficit does not have the "sight" to view the goings on of his earthly charge. Consequently his superior, Joseph, must help him "see." Joseph tells him, "If you ever get your wings you'll be able to see by yourself."

Clarence saves his charge by jumping off the bridge from which George is contemplating suicide, knowing full well that George will instead save him. In a wonderfully wry exchange, a shivering Bailey begins: "Who are you?"

Clarence: "I told you. I'm your guardian angel. I know everything about you."

George: "Well, you look about like the kind of an angel I'd get. Sort of a fallen angel aren't ya? What happened to your wings?"

Clarence: "I haven't won my wings yet. That's why I'm an angel second-class."

George: "I don't know whether I like it very much bein' seen around an angel without any wings."

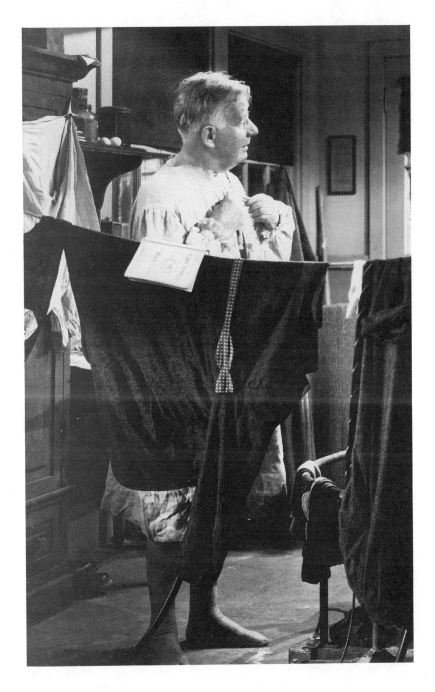

CLARENCE ODDBODY, THE
LOVABLE, BEFUDDLED
ANGEL SECOND-CLASS
FROM *IT'S A WONDERFUL LIFE.*
(RKO; COURTESY THE
KOBAL COLLECTION)

Clarence, realizing that it is not going to be easy making George understand just how much of an effect his life has had on those around him, decides to grant him his wish: that he had never been born. So their night journey begins.

With history erased, Clarence, drolly played by Henry Travers, takes George on an eye-opening sojourn. Bedford Falls, instead of the hopeful town that George and his family helped create, is a frighteningly decadent Sodom and Gomorrah under the thumb of the pontificating town villain, Henry Potter.

George, so dismayed by what he sees, and the people he encounters that don't recognize him, comes to the realization that indeed, he has made quite a contribution to his small world. "You see George," says Clarence, "you really had a wonderful life."

George becomes a believer and prays, "Please God let me live again!" His life, his family is restored and Clarence's job is finished. In a most touching final scene, amidst the swelling sounds of "Hark the herald angels sing," we hear the tinkling of a bell on the Bailey's Christmas tree. Zuzu, the smallest Bailey, explains, "Teacher says every time a bell rings an angel gets his wings." And George, echoing our own sentiments, whispers, "Atta boy Clarence!"

Sources:
Parish, James Robert. *Ghosts and Angels in Hollywood Films.* Jefferson, N.C.: McFarland & Co., 1994.

Collective Unconscious

The concept of the collective unconscious was postulated by **Carl Gustav Jung,** and can be used to explain the experience of angelic encounters, as well as help understand why the archetype of the angel should be so appealing. According to this famous Swiss psychiatrist, the collective unconscious is the storehouse of myths and symbols to which all human beings have access. It is a necessary and normal component of the psyche, from which archetypal symbols emerge in response to certain experiences—particularly in response to conflicts—as tools to help cope and give meaning. In their various roles as messengers from beyond, as guardians, and as spiritual helpers, angels can embody more than one archetypal meaning. Similarly, **demons** (as fallen angels) can also embody various negative meanings.

Jung's unique contribution to modern psychology begins with the observation that the basic structure of many symbols and myths are nearly universal, even between cultures that have no historical connection. Most traditional societies, for example, recount hero myths, utilize circles to represent wholeness, or associate the sky with transcendence.

Jung theorized that this universality results from unconscious patterns (genetic or quasi-genetic predispositions) that we inherit from our distant ancestors. The reservoir of these patterns constitutes a collective unconscious, distinct from the individual, personal unconscious.

Jung referred to the unconscious, predisposing patterns for particular myths and symbols as archetypes. Hence one can talk about the mandala (i.e., the circle) archetype, the hero archetype, or the angel (or demon) archetype. Jung asserted that his notions of the collective unconscious and the archetypes were on par with the theory of instinct.

Jung's ideas have sometimes been cited to explain certain experiences or certain cultural-historical facts that seem to indicate the existence of a spiritual dimension, and subsequently the inhabitants of such spiritual dimensions—angels and demons. On the other hand, the fact that different cultures at different periods of time all report similar beings might also indicate that such phenomena reflect archetypal patterns in the human mind rather than that angelic spirits truly exist.

Sources:

Eliade, Mircea, ed. *Encyclopedia of Religion.* 16 vols. New York: Macmillan, 1987.

Hostie, Raymond S. J. *Religion and the Psychology of Jung.* New York: Sheed & Ward, 1957.

MacGregor, Geddes. *Angels: Ministers of Grace.* New York: Paragon House, 1988.

Samuels, Andrew, Bani Shorter, and Fred Plaut. *A Critical Dictionary of Jungian Analysis.* London: Routledge & Kegan Paul, 1986.

Color, Angels and

Color has long been one attribute strongly associated with angelic visions. Color is actually the saturation and the brightness of reflected light upon an object, therefore the angelic vision can portray many color sensations through the human eye. Artists over the centuries have tried to accentuate the visual by adding luminous color surrounding the angel figure or including multi-hued **wings** and **halos.**

Within biblical reference the color white is used several times in association with an angelic presence. This is especially noted in the recounting of the resurrection sequence found within the Gospels. An example appears in Matt. 28:2–3, "And, behold, there was a great earthquake: for the angel of the Lord descended from heaven, and came and rolled back the stone from the door, and sat upon it. His countenance was like lightning, and his raiment white as snow."

There has also been some color associations assigned to the various ranks of angels. These can be looked upon only as an easier way of categorizing the positions of the angels, with no such reference found in biblical doctrine. The majority of those who have experienced visual visitation by angels do report a pervasion of a sensation of light. This light source has demonstrated many colors, the greatest being white.

It is often stated that when an angel descends to the earth, it brings with it a part of the light of the heavens, thus perhaps explaining the strong association of white to represent that light. Others who have had a close association or visitation with a stronger angelic presence, associate specific colors to the entire form. Many identify the color green with **Raphael,** perhaps to associate the healing of the earth; gold is widely connected with **Gabriel,** perhaps to draw emphasis to his divine messages; **Michael** is often portrayed in shades of blue to show his protection and solidarity to the heavens, and perhaps in reference to the peacock feathers usually associated with this figure.

When someone sees an angel they bring their own perceptions to the forefront. Each angelic visual is different, therefore one cannot designate a specific color to an angel or to all angelic beings. Artistic license is often asserted to create the angelic visuals so common to us today, but again, these are individual perceptions and should be viewed as such.

Sources:

Day, Leonard C. Letter to author, 26 June 1995.
Hauck, Rex, ed. *Angels: The Mysterious Messengers.* New York: Ballantine, 1994.

Communication with Angels

One broad area of agreement in all world religions is that communication between this world and the spiritual world is possible. Such communications are an important part of traditional as well as contemporary angel lore and direct communication with angels has been a viable link with the angelic world throughout the centuries.

Angels can communicate with people in three distinct ways. Communication from an angel can first be experienced through what is referred to as an audio presentation. This communication is heard by the receiver usually in an awakened state. Some who have related such an experience tell of a buzzing sensation or music before and after the message has been presented. The message of an audio communication usually relates joyous tidings or warns of approaching dangers. A biblical reference of an audio presentation is found in Luke 2:9–14 with the announcement to the shepherds of Jesus' birth:

And, lo, the angel of the Lord came upon them, and the glory of the Lord shone round about them: and they were sore afraid. And the angel said unto them, "Fear not; for, behold, I bring you good tidings of great joy, which shall be to all people. For unto you is born this day in the city of David a Savior, which is Christ the Lord. And this shall be a sign unto you; Ye shall find the babe wrapped in swaddling clothes, lying in a manger." And suddenly there was with the angel a multitude of the heavenly host praising God, and saying, "Glory to God in the highest, and on earth peace, good will toward men."

Angels also communicate with man through dreams. The idea that such communication should take place during sleep is a natural consequence of the nature of the dream state, during which we seem to enter a confused realm parallel to the world experienced in our waking consciousness. Usually the communication of the angels through a dream will refer to the welfare of others or will address an approaching concern.

Angelic encounters may occur during a sequence of dreams. These messages may come rapidly, within hours or days of each other, or they may be projected over the course of months or even years. A classical biblical reference to the dream sequence is that of Joseph, husband of **Mary,** whose dream sequence involved the birth and protection of Jesus Christ. The angel **Gabriel** appears to Joseph and says, "Joseph son of David, do not be afraid to take Mary home as your wife, because what is conceived in her is from the Holy Spirit. She will give birth to a son, and you are to give him the name Jesus, because he will save his people from their sins" (Matt. 1:20–21).

Angels may also relate their message in a solitary dream, such as in the case of **Jacob** and the dream of the ladder to heaven depicting angels ascending and descending:

And he dreamed that there was a ladder set up on the earth, and the top of it reached to heaven. And behold, the angels of God were ascending and descending on it! And behold, the Lord stood above it and said, "I am the Lord, the God of Abraham your father and the God of Isaac; the land on which you lie I will give to you and your descendants; . . . I will not leave you until I have done that of which I have spoken to you." Then Jacob awoke from his sleep and said, "Surely the Lord is in this place and I did not know it." And he was afraid, and said, "how awesome is this place! This is none other than the house of God, and this is the gate of heaven."

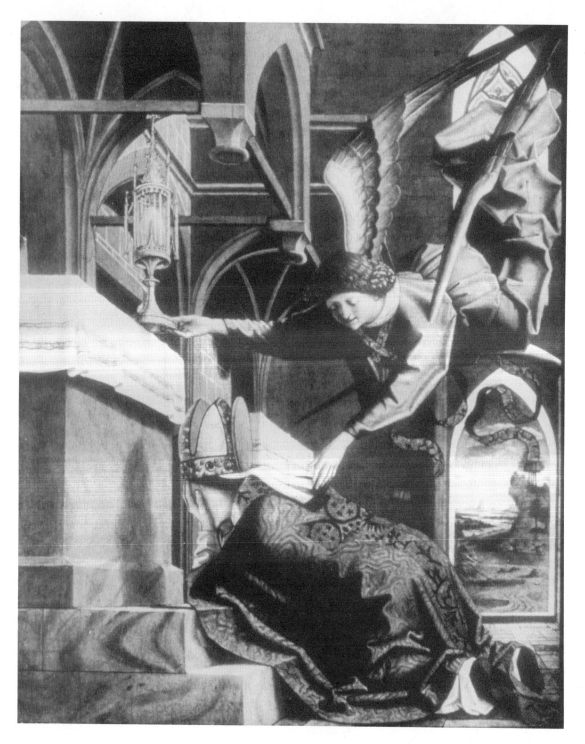

ANGEL MOVING AN ALTARPIECE IN ANSWER TO PRAYER OF KNEELING BISHOP, PERHAPS ST. WOLFGANG OR ST. AUGUSTINE (CA. 1475–79). (COURTESY ARAS)

other than the house of God, and this is the gate of heaven."
(Gen. 28:12–17)

Angels also communicate via the direct visual approach. Through this avenue an angel appears as an image and delivers his message in person. The angel as messenger wishes to draw very little attention to himself and so may take on a very unassuming presence. The message of the visual is very simple and direct and usually involves the person to whom it is presented. Biblical examples of the angelic visual communication is related in the Old Testament story of **Abraham** and Sarah and the birth of Isaac (Genesis 18) and in the New Testament Annunciation to Mary concerning the conception and birth of Jesus (Luke 1:26–38).

It must be stressed that communication with angels at any level—audio, dream, or visual—is only possible through the understanding and acceptance of the human spirit. Vital communication can be sent through the angels if we are open to the messengers and the messages.

—*Leonard Day*

Sources:
Adler, Mortimer J. *The Angels and Us*. New York: Macmillan, 1982.
Church, F. Forrester. *Entertaining Angels: A Guide to Heaven for Atheists & True Believers*. San Francisco: Harper & Row, 1987.
Day, Leonard C. Letter to author, 26 June 1995.
De Becker, Raymond. *The Understanding of Dreams or the Machinations of the Night*. London: George Allen & Unwin, 1968.

Constellations

Constellations named after angels are a rarity today, when constellations are commonly named for Greek and Roman mythological figures. However Judeo-Christian folklore did enter into astronomy in the past. The constellation that we know as Orion today was known to the ancient Jews as Gibbor the Giant, and was identified as **Nimrod,** the hunter referred to in the book of Genesis. Nimrod was believed by some to be the son of a fallen angel who was hung in heaven by God as punishment for trying to storm heaven. There have been attempts in the past, particularly in the 1600s, to replace the Greco-Roman star patterns with Bible-oriented constellations. The Biblical School of Atlas Makers turned the Big Dipper (Ursus Major) into the archangel **Michael.** The constellations Hydrus and Tucana and the Lesser Megellanic Cloud were combined to form a new constellation, **Raphael** the archangel.

"THE PROTECTING ONE," BY
JONATHAN W. DAY (1994).
(COURTESY OF THE ARTIST)

Sources:

Krupp, E. C. *Beyond the Blue Horizon.* New York: HarperCollins, 1991.

MacGregor, Geddes. *Angels: Ministers of Grace.* New York: Paragon House, 1988.

Contemporary Angel Artists

There are many contemporary artists who have a special affinity for angels and whose art is either entirely or largely devoted to angels as a subject.

Thierry Chatelan

Born in Casablanca, Morocco, of French parents, Chatelan finds inspiration in his paintings through mythology, primitive cultures, and Jungian psychology. After some years in Paris, he moved to San Diego, California, where he is currently working as an artist. Among his works are *Ebony Moon,* which evokes the traditions of the Peul nomadic tribe of Mali, and *Maheo,* which depicts the American Indian myth of creation of the Earth thanks to the Spirit Maheo.

Jonathan W. Day

The youngest of a new crop of contemporary artists, Day is just beginning his career. Day has painted for several years and has exhibited in a number of shows. His work uses a boldness of color, which makes his angel subjects so appealing.

Peggy Sue Florio

Born in Nebraska, Peggy Sue Florio lives in California where she works as an artist. Her paintings, cards, stationery, and furnishings emphasize the theme of angels, with their spiritual dimensions, and healing power. Florio is also a contributor to the magazine *Angel Times.*

Glenda Green (Youritzin)

Glenda Green obtained a degree in art history in 1970 and has since worked as an artist and art curator in New York, Oklahoma, and Texas. Her paintings depicting angel visions became very popular through the numerous exhibitions in public permanent collections as well as in solo museum and group displays throughout the United States.

Karen M. Haughey

Karen M. Haughey, who was born and grew up in the San Francisco Bay area, is a prolific artist painting mostly angels and mermaids. She also works as a teacher of her technique (that combines the use of water color, pastels, and collage). She is affiliated with the Society of Western Artists, the Oakland Association, Las Juntas Arts Association, Sun Gallery of Hayward, the Fremont Cultural Arts Council, and the Fremont Arts Association.

ANGELIC LOVE BY
GLENDA GREEN
(OIL ON CANVAS, 1995).

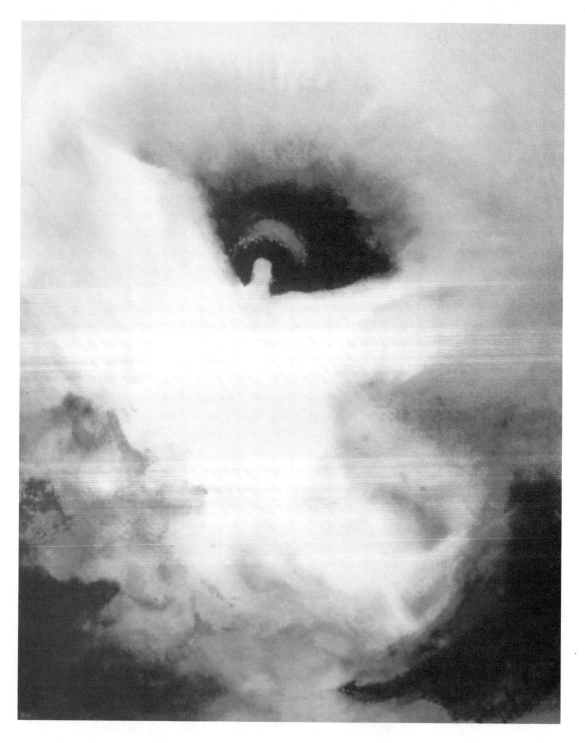

ARCHANGEL MICHAEL BY KARYN MARTIN-KURI. (WATERCOLOR, 1983).

Antoinette Bittar Jabbour

Antoinette Bittar Jabbour, whose art name is "Noon" (as this was initially the time when her creativity inspired her), graduated from the Willsey Institute of Interior Design in New York. Her paintings, which focus primarily on people's relationships and family ties, have been exhibited in the U.S. as well as in Europe, and her work has appeared in *L'Amateur d'Art,* a Paris art publication.

Gary Markowitz

Gary Markowitz, born in Kailu Kona, Hawaii, has for years been devoted to the practice of meditation and art. But Markowitz found his true inspiration when he discovered his new reality as a channeler of angel messages. Since then he has produced what came to be called "Automatic Art," i.e., his reinterpretation of the messages channeled through him from angelic entities. His art is based on the representation of these messages within a mythical context that refers primarily to the ancient and pre-Christian culture and symbology.

K. Martin-Kuri

The uniqueness of Karyn Martin-Kuri's artwork arises from a lifetime of conscious experience working with angels combined with thirty years lecturing and researching the subject. Her technique of painting creates an extraordinary radiance that shines through soft veils of color, forming heavenly images that are distinctly a new style of artwork. She has been called a visionary similar to **William Blake,** with the colors and radiance of her paintings similar to Monet and Turner. Her works in oil and watercolor with chalk pastel are collected around the world, and are recognized for their remarkable heavenly quality.

Martin-Kuri works exclusively by commission and, as well as painting a wide range of spiritual images, she became the first professional artist to paint guardian angels of individuals and organizations. She receives commissions from organizations seeking to provide soothing and uplifting images for the work environment. The combination of her painting, lecturing, and writing (Ballantine Books will, in 1996, release her art book *Living with Angels,* as well as *The Angels Are Calling: A Message for the Millennium*) and decades of helping people connect with angels has led to her being recognized as a sage in the field of angelology. Martin-Kuri is also president of **Twenty-Eight Angels, Inc.;** P.O. Box 116, Free Union, VA 22940; 1-800-28ANGELS.

Sandra Martindale

Martindale is a self-taught artist who paints angels who "come and pose" for her. Usually she paints the guardian angels of other people, using prayer and meditation to see the angel who guides the person. In addition to serving as her subjects, angels also guide Sandra in her painting. Sandra says that at times she feels almost like a spectator, with the angels themselves doing the painting. At other times, if she is unsure how to paint a particular feature, she feels that her angels give her a lesson in what she needs.

Sources:

Freeman, Eileen Elias. "Angels in Contemporary Art," *AngelWatch*. August 1993.

Cottingley Fairies

Belief in **fairies** has inspired folklore, literature, and the imagination of children throughout the world. However, the question of empirical evidence for the existence of fairies did not arouse serious consideration until the early twentieth century, when controversy erupted in response to the claims of two young English girls to have actually photographed fairies. The two girls, Francis Griffiths and Elsie Wright, friends and cousins, lived in Cottingley, Yorkshire. The Cottingley fairies incident began when they showed Elsie Wright's father a picture of four tiny fairies or angels dancing around her. About a year later the two girls took another photograph of a **gnome** approaching Elsie. In all, five photographs of alleged fairies were taken between 1917 and 1920.

In 1920 the news of these photographs was picked up in **Theosophical** circles through Elsie's mother, eventually reaching the ear of Sir Arthur Conan Doyle, author of Sherlock Holmes stories and a convinced **Spiritualist.** In the debate over the authenticity of the photographs, Doyle argued for their validity. He wrote articles and even a book, *The Coming of the Fairies* about the case.

Efforts to prove the photographs fraudulent were unsuccessful for more than sixty years. In the early 1970s, however, Elsie Wright wrote a letter admitting they were fake. The letter did not raise much controversy, however, until the early 1980s, when the case was reinvestigated by Geoffrey Crawley, editor of the *British Journal of Photography*. Crawley eventually elicited a public confession of the two women, who revealed that they had intended to maintain their secret until the death of their

"FAIRY OFFERING A POSY TO ELSIE" FROM *THE COMING OF THE FAIRIES*. (COURTESY ARC)

"FRANCES AND THE LEAPING FAIRY" FROM *THE COMING OF THE FAIRIES*. (COURTESY ARC)

most convinced supporters, Doyle and some of the first Theosophists to take them seriously.

The techniques used to create the fairy pictures involved single- and double-exposure, some of which were even shot unintentionally. Elsie Wright and Francis Griffiths never did complete their autobiographies, in which they had promised to explain exactly how the photographs were produced.

Sources:

Clark, Jerome. *Encyclopedia of Strange and Unexplained Physical Phenomena*. Detroit, Mich.: Gale Research, 1993.

Doyle, Arthur Conan. *The Coming of the Fairies*. New York: George H. Doran, 1922.

Cupid

Cupid is the Roman god of love, commonly identified with the Greek **Eros,** and son of Venus (Aphrodite), the love goddess. He is frequently depicted as a beautiful winged boy with bow and arrows, which arouse love in those they strike. Like love itself, he is described as erratic and mischievous.

Eros is certainly one of the oldest gods of Greece, though Homer does not mention him. The first traces of him are found in Hesiod, according to whom he is one of the three primal beings out of which the world was formed: Gaea, Chaos, and Eros—that is, Mother Earth, Primordial Matter, and Love.

Homer had no use for Cupid as he could not be fitted into the great family of gods. This difficulty proved a problem to a greater or lesser extent throughout Greek and Roman mythological poetry. Sometimes Aphrodite/Venus is named as his mother, sometimes Artemis/Diana. Ares/Mars and Hermes/Mercury are both suggested as his father.

In the classical period Cupid is given human shape, and all later artists show him as a youth just attaining puberty. From the very beginning he is almost invariably represented with **wings.** This indicates that he belongs to the category of beings called **demons,** who fly between the world and the sky, the lower and the upper regions, connecting what is above with that below (the defining characteristic of angels).

From the very earliest times the Greek Eros dominated gods and men, not with normal weapons but with a flower or a lyre held in his hand. Throughout the ages, fertility symbols, such as the hare, the duck, and the goose, were added to his figure. The great dramatist Euripides was the first to put a bow and arrow, the weapons of Diana, his putative mother, in his hands. But he always uses them to orchestrate romance, not for war.

Cupid, or Amor, the Roman counterpart of Eros, has strongly marked human characteristics, owing to the influence of the Alexandrian poets and artists. He is less of a god and more of a mischievous child. His name means desire. Apuleius describes him as "that very wicked boy, with neither manners nor respect for the decencies." In earlier times, however, he was a more powerful god. It was believed that his influence extended not only over the heavens and the sea but even to the underworld. He was widely venerated, and prayers and sacrifices were offered to him daily.

According to some authorities, there were two Cupids, one of whom, the son of Jupiter and Venus, was a lively and pleasant youth,

Cupid

According to legend Cupid wets with blood the stone on which he sharpens his arrows.

while the other, the offspring of Night and Erebus, was given to debauchery and riotous living. Cicero mentions three Cupids, their parentage ascribed to Mercury and Diana, Mercury and Venus, and Mars and Venus. In common with other immortals, Cupid had the power to change his shape at will: in Virgil's *Aeneid* he assumes the form of Ascanius at the request of his mother, Venus, and goes to the court of Dido, where he inspires the queen with love. Like Eros, Cupid is vain and cruel, and the Roman poet Ovid speaks of his "savage spite." It is in the legend of Cupid and Psyche, as told by Apuleius, that Cupid is shown at his most tender and humane, since, for once, he is made to experience the suffering that he has inflicted on others.

The god of love in his manifold shapes soon began to be conceived of in the plural and to be called *erotes-amorini* and later *amoretti* instead of Eros-Amor. In late antiquity the erotes (the plural of eros) accompanied men and gods throughout their lives and even into the underworld. This idea corresponded to the Roman concept of the genii, male **guardian spirits** who were supposed to accompany the soul entrusted to them through-

CUPID, THE ROMAN GOD OF LOVE.

out life. The early Christians had no difficulty accepting figures like these literally, for they shared with the world of antiquity the belief in guardian spirits that accompanied people throughout life and led the soul to the next world after death. The early Christians also gave the shape of children to the spirits, thus bestowing an ancient symbol of eternal youth on these lofty angels, who, according to the word of Christ, gaze forever on the face of the heavenly Father.

Sources:

Cavendish, Richard. *Man, Myth & Magic: The Illustrated Encyclopedia of Mythology, Religion and the Unknown.* New York: Marshall Cavendish, 1995.

Kunstmann, Josef. *The Transformation of Eros.* Philadelphia: Dufour Editions, 1965.

The devil is an angel too.

—Miguel de Unamuno

(y Jugo), *Two Mothers*

Daemon (Daimon)

Daemon (Greek for "soul"), is the source for the English word demon. It was a complex term that could refer to more than one type of spirit entity, and ultimately came to be associated with invisible spirits (both good and evil) that occupied the ethereal spaces between God and humanity. These were beings that flew between the world and the sky, the lower and the upper regions, connecting what was above with what was below, acting as sort of **guardian angels.**

The Greek notion of daemons as personal familiar spirits was originally derived from similar notions widespread throughout the Near East—from **Greeks** to Babylonians, from **Egyptians** to Persians. Sometimes one central spirit became the leading principle, and was called the archetype of the Anthropos—the Self in human form, often experienced as an inner guide. The daemon of Socrates, described by Plato as Socrates' good spirit, is the most familiar example of these entities. This spirit manifested as a figure or a voice, which forbade the philosopher from doing certain things and encouraged him to undertake others. A later variation of this basic idea is that of a guardian spirit who mediates between the spirit world and man, bringing dreams and foretelling the future.

Another context in which the daemon is mentioned in the early Platonic dialogues is in connection with love—**Eros.** According to Socrates, Eros is not the beautiful beloved, but is, rather, the spirit who inspires the lover, giving the lover his divine madness. Eros is neither mortal nor immortal, but the spirit who interprets and conveys messages back and forth between men and gods. He is described as a "great spirit—daemon—and like all spirits a being intermediate between the divine and the mortal."

The role of daemons was of considerable importance in Plutarch's universe. They were regarded as a crucial intermediary between the gods and humanity, intervening in the affairs of human life in ways that would be unworthy of more exalted beings. In the *De defectu oraculorum,* Plutarch's chief concern is the way daemons administer the oracles, although he also considers them in the much wider context of mythology in general. Some daemons are evil, and Plutarch's belief in them is the basis behind the story of Typhon and the other giants in mythology—the fallen daemons confined in bodies as a punishment.

The ancient Jewish philosopher Philo said that air was the region inhabited by incorporeal souls, which the philosophers call daemons, but which the Scriptures more appropriately call angels.

When the Hebrew Scriptures were being translated from Hebrew to Greek, the translators apparently considered using the word *daemon* to translate the Hebrew *malakh* (angel, a word literally meaning "messenger"). However, because of the complexity and moral ambivalence of the Greek term, the translators chose *angelos,* Greek for "messenger."

Sources:

Bemrose, Stephen. *Dante's Angelic Intelligences: Their Importance in the Cosmos and in Pre-Christian Religion.* Rome: Edizioni di Storia e Letteratura, 1983.

Eliade, Mircea, ed. *Encyclopedia of Religion.* 16 vols. New York: Macmillan, 1987.

Godwin, Malcolm. *Angels: An Endangered Species.* New York: Simon and Schuster, 1990.

Kunstmann, Josef. *The Transformation of Eros.* Philadelphia: Dufour Editions, 1965.

Wilson, Peter Lamborn. *Angels.* New York: Pantheon Books, 1980.

Dante Alighieri

The Italian poet, philosopher, and theologian Dante Alighieri (1265–1321), whose epic poems are filled with the ponderings of angelic hierarchies, was born in Florence to a family of lesser nobility. The essential facts of his early life are recorded in *The New Life* (ca. 1293), about his youthful, idealistic love for Beatrice Portinari.

Dante played an important role in Florentine civic and political life. He was also a leader on the imperial side in the struggle between the Guelfs and the Ghibellines, the partisans of the pope and the emperor, respectively, who were fighting for jurisdiction in Italy. When the rival party splintered into two factions, however, he decided to support the antipapal policy of the White Guelfs. After the Blacks took over the city in 1301, under the wing of Charles de Valois, Dante was exiled and his life of wandering from court to court of medieval Italy began.

During his exile, he wrote the *Convivio,* his chief work in Italian prose, inspired by the reading of Cicero and Boethius; the Latin *De vulgari eloquentia,* a treatise about the preeminence of the Italian vernacular and the definition of the highest form of Italian lyrical poetry, the *Canzone;* and the *De Monarchia,* an eloquent defense of the imperial principle and Dante's most original contribution to philosophical thought.

The tenor of his times, as well as his own inner anguishes, was Dante's primary source of inspiration for his masterpiece, *The Divine Comedy* (1472), an allegory of human existence and destiny in the form of the pilgrimage of the soul after death. Dante himself is the pilgrim on the visionary journey through Hell, Purgatory, and Heaven, during a week at Easter in the year 1300 when, at the age of thirty-five, he feels lost in the "dark wood" of his own moral confusion. The Roman poet Virgil, representing secular learning, is his guide through the depths of Hell and up the "mountain of purgatory," and Beatrice, representing the higher divine inspiration, leads him to Heaven and to the inexpressible divine source of all love, which "moves the sun and all the stars."

Dante adopted a punitive hell and added a purgatory for those who were not cut off from hope. Hell, in Dante's scheme, corresponding to the general medieval view of the world, is placed in the interior of the earth and is portrayed as the place of eternal isolation of the soul. It consists of nine concentric circles that, from the hemisphere of the earth and across the river Acheron, progressively diminish in circumference, forming an inverted cone ending in the center of the earth. In each circle, representing the nature and effects of sin, a distinct class of sinners undergo a particular torment according to the nature and gravity of their wrongdoings.

According to Dante's vision, when **Satan** fell from Heaven, he struck the earth at the antipodes of Jerusalem and tore through its substance as far as the center, where he remains fixed for all time, a three-faced monster champing at the three archsinners against church and state,

Judas Iscariot, Brutus, and Cassius. Extreme torture is inflicted by cold, not heat. Satan's wings, perpetually beating, send forth an icy blast that freezes the river Cocytus to a glassy hardness, and in it are immured the final four grades of sinners.

A hidden path connects the center of the earth to Purgatory, the place of expiatory purification and preparation for the life of eternal blessedness. It is imagined as a mountain formed by **Lucifer** as he fell from Heaven into the abyss of Hell, and it is antipodal to Jerusalem and Mount Calvary, in the center of the Southern Hemisphere. After the ante-purgatory, where are placed the excommunicated and the belated penitents, and passage through **Peter**'s gate come seven encircling terraces, which rise in succession with diminished circuit as they approach the summit. Each of the cornices corresponds to the seven deadly sins, from which the soul is purged through the expiatory labor of climbing the Mountain of Purgatory.

DEVILS AND VIRGIL BY GUSTAVE DORÉ. ILLUSTRATION FOR DANTE'S DIVINE COMEDY.

Heaven, in Dante's view a terrestrial paradise, is reached through a final wall of flames. Inside are two streams that wash away the remembrance of sin and strengthen the remembrance of good deeds. Dante's Paradise, constructed according to the Ptolemaic system of cosmography, consists of nine moving heavens concentric with the earth, the fixed center of the universe, around which they revolve at a velocity proportional to their distance from the earth. Each heaven is presided over by one of the angelic orders and exercises its special influence on human beings and their affairs. The seven lowest are the heavens of the planets: the Moon, Mercury, Venus, the Sun, Mars, Jupiter, and Saturn. The eighth heaven, the sphere of the fixed stars, is the highest visible region of the celestial world; and the ninth heaven, the primum mobile, governs the general motion of the heavens from east to west, and by it all place and time are ultimately measured. Finally, beyond and outside the heavens, lies the Empyrean, where there is neither time nor place, but light only, and which is the special abode of the Deity and the saints.

According to Dante, a hierarchical interdependence exists between the angels. One order of angels acts upon those below it, inspiring them to contemplate God; and the lower intelligences receive illumination from those above, and in turn reflect it, like mirrors, to those below them. Similarly, there is a hierarchical downward transmission of power between the heavenly spheres moved by the angels. Like all other creatures, angels owe their being to God, to that point of light around which Dante sees them spinning.

Dante believed that angels are incorporeal spiritual substances. He asserts that angels are pure form, and he frequently alleges that they are immortal and were directly created by God. Dante's angels are purely intellectual beings, lacking all sensation. After all, their primary purpose is to contemplate God.

Dante is conscious of the angels' limitations; they are included, together with human souls, among the intelligences whose knowledge is less perfect than God's. Indeed, just like humans, they have as part of their nature an appropriate limitation on the desire to know. In his epic poem *Paradiso* (1310) we are told that not even the seraph with the clearest vision of God could answer Dante's question about predestination.

Dante is fascinated by the similarities between angels and men. He is very conscious of the affinity between them, as well as their differences. He says that angelic nature is perfectly intellectual, and so the separated intelligences contemplate constantly, as opposed to humans, with whom such contemplation is intermittent. Dante believes that angels possess in common with men not only intellect but also will, and that this will is essentially free. The prayer of the penitent proud on the first terrace of purgatory might seem to suggest that the angels have sacrificed this will to God, but this does not mean that they are deprived of it.

In *Paradiso,* Dante puts strong emphasis upon the angels as sphere-movers, although he does not believe that all the angels are movers, since there are many who simply spend their time in contemplation. Nothing is said in *Paradiso* about how the angels move the heavens, but Dante discusses this in Convivio, where he says that they move simply by understanding, and that they touch their spheres, not corporeally, but through mind power. Dante's spheres do not merely move; they, and thus the angels that operate via them, exercise a powerful influence upon the world.

The final intuitive vision of the divine will in Dante's poem is the last step of an itinerary that leads both the author and the reader through a process of conversion, as well as a deep investigation of human nature.

—*Michela Zonta*

Sources:

Bemrose, Stephen. *Dante's Angelic Intelligences: Their Importance in the Cosmos and in Pre-Christian Religion.* Rome: Edizioni di Storia e Letteratura, 1983.

Edwards Paul, ed. *The Encyclopedia of Philosophy.* New York: Macmillan, 1967.

Eliade, Mircea, ed. *Encyclopedia of Religion.* 16 vols. New York: Macmillan, 1987.

MacGregor, Geddes. *Angels: Ministers of Grace.* New York: Paragon House, 1988.

Toynbee, Paget. *Dante Alighieri: His Life and Works.* New York, Harper & Row, 1965.

Day, Leonard C.

Leonard C. Day, known as the "Angel Man of the South," is a researcher and lecturer on the realm of angels. He was born and raised in the small community of Ellis, Kansas and received his bachelor of science degree in art education and master of arts from Fort Hays State University in Hays, Kansas.

Day began his career as a museum curator and director in 1972 while doing a tour of duty at the Naval Memorial Museum in Washington, D.C. During his tour he was trained as an art conservationist and assisted in the care and preservation of the paintings in the White House and the Senate buildings. Since being discharged from the Navy, Day has served as the executive director and curator of the Ellis County Historical Society in Hays, Kansas and executive director of the High Point Histori-

SPIRIT CARRIER BY LEONARD DAY (WATERCOLOR, 1990s).
(COURTESY OF THE ARTIST)

cal Society in High Point, North Carolina. In 1992 he established his own art conservation, restoration, and appraisal firm. He is a member of the American Institute of Conservationists and is certified in painting, textile, and porcelain conservation and appraisal. He is also a freelance illustrator.

Day began his research into angels in 1992. Coming from a strong Catholic background in which allusion to angels was very common, he was surprised to find angels very rarely mentioned in general reference sources. This intrigued him and led him on the road to discovery. His research eventually led to the development of several class-series studies ranging from angels in art—depicting the stylistic changes in angel representations over the decades—to angel encounters in today's world. Day has presented countless lectures, classes, and workshops on angels. Currently he is conducting interviews and gathering research for books of his own on angels in art and angelic encounters in deathbed visions. Leonard Day has been married for twenty-three years. The Days are the parents of two sons and reside in High Point, North Carolina.

Sources:
Day, Leonard C. Letter to author, 26 April 1995.

Days of the Week (Angels and the)

In ancient times **astrology** was a universal language or symbolic code that was used to interpret every imaginable phenomenon. As far back as Roman times, the days of the week were correlated with the traditional planets (the Sun, the Moon, and the five planets visible to the naked eye). Monday is ruled (see **rulership**) by the Moon ("Moonday"), Tuesday by Mars, Wednesday by Mercury, Thursday by Jupiter, Friday by Venus, Saturday by Saturday ("Saturnday"), and Sunday by the Sun ("Sunday"). In ancient times an activity ruled by a particular planet was said to be enhanced when carried out on a day ruled by that planet (e.g., Mercury-ruled Wednesday was good for writing and sending letters—activities ruled by the planet Mercury).

In later European history angels came to be associated with almost every aspect of daily life in a manner similar to astrology. Even the same metaphor of rulership was utilized, with angels said to rule various objects and cycles. Through this and other connections, astrology and **angelology** became associated. With respect to angels and days of the week, the traditional associations are as follows:

Day of the Week	Angel
Sunday (Sun)	Michael

Monday (Moon)	Gabriel
Tuesday (Mars)	Sammael
Wednesday (Mercury)	Raphael
Thursday (Jupiter)	Sachiel
Friday (Venus)	Anael
Saturday (Saturn)	Cassiel

Sunday

Michael, whose name means "who is as God," is the angel who rules Sunday, the day associated with the Sun. In astrology the Sun is said to rule the sign Leo, which indicates they share certain characteristics. Leo is the sign of the king, the central personality of a country and the person responsible for overseeing the kingdom, coordinating its activities, and administering justice. Such a description aptly fits Michael, who in postbiblical **Jewish, Christian,** and **Islamic** writings ranks as the greatest of all angels. He also administers justice as the angel of the Last Judgment, the "weigher of souls." In addition, Michael is chief of **archangels** and chief of the order of **virtues.**

Monday

The angel and archangel for Monday, which is associated with the Moon, is **Gabriel,** whose name means "God is my strength." In astrology the Moon is associated with women and childbirth; it also represents the principle of creativity in the sense of giving birth to ideas. Thus the correlation between the Moon and Gabriel is fitting since Gabriel, the chief ambassador to humanity, announced the conception of Christ to the Virgin **Mary,** and **Muhammad** claimed that Gabriel dictated the Koran to him (thus giving birth to a new religion).

Tuesday

Sammael is the ruler of Tuesday, the day associated with Mars. In astrology Mars is associated with aggression, conflict, and emotional passion, as well as with physical skills. Sammael (whose name is an amalgam of *sam,* "poison," and *el,* "angel") is an angel of death, the prince of demons, and a magician in rabbinic literature. In the *Sayings of Rabbi Eliezer* he is charged with being the one, who in the guise of a serpent, tempted Eve, seduced her, and became the father of Cain. In the **Zohar** Sammael is the dark angel who wrestled with **Jacob** at Peniel.

In Longfellow's *The Golden Legend,* Judas Iscariot explains to the rabbi why the dogs howl at night: "In the Rabbinical book it sayeth / The dogs howl when, with icy breath, / Great Sammael, the Angel of Death, / Takes through the town his flight."

Wednesday

Raphael, "the Shining one who heals," rules Wednesday, associated with Mercury. Traits associated with the planet Mercury (as with the Roman god) include travel and communication. According to **Sophy Burnham** (*A Book of Angels*), Raphael is especially concerned with pilgrims—not only travelers but those on pilgrimages to communicate with God. He is portrayed with staff and sandals, a water gourd, and a wallet strapped over his shoulder. In the Book of **Tobit,** Raphael acts as companion and guide to Tobit's son, Tobias, revealing himself only at the end as a servant of the four subprinces of the infernal empire.

Thursday

Sachiel, whose name means "covering of God," is frequently described as ruler of Thursday, the day associated with Jupiter. He is a presiding spirit of the planet Jupiter and an angel of the order of **cherubim.** He is invoked from the south (also the west.)

In the lore of witchcraft and black magic he is described as a servant of the four subprinces of the infernal empire.

Friday

Anael, chief of the order of **principalities** and one of the seven angels of the Creation, is ruler of Friday. He thus exercises dominion over the planet Venus, and as ruler of the planet of love he is concerned with human sexuality. (In Longfellow's *The Golden Legend,* Anael is referred to as the angel of "the Star of Love.")

Saturday

Cassiel is one of the rulers of the planet Saturn, associated with Saturday. He is known as the angel of solitudes and tears, perhaps reflecting a saturnine temperament given to moroseness and sullenness. He is also sometimes called the angel of temperance, and the planet Saturn is strongly associated with the social order. It is an embodiment of the principle of stability, and the opposite of upheaval.

Cassiel is one of the princes of the order of **powers.** In Francis Barrett's *The Magus* he is pictured as a bearded **jinn** riding a dragon.

Sources:

Burnham, Sophy. *A Book of Angels*. New York: Ballantine Books, 1990.

Davidson, Gustav. *A Dictionary of Angels: Including the Fallen Angels*. 1967. Reprint. New York: Free Press.

Godwin, Malcolm. *Angels: An Endangered Species*. New York: Simon and Schuster, 1990.

Hall, Manly P. *Astrological Keywords*. 1958. Reprint. Savage, Md.: Littlefield Adams, 1975.

Longfellow, Henry Wadsworth. *Poetical Works*. 6 vols. Boston: Houghton, 1904.

Dead Sea Scrolls

In 1947 a shepherd searching for a lost member of his flock discovered seven ancient scrolls, dating from 100 B.C. to A.D. 68, that had been sealed in jars and hidden in caves near the Dead Sea in Israel. This discovery led to others, and eventually eleven scroll-yielding caves and a habita-

THE MAGIC SEALS ASSOCIATED WITH THE SEVEN ANGELS OF THE SEVEN DAYS OF THE WEEK.

Michael.

Gabriel.

Samael.

Raphaël.

Sachiel.

Anaël.

Cassiel.

tion site were uncovered. In all, hundreds of manuscripts were found, including copies of most of the books of the Old Testament. The initial discovery of the seven scrolls was greeted by the general public with excitement because of the scrolls' mention of a "teacher of righteousness," which some early investigators mistakenly thought might be a reference to Jesus Christ. Most scholars now agree that the Dead Sea Scrolls, as they came to be called, are the library of the Essenes, an **apocalyptic** Jewish sect with their roots in the pietists (the Hasidim, not to be confused with contemporary Hasidism) of the Maccabean era. They withdrew from society and in the middle of the second century B.C. established a monastery on the shores of the Dead Sea at Qumran, where they had a community until they attacked during the war with the Romans in A.D. 66–70.

In stark contrast to other forms of **Judaism** and to early **Christianity,** the Essenes believed in the notion of an immortal soul. In their very un-Jewish antagonism toward the flesh, as well as in certain of their notions of the soul, they appear to have been influenced by **Gnosticism,** or by one of the other Neoplatonic mystery religions of the Hellenistic period.

Many of the surviving Dead Sea Scrolls are characterized by an apocalyptic, endtime emphasis that often pictures a supernatural redemption at the hands of God and his angels, a trait they share with the roughly contemporaneous writings of the **Apocrypha** and the Pseudepigrapha. They also portray the human soul as a battleground where angels of light and angels of darkness attempt to exert influence over human action for good or for ill:

> Through the Angel of Darkness, even those who practice righteousness are made liable to error. . . . All of the spirits that attend upon him are bent on causing the sons of light to stumble. Howbeit, the God of Israel and the Angel of His truth are always there to help the sons of light. (Gaster, pp. 43–44)

In this belief, they appear to have been influenced, directly or indirectly, by **Zoroastrianism.**

Sources:

Gaster, Theodore. *The Dead Sea Scriptures in English Translation.* New York: Doubleday, 1956.

Margolies, Morris B. *A Gathering of Angels: Angels in Jewish Life and Literature.* New York: Ballantine, 1994.

Turner, Alice K. *The History of Hell.* New York: Harcourt Brace, 1993.

Deathbed Visions

Deathbed visions are experienced by people very close to death during which they see deceased relatives or religious figures. Such visions share certain characteristics with mystical experiences, such as a strong sense of the sacred and a feeling of profound peace. Deathbed visions are usually characterized by radiant lights, scenes of great beauty, and, especially, the appearance of beings of light, whose purpose is to escort the deceased to the afterworld.

Angels are one kind of being regularly encountered during such visions. In his book *Angels: God's Secret Agents,* evangelist **Billy Graham** recounts a number of cases in which the dying report that they see angels and hear them singing their praises to God in heaven. Graham, citing the biblical account of Lazarus (Luke 16), is convinced that he, too, "will actually be taken by angels into the presence of God."

Swedish theologian **Emanuel Swedenbörg** (*Heaven and Hell*) believed that the soul crosses into the "kingdom of the Spirits" after death, and wrote about the spirits who receive the new arrivals: "They perform this task with great delicacy, granting the new arrival complete freedom. Above all, they transmit a feeling of great love and make the new arrival aware of the presence of a friend, someone who knows and can explain everything."

Those who have witnessed such deathbed occurrences relate similar characteristics. As the deathbed vision accelerates many have shared that the light they encounter radiates a warmth or a security that draws them ever closer to the original source. With the light also comes a vision of beautiful gardens or open fields, that adds to the sense of peace and security.

According to angel researcher **Leonard Day,** who has been called upon to assist the dying, a very high percentage do speak of the presence of angels. A trend, according to Day, is for the person to actually mention the presence of two angels, one presenting a more radiant glow than the other. Day believes the angel of brighter light to be the individual's **guardian angel.** This angel is usually in close proximity to the person and offers soothing words of consolation. The other angel usually remains at a distance, standing in the corner or behind the first angel. For Day, this other angel represents the **angel of death.**

Those who recount their visions do not refer to the angel of death as the foreboding apparition so commonly portrayed across the centuries. In reality, according to Day, it is perhaps the most gentle and sensitive angel within God's creation. Those who have shared their encounter with this angel, describe it as dark, very quiet, and not at all menacing. According to Day, it is the responsibility of the angel of death to summon the departed spirit into the care of the guardian angel so the journey to the "other side" can begin.

Deathbed Visions

The angel of the north star is said to preside over the scales in which the human soul is weighed at the death of the body.

Sources:

Barrett, Sir William. *Death-Bed Visions: The Psychical Experiences of the Dying.* 1926. Reprint. Northhamptonshire, England: Aquarian Press, 1986.

Day, Leonard C. Letter to author, 26 June 1995.

Graham, Billy. *Angels: God's Secret Agents.* Dallas: Word Publishing, 1994.

Giovetti, Paola. *Angels: The Role of Celestial Guardians and Beings of Light.* Translated by Toby McCormick. York Beach, Maine: Samuel Weiser, 1989.

Demiurge

The Demiurge is the chief **archon** (evil spiritual being), who creates the world in the Gnostic system. **Gnosticism** was a movement and school of thought prominent in the Hellenistic Mediterranean world that influenced paganism, **Judaism,** and **Christianity.** According to the Gnostic myth of creation, **Sophia,** one of the good spiritual beings **(aeons)** residing in the *pleroma* (the pure spiritual realm), inadvertently created another entity—often called Yaldabaoth—who created our material world (Robinson, p. 9f). This evil deity, designated the Demiurge (a term originally used by Plato in the *Timaeus* to refer to a demigod who created the world), also created the human body in order to trap human spirits in the physical world. Our true home is the pleroma, however, to which we seek to return even as the archons try to prevent us from doing so.

A standard tenet of Gnostic Christianity was that Yahweh, the God of the Old Testament, and the evil Demiurge are one and the same. Pointing to the discrepancy between the jealous, vengeful God of the Old Testament and the teachings of the gentle Jesus, the Gnostics asserted that Jesus was a teacher sent from the pleroma to guide us back to our true home, and that the "Father" to which he referred was different from Yahweh.

Sources:

Layton, Bentley. *The Gnostic Scriptures.* Garden City, N.Y.: Doubleday, 1987.

Robinson, James M. *The Nag Hammadi Library.* 1977. Reprint. New York: Harper & Row, 1981.

Ronner, John. *Know Your Angels: The Angel Almanac with Biographies of 100 Prominent Angels in Legend and Folklore, and Much More.* Murfreesboro, Tenn.: Mamre Press, 1993.

Devas

The word *deva* has two distinct meanings, both related to contemporary **angelology.** In the first meaning, devas are the demigods of **Hinduism** and **Buddhism.** In the second, devas are the angel-like beings of **Theosophy,** which have been adopted into the worldview of the contemporary **New Age** metaphysical subculture.

Hindu and Buddhist Devas

Around 1000–1500 B.C. a group of **Indo-Europeans** invaded India through the northern mountain passes, destroyed whatever written records might have remained from the original civilization, and settled in northern India. The worldview of these invaders, who called themselves Aryans, was vastly different from what later became Hinduism. In addition to other changes, the principal gods of the Vedic pantheon were supplanted by new ones. Because of the tendency of Hinduism to keep earlier layers of its own tradition, however, the Vedic gods were retained in the form of lower-level demigods, referred to as devas.

As embodied in such classical Hindu mythological texts as the Puranas, devas are far more complex than Western angels. Nevertheless, some devas occasionally perform messenger tasks for the higher deities, making them comparable to angels. Early Buddhism, on the other hand, retained a belief in the older divinities of the Vedic pantheon but denied their importance in helping the aspirant achieve Buddhism's ultimate goal—liberation from the cycle of death and rebirth (i.e., terminating the process of reincarnation). Thus, as in later Hinduism, the Vedic gods and goddesses—the devas—came to play a role in Buddhist thought and mythology somewhat comparable to that of Western angels.

New Age Devas

Partially because of the association of some devas with the forces of nature, the term *deva* was adopted in nineteenth-century Theosophy to denote the class of spiritual beings believed to have formed and to control the manifest world. Theosophists further assert that the devas of the East correspond with the angels of the West but have many more functions.

In particular, devas oversee natural forces and are responsible for building up forms on inner planes as well as on the physical plane. According to this theory, there are two distinct lines of spiritual evolution, one going from the mineral, through the animal, to the human and beyond; the other going from **elemental** spirits, through **fairies,** to angels (devas) and beyond. Beings in the devic line are responsible for creating forms, which allows other beings to evolve spiritually. In the words of one of the founders of **Findhorn:**

> [Devas constitute] a whole hierarchy of beings, from the earthiest gnome to the highest archangel, and are a sister evolution to the human on earth. The devas hold the archetypal pattern and plan for all forms around us, and they direct the

energy needed for materializing them. The physical bodies of minerals, vegetables, animals and humans are all energy brought into form through the work of the devic kingdom. (*The Findhorn Garden,* p. 58)

In the theosophical view, everything is ultimately spirit, and it is only through devic activity that the physical world of our everyday experience is created. William Bloom, a contemporary metaphysical writer, explains this view by drawing an analogy to atomic theory: all material objects are composed of minute electrically charged particles in motion. Bloom asserts that:

> *Devic essence* bridges between the constantly moving electric charges to produce the matter we can see and touch. . . . Without devic essence there would be no coherence to manifest life—just an ocean of unconnected electric charges. *All* form is a mixture of, a relationship between, devic essence and atomic electric charges. (*Devas, Fairies and Angels,* p. 3)

In other words, beings in the devic lifestream—beings from elementals to **archangels**—provide both a *pattern* and an active, constituting activity for matter that allows diverse forms to manifest as tangible material objects. These patterns include everything from plants and mountains to the bodies of animals and human beings. Thus both lines of spiritual evolution—that from the mineral to the human and beyond, and that from elemental spirits to devas and beyond—"are interdependent in the structure of all manifest life. Their relationship is interwoven and patterned from an extremely deep level of creation" (Bloom, p. 5).

That devic activity takes place all around us without our awareness is explained in terms of differing rates of vibration: devas are normally invisible to us because they exist at a higher, imperceptible rate of vibration—like the high-pitched sounds of a dog whistle that cannot be heard by human ears.

The Findhorn community in northern Scotland became well known in New Age and metaphysical circles as a result of its members participation in a vegetable garden experiment in which they attempted to cooperate with the nature devas in creating the garden. Communicating with these spirits in a mediumistic (**Spiritualistic**) fashion, they claimed to receive gardening advice from the devas that allowed them to grow gigantic vegetables in an environment that otherwise was not particularly hospitable to gardening.

Findhorn attracted such attention that it left an indelible impression on many people's perceptions of devas. In particular, the emphasis on nature devas caused many to overlook the importance of other kinds of

Devas

According to St. Bartholomew angels are often accompanied by a lingering fragrance in the air such as flowers or pine.

devas, such as those who were said to function as **guardian angels** for both human beings and collectivities (e.g., the devas of nations or ethnic groups).

Sources:

Bloom, William. *Devas, Fairies and Angels: A Modern Approach.* Glastonbury, England: Gothic Image Publications, 1986.

Eliade, Mircea, ed. *Encyclopedia of Religion.* 16 vols. New York: Macmillan, 1987.

Findhorn Community. *The Findhorn Garden.* New York: Harper & Row, 1975.

MacGregor, Geddes. *Angels: Ministers of Grace.* New York: Paragon House, 1988.

Parisen, Maria. *Angels & Mortals: Their Co-Creative Power.* Wheaton, Ill.: Quest, 1990.

Zimmer, Heinrich. *Philosophies of India.* 1951. Reprint. New York: Macmillan, 1987.

Devidasi

Devidasi (or *devadasi*) is an Indian term meaning servant or slave (*das*) of a god (*deva*) or goddess (*devi*). It refers primarily to the dancing girls who were traditionally attached to certain Hindu temples. The term later became interchangeable with *prostitute* because of the practice of temple prostitution—often engaged in by the devidasis—in medieval **Hinduism.** The term has also been used to denote heavenly dancing girls, and is thus used interchangeably with **apsara**, a type of Hindu demigoddess frequently compared with angels.

Sources:

Ronner, John. *Know Your Angels: The Angel Almanac with Biographies of 100 Prominent Angels in Legend and Folklore, and Much More.* Murfreesboro, Tenn.: Mamre Press, 1993.

Stutley, Margaret, and James Stutley. *Harper's Dictionary of Hinduism: Its Mythology, Folklore, Philosophy, Literature, and History.* New York: Harper & Row, 1977.

Devils, Demons, and Fallen Angels

Any thorough or systematic discussion of angels must include a discussion of the so-called fallen angels, namely, devils and demons. Although the two words are often used interchangeably for evil spiritual entities, the original meanings of *devil* (from Greek *diabolos,* to throw across, slander) and *demon* (from Greek *daemon,* spirit) were somewhat more complex.

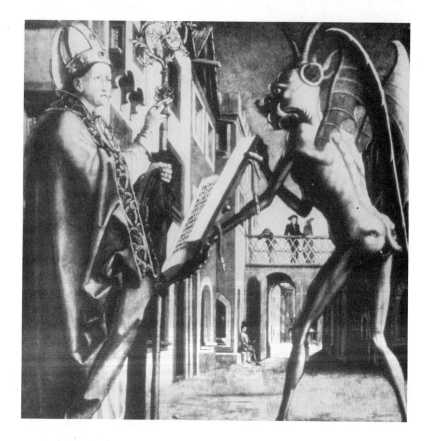

BISHOP SAINT ENCOUNTERING A FANGED, WINGED DEVIL BY MICHAEL PACHER
(OUTER SIDE OF THE WINGS OF THE FATHERS OF THE CHURCH ALTAR, MUNICH,
CA. 1435–98). (COURTESY ARAS)

Devils have always had a negative connotation in Western religions as evil forces, but the word *devil* has the same Indo-European root as the Hindu-Buddhist term *deva,* which roughly approximates the Western angel.

Daemons, on the other hand, were ancient **Greek** tutelary spirits of either good or bad nature. The Greek word *daemon* was introduced in the Roman and Hellenistic world to indicate evil forces, and it thus entered early **Christian** writings with the negative connotation of impure spirits.

The Judeo-Christian tradition elaborated the concept of the Devil as the fallen angel who tempted **Adam** and Eve and was forever banished from Paradise. Christian literature also drew upon the depiction of evil spirits in Jewish, Persian, and **Mesopotamian** legends.

In the Christian tradition, devils acquired employment tormenting the souls of the damned in the underworld (although the earliest Christian idea was that stern, righteous angels tormented the damned). As these ideas evolved and the righteous angels were removed from hell, **Satan,** ruler of all other devils, became king of the underworld. Hell then became the headquarters or central staging area from which demonic forces launched assaults against those on earth, attempting to snare human souls and otherwise spoil God's creation.

There are two stories of how these former angels fell from grace. In the most commonly accepted narrative of events, Satan, formerly one of God's favorite angels, leads a rebellion against God. As one might anticipate, Satan loses, and he and the angels who follow him (one-third of the celestial host, by some accounts) are tossed out of heaven. The early Christians and contemporaneous Jews, however, were familiar with a very different story, in which the angels fall via their lust for human women. A fragment of this tale was incorporated into a brief passage in Scripture that alludes to "the sons of God" (i.e., the angels), who, viewing beautiful human women, took them for wives. (Gen. 6:2). This latter tale was elaborated on in such noncanonical writings as the **Book of Enoch.**

Sources:

Baskin, Wade. *Dictionary of Satanism*. New York: Philosophical Library, 1962.
Masello, Robert. *Fallen Angels . . . and Spirits of the Dark*. New York: Perigree, 1994.
Prophet, Elizabeth Clare. *Forbidden Mysteries of Enoch: Fallen Angels and the Origins of Evil*. Livingston, Mont.: Summit University Press, 1983.
Turner, Alice K. *The History of Hell*. New York: Harcourt Brace, 1993.
Wilson, Peter Lamborn. *Angels*. New York: Pantheon Books, 1980.

Dionysius the Areopagite

The early sixth-century writings of the mystical theologian Dionysius the Areopagite had a significant impact on classical Christian **angelology.** Some erroneously claim he was the philosopher converted by St. Paul on the Athenian Areopagus, however he is known to scholars today as Dionysius the Pseudo-Areopagite or the Pseudo-Dionysius, to distinguish him from the New Testament Dionysius. His Neoplatonism is evident in both the concept and the terminology of *The Celestial Hierarchy,* the most influential treatise in Christian angelology, and in his treatises *The Divine Names,* and *Ten Letters.*

The Dionysian scheme describes nine **choirs** of angels, grouped into three **hierarchies.** In descending order of closeness to God they are:

First Hierarchy	Second Hierarchy	Third Hierarchy
seraphim	dominions	principalities
cherubim	virtues	archangels
thrones	powers	angels

Only the last two choirs have contact with human beings; in them are placed all of the angels, named and unnamed, of the biblical tradition.

According to Dionysius each name of the choirs indicates its divine nature. For example, the name of the seraphim means both "those that burn" and "those that warm." Dionysius explains that the seraphim are in continuous revolution around God, thus the heat that they emit is like lightning.

The name **cherubim** means "fullness of knowledge" or "effusion of wisdom." This choir has the power to know and contemplate God, and the capacity to understand and communicate divine knowledge.

The term **thrones,** or the "many eyed ones," is an indication of their close proximity to the throne of God. This is the order closest to God and they receive directly from him divine perfection and awareness.

The holy **dominions** have the power to elevate themselves and are liberated from all earthly desires and yearnings. It is their job to regulate the duties of the angels.

The name of the **virtues** indicates a firm and steadfast courage in all angelic activities. Known as the "brilliant" or "shining ones," the virtues are associated with acts of heroism.

The **powers** are on the same level as the dominions and virtues, and possess the power and intelligence that is subordinate only to God. They keep the universe in balance.

The order of **angels** is closest to human kind. It is the job of this order to act as guardians and messengers, and at its helm is placed Michael, prince of the Jewish people, who leads all the angels in their posts as guardians of nations. In fact, according to Dionysius, God established the boundaries of the nations according to the number of the angels.

According to another Pseudo-Dionysian work, *The Ecclesiastical Hierarchy,* the angelic orders are reflected in the structure of the earthly Church, and thus form a continuum between God and the believer. The Dionysian scheme bears a curious resemblance to the Gnostic order of angels criticized by the second-century saint Irenaeus; both systems may reflect Persian angelology passed on through the biblical and rabbinic literature of postexilic Judaism.

Sources:

Bemrose, Stephen. *Dante's Angelic Intelligences: Their Importance in the Cosmos and in Pre-Christian Religion.* Rome: Edizioni di Storia e Letteratura, 1983.

Dionysius the Areopagite. *The Celestial Hierarchies.* Godalmins, Surrey, UK: The Shrine of Wisdom, 1949.

————. *The Mystical Theology and the Celestial Hierarchies.* Godalmins, Surrey, UK: The Shrine of Wisdom, 1949.

Giovetti, Paola. *Angels: The Role of Celestial Guardians and Beings of Light.* Translated by Toby McCormick. York Beach, Maine: Samuel Weiser, 1993.

MacGregor, Geddes. *Angels: Ministers of Grace.* New York: Paragon House, 1988.

Strayer, Joseph R., ed. *Dictionary of the Middle Ages.* 13 vols. New York: Scribner, 1982–89.

Directions (Angels of the)

Almost every traditional society invests special significance in the four cardinal directions—north, south, east, and west. The directions are the dwelling places of specific gods or other spiritual beings, who often "rule" the energies specifically associated with the directions. Today all sense of the sacrality of the directions has virtually been lost. One of the few sources offering a dim reflection of this rather archaic way of viewing the world is the popular movie *The Wizard of Oz,* which aligns specific "witches" with each of the directions.

Traditionally, the four principal **archangels** were associated with the four directions. It was believed that **Raphael** ruled the east, **Michael** the south, **Gabriel** the west, and **Uriel** the north. These traditional associations survive in ritual **magic,** in which the power of the archangels is invoked when drawing a magic circle.

Sources:

Cavendish, Richard. *The Black Arts.* New York: Capricorn Books, 1967.

Guiley, Rosemary Ellen. *The Encyclopedia of Witches and Witchcraft.* New York: Facts on File, 1989.

Djibril

Djibril (also Jibril or Jabril, among other variant spellings) is **Gabriel**'s name in **Islam.** He is looked upon as a **guardian angel,** has huge green wings, and bears the inscription "There is no God but God, and **Muhammad** is the Prophet of God" between his eyes. Djibril is said to have presented himself before the prophet Muhammad on "the Night of Power and Glory" and dictated to him the sacred words of the Koran. Djibril also led Muhammad (who rode upon a winged magic mule with the face of a woman) to the Islamic shrine known as the Dome of the Rock, where Muhammad ascended a golden ladder to the heavens. Along the way, he passed by Isa and Idris (Jesus and Hermes), **Adam, Abraham,** Moses, and the archangel **Michael.** Muhammad later arrived at a vast sea of golden light where he was enlightened to divine truth. He then returned to earth.

In Islamic legend, Djibril has at least six hundred wings, and the sun is placed between his two eyes. Djibril is also said to have been helpful and sympathetic to Adam after he fell from grace. He instructed Adam in the arts and escorted him to Mecca, where he trained him in pilgrimage rituals. Djibril is known in Persian lore as both Serosh, "the message-bringer," and Bahram, "the mightiest of all the angels."

Sources:

Davidson, Gustav. *A Dictionary of Angels: Including the Fallen Angels.* 1967. Reprint. New York: Free Press, 1971.

Glassé, Cyril. *The Concise Encyclopedia of Islam.* San Francisco: Harper San Francisco, 1989.

Ronner, John. *Know Your Angels: The Angel Almanac with Biographies of 100 Prominent Angels In Legend and Folklore, and Much More.* Murfreesboro, Tenn.: Mamre Press, 1993.

Dominions (Dominations)

The dominions may be the first realm of beings given executive free will to manage the daily functioning of the universe. **Dionysius** says that this realm "regulates the angels," who are constantly aspiring to lordship, although the first three **choirs** (**seraphim, cherubim,** and **thrones**) are so closely dedicated to serving only God that they do not require supervision. Also, according to Dionysius, the mercy of God manifests through them, which is why scholars sometimes refer to the dominions as channels of mercy.

A friend of God's named **Raguel** is reportedly the being in charge of this realm. Traditionally Raguel is thought to have transported **Enoch,** while still in the flesh, to heaven (Gen. 5:24). (In other literature, however, the angel Anafiel is credited with this feat.) In a 1966 opera at St. George's Church in New York, Raguel was cast as an angel of the **principalities,** however in most references, he belongs to the choir of dominions.

According to Jewish legend, the success or failure of nations was decided by their respective guardian angels. The dominions were the choir from which the angels who had "dominion" over the countries were drawn. The appellation *dominion,* according to Hermes Trismegistus, was taken from the name of the oldest angel, Dominion.

Sources:

Davidson, Gustav. *A Dictionary of Angels: Including the Fallen Angels.* 1967. New York: Free Press, 1971.

Godwin, Malcolm. *Angels: An Endangered Species.* New York: Simon and Schuster, 1990.

Mansfield, Richard. *Angels: An Introduction to the Angelic Hierarchy.* Encinitas, Calif.: Estuary Publications, 1994.

Dragons

Often depicted as a mix of several creatures, the dragon is a fantastic beast found in mythology and folklore worldwide. In Oriental mythologies the dragon is seen as a beneficent animal and is often a symbol or a portent of prosperity, whereas in most European mythologies it is viewed as a demonic beast hostile to man. In Christian symbolism, for instance, the dragon represents the chief of the fallen angels, the Devil.

ENGRAVING OF MICHAEL SLAYING THE DRAGON BY MARTIN SCHONGAUER (1470). (COURTESY ARAS)

One inspiration for the Christian Devil via Hebrew Scriptures (the Old Testament) is the Babylonian female dragon monster known as Tiamet. In early Christian thought, the Devil as dragon has taken on the allegorical role of representing the Antichrist, or, more generally, evil passions, paganism, or the oppressive powers of this world. In the Book of Revelation, chapter 12, he is described as big and red, with seven heads and ten horns.

In the **war in heaven,** the archangel **Michael** is usually represented as the slayer of the dragon, and his angels fight against the dragon and his angels. "The great dragon was thrown down, that ancient serpent who is called Devil and Satan, the deceiver of the whole world; he was thrown down to the earth, and his angels were thrown down with him."

In Hebrew Scriptures, in the battle between God and the dragon, Yahweh is depicted as a storm god. At his coming "the earth trembled, and the heavens dropped, yea, the clouds dropped water, the mountains quaked before the Lord" (Judg. 5:4–5). "Thou didst break the heads of the dragons on the waters," says the psalmist in Ps. 74:13, and "the Lord . . . shall slay the dragon that is in the sea," declares Isa. 27:1. Moreover, according to Ps. 91:13, the saints will "trample the dragon under their feet." The battle between Yahweh and the dragon is very popular in the visions of the later Hebrew prophets, although the dragon usually embodies a purely symbolic meaning as the enemy of Israel, that is, the Assyrians, the Babylonians, or the **Egyptians.**

An account of God's hostility toward Pharaoh is reported by the prophet **Ezekiel,** who speaks of Pharaoh as "the great dragon that lies in the midst of his streams," into whose jaws he will put hooks and whom he will have thrown into the wilderness. Elsewhere in the Old Testament, the dragon is also a symbol of mourning and desolation.

One of the most discussed chapters of the Old Testament is Daniel 7, which reports a dream, alleged to have occurred in the first year of Belshazzar, king of Babylon, in which Daniel sees the four winds of heaven stirring up the great sea. Out of the sea emerge, one after the other, a series of beasts, four in number, all of fabulous form. The fourth beast, in particular, is especially terrible and has ten horns. The four beasts represent in succession the Babylonian, Median, Persian, and Hellenistic empires.

In **Gnosticism,** the dragon is a symbol for the angel of dawn.

Sources:

Cavendish, Richard. *Man, Myth & Magic: The Illustrated Encyclopedia of Mythology, Religion and the Unknown.* New York: Marshall Cavendish, 1995.

Davidson, Gustav. *A Dictionary of Angels: Including the Fallen Angels.* 1967. Reprint. New York: Free Press, 1971.

Day, John. *God's Conflict with the Dragon and the Sea: Echoes of a Canaanite Myth in the Old Testament.* Cambridge: Cambridge University Press, 1985.

Mercatante, Anthony S. *The Facts on File Encyclopedia of World Mythology and Legend.* New York: Facts on File, 1988.

Dubbiel

Dubbiel (also Dubiel or Dobiel) is known as the **guardian angel** of Persia. A full account of the legend describing Dubbiel's exploits is told in the scholarly work *Fallen Angels,* by Bernard J. Bamberger. In brief, the story is as follows.

In ancient times, the fate of each nation was determined by the actions of the guardian angel that represented that nation in heaven. The angels would battle with one another to win favor with God, who would decide upon the destiny of the nations in question.

In this instance, the guardian angel for Israel, **Gabriel,** was in disfavor with God because of an attempt by the angel to intervene when an angry God decided to destroy Israel. Gabriel's efforts to stop God were partially successful; although much of Israel was devastated, some Jewish noblemen were saved and taken into captivity in Babylon.

Dubbiel was then allowed to take Gabriel's place in God's inner circle, and immediately took advantage of the situation. Soon he had arranged for great amounts of territory on earth to be conquered by Persia, and the great expansion of the Persian Empire during the 500s through the 300s B.C. was accredited to Dubbiel's work in heaven during this time. His position of power lasted only twenty-one days, however, before Gabriel convinced God to let him resume his original place, forcing out the ambitious Dubbiel.

Sources:

Bamberger, Bernard J. *Fallen Angels.* Philadelphia: Jewish Publication Society of America, 1952.

Davidson, Gustav. *A Dictionary of Angels: Including the Fallen Angels.* 1967. Reprint. New York: Free Press, 1971.

Ronner, John. *Know Your Angels: The Angel Almanac with Biographies of 100 Prominent Angels in Legend and Folklore, and Much More.* Murfreesboro, Tenn.: Mamre Press, 1993.

Dwarfs

Dwarfs are a form of German **fairy.** Because of the diminutive size of most fairies and because the term *dwarf* has come to mean "tiny," many other species of small spiritual beings have been referred to as dwarfs. It is said that the Isle of Rügen has black and white dwarfs.

Sources:

Briggs, Katharine. *An Encyclopedia of Fairies.* New York: Pantheon, 1976.

McCoy, Edwin. *A Witch's Guide to Faery Folk.* St. Paul, Minn.: Llewellyn Publications, 1994.

An actually existing fly is more important than a possibly existing angel.

—Ralph Waldo Emerson

Egypt

In polytheistic religions such as those of ancient Egypt, the line between gods and angels was a thin one, and representations of winged figures was very common. For instance, Isis, the protectress, virgin, and mother, manifests as an angel, her wings spread to enfold her worshipers in the sleep of unity, or perhaps to reveal her role as the **angel of death.**

The god Horus is represented as a falcon, or as a falcon-headed man, sometimes wearing a solar disc. One of his most important manifestations is as Horus of Behtet, represented as a solar disc with falcon's wings, a figure frequently carved over the doors of temples. The goddess Nut is represented as a woman with wings outspread or folded around her body, wearing upon her head the hieroglyph of her name, or as a woman with elongated body, stooping so that her hands touch the ground. She is a goddess of the sky and consort of Geb.

An element of mortals that was believed to survive death was the *ba,* or the soul. Depicted as a human-headed bird, the ba was an animating force that could leave the dead body and travel at will outside the tomb to visit places that the deceased enjoyed while alive. The ba returned periodically to the tomb to feed upon the funerary offerings.

THE FOUR-WINGED EGYPTIAN
GOD KHONSU. (COURTESY ARAS)

The idea of a unique angelic species probably derived ultimately from the influence of Egyptian, Sumerian, Babylonian, and Persian views of supernatural beings. This interaction of ideas produced the familiar image of the winged messenger of God. For example, in Chaldea **Michael** was considered the angel of the Last Judgment and the "weigher of souls" and, as such, was a descendent of Anubis, the jackal-headed deity who weighed the hearts of the deceased when the tribes of Israel were in captivity in Egypt. Anubis was identified with Sirius, the Dog Star, which is the most important star in the Egyptian sky. As god of the Egyptian underworld, Anubis was associated with the Indo-European god **Hermes,** especially in his role as **psychopomp,** conductor of souls.

—*Michela Zonta*

Sources:

David, A. Rosalie. *The Ancient Egyptians: Religious Beliefs and Practices.* London: Routledge & Kegan Paul, 1982.

Godwin, Malcolm. *Angels: An Endangered Species.* New York: Simon and Schuster, 1990.

Shorter, Alan W. *The Egyptian Gods: A Handbook.* London: Routledge & Kegan Paul, 1937.

Wilson, Peter Lamborn. *Angels: Messengers of Gods.* London: Thames and Hudson, 1980.

Elementals

The term *element* has come to be associated with the chemical elements. Prior to the modern era, and dating back at least as far as the ancient **Greeks,** this term referred to the four classical elements of earth, air, water, and fire. It seems that by these "elements" the ancients meant "states of matter": solid, gas, liquid, and (for lack of a better term) energy.

The Western occult tradition has postulated that these "states" are the result of the activity of small, invisible spirits termed *elementals.* While some branches of the occult tradition view elementals as transitory and soulless, others see them as conscious life forms that evolve into **fairies** and **devas** (angels). The task of the elementals, like that of the nature devas, is to build up forms in the natural world, thus providing an arena in which other beings, such as human souls, can evolve spiritually.

The names of the elemental spirits and the archangels said to **rule** them (in at least some schemas) are as follows:

Element	Elemental Beings	Ruling Archangel
Earth	**Gnomes**	**Uriel**
Water	**Undines**	**Gabriel**
Air	**Sylphs**	**Raphael**
Fire	**Salamanders**	**Michael**

Sources:

Andrews, Ted. *Enchantment of the Faerie Realm: Communicate with Nature Spirits & Elementals.* St. Paul, Minn.: Llewellyn Publications, 1993.

Shepard, Leslie A., ed. *Encyclopedia of Occultism & Parapsychology.* Detroit, Mich.: Gale Research, 1991.

Elijah

Elijah is one of the more famous Hebrew prophets, with whom much fantastic lore is associated. So entrenched in mythic lore is this prophet, that he has taken on decidedly angelic proportions. In the **Bible,** Elijah is the prophet who bests the priests of Baal in a contest of supernatural power between their god and the God of Israel.

Scripture records (2 Kings 2:11–12) that, at the end of his life, Elijah was taken up to heaven in a chariot of fire without having to die. Like **Enoch** before him, who was translated bodily into heaven and became an angel, Elijah is supposed to have been transformed into the angel **Sandalphon.**

Elijah is considered the harbinger of the Messiah's return according to Mal. 3:23: "Behold, I will send the prophet Elijah to you before the coming of the awesome, fearful day of the Lord." Because of this role as precursor and preparer for the Lord, the Christian church appropriated Elijah and claimed him to be reincarnated in the guise of **John the Baptist.** In his role as messianic herald, at the End of Days, Elijah will "blow the *shofar,* revealing the Primal Light of Creation, reviving the dead, and rebuilding the Temple. His arrival will banish all evil from the earth" (Frankel, p. 48).

Jewish tradition has assigned Elijah the role of **guardian angel** to newborn children and young people who die early in life. His legend has so grown in proportion that he is considered a kind of miracle worker or fairy godfather who intervenes in times of marital trouble, grants wishes, and in essence, performs all the true functions of an angel. Jewish Cabalists even assert that Elijah originally was an angel created out of the Tree of Life, who frequently returns to holy residents of earth to explain the mysteries of the Torah.

ELIJAH FED BY AN ANGEL IN THE DESERT BY DIRK BOUTS (CA. 1464–67). (COURTESY ARAS)

Sources:

Frankel, Ellen, and Betsy Platkin Teutsch. *The Encyclopedia of Jewish Symbols*. Northvale, N.J.: Jason Aronson, 1992.

Gaster, Theodore. *Myth, Legend, and Custom in the Old Testament*. New York: Harper & Roe, 1969.

Margolies, Morris B. *A Gathering of Angels: Angels in Jewish Life and Literature*. New York: Ballantine, 1994.

Schwartz, Howard. *Gabriel's Palace: Jewish Mystical Tales*. New York: Oxford University Press, 1993.

Elohim

Elohim is a Hebrew term that has multiple meanings. It is among the two well-known Hebrew names for God, the other being *Eloha*. Eloha occurs in the book of Job in this singular form and refers to the God of Israel. Elohim, translated literally "God," is the name for God that appears most often in the Bible. It usually refers to the God of Israel but can be used to connote a pagan deity, even a "goddess." While Elohim is plural in form, it is treated as a singular noun, although again it can refer to pagan "gods."

Elohim is also used to refer to spirits of the departed, as in 1 Sam. 28:13, where the woman of Endor tells Saul she saw gods ascending out of the earth. Elsewhere Elohim is the name of an angel, as recorded in Deuteronomy.

The elohim rank ninth in the Mirandola listing of the celestial **hierarchies**. Elohim is the name of the seventh of the ten **sefiroth** and corresponds to *netzach,* or victory, in the *Book of Formation.* **Rudolf Steiner** equates the icxusai (spirits of form) of his own hierarchy with the elohim. Elohim are also represented in art, as in **William Blake**'s drawing entitled *Elohim Giving Life to Adam.*

Sources:
MacGregor, Geddes. *Angels: Ministers of Grace*. New York: Paragon House Publishers, 1988.

Margolies, Morris B. *A Gathering of Angels: Angels in Jewish Life and Literature*. New York: Ballantine, 1994.

Parisen, Maria. *Angels & Mortals: Their Co-Creative Power*. Wheaton, Ill.: Quest Books, 1990.

Elves

Elves, also called *elbs, erls,* or *mannikins,* were originally Scandinavian **fairies,** which explains their connection with the North Pole and Santa Claus. The name was, however, imported into Great Britain, and used to designate special classes of fairies. Specifically, in Scotland, fairies as large as humans were termed elves, and fairyland was called *Elfame.* By way of contrast, in England the term was used to designate the so-called *trooping fairies,* namely fairies who liked to congregate in groups (as opposed to *solitary fairies*). Relevant folklore portrays them as skillful spinners and sewers. They are associated with mice in some fairy tales.

Sources:

Briggs, Katharine. *An Encyclopedia of Fairies.* New York: Pantheon, 1976.
McCoy, Edwin. *A Witch's Guide to Faery Folk.* St. Paul, Minn.: Llewellyn, 1994.

Enoch, Book of

Enoch is mentioned in Genesis as the father of Methuselah, the oldest of the long-lived descendants of **Adam.** In a pattern that was typical of the intertestamental period, several books (none ever accepted as canonical) were composed in the name of Enoch. These works, especially the Book of Enoch, are extremely important for the angel lore they contain. The Book of Enoch is sometimes referred to as 1 Enoch to distinguish it from the Book of the Secrets of Enoch, which is often called 2 Enoch. 1 Enoch and 2 Enoch are also sometimes called, respectively, the Ethiopic Enoch and the Slavonic Enoch, after the earliest languages in which complete copies of these books were found.

The most important angel narrative in the Book of Enoch is the tale of a group of two hundred angels who lusted after mortal women, fell from grace, and subsequently became devils after leaving their heavenly abode under the leadership of the angel **Semyaza.** These angels also encouraged other sinful activities by teaching humans about such things as cosmetics (encouraging vanity) and weapons (promoting war). The core of the narrative is contained in chapter 7:

> It happened after the sons of men had multiplied in those days, that daughters were born to them elegant and beautiful. And when the angels, the sons of heaven, beheld them, they became enamored of them, saying to each other: Come, let us select for ourselves wives from the progeny of men, and let us beget children. (7:1–2)

> Then they took wives, each choosing for himself; whom they began to approach, and with whom they cohabited; teaching them sorcery, incantation, and the dividing of roots and trees. And they conceiving brought forth giants; whose stature was each three hundred cubits. These devoured all which the labor of men produced; until it became impossible to feed

them; when they turned themselves against men, in order to devour them. (7:10–13)

When earth was in complete anarchy, God sent the archangel **Michael** down from heaven to confine the corrupt angels in the valleys of earth until doomsday. The giants that these angels fathered (the **Nephilim**) went on wreaking havoc until, according to such sources as the **Book of Jubilees,** they were wiped out in the Flood. Scripture, however, records later post-Flood tribes of giants who were descendants of the Nephilim (e.g., Num. 13:33; Deut. 2:11; Josh. 12:4).

This story, which at one time was widely known, eventually disappeared from popular folklore because it clashed with the official church position, which was that angels were beings of pure spirit and thus could not engage in sexual intercourse. Gen. 6:2–4 alludes to the Enoch tale, stating that the "sons of God" (which, in the context of the Book of Enoch, are angels) took mortal women as wives.

THE APOTHEOSIS OF EMPEROR ANTONIUS PIUS AND EMPRESS FAUSTINA. PARALLEL TO THE JEWISH NOTION THAT ENOCH WAS TRANSMUTED INTO AN ANGEL, THE ANCIENT ROMANS BELIEVED THAT THEIR ROYALTY WOULD BE TRANSFORMED INTO DEMI-GODS. (ROME, CA. 161 A.D.). (COURTESY ARAS)

The early church fathers clearly regarded the Book of Enoch as Scripture, which is evident in many places in the New Testament canon. The Epistle of Jude, for example, refers directly to 1 Enoch when he states that "Enoch also, the seventh from Adam, prophesied of these, saying, Behold the Lord cometh with ten thousands of his saints, to execute judgment upon all . . ." (Jude 1:14–15).

According to the Hebrew Book of Enoch, God took Enoch and translated him directly to heaven, where his body was transformed into flame and he became the angel **Metatron.**

This tale about Enoch ascending bodily to heaven is based on a brief scriptural allusion in Genesis, where it states that "Enoch walked with God; and he was not, for God took him" (5:24). (This contrasts with statements about the other patriarchs, who Scripture asserts simply died.) Among other heavenly tasks, Enoch became high priest of the heavenly temple and minister of wisdom, who holds the keys to the divine mysteries. It is perhaps because of these exalted positions that Enoch was attributed with the authorship of 1 and 2 Enoch.

Sources:

The Book of Enoch. Translated by Richard Laurence. Thousand Oaks, Calif.: Artisan Sales, 1980. (Originally published 1882).

Giovetti, Paola. *Angels: The Role of Celestial Guardians and Beings of Light.* Translated by Toby McCormick. York Beach, Maine: Samuel Weiser, 1993.

Margolies, Morris B. *A Gathering of Angels: Angels in Jewish Life and Literature.* New York: Ballantine, 1994.

Prophet, Elizabeth Clare. *Forbidden Mysteries of Enoch: Fallen Angels and the Origins of Evil.* Rev. ed. Livingston, Mont.: Summit University Press, 1992.

Eros

Angels are predominantly considered messengers of god in the great monotheistic faiths of the West—**Zoroastrianism, Judaism, Christianity,** and **Islam.** In contrast, among polytheistic systems, gods and goddesses themselves often serve as message bearers. In the earlier pantheistic religions of the Mediterranean and the Middle East there were many gods and demigods who served as divine messengers, along with lesser divinities who in one way or another became paradigms for later angels.

One of these forerunners was the Greek god Eros, who was the direct model for **Cupid**—the familiar child angel of romantic love. Like Cupid, Eros sported wings and shot arrows, though the emotions aroused by Eros's arrows were more purely sexual than the gentler emotions associated with Cupid. Befitting his association with the passions, Eros was portrayed in art as a young, handsome, athletic man. Eros did not metamorphose into the child-like Cupid until the Hellenistic period.

Sources:

Grant, Michael, and John Hazel. *Who's Who in Classical Mythology.* New York: Oxford University Press, 1993.

Tripp, Edward. *The Meridian Handbook of Classical Mythology.* New York: New American Library, 1970.

Eschatology

As we approach the end of the second millennium, a diverse range of religious thinkers have been prompted to speculate that humanity—and, indeed, the entire earth—is nearing the endtime, when life and the world as we know it will be completely destroyed or transformed. Seeing the hand of God in every event that foreshadows this terminus of history, people who live in anticipation of the end often perceive angels at work behind the scenes, both in the lives of individuals and on the stage of world events. The Book of Revelation, which contains an outline of endtime events, pictures angels as God's agents of destruction.

A SMILING, BOYISH EROS AS REPRESENTED BY MICHELANGELO MERISI DA CARAVAGGIO IN *AMOR VICTORIOUS* (CA. 1598–99). (COURTESY ARAS)

Eschatology, "the study of the last things," is the technical theological term for the study of the end of time. Religious eschatology always involves the idea of redemption or salvation, and is a part of the doctrine of most world religions. **Zoroastrianism,** which decisively influenced **Judaism, Christianity,** and **Islam,** was the first historical religion to include a battle between good and evil forces—including good and evil angels—as an essential part of its endtime scenario. Once the forces of light have completely overturned darkness, the resurrection of the dead and the restoration of Paradise will occur.

Early Jewish eschatology as documented in the prophecies of the Old Testament aimed at the restoration of the golden age. Persian and Hellenistic ideas particularly influenced Judaism during the first diasporas, leading to the development of a number of different messianic and apocalyptic ideas. These ideas sometimes contradicted one another, and only in later centuries were they harmonized into a coherent system. The Messiah who is expected to come is a descendant of the House of David, a divine being referred to as the Son of Man.

Sources:

Gaster, Theodore. *The Dead Sea Scriptures in English Translation*. New York: Doubleday, 1956.

Margolies, Morris B. *A Gathering of Angels: Angels in Jewish Life and Literature*. New York: Ballantine, 1994.

Morris, Henry M. *The Revelation Record: A Scientific and Devotional Commentary on the Book of Revelation*. Wheaton, Ill.: Tyndale House, 1983.

Turner, Alice K. *The History of Hell*. New York: Harcourt Brace, 1993.

Ethnarchs

In the same way that individual human beings have **guardian angels,** so larger groups are watched over by particular angels. These angels are traditionally referred to as ethnarchs. The earliest biblical evidence that angels are in charge of nations appears in Daniel, chapters 10 and 12. Michael is described as "the great prince who has charge of your people." In Jewish legend seventy distinct nations emerged out of the debacle at the Tower of Babel, and God appointed an angel to watch over each nation. Jewish legend further asserts that all of the ethnarchs except **Michael,** guardian of Israel, fell and became evil angels. Among these fallen angels are **Dubbiel,** guardian of Persia, **Rahab,** guardian of Egypt, and **Sammael,** guardian of Rome. Despite their supposedly fallen state, God is able to direct the course of nations by issuing commands to their angels. Portugal is the only country to celebrate a feast in honor of its angel, on the third Sunday in July.

Sources:

Cavendish, Richard. *Man, Myth & Magic: The Illustrated Encyclopedia of Mythology, Religion and the Unknown*. New York: Marshall Cavendish, 1995.

Davidson, Gustav. *A Dictionary of Angels: Including the Fallen Angels*. 1967. Reprint. New York: Free Press, 1971.

Ronner, John. *Know Your Angels: The Angel Almanac with Biographies of 100 Prominent Angels in Legend and Folklore, and Much More*. Murfreesboro, Tenn.: Mamre Press, 1993.

Evangelical Authors

Evangelicalism is a Protestant movement emphasizing the Bible as authoritative and reliable, involving personal trust in Christ and in his work. It also emphasizes a spiritually transformed life marked by moral conduct, personal devotion, Bible study, and prayer.

The term *evangelical* refers in particular to a distinct movement that emerged from the religious awakenings of the eighteenth and early nineteenth centuries in the United States (which remained the place where this movement had its greatest impact), England, and the British Empire. This movement brought together several others, such as New England Puritanism, continental pietism, revivalist Presbyterianism, Baptist antiestablishment democratic impulses, Calvinist revivalism, and Methodism.

American evangelicalism emphasizes conversion experiences evidenced by lives freed from vices. Evangelicals also promote revivals and missions and view the church as a voluntary association of believers founded upon the authority of the Bible alone.

In recent years several evangelical authors, including **Billy Graham** (America's leading evangelist), Marilynn Carlson, William D. Webber, Gary Kinnaman, and Ron Rhodes, have investigated the nature and the role of angels, reporting a variety of accounts of encounters with them. Their books provide thoroughly biblical guides to the world of angels and are filled with stories of personal experiences that fit into the scheme of biblical **angelology.**

Evangelical authors generally agree with the theory that God created the angels—countless thousands of them—some time before he created the physical universe. A **war in heaven** resulted in the expulsion of **Satan** and his angels. Humans were created later, in God's image, but a little lower than the angels in the order of being. Regarded as messengers of God, the good angels serve him as well as his people, whereas evil angels serve Satan and his purposes. God provides assistance for his people in their spiritual conflicts through the actions of the multitude of angels at his command, who provide unseen aid on the humanity's behalf. Evangelicals are united in asserting that, although the Bible does not gives us much information about angels, its teachings should be a source of comfort and strength for men in every circumstance.

—*Michela Zonta*

Sources:

Graham, Billy. *Angels: God's Secret Agents*. 1975. Reprint. Dallas: Word Publishing, 1994.

Kinnaman, Gary. *Angels: Dark and Light*. Ann Arbor, Mich.: Servant Publications, 1994.

Rhodes, Ron. *Angels Among Us: Separating Truth From Fiction*. Eugene, Oreg.: Harvest House, 1994.

Webber, Marylinn Carlson, and William D. Webber. *A Rustle of Angels: Stories About Angels in Real-Life and Scripture*. Grand Rapids, Mich.: Zondervan, 1994.

Evolution of Angels

Angels have traditionally been viewed as perfect, eternal beings who remain in a constant state of grace thus causing "evolution of angels" to sound rather like an oxymoron. In contrast to this static view of traditional religion, however, contemporary occult/metaphysical spirituality emphasizes gradual growth, expansion of consciousness, and learning across time, including growth across many different lifetimes. Reincarnation, for instance, is viewed positively as a series of opportunities for expanded spiritual growth. This gradual spiritual expansion constitutes a kind of evolution of the soul, and the metaphor of spiritual evolution is often expressed in the literature of this subculture.

The notion of evolving angels is rooted in certain theosophical ideas about **devas,** the rough equivalent of angels in theosophical lore. Some strands of **Theosophy** view devas as human souls who have, through the process of reincarnation, evolved into higher, spiritual beings. Other strands, such as the Theosophy of Alice Bailey's Arcane School, place the devas on a separate evolutionary path. In particular, Bailey sees devas as evolving from elemental spirits and **fairies,** rather than from human forms.

The notion of souls "incarnating" as fairies and angels necessarily implies that these beings have *bodies,* however refined and spiritualized. This notion also raises the possibility that angels or other spirits can "cross over" and reincarnate in human bodies; some contemporary **New Age** teachers assert that devas sometimes incarnate as human beings.

The teachings of Mormonism also point to angels who undergo an evolutionary process. One type, in particular, is referred to as a "spirit child of the Eternal Father who has not yet been born on the earth but is intended for earthly mortality" (Ludlow, p. 40). An example would be the angel who appeared to **Adam** (Moses 5:6–8).

A second type of evolutionary spirit is known as a translated being. **Enoch,** Moses, and **Elijah,** who were all translated bodily to heaven would fit this category. According to Mormon church founder Joseph Smith, "These translated beings are designated for future missions."

A third kind of angel is described as an angel "who completed his mortal existence but whose labor continues in the spirit world while he awaits the resurrection of the body" (Ludlow, p. 41). Reference is made to such beings in Heb. 12:22–23 as "the spirits of just men made perfect."

The final type of evolutionary being is referred to as "resurrected personages, having bodies of flesh and bones." These resurrected angels, according to Smith, "have advanced further in light and glory than spirits." Saint John, in Rev. 14:6, writes, "And I saw another angel fly in the midst of heaven, having the everlasting gospel to preach unto them that dwell on the earth, and to every nation, and kindred, and tongue, and people." It was, in fact, a resurrected angel, **Moroni,** who revealed the Book of Mormon to Prophet Joseph Smith.

Sources:

Banerjee, H. N., and W. C. Oursler. *Lives Unlimited: Reincarnation East and West.* New York: Doubleday, 1974.

Hall, Manly Palmer. *Reincarnation: The Cycle of Necessity.* Los Angeles: Philosophical Research Society, 1956.

Head, Joseph, and S. L. Cranston, eds. *Reincarnation in World Thought.* New York: Crown, 1967.

Ludlow, Daniel H. *Encyclopedia of Mormonism.* Vol. 1. New York: Macmillan, 1992.

Ezekiel

In building their empire, the Babylonians followed a policy of relocating populations as a way of preventing rebellions. After they conquered Judah in 605 B.C., they moved the upper class of Jewish society to Babylonia. For the Jews, the worship of God in the temple at Jerusalem was essential to their faith. After all, it was there that the Ark of the Covenant was housed. Thus, this relocation posed a challenge to their traditional understanding of religion. It is in this context that the prophet Ezekiel's vision and message in the Book of the Prophet Ezekiel have been interpreted by biblical scholars.

THE FANTASTIC VISION OF EZEKIEL AS DEPICTED IN THE SEVENTEENTH-CENTURY BEAR BIBLE. (COURTESY ARAS)

In Ezekiel's fantastic vision four creatures appear who support God's throne and who symbolize the four directions, a symbolic allusion to God's omnipresence. Ezekiel also mentions that beside each creature is a wheel with rims and spokes, the rims full of eyes. Wheels are symbols of mobility and the eyes reflect God's all-seeing power in the world. The implicit message is clear—God does not exist in a stationary throne in a temple; he is everywhere and can thus be worshiped anywhere. This was an essential message to a people who had been exiled from the promised land and their sacred place of worship destroyed.

The first part of Ezekiel's vision contains description of the four creatures. This description later became the basis for the Christian iconography of **thrones,** the third **choir** in the nine-rung hierarchy of angels originally laid out by **Dionysius the Areopagite.** Ezekiel's vision begins thus:

As I looked, behold, a stormy wind came out of the north, and a great cloud, with brightness round about it, and fire flashing forth continually, and in the midst of the fire, as it were gleaming bronze. And from the midst of it came the likeness of four living creatures. And this was their appearance: they had the form of men, but each had four faces, and each of them had four wings. Their legs were straight, and the soles of their feet were like the sole of a calf's foot; and they sparkled like burnished bronze. Under their wings on their four sides they had human hands, and the four had their faces and their wings thus: their wings touched one another; they went every one straight forward, without turning as they went. (Ezek. 1:4–9)

It is important to note the four faces of each creature: the face of a human being, a lion, an ox, and an eagle. These represent the four highest forms of the various realms of creation: the face of man, as the supreme being, faces forward; the lion is the king of the wild beasts; the ox is at the fore of domesticated animals; and the eagle is the king of the skies. Besides providing the visual model for throne angels, Ezekiel's vision has sometimes been interpreted as the vision of some great flying machine, or **UFO.**

Sources:

The Illustrated Bible Dictionary. Sydney, Australia: Hodder and Stoughton, 1980.

Ferguson, Everett, ed. *Encyclopedia of Early Christianity.* New York: Garland, 1990.

For fools rush in where

angels fear to tread.

—Alexander Pope, 1711

Fairies

Fairies are a kind of nature spirit that, under different names and guises, are found in every part of the world. Often pictured as small humanoid beings with wings, they look like mini angels. Unlike angels, however, fairies have always had an ambivalent relationship with humanity. As nature spirits concerned with natural processes, they do not normally seek out human contact, but, when they take a liking to someone, they will help that person in various ways. Sometimes, however, they are pictured as mischievous beings who enjoy playing pranks.

Because the church did not have room in its worldview for morally neutral spiritual beings who were neither good nor evil, fairies were rejected as agents of **Satan.** Traditional religious authorities were thus responsible for driving a wedge between fairies and angels, and the rather obvious family resemblance between them has been obscured ever since.

We can acquire a fresh perspective on the fairy-angel connection by shifting our attention away from church lore and examining these spiritual beings through the lens of **Theosophy.** Theosophy refers to the particular synthesis of ideas from the philosophical systems of China and India, and the works of the **Gnostics,** the Neoplatonists and the Cabalists, manifested in the Theosophical Society, which was founded in New York in 1875 by Madame Helena Blavatsky. At the core of Theosophy is a teaching of "spiritual evolution," which portrays human souls as developing their inner potentials, freeing themselves from matter and returning to the Source of All, with increased consciousness.

According to Theosophists the cosmos is populated with innumerable spiritual entities. A significant class of these entities are what Theosophists call the **devas,** which is a Sanskrit term for the demi-gods of **Hinduism** and **Buddhism.** These devas are the Theosophical equivalents of angels. In addition to the functions traditionally attributed to angels (e.g., serving as **guardian spirits**), devas oversee natural forces and are responsible for building up forms on inner planes as well as on the physical plane. Some strands of Theosophy view devas as human souls who have, through the process of reincarnation, evolved into higher, spiritual beings. Other strands place the devas on a separate evolutionary path, viewing devas as the prototypes of angels.

Fairy (*faye* in Old English) is thought to be derived from *Fata,* the name of the Greek goddess of fate. *Fay-erie* was originally the "erie" state of enchantment that could be induced by the fays, and only later became interchangeable with the beings themselves. The fays were originally but one class of spirit being, and it was perhaps the general association of "little people" with enchantment that enabled the term *fairy* to become the generic term for fays, **brownies, elves, pixies,** and so forth.

Folklorists have advanced a number of theories to explain the source of belief in fairies. One plausible notion is that, particularly in pre-Christian Europe, fairies were originally the spirits of the dead. After Christianity was embraced, the Christian notion of what happened to the souls of the dead supplanted earlier beliefs. Rather than disappearing, however, the older folklore persisted, with the modification that the fairy spirits became entities independent of humanity, rather than spirits of the dead.

Another theory is that fairy lore represents a distant memory of an earlier and more primitive race (e.g., the aboriginal Picts of the British Isles) who continued to interact with the dominant invaders (e.g., the Celts) for many centuries before disappearing altogether. Yet another idea put forward is that the fairies are the gods of pre-Christian Europe, who were reduced to the diminished status of nature spirits after being supplanted by Christianity.

These theories fail to consider that roughly similar ideas of nature spirits can be found in traditional tribal societies all over the world where none of the foregoing conditions exist. However, in non-European traditional societies nature spirits do not interact as intensively with humanity as they do in European folklore, which indicates that one or more of these theories may at least partially explain some aspects of fairy belief.

A look at some of the themes explored in Katharine Briggs's comprehensive *Encyclopedia of Fairies* (1976) demonstrates the intensive interaction ascribed to humans and fairies through the ages: fairy borrowing, fairy thefts, dependence of fairies upon mortals, fairy brides, fairy loans. . . . A close examination of this folklore makes some of the proposed theories, such as the notion that fairy lore is a residual memory of interactions with a more primitive race, seem plausible.

Sources:

Briggs, Katharine. *An Encyclopedia of Fairies.* New York: Pantheon, 1976.
McCoy, Edwin. *A Witch's Guide to Faery Folk.* St. Paul, Minn.: Llewellyn, 1994.
Shepard, Leslie A., ed. *Encyclopedia of Occultism & Parapsychology.* 3d ed. Detroit, Mich.: Gale Research, 1991.

The Fall of the Angels

In theology, the Fall refers to humanity's fall from grace into sin. The Fall is responsible for *original sin,* meaning that everyone is born in sin—and thus in need of salvation—because of **Adam** and Eve's disobedience of God's command not to eat of the Tree of Knowledge of Good and Evil in the Garden of Eden. Simply by being born into this world, every human being inherits the sin of our distant ancestors. Many contemporary theologians have reinterpreted the story of the Fall less literally, but this is the essence of the biblical narrative.

Less well known is the story of the fall of the angels. For whatever reason—some accounts say that **Lucifer** was jealous of God's love of Adam, but in any event it was some form of pride—Lucifer declared himself as great as God and led a rebellion of angels against the celestial order. Defeated, the Devil and his followers were tossed out of heaven and subsequently have continued to war against God by attempting to ruin God's creation, the earth. Traditional theology even portrays the serpent that conversed with Eve in the garden as Satan in disguise, thus attributing to the fallen prince of angels responsibility for humankind's fall.

A less well known alternative narrative, which is best preserved in the apocalyptic **Book of Enoch,** is that a group of angels lusted after mortal women. They then fell after leaving their heavenly abode and copulating with them. This story, which at one time was widely known, eventually disappeared from popular folklore because it clashed with the

THE FALL OF SATAN AND HIS LEGIONS BY GUSTAVE DORÉ. ILLUSTRATION FOR
MILTON'S *PARADISE LOST.*

official church position (or what became the official position by the late Middle Ages), which was that angels are beings of pure spirit and thus do not engage in sexual intercourse. A brief allusion to the Enoch tale can be found in Gen. 6:2–4, where it says that the "sons of God" (which, when seen through the lens of the Book of Enoch, are angels) took mortal women as wives.

One contemporary religious leader, **Elizabeth Clare Prophet,** has reexamined these ancient stories of fallen angels—particularly the Book of Enoch and other early works—and concluded that there were actually two distinct celestial falls: that of Lucifer and the rebellious angels and that of the angels who copulated with human women. This bit of speculative theology, as well as the full passages from the relevant apocryphal books, is contained in Prophet's fascinating *Forbidden Mysteries of Enoch: Fallen Angels and the Origins of Evil.*

Malcolm Godwin in *Angels: An Endangered Species* recounts four additional versions of the fall of the angels. The first legend surrounds the "shadow of God," where the Devil at first is the dark aspect of God turned toward humanity. This dark force eventually evolved in Hebrew tradition to become a separate entity with his own free will, and by the time of the New Testament, became Satan, direct opponent to God.

The second legend was introduced by **Origen** (ca. 185–254), the greatest biblical scholar of the patristic period. Origen asserted that angels were created with free will, and that some eventually migrated away from the Original Source (God). Those who drifted into the lower air took on human bodies; those who drifted farthest away became demons.

The **War in Heaven** is a third legend that may account for the fall of the angels. On the second day of creation a tremendous battle took place between two factions of angelic beings. The first group was created by God and given the Grace to pursue goodness. The second was equal in strength but were devoid of God's Grace, and thus had the ability to choose sin. **Michael,** at the helm of the good angels, conquered the sinners from heaven, among them Lucifer, who took with him one-third of the legions of angels.

A fourth alternative concerns the birth and passion of Christ. Already banished from heaven and given free reign to tempt and punish mankind, Satan is confronted with the Divine in the form of Jesus Christ. In essence, the fallen angel commits the ultimate transgression by attempting to befoul that which is most Divine. Christ emerges victorious and Satan furiously resolves to increase his devilish pursuits. In response Christ hurls him into hell and the archangel Michael binds him fast.

Sources:

Davidson, Gustav. *A Dictionary of Angels: Including the Fallen Angels.* 1967. Reprint. New York: Free Press, 1971.

Godwin, Malcolm. *Angels: An Endangered Species.* New York: Simon and Schuster, 1990.

Masello, Robert. *Fallen Angels . . . and Spirits of the Dark.* New York: Perigree, 1994.

Prophet, Elizabeth Clare. *Forbidden Mysteries of Enoch: Fallen Angels and the Origins of Evil.* 1983. Reprint. Livingston, Mont.: Summit University Press, 1992.

Fallen Angels *See: Devils, Demons, and Fallen Angels*

Familiars

Familiars are low-level **demons,** sometimes classified as **imps,** that do the bidding of witches. They usually take the form of animals—particularly cats, dogs, owls, and mice—and are sometimes conceptualized as having the power to change shape. Cats are an especially favored form, which explains the periodic cat massacres that swept through Europe during the Middle Ages.

Familiars are said to be given to witches by the Devil or by other witches. They require blood, and their masters either sacrifice animals for them or provide blood to them directly through protuberances on the surface of their own skin, called "witch's teats" or "witch's marks." In addition to aiding witches by carrying their bewitchments to the intended victims, familiars also act as the infernal equivalent of **guardian angels,** providing witches with protection from attacks. Among modern neopagan witches, familiars have been reinterpreted as animal companions that are psychically sensitive enough to aid witches in their craft.

Sources:

Guiley, Rosemary Ellen. *The Encyclopedia of Witches and Witchcraft.* New York: Facts on File, 1989.

Masello, Robert. *Fallen Angels . . . Spirits of the Dark.* New York: Perigee, 1994.

Fate

The Greek Fates are considered precursors to angels because, as divinities of destiny and messengers of the gods, they were usually depicted with **wings.** According to the mythographer Hesiod their names were Atropos (Inevitable), Lachesis (Apportioner of Lots), and Clotho

THE FATES. ILLUSTRATION FOR DANTE'S *DIVINE COMEDY* BY GUSTAVE DORÉ (1861–68).

(the Spinner; related to the image of "spinning" one's destiny). Their Greek name, *Moirai,* means "parts" or "allotted portion." According to mythology the Fates are present at the birth of human beings and allot their fate at the moment of birth. It is interesting to note that this function links them to the **theosophical** notion of **Lipikas,** angelic beings that regulate the karma (a notion related to fate) of individual human beings prior to their birth.

Sources:

Grant, Michael, and John Hazel. *Who's Who in Classical Mythology.* New York: Oxford University Press, 1993.

Tripp, Edward. *The Meridian Handbook of Classical Mythology.* New York: New American Library, 1970.

Final Judgment

Western religions propagate the idea of an **apocalyptic** final Judgment Day, held at the end of time, which culminates in the resurrection of the righteous for life in Paradise and the resurrection of sinners for either extinction or eternal damnation. In Western religions, the notion of a final judgment originated in **Zoroastrianism.** Many of the components of the Zoroastrian vision of the end times—a final battle between good and evil, judgment of the wicked, resurrection of the dead—were adopted by Jewish apocalyptic thinkers. From texts composed by these apocalypticists, such notions were adopted into **Christianity** and **Islam.**

Angels have always played a central role in apocalyptic, endtime scenarios. Although God may issue the commands, it is his angels who carry out the tasks. As a dramatic, supernatural intervention into human history and a radical departure from the usual order of the world, it is natural that the final judgment should entail the visible manifestation of normally unseen spiritual forces on the world stage.

THE SEVEN ANGELS WITH THE SEVEN PLAGUES.

In the Book of Revelation, which is the one true apocalyptic book incorporated into the New Testament, angels carry out God's directions to wreak havoc on the earth:

> Then I heard a loud voice from the temple telling the seven angels, "Go and pour out on the earth the seven bowls of the wrath of God." So the first angel went and poured his bowl on the earth, and foul and evil sores came upon the men who bore the mark of the beast and worshiped its image. (Rev. 16:1–2)

Needless to say, the impact of the contents of the other six bowls are no less unpleasant than the first. When individuals finally come before the Throne of Judgment in the Book of Revelations' account, the damned are tossed into the lake of fire:

> [I]f any one's name was not found written in the book of life, he was thrown into the lake of fire (Rev. 20:15).

And while Scripture does not say who does the throwing, it clear that God's angels perform the task of executioners.

Judgment Day is also a day of reckoning for the fallen angels, who are similarly judged and punished:

> For God spared not the angels that sinned, but cast them down to Hell, and delivered them into chains of darkness to be reserved unto judgment. (2 Pet. 2:4)

Sources:

Eliade, Mircea. *Encyclopedia of Religion.* 16 vols. New York: Macmillan, 1987.

Morris, Henry M. *The Revelation Record: A Scientific and Devotional Commentary on the Book of Revelation.* Wheaton, Ill.: Tyndale House, 1983.

Turner, Alice K. *The History of Hell.* New York: Harcourt Brace, 1993.

Van Der Leeuw, G., trans. *Religion in Essence and Manifestation.* Vol. 1. Gloucester, Mass.: Peter Smith, 1967.

Findhorn

A major source of the current New Age interest in angels seems to be Findhorn, a community in northern Scotland that came to the attention of the occult/metaphysical subculture in the late 1960s. The early Findhorn community focused around a highly successful vegetable garden in which, residents claimed, community members were engaged in a unique cooperative arrangement with agricultural **devas**—nature spirits said to be particularly associated with various plants and landscape features.

Thus, the devas, whom **Theosophists** had long identified with the angels of Western religious traditions, entered **New Age** consciousness, although it would be more than two decades before they would occupy center stage.

The Findhorn Community was conceived in late 1962 when Eileen and Peter Caddy and Dorothy Maclean moved into a mobile home at the Findhorn Bay Caravan Park on Moray Firth in Scotland. The three were unemployed and living on a small government relief allotment when they began a garden, a seemingly impossible task given their far northern location and the fact that they were living on sand rather than true soil. Soon after starting the garden Dorothy Maclean made contact with the devas.

Maclean was told by the first deva she contacted that the garden would succeed if they cooperated with the devas by seeking their advice. Peter Caddy, who was in charge of gardening, would present his practical questions (such as how far apart plants should be and how often to water them) to Maclean and she would get an answer from the appropriate deva and report back to him. Following the advice of the devas, the garden at Findhorn flourished and produced an abundance of fruits and vegetables. Gardening experts visited Findhorn and found the garden's production to be little short of miraculous. Other people of theosophical or spiritualistic bent joined the community and they began to think of themselves as an experiment in cooperation between devas and humans. Sir George Trevelyan, author and head of the Wrekin Trust, said of the Findhorn Community, "The possibility of cooperation with the devas should be investigated seriously. The time has come when this can be spoken of more openly. The phenomenon of a group of amateurs doing this forces it into our attention. Many people are not ready to understand, and that enough should understand and act on it is possibly of critical importance in the present world situation."

Sources:

Bloom, William. *Devas, Fairies and Angels: A Modern Approach.* Somerset: Gothic Image Publications, 1986.
The Findhorn Community. *The Findhorn Garden.* New York: HarperPerennial, 1975.
Lewis, James R., and J. Gordon Melton, eds. *Perspectives on the New Age.* Albany: State University of New York Press, 1992.

First Church of Angels

The First Church of Angels is a metaphysically oriented church originally founded as the Church of Self Discovery in 1969 by Rev.

Dorie D'Angelo, who wrote a book entitled *Living with Angels*. When Dorie D'Angelo died in 1984, her work was continued by her husband, Rev. André D'Angelo. The core of the church's ministry is not worship services in the usual sense, but rather "angel power healing circles," which feature metaphysical healing purportedly mediated by angels. Besides the healing circles, D'Angelo provides individuals with "angel power readings." The church also publishes a newsletter, *Angel Power*. Address: Rev. André D'Angelo, P.O. Box 4713, Carmel, CA 93921.

Source:
Freeman, Eileen. "The First Church of Angels." *AngelWatch* (November–December 1992):11.

Fravashi

The religion of **Zoroastrianism** is the source of the notion of angels as agents of God (rather than as demigods). Zoroastrianism originated in Persia (modern Iran), but most contemporary Zoroastrians reside in India, where they are known as Parsees. The principal angelic beings in this tradition are the **holy immortals**, who are regarded as **archangels**, and the **yazatas**, or angels. Yet another group of angelic beings are the fravashi. They seem to have originally been spirits of the ancestors, but gradually developed into **guardian spirits,** of both human beings and celestial beings. The fravashi is also the immortal part of the human being that remains in heaven while the individual is incarnate on the earth.

It is said that when a Zoroastrian child is born, his or her fravashi accompanies them to earth and acts as a guardian spirit throughout their life, finally helping them through the trial that accompanies death.

Sources:
Noss, John B. *Man's Religions*. 4th ed. New York: Macmillan, 1969.
Freeman, Eileen E. "Do You Have Your Own Fravashi—Angels in Ancient Persia." *AngelWatch* (June 1993).
Ronner, John. *Know Your Angels: The Angel Almanac with Biographies of 100 Prominent Angels in Legend and Folklore, and Much More*. Murfreesboro, Tenn.: Mamre Press, 1993.

Freeman, Eileen Elias

Eileen Elias Freeman is the director of the AngelWatch™ Foundation, Inc., a nonprofit organization that serves as a major resource center on the topic of angels, and the editor and publisher of its bimonthly newsletter, *AngelWatch*. She is the best-selling author of *Touched by*

Angels, (1992) *Angelic Healing,* (1994) and *The Angel's Little Instruction Book* (1994). She holds a bachelor of arts degree in comparative religion from Barnard College and a master's degree in theology from the University of Notre Dame.

Eileen Freeman's life has indeed been touched by angels. When she was five years old her much-loved grandmother died. She had always been a very fearful child, but when her grandmother died her fears mounted to the point that she could not sleep at night. One night she was sitting up in bed when a light started growing at its foot. As she watched, the growing light began to take human form. The being, who identified himself as Eileen's **guardian angel,** looked at the young Eileen and told her not to be afraid, that her grandmother was happy in heaven with God and the people she loved.

Freeman wrote *Touched by Angels* to show the many ways angels affect the lives of humans. In the book she shares accounts of people whose lives have been changed by angels, including her own. One of the most important things she conveys is that when angels come into people's lives, they come to bring an important message, not for any trivial reason.

When Freeman was in college, she was again touched by an angel, quite literally this time. She was entering the apartment building of a friend when she felt a hand on her shoulder that pulled her back. She turned around but no one was there. She again started to go into the building, but was again stopped. This time she heard a voice telling her that it would not be wise for her to enter the building at that time. When she called her friend later that day he told her that a woman had been stabbed to death in the elevator by a drug dealer.

It was as a result of these encounters with angels that Eileen Freeman founded the nonprofit AngelWatch Foundation, whose purpose is to search for evidence of angelic activity in the world, and to disseminate the information as widely as possible.

Later in her life, while preparing to be hospitalized for major surgery, Eileen Freeman was again touched by an angelic presence. She suffered a violent reaction to an antibiotic and was visited by an angel who embraced her with light and warmth and peace. Within an hour, she began to heal. It was because of this experience that Eileen wrote *Angelic Healing: Working with Your Angels to Heal Your Life.* In addition to her own experiences, Eileen relates the real-life stories of many other people who have been healed through the intervention of angels.

Sources:

Freeman, Eileen Elias. *Angelic Healing: Working with Your Angels to Heal Your Life*. New York: Warner Books, 1994.

Hauch, Rex, editor. *Angels: The Mysterious Messengers*. New York: Ballantine Books, 1994.

Fylgir

Fylgja (follower; plural, *fylgir*) is an ancient Germanic term referring to an entity that is simultaneously a **guardian spirit** and a projection of the individual's own soul (not unlike the **Zoroastrian** idea of an individual **fravashi**). It was believed that the fylgja was encountered outside one's body in the form of an animal that reflected the individual's character. Thus, a visionary might see his fylgja in the form of an eagle, a schemer might encounter his projected soul in the form of a weasel, and so on. In precarious situations, the fylgja traveled before the embodied person as a kind of **guardian angel.** Normally invisible, a person's fylgja might be encountered in dreams or at death. If the fylgja was killed, it indicated the person's imminent death.

Sources:

McCoy, Edwin. *A Witch's Guide to Faery Folk.* St. Paul, Minn.: Llewellyn Publications, 1994.

Ronner, John. *Know Your Angels: The Angel Almanac with Biographies of 100 Prominent Angels in Legend and Folklore, and Much More.* Murfreesboro, Tenn.: Mamre Press, 1993.

I shall probably never know my guardian angel, and though once I sought him earnestly, now I don't want to know him.

—Paul Leroy Robeson

Gabriel

Gabriel, one of the four **archangels** named in Hebrew tradition, is considered one of the two highest-ranking angels in Judeo-Christian and **Islamic** religious lore. Apart from **Michael,** he is the only angel mentioned by name in the Old Testament.

The name Gabriel, which means "God is my strength," is of Chaldean origin and was unknown to the Jews prior to Babylonian captivity. In the original listing of 119 angels of the Parsees, Gabriel's name is missing. The Sumerian root of the word *gabri* is *gbr* or *gubernator,* meaning "steersman" or "governor." Gabriel, who is described as possessing 140 pairs of wings, is the governor of Eden and ruler of the **cherubim.** He is the angel of the Annunciation and the Resurrection, as well as an angel of mercy, vengeance, death, and revelation.

Gabriel is a unique archangel in the sense that it is almost certain that she is the only female in the higher echelons. In addition, Gabriel is said to sit on the left hand side of God, whose dwelling is popularly believed to be residing in the seventh heaven (or, sometimes, the tenth heaven). This is further evidence of her being female. The essentially female character of Gabriel is once again confirmed in popular lore, which tells of how she takes the invariably protesting soul from paradise, and instructs it for the nine months while it remains in the womb of its mother.

Muhammad claimed it was Gabriel—**Djibril** in Arabic—who dictated the Koran to him, sura by sura. Muslims consider Gabriel the spirit of truth, but devout Muslims would hardly agree to his female gender.

Jewish legend claims that it was Gabriel who dealt death and destruction to such sinful cities as Sodom and Gomorrah. According to Talmud Sanhedrin 95b, it was also Gabriel who prevented Queen Vashti from appearing naked before King Ahasuerus and his guests in order to bring about the election of Esther in her place. Moreover, according to Jewish legend the three holy men Hananiah, Mishael, and Azariah were rescued from the furnace by Gabriel, although Michael is credited in other sources.

In Daniel, chapter 8, Daniel falls on his face before Gabriel to learn the meaning of the encounter between the ram and the heg-he-goat (the oracle of the Persians being overthrown by the Greeks). Gabriel later appears again to Daniel to tell him of the coming of the Messiah, a message that half a millennium later he repeats to **Mary** in the Annunciation.

Gabriel is identified by Cabalists as "the man clothed in linen" in Dan. 10:5–21. She is the prince of justice in rabbinic literature, whereas she is called the angel of war by **Origen** in *De Principiis* I, 81. Jerome equates Gabriel with Hamon, and according to **Milton,** Gabriel is chief of the angelic guards placed over Paradise. Gabriel is identified as the man-God-angel who wrestled with Jacob at Peniel, although this antagonist has often been identified with other angels.

According to an Islamic legend, when the dust from the hoofprints of Gabriel's horse was thrown into the mouth of the golden calf (Exodus, chapter 32), the calf at once became animated. Some Christian critics have claimed that Muhammad confused Gabriel with the **Holy Ghost.** Bernard Bamberger, in *Fallen Angels* (1952), asserts that Gabriel once fell into disgrace for "not obeying a command exactly as given, and remained for a while outside the heavenly Curtain."

In Midrash Eleh Ezkerah, Gabriel figures in the tale of the legendary ten Jewish sages, one of whom, Rabbi Ishmael, ascends to heaven and asks Gabriel why they merit death. She replies that they are atoning for the sin of the ten sons of Jacob who sold Joseph into slavery.

According to the testimony of **Joan of Arc,** Gabriel inspired her to go to the succor of the king of France and also persuaded her to help the Dauphin. In *The Golden Legend* (1851) Longfellow depicts Gabriel as

IN THIS ANNUNCIATION BY AN UNKNOWN ARTIST OF THE "ALTARPIECE OF THE LIFE OF THE VIRGIN," THE ANGEL GABRIEL UNFURLS THE SCROLL ANNOUNCING THE IMPENDING BIRTH OF CHRIST (COLOGNE CATHEDRAL, CA. 1360). (COURTESY ARAS)

GABRIEL IS DECIDEDLY FEMININE IN THIS 1920s ILLUSTRATION. NOTE THAT SHE IS CARRYING A FLOWER RATHER THAN A SCEPTER. (COURTESY LEONARD DAY)

the angel of the moon, who brings humanity the gift of hope. In more recent times Gabriel is the angel who allegedly visited Father George Rapp, leader of the 2nd Advent community in New Harmony, Indiana, and left his footprint on a limestone slab preserved in the yard of the Maclure-Owen residence in that city.

Considered the chief ambassador of God to humanity, Gabriel is most commonly portrayed pursuing this role and therefore in the company of the recipient of one or other of her missions. In Christian art the most common of these themes is the Annunciation, when the angel reveals to Mary that she is to be the Mother of the Christ. **Rembrandt,** among others, painted a canvas of the celebrated encounter. In earlier paintings of this great event, Gabriel is usually pictured as a majestic fig-

A SOMEWHAT
ANDROGYNOUS, ETHEREAL
GABRIEL IS DEPICTED IN THIS
DETAIL OF *THE
ANNUNCIATION* BY THE
ITALIAN MANNERIST
JACOPO DA PONTORMO
(1494–1557). (CAPPONI
CHAPEL, FLORENCE, ITALY)

ure, richly attired, sometimes wearing a crown and bearing a scepter. Her
right hand is usually extended in salutation, while the Virgin Mary sits
submissively. However, from about the fourteenth century, the roles are

somewhat reversed, in that Mary becomes the more prominent of the two figures, as though already Queen of the Angels and Gabriel therefore her dutiful subject. In these later depictions Gabriel carries, instead of the scepter, a lily as a symbol of the purity of the Virgin or sometimes a scroll inscribed with the opening words, in Latin, of the Ave Maria.

Sources:

Bamberger, Bernard J. *Fallen Angels*. Philadelphia: The Jewish Publication Society of America, 1952.

Godwin, Malcolm. *Angels: An Endangered Species*. New York: Simon and Schuster, 1990.

Longfellow, Henry Wadsworth. *Poetical Works*. 6 vols. Boston: Houghton, 1904.

MacGregor, Geddes. *Angels: Ministers of Grace*. New York: Paragon House, 1988.

Gandharvas

Angels are most prominent in monotheistic traditions, which need intermediaries between an exalted divinity and humanity. Mediating beings are less important for religious systems with many deities, because, in most such belief systems, the gods or goddesses themselves can manifest in the world without contradicting their basic nature. In their attempts to discover parallel beings in other religions, contemporary researchers studying angels often mention an unusual **Hindu/Buddhist** spirit being traditionally referred to as a gandharva.

Gandharvas are frequently mentioned in the Vedas, the oldest body of Hindu religious literature. It is difficult to determine the precise meaning or set of meanings the term *gandharva* had in the early Vedic period. By the time of the emergence of classical Hinduism, gandharvas had come to be regarded primarily as the musicians of heaven. Their status as celestial musicians and their depiction as winged men are the only two characteristics that might lead one to associate them with Western angels. Otherwise, their activities are decidedly nonangelic.

For example, they are said to take particular interest in sex, and are also said to be married to the **apsaras,** the Hindu equivalent of wood nymphs. Their sexual appetite is such an important part of their identity that gandharva "marriages" are unions brought about by affection, without the benefit of any formal marriage rite. In the time of Buddha, it was believed that it was necessary for a gandharva to be present before conception was possible. In the Vedas, gandharvas are described variously as atmospheric deities associated with rain clouds and as nature spirits living in the trees. The Atharva Veda even contains incantations designed to ban gandharvas from sacrificial rites, which indicates that they were originally beings to be feared. Without the appropriate propitiatory offerings, they could even cause madness.

Sources:

McCoy, Edwin. *A Witch's Guide to Faery Folk.* St. Paul, Minn.: Llewellyn Publications, 1994.

Stutley, Margaret, and James Stutley. *Harper's Dictionary of Hinduism: Its Mythology, Folklore, Philosophy, Literature, and History.* New York: Harper & Row, 1977.

Sykes, Egerton. *Who's Who: Non-Classical Mythology.* Rev. ed. New York: Oxford University Press, 1993.

Gender of Angels

The gender of angels is often disputed. Angels are perceived as either male or female by people who feel they have actually seen them or feel that they have a **guardian angel.** Theologians, on the other hand, have usually considered angels to be androgynous, or to be neither distinctly male nor female, but to combine maleness and femaleness in perfect wholeness. The words of Jesus according to the Apostle Matthew confirm this. The case of a woman who was widowed and married more than once was brought up and Jesus was asked whose wife the woman would be at the resurrection. Jesus replied, "At the resurrection men and women do not marry; they are like angels in heaven" (Matt. 22:30). Artists commonly portray angels without distinct sexuality, sometimes portraying them in a prepubescent human form. The only angel commonly thought to be of the female, however, is the archangel **Gabriel,** who is commonly depicted with decidedly feminine features.

Sources:

Edward, Paul, ed. *The Encyclopedia of Philosophy.* New York: Macmillan, 1967.

Giovetti, Paola. *Angels: The Role of Celestial Guardians and Beings of Light.* Translated by Toby McCormick. York Beach, Maine: Samuel Weiser, 1993.

Ghosts and Angels

There is a widespread tendency to confuse angels with the departed spirits of human beings—departed spirits that have traditionally been referred to as ghosts. Ghosts are believed to be the souls of the dead who stay close to the earthly realm due to some upsetting aspect of their death or their own addiction to physical existence. Etymologically, *ghost* is linked to the German word *geist,* "spirit," thus indicating a broader connotation of the original word.

Ghosts are viewed differently in different civilizations. In the West, ghosts are traditionally considered frightening, a source of evil or a demonic force. The "role" of ghosts expanded in the nineteenth century with the birth of **Spiritualism** and its systematic approach to mediumship. Mediums, intermediaries who can communicate with spirits, began to portray ghosts as helpful entities who remain on earth to aid their loved ones or to reveal some sort of truth. Because they were cast in a sort of "messenger" role, it was natural that confusion between ghosts and angels should arise. Traditionally, however, there are several beliefs that separate the two: angels are a separate order of creation and have never incarnated in a human body; angels are considered residents of heaven and are always on a mission when they are on earth, whereas ghosts are not by any means always on a mission when earthbound.

Sources:

Cavendish, Richard, ed. *Encyclopedia of the Unexplained: Magic, Occultism and Parapsychology.* London: Arkana Penguin Books, 1989.

Guiley, Rosemary Ellen. *The Encyclopedia of Ghosts and Spirits.* New York: Facts on File, 1992.

Giotto

Traditionally, Giotto di Bondone (ca. 1267–1337) is known as the hero of a naturalistic revolution that supposedly broke all bonds with the **Middle Ages** and laid the foundations of modern painting. He is recognized as the first genius of art in the Italian Renaissance. His work can be considered a synthesis of the discordant traditions of the Middle Ages in the East and the West, from which traditions of Italian art sprang.

Giotto di Bondone was born of a family of peasant stock around 1267 in a village in the Mugello area called Colle di Vespignano, a few miles north of Florence. Between 1285 and 1290 he is thought to have been apprenticed to Cimabue at Florence and to have traveled for the first time to Rome.

In 1291 he started working in the Upper Church of San Francesco in Assisi (Old and New Testament Cycles) on the uppermost tier of the walls, in the first two bays near the entrance, and in 1297–99 he painted the Franciscan Cycle in San Francesco. In 1300 he went to Rome, where he painted *Boniface the VIII Proclaims the Jubilee* in the basilica of St. John Lateran. During 1304–6 he painted the frescoes in the Arena Chapel of the Scrovegni family in Padua. In the following years he went to Florence several times, and in 1327 he enrolled in the guild of Physicians and Apothecaries, to which artists had only recently been admitted.

Various documents testify that between 1329 and 1333 Giotto was in Naples, where he worked at the court of Robert of Anjou and was admitted to the circle of the king's intimate friends. In 1334 the Florentine republic appointed him master of the works of the of the cathedral and architect of the city walls and fortifications. He died in Florence in 1337.

During the first three centuries of **Christianity** the representation of angels was not permissible, and it is interesting that until the tenth century angels in art were curiously draped. Giotto was the first to approach the ideal representation of angels. His *Birth of the Madonna* (1304–6) in the Scrovegni (also known as the Arena) Chapel in Padua shows two naked erotes carrying a cockle-shaped medallion with a bust of Christ. This is an entirely new use of the classical sarcophagus motif. Angels are also represented in Giotto's picture of the Crucifixion, in which he introduced an element of absurdity by depicting extremely human little angels tearing open their little breasts in despair. In the *Crucifixion,* found in the Scrovegni Chapel at Padua, the angel's full-throated lament in the sky tends to expand beyond all reasonable proportions if compared to the compact little group in the lower area around the crucified.

For a long time there were no pictures of the Resurrection, its treatment being confined to carvings in ivory, on shrines, and on other small objects. The Resurrection was first painted by Giotto, as one of a series of small pictures upon a press for the sacred vessels in the Church of Santa Croce in Florence (1297–1305). In this picture, however, there are no angels. As with his fresco of the Resurrection, in *The Ascension,* painted on the walls of the Scrovegni Chapel in Padua, Giotto attempted to represent the scene in accordance with scriptural description. In the center of the lower part of the picture are two angels who with raised hands direct the attention of the kneeling Virgin and groups of apostles, also kneeling, to Christ, already soaring far above them, accompanied by numerous worshiping angels on both sides at some distance from him. This fresco is much injured but is highly valued for the sublimity of its composition.

The *Stigmata of St. Francis* (1300) shows St. Francis, who, as he prays on the slope of Mount Vernia, sees the Savior in the form of a crucified seraph and is impressed miraculously on his hands, feet, and right side with the stigmata of the Cross, as suffered by Jesus. The power of this vision is so overwhelming that blood flows from the palms and feet of the visionary, who for that moment is truly Christ himself. In the *Annunciation to St. Anne,* in the Scrovegni Chapel, the angel tells Anne that she will give birth to a child. A beautiful angel is represented in the *Sacrifice of Joachim,* and in *Joachim's Dream* an angel appears to him in a dream and bids him go to Jerusalem, where by the Golden Gate he will find his wife.

GIOTTO'S *MOURNING THE DEAD CHRIST* (WALL PAINTING IN THE ARENA CHAPEL, PADUA, CA. 1306). (COURTESY ARAS)

Several angels surrounding God are depicted in the upper part of the *Annunciation* (Scrovegni Chapel), and the archangel Gabriel is represented in the lower compartments, visiting the Virgin and announcing to her that soon she will bear a divine child. *Mourning the Dead Christ,* in which the two Marys, the apostles, and several angels grieve over Christ's body, is the most famous fresco of the whole cycle.

Multitudes of angels are portrayed in the *Triumphal Arch,* and in the *Last Judgment,* a fresco which takes up the whole inner wall of the Scrovegni Chapel's front. In the upper part heaven is portrayed, with angels and apostles; below are the elect led by the Virgin; on the lower right is hell. At the center, lower area to the left of the Cross is the offering of the chapel to the Virgin.

Both the mosaics titled *Angel* (1310) are part of the original Navicella mosaic by Giotto in the portico of St. Peter's Cathedral in Rome. They represent St. Peter sailing in a storm and the Savior preventing him and his ship from sinking. The two angels reproduced on these mosaics, with their rich, graduated colors, were probably on the two sides of an inscription under the Navicella. Angels are also depicted in *St. John on Patmos* (the Peruzzi Chapel in the Church of Sta Croce, Florence, 1310), which shows John, who, relegated to the isle of Patmos, sees in a dream Jesus holding a scythe, the angel calling on time to reap, the travailing woman pursued by a dragon, the mystic child in its cradle, the angels, and the four beasts.

Sources:

Berefel, Gunnar. *A Study on the Winged Angel: The Origin of a Motif.* Stockholm: Almqvist & Wiksell, 1968.

Baccheschi, Edi. *The Complete Paintings of Giotto.* New York: Henry M. Abrams, 1966.

MacGregor, Geddes. *Angels: Ministers of Grace.* New York: Paragon House, 1988.

Salvini, Roberto. *All the Paintings of Giotto.* 2 vols. New York: Hawthorn Books, 1963.

Gnome

A gnome's life-span averages 400 years.

Gnomes

Gnomes are a form of dwarf **fairy,** and are associated with the element earth. They are said to reside in deep forests, in the roots of ancient oak trees, and are supposedly occupied with the healing and protection of wild animals. They reach maturity early and are thus often pictured as quite old. In the **occult** tradition, earth is traditionally associated with the physical body, and earth **elementals** (gnomes) are said to work with human beings to maintain physical health.

As the archetypal spirits of the earth element, gnomes are occupied with maintaining the physical structure of the planet. In ceremonial magic, gnomes are the earth elementals of the North who are called upon to witness rituals. The task of the elementals, like that of the nature **devas,** is to build up forms in the natural world, thus providing an arena in which other beings, such as human souls, can spiritually evolve. Some occultists view elementals as soulless entities who simply disappear at death, but others see them as spirits who eventually evolve into devas (angels). Because of their association with earth, the gnomes are under the **rulership** of the archangel **Uriel.**

Sources:

Andrews, Ted. *Enchantment of the Faerie Realm: Communicate with Nature Spirits & Elementals.* St. Paul, Minn.: Llewellyn Publications, 1993.

McCoy, Edwin. *A Witch's Guide to Faery Folk*. St. Paul, Minn.: Llewellyn
   Publications, 1994.

Gnosticism

Gnosticism embodies a complex of related sects and religious writings that together constituted a major movement in the early centuries of the Christian era. Although the thoughtway of Gnosticism was not exclusively Christian, Gnostic Christianity was a significant competitor with what became the Christian mainstream. The numerous beings with which Gnosticism populated the cosmos and the higher spiritual realms influenced later conceptualizations of angels and **demons.**

Gnosticism propagated the idea that this world is the product of an evil deity—the **Demiurge**—who traps human spirits in the prison of the physical world. Our true home is the *pleroma,* the absolute spirit, to which we should seek to return by rejecting this material world and abstaining from the pleasures of the flesh. Unlike **Christianity,** in which one is saved by faith, in this school of thought one was saved by proper intellectual insight, or *gnosis,* which is secret knowledge imparted to Gnostics. Gnosticism in the original sense died out before the **Middle Ages,** but the term continued to be used to refer to any departure from orthodoxy the Church judged to be too world-denying or that seemed to stress mental insight over faith as the essential mode of salvation.

Two distinct types of entities are associated with Gnosticism: **aeons** and **archons.** The aeons are the higher spiritual beings who reside in the pleroma. In one common schema—discussed by the anti-Gnostic Church writer Irenaeus—there were thirty aeons, arranged in fifteen pairs, from Depth and Silence to Theletos (Desire) and **Sophia** (Wisdom). Sophia, the lowest aeon, desired to know Depth (in some accounts, she desired to know herself). Her unfulfilled desire caused her to give birth to another entity—often called Yaldabaoth—who created our material world. This creation involved the emanation of the seven levels of the classical cosmos. The archons are the rulers who govern each of these levels and act as guardians preventing the sparks of light (i.e., the divine essence of individual human beings) from returning to the pleroma. Part of the knowledge imparted to the Gnostics is information on how to bypass these archons.

Sources:

Layton, Bentley. *The Gnostic Scriptures*. Garden City, N.Y.: Doubleday, 1987.
Robinson, James M., ed. *The Nag Hammadi Library*. 1977. Reprint. New
   York: Harper & Row, 1981.
Turner, Alice K. *The History of Hell*. New York: Harcourt Brace, 1993.

Goblins

In contemporary English, *goblin* connotes an evil spirit, sort of a small **demon.** Originally goblins were a grotesque tribe of **fairies** who delighted in frightening people with malicious pranks, such as the kind of activities one associates with poltergeists. They could, however, also be helpful around a house, in the same way that **brownies** could be helpful. The expanded term *hobgoblin* was originally reserved for helpful goblins. However, perhaps because the Puritans used goblin and hobgoblin to designate evil spirits, both words eventually acquired demonic connotations.

Sources:

Guiley, Rosemary Ellen. *The Encyclopedia of Ghosts and Spirits.* New York: Facts on File, 1992.

Masello, Robert. *Fallen Angels . . . and Spirits of the Dark.* New York: Perigee, 1994.

Graham, Billy

America's leading evangelist and angel advocate, William (Billy) Franklin Graham, Jr., was born on November 7, 1918, in Charlotte, North Carolina. During his early teen years he showed little evidence of any great interest in religion, even though he was friendly with and had great respect for the McMakin brothers, children of the Graham's intensely religious sharecropper.

The September before Graham's sixteenth birthday, Mordecai Ham, a well-known evangelist, traveled to Charlotte to hold a series of meetings that Graham attended. He was very impressed by Ham's words and message, and one night believed he felt the presence of Christ. This experience eventually led to his conversion. He undertook formal Bible training, and when he graduated from Sharon High School he enrolled at Bob Jones College in Cleveland, Tennessee, and in 1937 at the Florida Bible Institute.

Upon graduation from Florida Bible Institute, Graham went north to Wheaton College in Illinois for the fall semester of 1940. Wheaton College was a highly respected educational institution that ranked first among the evangelical colleges of its day. There he met Ruth Bell, daughter of missionaries, who married him in 1943. After graduating, he accepted the pastorate of a small Baptist church in Western Springs, Illinois, and in October 1943 he accepted Torrey Johnson's offer to participate in the organization called Youth for Christ and to take over responsibility for the organization's radio program.

Early in 1949 he received the most important invitation of his career, when a group of Los Angeles businessmen asked him to come to their city in September to conduct a series of evangelistic meetings. In the same period he was struggling with the question of the authority of the Scriptures; he eventually decided to accept the authority of the Bible on faith and not demand rational or intellectual proofs for its trustworthiness. After the Los Angeles sessions, Graham held well-attended meetings in New England and the South, and by the early 1950s he had a national following. The tremendous response caused Graham to set up a formal organization known as the Billy Graham Evangelistic Association.

In the early 1950s while he was busy establishing his association and holding crusades in American cities, his activities were being watched with interest overseas, and in 1953 he was invited to London for a crusade that opened on March 1, 1954. Almost 40,000 people made decisions for Christ during the London Crusade, after which Graham decided to go ahead with his scheduled visits to continental Europe. He visited Scotland, Scandinavia, and Germany, as well as Canada, in 1955, and the following January he spoke before more than 800,000 people in an eight-week crusade in India. Then in the spring of 1957 Graham held his famous crusade in New York's Madison Square.

EVANGELIST BILLY GRAHAM

In the spring of 1959 he and his team flew to Australia for a series of meetings, and in the 1960s, which seemed to hold great promise for a continuation of Graham's crusade efforts, he held meetings in many of the world's largest and most important cities and reconfirmed his standing as the greatest evangelist of the age.

In the 1970s Graham continued his world travels, although he reduced his crusade schedule to dedicate more energy to television programs. Among his best-selling books are *Peace With God* (1953), *The Secret of Happiness* (1955), *How to Be Born Again* (1977), *The Holy Spirit: Activating God's Power in Your Life* (1978), *Approaching Hoofbeats: The Four Horsemen of the Apocalypse* (1983), *Hope for the Troubled Heart* (1991), and *Storm Warning: Deceptive Evil Looms on the Horizon* (1992).

Naturally, Billy Graham has long been involved with the subject of angels. His book *Angels: God's Secret Agents* (orig. publ. 1975) records his experiences as well as those of others who are convinced that at moments of special need they have been attended by angels. His work has been inspired by the teaching of the Scriptures, which testify that God has provided assistance for human beings in their spiritual conflicts through the actions of countless angels at his command. Although the Bible does not give us much information about angels, its teachings can be a source of comfort and strength for humanity in every circumstance.

Graham is convinced that angels exist and that they provide unseen aid on our behalf. His belief in angels is not influenced by accounts of dramatic visitations from angels. He believes in angels because the Bible says there are angels and because he has sensed their presence in his life on special occasions.

He asserts that angels, who think, feel, will, and display emotions, are "ministering servants" who can appear or remain invisible as they perform the tasks that God assigns them. As the Bible states, he believes that angels, like humans, were created by God and that their empire is as vast as God's creation. Although the activities of the Devil and his demons may seem to be intensifying in these days, Christians must never fail to sense the operation of angelic glory.

Graham does not equate angels with the **Holy Spirit.** Although they are mightier than humans, they are not gods and they do not possess God's attributes. Nevertheless, both angels and the Holy Spirit are at work to accomplish God's perfect will. Although they are glorious beings, they differ from regenerated man in significant ways. God is not called "Father" by angels, because, not having sinned, they need not be redeemed. In addition, Graham asserts that although the angels rejoice when people are saved and glorify God, who has redeemed them, they cannot testify personally to something they have not experienced, but can only point to the experiences of the redeemed and rejoice that God has saved them.

Angels do not marry or procreate, and they excel humankind in their knowledge, although they are not omniscient. Also, they enjoy far greater power than humans, but they are not omnipotent. Graham is convinced that angels have the capacity to employ heavenly celestial music, although the Scriptures do not directly say so.

Sources:

Graham, Billy. *Angels: God's Secret Agents*. 1975. Reprint. Dallas: Word Publishing, 1994.

Strober, Gerald S. *Billy Graham: His Life and Faith*. Waco, Tex.: Word Books, 1977.

Greece (Ancient)

In the earliest pantheistic religions of the Mediterranean and the Middle East, there were myriad gods and demigods who served as divine messengers, or other lesser divinities who in one way or another provided paradigms for later angels. Among these were the nine Muses, the Greek personifications of artistic and literary inspiration. It was said that the Muses had **wings** and, while not explicitly messengers of the gods, conveyed inspiration to mortals. The Greek **Fates,** divinities of destiny, were also pictured with wings.

One of the most important of these angel paradigms was **Hermes,** whose characteristics were later adopted by the Romans and attributed to the god Mercury, chief messenger of Zeus. Hermes was a god of good luck who protected people on journeys and led the spirits of the departed to the afterlife. The most relevant myth associated with Hermes is that he was traditionally represented as wearing a hat with wings as well as sandals with wings; he was thus one of the classical sources of the convention that God's messengers wore wings.

Plato in the *Phaedrus* implies that both the gods and the souls of men are winged. But the being who above all others must be winged is the one who is neither god nor man, but an intermediary between the two, a messenger—in Greek, *angelos*. Plato relates Socrates' notion of the winged spirit:

> Thus when it is perfect and winged it journeys on high and controls the whole world: but one that has shed its wings sinks down until it can fasten on something solid. . . . The natural property of a wing is to raise that which is heavy and carry it aloft to the region where the gods dwell: and more than any other bodily part it shares in the divine nature.

This Platonic expression may have had some influence on later conceptualizations of angels and their appearance. The classical idea of wings as a symbol of speed, as the attribute of a being occupying an intermediate position between mortals and gods, and as symbol of spirituality lies at the root of the investment of Christian angels with wings.

The essence of Christian **angelology,** which can be considered an adaptation of a Greco-Oriental inheritance, was based on the persistent need for agents to explain certain events to which theologians did not suppose God to condescend and to which humanity was not equal.

NEMESIS OR FORTUNA BY ALBRECHT DÜRER (CA. 1502). IT IS EASY TO SEE HOW THIS MAGNIFICENTLY WINGED GODDESS, HOVERING IN THE HEAVENS, WAS A PRECURSOR TO THE CHRISTIAN NOTION OF WINGED ANGEL MESSENGERS.

To explain such acts and the events of nature, both the ordered and the random, the internal and the external, Christian theologians had available to them the pagan concepts of rational agents above humanity and beneath God, who out of obedience or revolt or innate impulse invisibly controlled the events God left to them.

Plato's doctrine of separable forms and the myths about superior beings, in which he delighted, produced more kinds of invisibles than the scriptural idea of angels could accommodate or a monistic religion tolerate. On the other hand, Aristotle's rejection of separable forms and disinclination to allegorize led some of his followers to discount separate intelligences almost altogether. Plato stressed heavenly order as evidence of intelligence in celestial bodies, and Aristotle confirmed Plato's ascription of intelligent forces to the moving spheres of heaven.

According to later angelologists, Aristotle's view was very close to Plato's. The spheres have "movers," Aristotle argued, because their perfect circular movements must each be caused by a substance both unmovable in itself and eternal, since the heavenly bodies are eternal in their motions and so could be moved only by what is itself eternal and unmovable. He did not say that these substances were persons, but he did say that we must not think of the stars as mere inanimate bodies, but rather as experiencing life and action. This was enough to prompt Christian angelologists up to the middle of the seventeenth century to cite Aristotle as believing in at least the angels of the celestial spheres.

Sources:

Grant, Michael, and John Hazel. *Who's Who in Classical Mythology.* New York: Oxford University Press, 1993.

MacGregor, Geddes. *Angels: Ministers of Grace.* New York: Paragon House Publishers, 1988.

Plato. *Phaedrus.* With an introduction and commentary by R. Hackforth. Cambridge University Press, 1952.

Schneiderman, Stuart. *An Angel Passes. How the Sexes Became Undivided.* New York: New York University Press, 1988.

West, Robert H. *Milton and the Angels.* Athens: University of Georgia Press, 1955.

Wilson, Peter Lamborn. *Angels.* New York: Pantheon Books, 1980.

Gremlins

Gremlins are technological **fairies,** associated particularly, but not exclusively, with airplanes. Traditional fairies, who are usually thought of as connected with nature, are said to dislike technology, but gremlins seem to have adapted to the modern age. Some sources claim that gremlins are spirits of the air, others that they live underground around airfields. While description varies, they are usually pictured as being about a foot tall, green in color, with large fuzzy ears, and webbed feet (with which to cling to airplane wings). They sometimes go about naked, or may be clothed like aviators, with suction cups on the bottoms of their boots.

At the beginning of the air age, aircraft struck the human imagination as quasi-mystical devices, at once of earth and of the celestial regions. Aviators' vague (and not-so-vague) fears stimulated overactive imaginations to perceive prankish spirits who let air out of tires, stalled engines, bored holes in the side of airplanes, bit through cables, and emptied gas tanks (gremlins were said to drink petrol).

The term "gremlin" originated from Grimm's *Fairy Tales*. While first perceived aboard British military aircraft during the second world war, they did not receive their name until 1939. During that year, a British bomber squadron stationed in India was experiencing a rash of what seemed like sabotage against their aircraft. Never able to locate human culprits, they resorted to blaming damage to the pranks of spirits they came to call gremlins.

Gremlins did not, however, always work against the best interests of the craft on which they stowed away—some incidents of miraculous rescue have, for instance, been attributed to the action of these technological fairies. It should also be noted that gremlins have moved well beyond the aviation field and into other areas of technological activity, from factories to computers.

Sources:

Guiley, Rosemary Ellen. *The Encyclopedia of Ghosts and Spirits*. New York: Facts on File, 1992.
Masello, Robert. *Fallen Angels . . . and Spirits of the Dark*. New York: Perigee, 1994.

Guardian Angels

Man's concept of a spirit guardian is probably as old as the human race. In ancient **Mesopotamia** people believed they had personal gods, called *massar sulmi* ("the guardian of man's welfare"). Zoroastrians called these protective spirits *fravashis*. Greeks believed a familiar spirit called a *daemon* was assigned to each person at birth and guided that person through life. The Japanese also had a guiding spirit, a *kami,* and pre-Christian Romans believed each man had a guardian *genius* and each woman a *juno*.

GUARDIAN ANGEL (DETAIL FROM SUMMIT UNIVERSITY PRESS FLYER, COURTESY KALI PRODUCTIONS)

In Teutonic tradition, a spirit guide is assigned to every individual at birth and remains with their charge throughout his or her life. An interesting bit of folklore is held by the Armenians who claim that an infant's guardian angel trims the baby's nails and brings a smile to its lips when they play together. The spirit returns to heaven when the child is older.

Early Christian theologian **Origen** (ca. A.D. 235) held the view that each person had a good angel to guide him and an evil one to tempt him throughout life. This view was also popular in Jewish tradition and in Roman literature.

Even though influential sixth-century theologians **Pseudo-Diony-sius** and Pope Gregory the Great never mentioned personal guardian angels in their writings on **angelology,** belief in such guardians was widespread during the **Middle Ages.** Thirteenth-century religious philosopher

St. **Thomas Aquinas** taught that the individual has a guardian angel close at hand throughout life. Christian Puritan writer Increase Mather (1639–1723), in *Angelographia* states, "Angels both good and bad have a greater influence on this world than men are generally aware of. We ought to admire the grace of God toward us sinful creatures in that He hath appointed His holy angels to guard us against mischiefs of wicked spirits who are always intending our hurt both to our bodies and to our souls."

Catholic Teachings

It is not part of the dogma of the Catholic Church, but Catholics are taught that each person has a guardian angel who protects and watches over him or her. As children, Catholics learn this prayer: "Angel of God who are my guardian, enlighten, watch over, support and rule me, who was entrusted to you by the heavenly piety. Amen."

For her book *Angels: The Role of Celestial Guardians and Beings of Light,* Paola Giovetti interviewed Father Eugenio Ferrarotti of Genoa, who says he has made contact with his guardian angel through automatic writing. When asked whether the existence of guardian angels is the official teaching of the church, Fr. Ferrarotti answered, "Of course, it's an element of faith. There are about three hundred mentions of angels in the Scriptures, and Jesus himself speaks of them. Therefore, to remain silent today on the presence of angels amounts to belittling slightly the word of the Lord, censuring it and interpreting it incorrectly. Devotion to our guardian angels should come immediately after that for the Holy Trinity, Jesus, and the Madonna." Fr. Ferrarotti also claims angels are a gift from God, given at the moment the soul issues from God and remaining at the person's side until after death. "Yes, there are angels all around us," he affirms; "they enlighten us, protect, rule, and defend us on our return journey to the Heavenly Father."

The Roman Catholic Church celebrates a feast day to the guardian angels on October 2. Catholicism holds that every country, city, town, village, parish, and family has its own guardian angel, as do altars, churches, dioceses, and religious institutions.

According to the Catholic publication *Saint Michael and the Angels,* the personal guardian angels' ministry consists of warding off dangers to body and soul; preventing Satan's suggesting evil thoughts, and removing occasions of sin; enlightening and instructing the charge and fostering holy thoughts and pious desires; offering the person's prayers to God and praying for him or her; correcting the charge if he or she sins; and helping the individual in the agony of death and conducting the soul to **heaven** or to **purgatory.**

Guardian Angels in the Bible

The story of the archangel **Raphael** as he guides the youth Tobias on his dangerous journey in the apocryphal **Book of Tobit** sets the stage for biblical guardian angels. Among biblical references to guardian angels is Heb. 1:14, where St. Paul says, "Are they all not ministering spirits, sent forth to minister for them who shall be heirs of salvation?" Dr. **Billy Graham,** Christian evangelist, cites in his book *Angels: God's Secret Agents* the classic example of an angel protector found in Acts 12:5–11. **Peter** is in prison awaiting execution because of his belief in the Gospel and the works of God. James, the brother of John, has already fallen victim to the executioner's axe. As Peter sleeps, an angel appears, enters the prison cell, and wakes Peter, telling him to prepare to escape. A light shines in the cell, Peter's chains fall off, he dresses and follows the angel outside, where the gates of the city open of their own accord and let them pass.

Ps. 91:11–12 speaks of guardian angels: "For he shall give his angels charge over thee, to keep thee and all thy ways. They shall bear thee up in their hands, lest thou dash thy foot against the stone." The angels are said to take special care of children. Jesus says in Matt. 18:10, "Take heed that ye despise not one of these little ones; for I say unto you, that in heaven their angels do always behold the face of my Father."

Churches, cities, and nations are also said to have guardian angels. In the Book of Revelation seven angels are assigned to minister to the seven churches, Ephesus, Smyrna, Pergamos, Thyatira, Sardis, Philadelphia, and Laodicea during the final days before the second coming of Christ.

On the Belief in Guardian Angels

Writer Michael Grosso, in the book *Angels and Mortals: Their Co-Creative Power,* writes that the belief in and reverence of guardian angels is "the collective outgrowth of thousands of years of unconscious psycho-mythical evolution." He cites biblical examples of the beginnings of this belief, such as in Exod. 23:20, when god tells Moses, "I myself will send an angel before you to guard you as you go and to bring you to the place that I have prepared. Give him reverence and listen to all that he says." According to Grosso the guardian angel is an *imago dei*—"an image or form of divine power"—and that Christ is the exclusive imago dei. Speaking of angelic cult in the Catholic Church, Grosso writes, "Popular movements that grow outside or parallel to the dogmas of the Church . . . are likely to reflect some deep psychic need." He theorizes that the cult of the guardian angel, like the cult of saints and of the Virgin

Mary, "may be seen as an attempt to overcome the remoteness and impersonality of God," to "shrink out distance from deity."

Writing about the last stage of the *Opus Sanctorum Angelorum* (the Work of the Holy Angels, a current movement in the Catholic Church that is devoted to angels), Grosso says, "all human beings, saints or sinners, Christians or pagans, enjoy the service of a guardian angel. The concept, in short, is archetypal: it applies to the psyche universally. The guardian angel is portrayed as existing 'face to face' with God. . . . In short, there is in every human being an unconscious inlet to the highest creative energies of the spirit."

Then Grosso takes another look—at the view of the philosopher Vico, called the philosopher of the imagination. "In a Vichian vein," Grosso writes, "we can say that angels exist insofar as we imaginally co-create them. . . . Angels are true to the extent that we make them true. That is our premise. It contrasts sharply with the traditional religion *and* with modern science." Grosso says that people in a time when the world is saturated with science, are hungry for fresh contact with renewing spirits, thus the popularity of archetypes (inherited ideas common to a race and existing in the subconscious) in the forms of psychic channeling, UFO contacts, near-death experiences, apparitions of Mary, and guardian angels. In these new times of return to the primal imagination, writes Grosso, "the gods and goddesses, the demons and fairies, the griffins and guardian angels we have trampled under the feet of scientific rationalism are returning with a vengeance." But he does not discount this experience of our collective psyche. Rather he asserts, "As this happens, opportunities for transforming ourselves in the image of our divinely human potentials—opportunities for soul-making—will multiply, with the help of our guardian angels."

How Angels Guard and Guide

While guardian angels can help humans even if they don't ask, it is best if the person does ask for help, says contemporary author Linda Georgian in her book *Your Guardian Angels*. She maintains that a person should think about the angels daily to communicate with them, and become aware of instinct and intuition since these gentle nudgings could be angels talking.

Angels will do all they can to help the humans in their care, but they cannot act against man's free will, according to angel lore. If a person wants angelic help, he will also have to strive to do what is right, including taking all possible care to be safe in difficult circumstances. Betty Malz, in her book *Angels Watching over Me,* uses the example of a

Guardian Angels

A well-known nineteenth-century children's poem is "Four angels to my bed, four angels round my head. One to watch and one to pray, and two to bear my soul away."

daredevil pilot who is killed in an accident to illustrate that people can, by choosing to take too many chances, deliberately move themselves out of the "safety zone," in which angels will protect them.

Sophy Burnham, in *A Book of Angels* considers the difficult question: If an angel can save one person, why not a troop of angels to save our world? "Why did spiritual beings not sweep over us to save mothers in Vietnam or Palestine from bombs and napalm burns, or babies from dying of disease? Why do not angels lift up planes shot down in war and hold them in their winged hands as a mother would in setting her baby in a crib?" Burnham asks. She answers, "Blood splatters on our earth. Blood fertilizes it. Blood of mankind shed by man. Is that why angels cannot interfere? . . . Are angels helpless against the rage of man?"

An account in Giovetti's book seems to bear out Burnham's conclusion. In peaceful settings angels perhaps *are* trying to save our world. Giovetti writes of the extraordinary events at **Findhorn,** on the coast of Scotland, where spirit **devas** led two women, a man, and three children to plant and grow fruits and vegetables of unheard-of variety and size in a cold, desolate spot that had only pebbly sand for soil. These spirit voices instructed Dorothy Maclean and Eileen Caddy in the harmonious and natural way to fertilize the earth and sow seed to care for and nourish each variety of grass, greens, and vegetables, and when and how to gather them. Begun as a small kitchen seed-plot, the "Findhorn phenomenon" eventually brought visitors from all over the world to see the magnificent garden cultivated by Maclean and the Caddy family. Some stayed to help and a community grew up at Findhorn. Today it is a school not only of gardening, but of life, where lectures and courses are given, showing people that it is possible to live healthy lives in harmony with nature and humanity and in tune with the spiritual dimension.

Another example in Giovetti's book is that of a young woman named Elisa, who lives in Rome. Elisa says she has always felt angels close to her and has seen them: "They are tall, luminous, made of pure light and sexless," she says, and they describe themselves as "beings of light, vibrating in the Divine Energy, pure and uncontaminated by thought." Since 1987 these beings have spoken to Elisa about the future of the human race urging her to arouse people's consciousness and get them to love, pray, and think positively so that the angels can help them to realize the divine plan for a harmonious earth.

Is It Really From the Angels?

Hundreds of people claim to receive not only protection but daily guidance from angels through dreams, visions, or voices. **Eileen Elias**

Freeman, editor of the *AngelWatch Newsletter* and author of *Touched by Angels: True Cases of Close Encounters of the Celestial Kind* (1993), lists some ways by which a person can tell whether a message actually comes from the angels. She says angelic messages are always loving, positive, and clear, even though they may be sobering. They do not leave the receiver with feelings of anxiety or unnamed fears, but with confidence and knowing from within that the message is right and true. Truly angelic messages, says Freeman, come only from God. If carrying out the message brings good in the life of the receiver and those around him, it came from the angels, and an angelic encounter will always leave the person changed for the better. Any being that can be summoned at will, with or without ritual, she says, is not an angel, for God alone sends the angels when the time is right.

Sources:

Burnham, Sophy. *A Book of Angels: Reflections on Angels Past and Present and True Stories of How They Touch Our Lives.* New York: Ballantine, 1990.

Freeman, Eileen Elias. *Touched by Angels: True Cases of Close Encounters of the Celestial Kind.* New York: Warner Books, 1993.

Gaster, Theodore H. *Myth, Legend, and Custom in the Old Testament.* New York: Harper & Row, 1969.

Georgian, Linda. *Your Guardian Angels: Use the Power of Angelic Messengers to Enrich and Empower Your Life.* New York: Simon & Schuster, 1994.

Giovetti, Paola. *Angels: The Role of Celestial Guardians and Beings of Light.* Translated by Toby McCormick. York Beach, Maine: Samuel Weiser, 1993.

Graham, Billy. *Angels: God's Secret Agents.* 1975. Reprint. Dallas, Word Publishing, 1994.

Grosso, Michael. "The Cult of the Guardian Angel." In *Angels and Mortals: Their Co-Creative Power.* Compiled by Maria Parisen. Wheaton, Ill.: Quest Books, 1990.

Malz, Betty. *Angels Watching Over Me.* Grand Rapids, Mich.: Chosen Books, 1986.

New Catholic Encyclopedia. Vol. 1. Washington, D.C.: Catholic University of America, 1981.

Saint Michael and the Angels. Compiled from Approved Sources. Rockford, Ill.: TAN Books, 1983.

Guardian Spirit (Shaman; Spirit Guide; Tutelary Spirit)

The contemporary interest in angels is built largely around **guardian angels,** a specific category of angelic beings said to be assigned to watch over each person. However, parallel notions of guardian or *tutelary* spirits are found worldwide in every culture—even in societies lacking belief in what we would readily call angels.

The function of these tutelary spirits is, in many cases, quite similar to the function of traditional angels. They watch over and protect individuals, and in some cultures, these spirits are believed to be attached to a person from birth. The manner in which these spirits manifest their guidance varies: often people refer to inexplicable "hunches" or intuitions, sometimes they receive visions or hear voices.

Possibly the most well known means of actually seeking a guardian spirit is the "vision quest" undertaken by certain Native American groups. In these societies, a standard component of the puberty rite (the formal transition from childhood to adulthood) is the ritual quest for a "revelation" (in the form of a dream or a vision) from the spirit world. It is the hope that this revelation will ultimately inspire in a young person a sense of purpose or identity, or it may steer the seeker toward his adult vocation. These rituals sometimes involve treks into the wilderness where the seeker fasts or engages in other activities likely to bring on visionary experiences. As part of the vision, initiates often acquire spirit helpers who take the form of animal spirits, deceased relatives, or personifications of the forces of nature. This link-up (meeting the spirit guardian) can be viewed as a wholly new relationship, or the conscious realization of a relationship that has existed since birth.

Shamans (healers or religious specialists of hunter/gatherer cultures), who may find their vocations during their adolescent vision quest—or, later, during a separate encounter with the otherworld—often have many spirit helpers. These helpers run the gamut from animal spirits to the spirits of departed shamans. With respect to animal helpers (one's "power animals," to use contemporary terminology) the relationship may be a totemic one, meaning that the initiate or shaman in some way participates in the nature of the animal. In other words, a person with an eagle spirit helper becomes "eagle-like," and someone with a bear helper becomes "bear-like."

There is, in particular, a correlation between the shaman's guardian spirits and traditional guardian angels. To the extent that such helpers are viewed as communication links between shamans and higher spirits, they function as true angels (whose defining characteristic is the job of message bearers).

A phenomenon with certain parallels to shamanism is contemporary **Spiritualism.** Among Spiritualists, whose religion is built around communication with the so-called dead, one finds similar notions of spirit guides or helpers—helpers who are often, but not always, deceased relatives. Individual mediums (people with exceptional sensitivity to the otherworld) often have many guides, much as the shaman has many spirit

Guardian Spirit (Shaman; Spirit Guide; Tutelary Spirit)

helpers. Despite this multiplicity, mediums will usually have one principle spirit—a master guide or "control"—who regulates contact with other spirits, and who thus serves as a kind of guardian spirit for the medium.

Sources:

Eliade, Mircea, ed. *Encyclopedia of Religion.* 16 vols. New York: Macmillan, 1987.

Hultkrantz, Ake. *Conceptions of the Soul Among North American Indians.* Stockholm: Ethnographic Museum of Sweden, 1953.

Lewis, James R. *The Encyclopedia of Afterlife Beliefs and Phenomena.* Detroit, Mich.: Gale Research, 1994.

Hadraniel

Hadraniel (or Hadarniel, among other variant spellings), meaning "majesty [or greatness] of God," is an angel assigned as gatekeeper at the second gate in heaven. He is supposed to be more than sixty myriads of parasangs (approximately 2.1 million miles) tall and a daunting figure to face.

When Moses arrived in heaven to get the Torah from God, it was said that he was speechless with awe at the sight of Hadraniel. Hadraniel didn't think that Moses should have the Torah, and made him weep in fear, which caused God to appear and reprimand Hadraniel for causing problems. Hadraniel quickly decided to behave and acted as a guide for Moses. This was a great help, because (according to Zoharic legend) "when Hadraniel proclaims the will of the lord, his voice penetrates through 200,000 firmaments." Also, according to the Revelation of Moses, "with every word from his (Hadraniel's) mouth go forth 12,000 flashes of lightning."

In **Gnosticism** Hadraniel is only one of seven subordinates to Jehuel, prince of fire (King, p. 15). In the Zohar I (55b), Hadraniel speaks to **Adam** about Adam's possession of the Book of the Angel Raziel, which was said to contain secret information that not even the angels knew.

Sources:

Davidson, Gustav. *A Dictionary of Angels: Including the Fallen Angels.* 1967. Reprint. New York: Free Press, 1971.

King, Charles William. *The Gnostics and Their Remains.* San Diego, Calif.: Wizards Bookshelf, 1982.

Liebes, Yehuda. *Studies in the Zohar.* Translated from the Hebrew by Arnold Schwartz, Stephanie Nakache, and Penina Peli. Albany, N.Y.: State University of New York Press, 1993.

Ronner, John. *Know Your Angels: The Angel Almanac with Biographies of 100 Prominent Angels in Legend and Folklore, and Much More.* Murfreesboro, Tenn.: Mamre Press, 1993.

Hafaza

The *hafaza* are **Islamic** angels who guard people against **jinn** (demons) and other evil spirits. According to legend, individuals have four hafaza attached to them, two who stand guard during the day and two who work the night shift. It is said that people are least protected during the twilight periods of both the morning and the evening. At these moments the guard changes, and the jinn attempt to make the most of this break to wreak havoc with individuals. These four guardian angels are also assigned the job of keeping record of each person's good and evil actions. Their logbooks will be used as evidence on the Day of Judgment.

Sources:

Davidson, Gustav. *A Dictionary of Angels: Including the Fallen Angels.* 1967. Reprint. New York: Free Press, 1971.

Glassé, Cyril. *The Concise Encyclopedia of Islam.* San Francisco: Harper San Francisco, 1989.

Halo (Nimbus; Aureole)

The halo (from a Greek term for the threshing floor where oxen moved around in a continuous circle) is a standard part of traditional religious iconography and was often drawn around the heads of religious figures such as Jesus, saints, and angels. Although contemporary artists tend to draw halos as thin circles of light that float over the subject's head like the brim of some sort of invisible hat, they were traditionally drawn as disks of gold (meant to imply a sphere of light radiating in every direction from the figure's head) against which the face was sketched. Halos symbolize holiness, innocence, and, sometimes, spiritual power (e.g., **Satan** was sometimes drawn with a halo of power in Byzantine art).

Halos have universal appeal and are found in the religious iconography of traditions as diverse as **Buddhism, Hinduism,** and the classical religions of the ancient Mediterranean. In Western religions, the halo

A HALO CAN BE A THIN CIRCLE AS IN *THE CRUCIFIXION* (MOSAIC MONASTERY CHURCH AT DAPHNE, GREECE, ELEVENTH CENTURY)

HALOS AS SOLID DISKS REINFORCE ASSOCIATION WITH THE CELESTIAL. DETAIL OF THE LINDISFARNE GOSPELS, CA. 687–698.

A HALO CONTAINING A CROSS IS USUALLY USED IN DEPICTIONS OF CHRIST (GIOTTO'S MEDALLION OF THE REDEEMER, CEILING VAULT OF THE SCROVEGNI CHAPEL, PADUA). (PHOTOS COURTESY ARAS)

seems to have originally been a representation of the solar disk, and hence of the Divinity's association with the celestial realms. Halos did not become part of the standard iconography of Christianity until the fourth century A.D., after which angels were frequently drawn with halos. In addition to the standard yellow-gold halo, halos are often depicted containing crosses, as well as with rays of light emanating from the subject's head.

Some contemporary writers in the **occult/metaphysical** tradition speculate that the halo is either the mental body or part of the astral body, a nonphysical "body" that surrounds the physical body. Individuals gifted with psychic sight are supposedly able to see this normally invisible "aura." It is even suggested that people who are "particularly holy" have noticeably luminous mental bodies, and the halos we see in art are, according to this school of thought, attempts to represent this experience.

Sources:
Cirlot, J. E. *A Dictionary of Symbols.* New York: Philosophical Library, 1971.

Cooper, J. C. *An Illustrated Encyclopaedia of Traditional Symbols.* 1978. Reprint. London: Thames and Hudson, 1992.

Ronner, John. *Know Your Angels: The Angel Almanac with Biographies of 100 Prominent Angels in Legend and Folklore, and Much More.* Murfreesboro, Tenn.: Mamre Press, 1993.

Harps and the Music of Heaven

Angels are often pictured wearing **halos** and white robes, seated on clouds, playing harps. This popular image stems partially from a tradition that views the chief occupation of angels as singing God's praises. (This tradition is so significant that the various ranks of angels are called **choirs.**) Why harps were chosen as the heavenly instrument par excellence appears to be based on the association between the Greek gods and the lyre, a harp-like musical instrument popular in ancient **Greece.**

Heavenly music is also associated with the so-called Music of the Spheres. Prior to the invention of the telescope and the Copernican revolution, it was generally believed that the earth was the stable center of the universe, around which the sun, moon, stars, and the five known planets revolved. Because the sun, moon, and planets moved along paths of their own, entirely independently of the stars, it was believed that they were "stuck" on a series of concentric, crystalline (i.e., transparent) spheres that revolved around the earth, between the earth and the stars. As these spheres moved it was said that they resonated with each other, much as the strings of a harp will do, thus producing the phenomenon referred to as the Music of the Spheres. This conception of the universe may thus have contributed to the idea that angels play harps rather than other kinds of instruments.

People who have had unusually vivid spiritual experiences sometimes report hearing heavenly music during them. One recent study of **near-death experiences,** for example, found that eleven percent of these people reported hearing celestial music. It is not illogical to postulate that the ancients also had such experiences, and these experiences may have also contributed to the notion that heaven was a musical place.

Sources:

MacGregor, Geddes. *Angels: Ministers of Grace.* New York: Paragon House, 1988.

Ronner, John. *Know Your Angels: The Angel Almanac with Biographies of 100 Prominent Angels in Legend and Folklore, and Much More.* Murfreesboro, Tenn.: Mamre Press, 1993.

Harut and Marut

Judaism, Christianity, and **Islam** all have angel lore related to angelic lust for human beings. Although the basic idea of spirit beings or demons having sex with human beings is very ancient, Judeo-Christian speculation on such ideas grew out of two short, obscure verses in Genesis (6:2 and 6:4) about the "sons of God" taking to wife the "daughters of men." In these rather strange verses, "sons of God" was taken to indicate angels. The traditional interpretation of these passages is that these sons of God are *fallen* angels.

Islam's version of this theme is a tale involving two angels mentioned in the Koran, Harut and Marut, although the Koranic reference contains no allusion to these angels' sexual misconduct. According to the story, humanity's seeming inability to avoid temptation and sin prompted the angels to make some uncomplimentary remarks about humankind. God responded that angels would fail as miserably as human beings if placed under the same conditions. In answer to God's challenge, Harut and Marut were chosen to go down to Earth, with strict instructions to avoid the most severe sins of murder, idolatry, alcohol, and illicit sexual relations.

Almost immediately, Harut and Marut were overcome by desire for an attractive woman. Caught in the act by a passerby, they killed him so that no one could testify to their sin. However, as one might anticipate, the all-knowing God was perfectly aware of their actions. Furthermore, he arranged it so that the angels in heaven would witness the reprehensive actions of their brothers on Earth.

Having miserably failed the test, Harut and Marut were punished by being hung upside down in a well in Babylon, this being preferable to eternal punishment in hell. The other angels had to admit that God was right, and, presumably, snide remarks about the weakness of humanity ceased to be made within the precincts of heaven. As for Harut and Marut, they occupied their time teaching sorcery to humanity, although they never failed to warn human beings of the ultimate consequence of practicing the forbidden arts.

Sources:

The Encyclopedia of Islam. Vol. 3. Leiden, Netherlands: E. J. Brill, 1978.

Glassé, Cyril. *The Concise Encyclopedia of Islam.* San Francisco: Harper San Francisco, 1989.

Ronner, John. *Know Your Angels: The Angel Almanac with Biographies of 100 Prominent Angels in Legend and Folklore, and Much More.* Murfreesboro, Tenn.: Mamre Press, 1993.

Hayyoth

Hayyoth, meaning "holy, heavenly beasts," are a class of **Merkabah** (Jewish mystical) angels, corresponding to the **cherubim** who reside in the seventh heaven. The hayyoth are also considered angels of fire who support the throne of Glory, each having, as reported by **Enoch,** four faces, four wings, and two thousand thrones.

According to **Ezekiel,** the Hayyoth were seen by the river Chebar, whereas the **Zohar** argues that they number thirty-six, constitute the "camp of Shekinah," uphold the universe, and break into songs of praise when they spread their wings. Abelson, in *Jewish Mysticism* (1913), asserts that they receive from above the holy effluence, which is eventually disseminated to the hayyoth, or movers of the wheels. It is said that the work of the contemporary painter Marc Chagall was considerably influenced by the prophet's vision of the hayyoth, and by the postbiblical lore on these angels.

Sources:

Abelson, J. *Jewish Mysticism.* London: G. Bell, 1913.

Davidson, Gustav. *A Dictionary of Angels: Including the Fallen Angels.* 1967. Reprint. New York: Free Press, 1971.

Liebes, Yehuda. *Studies in the Zohar.* Translated from the Hebrew by Arnold Schwarts, Stephanie Nakache, and Penina Peli. Albany, N.Y.: State University of New York Press, 1993.

Healing, Angelic

Angelic healing is the act of angels interacting with and inspiring humans to heal from physical, spiritual, or emotional afflictions. William Bloom, author of *Devas, Fairies and Angels: A Modern Approach,* has this to say: "There is a large school of Angels whose major focus is healing work. They do not themselves do dramatic acts of healing, but they provide an atmosphere of clarity, of comfort and of love, in which healing can take place. They are also capable of facilitating healing by directly helping the work of individual human healers."

Eileen Elias Freeman writes in *Angelic Healing: Working with Your Angels to Heal Your Life,* "Healing is a partnership that includes each of us, each of our angels, other people and their angels, and God, who binds us all together and who is the divine fire that lights all our candles, human and angelic. Certainly, God can and does heal people directly, and we have every right to ask God to work in that way. But it's been my experience that, most often, God heals us through each other, because we are a human family and we need to realize that we cannot live and die in isolation. And by 'each other,' I mean not only other human beings, but angels as well."

Although dynamic cure from physical disease is the most apparent form of healing, emotional healing manifests more subtly. Emotional healing involves a more inward focus and can be as insidious as any physical ailment. Often it is within the emotional arena that damage occurs over an extended period of time. Fear is the most debilitating hazard of mankind that erodes the stability of the emotions. Healing from God through his angels eliminates fear and substitutes confidence and direction. Throughout history, the salutation of an angel has been "fear not," for fear has to be removed to allow the message to be shared and heard. Thus, through the hands of the angels fear is dashed and healing can begin.

There are several distinct types of angelic healing. Angelic healing can be spontaneous, can be sought via prayer, and can be experienced indirectly when advice is given, which when followed can bring about positive results. Eileen Freeman and other angel enthusiasts have even developed angelic healing circles to help people, in cooperation with angels, heal the lives of those involved.

Healing

Number of people who received treatment last year from Andre D'Angelo, a healer who uses angelic energy: 2,000

Sources:

Bloom, William. *Devas, Fairies and Angels: A Modern Approach.* Somerset: Gothic Image Publications, 1986.

Day, Leonard C. Letter to author, 3 July 1995.

The Findhorn Community. *The Findhorn Garden.* New York: HarperPerennial, 1975.

Freeman, Eileen Elias. *Angelic Healing: Working with Your Angels to Heal Your Life.* New York: Warner Books, 1994.

Heaven and Hell

Most traditional cultures have postulated a three-level world: an upper world beyond the sky (above the "heavens") in which the gods of light dwell, a middle realm occupied by humanity, and a lower world beneath the earth in which gods of darkness reside. In certain religious traditions, particularly the familiar Western faiths, the gods of light became **angels** (at the service of one supremely good, monotheistic God) and the gods of darkness became **demons** (fallen angels). A natural consequence of this moral division is that the realm of reward in the afterlife was placed in the upper world with angels (heaven) and the realm of punishment in the lower world with the demons (hell). In the Christian tradi-

THE LADDER OF SALVATION STRETCHES FROM THE DEPTHS OF HELL TO THE HEIGHTS OF HEAVEN IN THIS DETAIL FROM A PAINTING AT ST. PAUL'S CHURCH AT CHALDON (LATE TWELFTH CENTURY). (COURTESY ARAS)

tion in particular, underworld devils acquire employment tormenting the souls of the damned, whereas upperworld angels become companions of the saved. This was not always the case: in early **Christianity** stern, righteous angels tortured sinners in the underworld.

An issue with which serious thinkers have grappled across the centuries is the fate of souls who, while not moral "athletes," have nevertheless not committed outrageous sins. This has led to the development of ideas of "intermediate" afterlife abodes in which "mixed" souls are purified (i.e., tormented by demons) and made fit for heaven. Catholic **purgatory** is the most well known of these realms, but the same basic idea is incorporated into other traditions. Yet another solution has been to postulate multiple heavens and hells, or "levels" of heaven and hell, in which good people and sinners are rewarded or punished according to the degree of their noble deeds or sins. One of the most well known examples is **Dante**'s *Inferno*. The heavenly hierarchy of levels also provided a structure for arranging the host of God's angels according to degrees of power and development.

Sources:

Eliade, Mircea, ed. *Encyclopedia of Religion.* 16 vols. New York: Macmillan, 1987.

McDannell, Colleen, and Bernhard Lang. *Heaven: A History.* 1988. Reprint. New York: Vintage, 1990.

New Catholic Encyclopedia. Vol. 1. Washington, D.C.: Catholic University of America, 1981.

Turner, Alice K. *The History of Hell.* New York: Harcourt Brace, 1993.

Hermes

One of the most important precursors of the modern-day notion of angel-as-messenger was the Greek Hermes (whose characteristics were later adopted by the Romans and attributed to the god Mercury), chief messenger of Zeus (the Roman Jupiter). As well as the god of science and commerce, Hermes was a god of good luck who protected people on journeys and led the spirits of the departed to the afterlife. He was also the patron divinity of merchants and thieves. Further, Hermes is said to have invented the lyre by stringing cords of linen through holes bored in a tortoise shell. There were nine cords in honor of the nine Muses.

Hermes was traditionally represented as wearing a hat with **wings** as well as sandals with wings, and thus, became one of the classical sources of the conventional assumption that God's messengers wore wings.

Sources:

Bulfinch, Thomas. *Bulfinch's Mythology.* New York: Gramercy Books, 1979.

Grant, Michael, and John Hazel. *Who's Who in Classical Mythology.* New York: Oxford University Press, 1993.

Tripp, Edward. *The Meridian Handbook of Classical Mythology.* New York: New American Library, 1970.

Hierarchy of Angels

In the ancient Western world, and particularly in the civilization of medieval Europe, it seemed natural that reality should be organized according to an ascending hierarchy of levels—a hierarchy that has been referred to as the Great Chain of Being. According to this argument, all of creation extends in a gradient fashion from the simplest organisms through more complex forms up to the human race. Unwilling to accept man as the pinnacle of creation, philosophers such as **Thomas Aquinas** and John Locke extended the chain upward to God. The enormous gap these philosophers found to exist on this ladder between human beings and God was their argument that an angelic kingdom ought to exist. This basic concept was not seriously challenged until the scientific revolution of the early modern era, which collapsed the West's traditional, ladderlike worldview into one level of matter in motion (or, in the case of those who continued to defend the reality of the spirit, into a comparatively simple duality of spirit and matter).

Given this view of reality, it was natural that the angels should be regarded as occupying a hierarchy of levels. One of the earliest schemas was that of the early sixth-century theologian **Dionysius the Areopagite.** His *Celestial Hierarchy* was the most influential treatise in Christian **angelology** and received added authority when adopted many centuries later by Thomas Aquinas. The Dionysian scheme describes nine **choirs** of angels, grouped into three hierarchies. In descending order they are as follows: **seraphim, cherubim, thrones; dominions, virtues, powers; principalities, archangels, angels.** Only the last two choirs have contact with human beings; in them are placed all of the angels, named and unnamed, of the biblical tradition.

According to another Dionysian work, *The Ecclesiastical Hierarchy,* the angelic orders are reflected in the structure of the earthly church, and also form a continuum between God and the believer.

Despite the popularity of the Dionysian schema, many others have been proffered by a wide variety of thinkers. Sometimes these are minor variations, such as in the work of **Dante,** who exchanges the places filled by the archangels and principalities in *The Celestial Hierarchy.* Other

DIONYSIAN HIERARCHY OF ANGELS

First order:
closest to God

SERAPHIM	"the fiery spirits" usually pictured with six wings and flames; they constantly sing God's praise and regulate heaven; led by Uriel
CHERUBIM	depicted with multi-eyed peacock's feathers to symbolize their all-knowing character; led by Jophiel
THRONES	"the many eyed ones" represented as wheels of fire to symbolize divine majesty; led by Japhkiel

Second order:
composed of the priest-princes of the court of heaven

DOMINIONS	carry scepter and sword to symbolize the divine power over all creation; led by Zadkiel
VIRTUES	the "brilliant" or "shining ones" are associated with acts of heroism; led by Haniel
POWERS	prevent the fallen angels from taking over the world and keep the universe in balance; led by Raphael

Third order:
constituted by the ministering angels

PRINCIPALITIES	represent the protectors of princes; guardian angels of cities, nations, and rulers; led by Camael
ARCHANGELS	carry God's messages to humans and command God's armies of angels in the constant battle with the "Sons of Darkness"; led by Michael
ANGELS	celestial beings closest to humans, they are the intermediaries between God and mortals

schemata are completely different, even in the names assigned to the various levels. In the **Zohar,** for example, we find the following hierarchy, in descending order:

1. Malachim
2. Erelim
3. Seraphim
4. Hayyoth
5. Ophanim
6. Hamshalim
7. Elim
8. Elohim
9. Bene Elohim
10. Ishim

Gustav Davidson, in the appendix of his *Dictionary of Angels* (1967), outlines thirteen such structures and alludes to several others. Despite this plethora of schemata, almost all contemporary authors writing about angels (with the notable exception of those with traditional Judaic and **Islamic** perspectives) refer exclusively to the Dionysian hierarchy. Even such an unorthodox author as **Rudolf Steiner** derives his schematic structure more or less directly from Dionysius.

Sources:

Davidson, Gustav. *A Dictionary of Angels: Including the Fallen Angels.* 1967. Reprint. New York: Free Press, 1971.
MacGregor, Geddes. *Angels: Ministers of Grace.* New York: Paragon House, 1988.
Parisen, Maria. *Angels & Mortals: Their Co-Creative Power.* Wheaton, Ill.: Quest, 1990.
Stayer, Joseph R., ed. *Dictionary of the Middle Ages.* 13 vols. New York: Scribner, 1982.

Hinduism

One religious tradition that has been of special importance for researchers studying angels is Hinduism, which has its roots in Brahmanism, the earliest historic religious tradition of the Indian subcontinent. Lacking a central religious body empowered to judge what is or is not proper belief and ritual, a complex variety of sects, movements, and practices find their place under the umbrella of Hinduism. Traditionally, only movements that explicitly rejected the nominal authority of the Vedas (India's most ancient layer of extant religious literature) and refused to follow caste guidelines were regarded as outside the fold (e.g., Sikhism, Jainism, and **Buddhism**). One trait of the Hindu tradition is that earlier strands of spiritual expression such as the Rig Veda and the Atharva Veda

THE HINDU GODS SHIVA
AND PARVATI ARE FLANKED
BY ANGELS IN THIS INDIAN
WATERCOLOR (CA. 1780).
(COURTESY ARAS)

have been retained and absorbed rather than discarded as new religious
forms emerge. This practice resulted in the transformation of the original
vedic deities into angelic **devas** of modern Hindu mythology.

Between 1500 and 1000 B.C., a group of aggressive pastoral peoples from central Asia invaded India through the northern mountain passes, destroyed whatever records might have remained from the original civilization, and settled in northern India. The worldview of these Aryan invaders has been preserved in the Rig Veda (ca. 1200–900 B.C.), a collection of 1,028 hymns to the Vedic deities. The Vedic religious vision was quite different from what later became Hinduism. In addition to other changes, the principal gods of the Vedic pantheon were supplanted by new gods. However, because of the tendency of Hinduism to keep earlier layers of its own tradition, the Vedic gods were retained in the form of lower-level demigods, referred to as devas.

As embodied in such classical mythological texts as the Puranas, devas are far more complex beings than are Western angels. Nevertheless, some devas occasionally performed messenger tasks for the higher deities, making them comparable to angels in certain respects. Contemporary studies of angels have particularly noted two types or classes of devas, **apsaras** and **gandharvas**, as embodying certain angel traits. Partially because of the association of some devas with the forces of nature, the term *deva* was adopted by nineteenth-century **Theosophy** for the class of spiritual beings they viewed as forming and controlling the manifest world. Theosophists further asserted that the devas of the East corresponded with the angels of the West. Thus, despite the wide variance between traditional southern Asian devas and Western angels, *deva* and *angel* are interchangeable terms in Theosophical circles, as well as the larger metaphysical/**New Age** subculture influenced by Theosophy.

Sources:

De Bary, Wm. Theodore, ed. *Sources of Indian Tradition*. Vol. 1. New York: Columbia University Press, 1958.

MacGregor, Geddes. *Angels: Ministers of Grace*. New York: Paragon House, 1988.

Parrinder, Geoffrey, ed. *World Religions From Ancient History to the Present* New York: Facts on File, 1983.

Organ, Troy Wilson. *Hinduism: Its Historical Development*. Woodbury, N.Y.: Barron's Educational Series, 1974.

Parisen, Maria. *Angels & Mortals: Their Co-Creative Power*. Wheaton, Ill.: Quest Books, 1990.

Zimmer, Heinrich. *Philosophies of India*. 1951. Reprint. New York: Macmillan, 1987.

Hocus Pocus

In certain medieval magic systems, Hocus Pocus was a spirit that manifested as a "prince on high" (i.e., an angel). In the 1600s "hocus pocus" was a name applied to any magician or juggler. The expression was perhaps originally sham Latin used by magicians performing tricks, very likely a perversion of the phrase from the Latin Mass, *Hoc est corpus meum* (This is my body). Numerous derivations come from the word including the English term *hoax*.

Sources:

Barnhart, Robert K., ed. *The Barnhart Dictionary of Etymology.* New York: H. W. Wilson, 1988.

Grant, R. M. *Gnosticism and Early Christianity.* New York: Columbia University Press, 1959.

The Oxford Dictionary of English Etymology. 1966. Reprint. New York: Oxford University Press, 1985.

Holidays, Angel

In the Catholic tradition, there are two holy days (the source of our word *holiday*) associated with angels: the Feast of **Guardian Angels,** celebrated on October 2, and St. Michael and All Angels (often called Michaelmas), celebrated on September 29. Before the church calendar was reformed in 1969, each of the three angels mentioned in the Bible had his own feast day, **Gabriel** on March 24, **Raphael** on October 24, and **Michael** on September 29. St. Michael's feast has thus become a combined holiday (like President's Day) that is now the celebration of all the angels. Interestingly, the Ethiopian and Egyptian Orthodox churches celebrate a feast on July 28 in honor of the fourth archangel, **Uriel.**

Sources:

Freeman, Eileen. "Michaelmas—Flowers, Springs and Geese." *AngelWatch* (September-October 1992).

Ronner, John. *Know Your Angels: The Angel Almanac with Biographies of 100 Prominent Angels in Legend and Folklore, and Much More.* Murfreesboro, Tenn.: Mamre Press, 1993.

Holy Immortals (Amesha Spentas)

Around 1000 B.C. the prophet Zoroaster reformulated the original polytheism of Persian religion into the first monotheism. Although little is known about the old Persian polytheism, apparently some of the old gods were demoted and retained as angels in Zoroaster's synthesis.

The struggle between good and evil occupies center stage in the **Zoroastrian** worldview. The god of light and the upper world, Ohrmazd or Ahura Mazda (Wise Lord), and his angels are locked in a cosmic struggle with the god of darkness and the lower world, Angra Mainyu or

Ahriman (Evil Spirit), and his demons. Every human being is urged to side with Ahura Mazda and his angels.

Chief among the Zoroastrian angels are the holy immortals (*amesha spentas*), the highest beings next to God in the Zoroastrian scheme of celestial inhabitants. These beings are named after qualities valued by Zoroastrians, and are usually numbered as six **archangels:**

Vohu Manah	(Good Thought or Good Sense)
Armaiti	(Piety or Harmony)
Ameretat	(Immortality)
Asha	(Righteousness or Truth)
Haurvatat	(Prosperity or Salvation)
Kshathra	(Power or Rulership)

This list is sometimes supplemented by a seventh, Saraosha (Obedience). Zoroaster originally regarded these beings as aspects of Ahura Mazda himself. Corresponding to these archangels of light are agents of the evil Angra Mainyu, such as Druj (the Lie), who was directly opposed to Asha.

The holy immortals played an important role in the religious experience of the founder. At the age of thirty, Zoroaster had a vision of Vohu Manah, who appeared to the prophet in a form nine times larger than an ordinary person. After questioning Zoroaster, Vohu Manah led his spirit into the heaven of Ahura Mazda, who was holding court with his angels. God then instructed the prophet in the principles of the true religion. Over the course of the following eight years, Zoroaster had a visionary experience with each of the archangels—experiences that allowed him to fill out the initial revelation into a complete religious system.

Sources:

Cohn, Norman. *Cosmos, Chaos and the World to Come: The Ancient Roots of Apocalyptic Faith.* New Haven: Yale University Press, 1993.

Eliade, Mircea, ed. *A History of Religious Ideas.* Vol. 1. Chicago: University of Chicago Press, 1978.

Noss, John B. *Man's Religions.* 4th ed. New York: Macmillan, 1969.

Holy Spirit (Holy Ghost)

The Christian mainstream, both Protestant and Catholic, has traditionally adhered to the notion of the Trinity, the idea that the one God manifests in three "modalities," the Father, Son, and Holy Spirit (or Holy Ghost). The Holy Spirit, as an aspect of the godhead, is not an angel—a creation of God—but is rather a direct expression of God. Although this is quite clear theoretically, in practical expression the Spirit manifests in ways that one might otherwise associate with angels.

In the Gospels, for example, Jesus tells his disciples not to worry about what to say when delivered up for trial. Rather, he asserts, they should "say whatever is given you in that hour, for it is not you who speak, but the Holy Spirit" (Mark 13:11). This kind of spiritual aid, in which someone is spontaneously given the right words to say, is a type of inspiration often attributed to angels. There are also many passages in the Acts of the Apostles in which the Holy Spirit speaks to or otherwise acts upon the early Christians in angel-like ways, for example, chapter 13, verse 2:

> While they were worshiping the Lord and fasting, the Holy
> Spirit said, "set apart for me Barnabas and Saul for the work
> to which I have called them."

Here, if "an angel appeared before them and said" were substituted for "the Holy Spirit said," the passage would not seem in any way odd or unorthodox.

In addition, the *Commentary on the Apocalypse of the Blessed John* indicates that "by the angel flying through the midst of heaven is signified the Holy Spirit."

Sources:

Ferguson, Everett, ed. *Encyclopedia of Early Christianity.* Vol. 846 of the Garland Reference Library of the Humanities. New York: Garland, 1990.

The Illustrated Bible Dictionary. Sydney, Australia: Hodder & Stoughton, 1980.

Richardson, Alan, and John Bowden, eds. *The Westminster Dictionary of Christian Theology.* Rev. ed. Philadelphia: Westminster Press, 1983.

Houri

In **Islam,** the houris are beautiful celestial maidens, created as a reward for the faithful in heaven. These companions of the saved are mentioned in a number of Koranic verses including the following:

> Surely for the godfearing awaits a place of security, gardens and
> vineyards, and maidens with swelling breasts . . . (78:31–34)

Some later interpreters viewed such verses as symbolizing spiritual states of rapture.

Sources:

Arberry, A. J. *The Koran Interpreted.* 1955. Reprint. New York: Macmillan, 1969.

Glassé, Cyril. *The Concise Encyclopedia of Islam.* San Francisco: Harper San Francisco, 1989.

Hours (Angels of the)

In traditional **astrology,** the period between sunrise and sunset was subdivided into hours, each ruled by a different **planet.** The heavenly bodies utilized were the seven traditional "planets" prior to the discovery of Uranus, including the Sun and the Moon. As with many other phases of astrology, these planetary hours were also associated with angels.

Traditional astrology stipulates that the day be divided into twelve equal segments between sunrise and sunset, which will thus vary in length according to the season. On a particular day, the first of these hours is ruled by the planet ruling that day of the week (see **rulership**). In other words, on Saturday, the first hour would be ruled by Saturn; on Sunday, the first hour would be ruled by the Sun; and so forth. The succeeding hours are ruled by the next planet in the following order: Saturn, Jupiter, Mars, the Sun, Venus, and the Moon. After reaching the Moon, one begins again with Saturn and repeats the same order.

THE DANCE OF THE HOURS BY GATANO PREVIATI (1899). (COURTESY ARC)

Ancient astrologers used their knowledge of the planetary hours to choose appropriate times for carrying out various activities. It was said, for example, that Paracelsus always chose to prepare chemical compounds on days and during hours when the ruling planet matched the therapeutic intent behind his compounds. The angels for the planetary hours are simultaneously the angels for the seven **days of the week,** as follows:

Monday (Moon)	Gabriel
Tuesday (Mars)	Sammael
Wednesday (Mercury)	Raphael
Thursday (Jupiter)	Sachiel
Friday (Venus)	Anael
Saturday (Saturn)	Cassiel
Sunday (Sun)	Michael

Not surprisingly, there are parallels between the astrological associations of the planets and the nature of the corresponding angels. Cassiel, for instance, is said to be the angel of solitude, tears, and temperance—all traditional attributes of the planet Saturn. Thus, an adherent of astrology would not schedule a party to begin during an hour ruled by Cassiel (Saturn).

Sources:

Davidson, Gustav. *A Dictionary of Angels: Including the Fallen Angels.* 1967. Reprint. New York: Free Press, 1971.

Hall, Manly P. *Astrological Keywords.* 1958. Reprint. Savage, Md.: Littlefield Adams, 1975.

Hypnos

The Greek god Hypnos (Sleep), son of Nyx (Night) and brother of **Thanatos** (Death), and from whom we derive the term *hypnosis,* was traditionally pictured as making his home in a dark, misty cave, through which flowed the River of Forgetfulness. He was surrounded by his numberless sons, the Dreams. As a messenger of the gods, Hypnos was pictured with **wings.** He had few myths associated with him—putting Zeus to sleep at the behest of Hera on several occasions and once helping his brother Thanatos carry the body of Apollo's son Sarpendon from a battlefield.

Sources:

Grant, Michael, and John Hazel. *Who's Who in Classical Mythology.* New York: Oxford University Press, 1993.

Tripp, Edward. *The Meridian Handbook of Classical Mythology.* New York: New American Library, 1970.

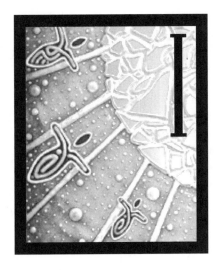

And the angel Israfel, who has the sweetest voice of all God's creatures.

—George Sale, Preliminary Discourse to the Koran

Iblis (Eblis)

All of the religions in the Judeo-Christian-Islamic complex share a similar idea about the origin of **Satan,** namely, that he was a prideful angel who was ejected from heaven. In his postcelestial career, Satan then took on the task of leading humanity astray. In **Judaism** and **Christianity,** Satan provokes a **war in heaven** in which he leads a revolt against God. He is, of course, defeated, and he and his followers are ejected from heaven. In **Islam,** the story is somewhat different.

In the Islamic tradition, there are three orders of beings—angels, who are made from light; **jinn,** who are made from fire; and human beings, who are made from clay. The angels were created first. When God created **Adam,** he commanded the angels to worship him. Iblis (often spelled Eblis) refused on the grounds that Adam, who, after all, was a mere creature of dust and dirt, was inferior to the angels. As punishment for his disobedience, Iblis was transformed from an angel into a jinn.

Subsequently, Iblis and other angels who shared his viewpoint were removed from their stations and exiled from heaven. They later became **demons,** with Iblis playing the role of the Islamic Satan. According to the Koran, Iblis's first misdeed was to lead Adam and Eve astray in the Garden of Eden. The Koran also notes that at the end of time Iblis and his hosts will be tossed into hell.

In an interesting variation on tradition, Sufis (Islamic mystics) reinterpreted Iblis's disobedience as an act of love for God, and as an act of obedience to the law that only God should be worshipped. To have bowed down to Adam, in other words, would have been to acknowledge another god, and thus have been an act of idolatry, a severe sin in the Muslim tradition. Iblis, according to this interpretation, was a true lover of God, and thus a Sufi. Iblis knew that the consequences of his actions would be punishment, but he preferred remaining true to his love of God (and accepting the consequences of being condemned to hell) to being untrue to his love of God and remaining in heaven.

Sources:

Davidson, Gustav. *A Dictionary of Angels: Including the Fallen Angels.* 1967. Reprint. New York: Free Press, 1971.
The Encyclopedia of Islam. Vol. 3. Leiden, Netherlands: E. J. Brill, 1978.
Glassé, Cyril. *The Concise Encyclopedia of Islam.* San Francisco: Harper San Francisco, 1989.
Ronner, John. *Know Your Angels: The Angels Almanac with Biographies of 100 Prominent Angels in Legend and Folklore, and Much More.* Murfreesboro, Tenn.: Mamre Press, 1993.

Iconography of Angels

Iconography is the set of conventional images or symbols associated with a subject, especially a religious or legendary subject. In most contemporary Western religions angels are symbolized as human figures with **wings,** white robes, **halos,** and sometimes harps. These components represent various angelic characteristics: wings signify that angels are celestial beings, white robes and halos symbolize purity and holiness, and harps indicate that angels are engaged in making music in God's praise.

The earliest records of the figure of an angel as commonly perceived today—as a winged messenger or mediator between heaven and earth—are found in the Middle Eastern religious traditions. In the city of Ur, near Babylon, which flourished around 2500 B.C., archaeologists have found a stele (an upright sculptured stone slab) depicting a winged figure descending from one of the seven heavens of Sumerian belief to pour water of life into the cup of a king.

The Babylonians also believed that each individual has a guardian being who intercedes with the gods on that person's behalf. **Cherubim,** one of the three orders of angels closest to God, are depicted in Assyrian iconography as winged creatures with either human or lion faces and the bodies of sphinxes, eagles, or bulls.

Early **Christian** angel iconography became considerably more complex. The earliest angels were portrayed as young, masculine, and virile. This convention began to change in the Gothic period as artists started to depict angels as the embodiment of ideal beauty, which led, in turn, to the purely feminine angel of the Renaissance.

The convention of angels wearing white robes goes back to the earliest period. As Christianity spread across the Roman Empire, angels were sometimes represented garbed in white togas like those of the Roman senators to give them an air of dignity. In the Byzantine period angels sometimes appeared in the uniform of imperial court guards. In the **Middle Ages,** angels were often depicted with a scepter, a diadem, or a codex—all symbolic of divine power and authority.

It was not until the fourth century of the Christian era that angels acquired wings. Following classical conventions, winged figures were the messengers of the gods to humanity, as in the traditional representations of Mercury and **Nike,** the goddess of victory. The earliest example of a winged human figure in Christianity is found in S. Pudenziana in Rome as the symbol of St. Matthew.

It was also not until the fourth century that halos became part of the standard iconography of Christianity. Halos symbolize holiness, innocence, and sometimes spiritual power. The halo seems to have originally been a representation of the solar disk, and hence of the divinity's association with the celestial realms.

Depending on the artist's purpose, angels were represented in ways that contributed to the larger theme of the painting, mural, or sculpture. An angel reflecting an attitude of adoration, for instance, might carry a musical instrument (symbolizing praise) or swing a censer (representing prayer). Angels might also carry a lily (symbolizing purity), a palm leaf (victory), a scepter (God's kingship), a flaming sword (judgment), or a trumpet (the voice of God).

The nine angel **choirs** also have distinctive iconographic conventions that make it possible to distinguish, for instance, cherubim from **seraphim.** (See also **Architecture, Angels in; Art, Angels in**)

Sources:
Ferguson, Everett, ed. *Encyclopedia of Early Christianity.* Vol. 846 of the Garland Reference Library of the Humanities. New York: Garland, 1990.
New Catholic Encyclopedia. Vol. 1. 1967. Reprint. Washington, D. C.: Catholic University of America, 1981.
MacGregor, Geddes. *Angels: Ministers of Grace.* New York: Paragon House, 1988.

Imps

Imps are minor evil spirits, rather like infernal **fairies.** The word *imp* originally meant shoot or bud, which conveys the impression of imps as offshoots of **Satan.** Imps have also been described as the demonic equivalent of **guardian angels,** tempting humans to evil acts rather than inclining them to good deeds. Imps are errand boys who carry out the bidding of their master, and were also traditionally thought to be the **familiars** of witches.

In the words of one writer imps are "low-maintenance demons" and can be kept just about anywhere. Usually tiny in size, some are said to look like small people, others like moles or even toads. They require some feeding, and need, in particular, blood.

Sources:

Briggs, Katharine. *An Encyclopedia of Fairies*. New York: Pantheon, 1976.
Masello, Robert. *Fallen Angels . . . and Spirits of the Dark*. New York: Perigee, 1994.

Incubi and Succubi

The notion of spirit beings or demons who take the form of human beings to have sex with people is ancient. In Western angel lore, speculation on such ideas grew out of two short verses in chapter 6 of Genesis:

> The sons of God saw that the daughters of men were fair; and they took to wife such of them as they chose. (6:2)

> The Nephilim were on the earth in those days, and also afterward, when the sons of God came in to the daughters of men, and they bore children to them. These were the mighty men that were of old, the men of renown. (6:4)

In these rather strange verses, "sons of God" is taken to indicate angels. However, although Scripture does not condemn these actions, the traditional interpretation of these passages is that these sons of God are *fallen* angels. This interpretation provided biblical legitimation for the elaborate notions of incubi and succubi that later developed in the **Middle Ages.**

Incubi took the form of handsome men and seduced women, whereas succubi took the form of beautiful women and seduced men. Although sterile themselves, incubi could supposedly impregnate women with seed taken by succubi from men—a belief that was sometimes used to explain a pregnancy resulting from a secret affair. This type of explanation not only absolved the woman from charges of licentiousness, but, because the sperm was taken from a man, also saved the child from being slain as an offspring of a demon. Such explanations were also useful for explaining sexual dreams in a society where any form of illicit sex was viewed as demonic.

There were, however, other medieval traditions that asserted incubi could impregnate mortal women with their own seed and that succubi could become pregnant by mortal men. It was rumored, for instance, that Merlin the magician was the offspring of such a union. This notion of semidemonic children was useful for explaining such phenomena as deformed babies. Incubi were sometimes referred to as demon lovers. Also, some writers asserted that succubi were the same as the wood nymphs of European folklore.

Mortals who willingly responded to the seductive wiles of these beings risked damnation. A papal bull issued by Pope Innocent in 1484, for instance, asserted that "many persons of both sexes, forgetful of their own salvation, have abused incubi and succubi." Some of the church fathers, including St. Anthony, asserted that demons sometimes took the form of seductive naked women and tried to lure them away from their devotions. These experiences served to reinforce later assertions of the existence of succubi.

Sources:

Baskin, Wade. *Dictionary of Satanism.* New York: Philosophical Library, 1962.
Guiley, Rosemary Ellen. *The Encyclopedia of Witches and Witchcraft.* New York: Facts on File, 1989.
Masello, Robert. *Fallen Angels . . . and Spirits of the Dark.* New York: Perigee, 1994.
Prophet, Elizabeth Clare. *Forbidden Mysteries of Enoch: Fallen Angels and the Origins of Evil.* Livingston, Mont.: Summit University Press.

Indo-Europeans

Although there have been innumerable subsidiary sources, the angels and demons of Western religions are derived ultimately from the gods of the Indo-Europeans. *Indo-European* was originally a linguistic term referring to the Indo-European family of languages. This category of classification was created when it was discovered that almost all of the languages from Europe to India were related, indicating a common root language. This family resemblance is evident in similarities of vocabulary. For example, the Sanskrit/Hindi word *deva,* which refers to a certain class of gods and goddess, comes from the same root as the English words *deity* and *divine.* To explain this phenomenon, scholars have postulated that these similarities are the result of a group of people who at one time spoke the original (now lost) Indo-European language.

Efforts to reconstruct Indo-European religion and mythology, represented especially in the work of George Dumezil, have focused on finding common elements in the myths and religious practices of Indo-European peoples that are not found in other cultural complexes. It has been established, for example, that the Indo-Europeans divided their society into three groups of people, and that this tripartite division was reflected in their myth system. According to one line of thought, in at least some branches of the Indo-European family two distinct groups of divinities were worshipped by two different social groups. In the Persian/Indian wing of the Indo-Europeans, these two groups were termed *ahuras* (Persian)/**asuras** (Indian) and *daevas* (Persian)/**devas** (Indian). Perhaps because of ongoing conflict between the two social divisions, the ahuras became the angels and the devas the demons in **Zoroastrianism,** and the devas became demigods and the asuras became demons in **Hinduism.** This confusion is reflected in modern English, in which the term *divinity* and the term *devil* derive from the same root word, *deva* or *daeva.*

Sources:

Cohn, Norman. *Cosmos, Chaos and the World to Come: The Ancient Roots of Apocalyptic Faith.* New Haven, Conn.: Yale University Press, 1993.

Eliade, Mircea, ed. *A History of Religious Ideas.* Vol. 1. Chicago: University of Chicago Press, 1978.

Noss, John B. *Man's Religions.* 4th ed. New York: Macmillan, 1969.

Islam

Angels, as messengers between God and humanity, are particularly prominent in the monotheistic religions of the West. The latest of these religions is Islam which was founded in Arabia by the Prophet **Muhammad** in the year A.D. 622. After his death in 632, Islam spread to the surrounding areas and westward throughout North Africa and southern Spain. For centuries Muslim empires enjoyed what is referred to as the Golden Age of Islam where sciences, art and literature, theology, and jurisprudence flourished. Today, Islam still unites the Arab world and has become one of the fastest growing religions in the world, second in numbers only to Christianity.

Belief in angels plays an important role in Islam. In Sura 2, verse 177 of the Koran, the Muslim Holy Scriptures, it states: "It is not righteousness that you turn your faces toward east or west; but it is righteousness to believe in Allah and the Last Day, and the angels and the Book and the messengers." **Mala'ika** is the Islamic term for angel (*malaak,* singular). One of the chief functions of angels in Islam is the carrying of messages between humans and Allah, the God of Muslim worship. In the Koran, angels are spiritual beings created to solely serve, worship, and obey Allah. They are formed of light or fire and do not sin or fall into temptation. They do not have any vested administrative authority from God but rather are beings who are commanded to precisely execute the orders of Allah.

Angels have heavenly, unseen forms as well as earthly forms. On earth they appear to mankind in the form of humans. In the *Hadith* or Traditions of the Prophet as recorded and attested to by credible witnesses, there is an account by the Caliph Omar (one of the successors to the Prophet) stating that the Prophet Muhammad once encountered an unknown man with very dark hair and a very white face. This man sat down next to him and asked him a series of four questions regarding the pillars of belief for Islam, faith, piety, and the Day of Judgment. The man told the Prophet that his response to the first four matters was correct. However, concerning a fifth matter, the time of the Last Days, he stated specifically that no man shall know the exact time aside from the Creator Himself. When the man left, the Prophet realized that he had been visited by an angel of Allah.

Many different kinds of angels are regularly mentioned in the Koran. Some, including **Djibril (Gabriel)** and **Mikhail (Michael),** are also found in **Judaism** and **Christianity.** Djibril and Mikhail are two of four important Muslim **archangels,** the other two being **Israfil** and **Izra'il.** Djibril is of especial importance in Islam. It was Djibril who originally contacted the Prophet and dictated the holy words of the Koran to him on the "Night of Power and Glory" (*Leilat al-Qadar*). Djibril also conducted Muhammad on his journey to heaven, known as the "Night Journey" (*Leilat al-Isra'*). He is also recognized by some Muslims as the **Holy Spirit.**

Djibril's primary task is that of messenger. The task of the other archangels differs. Mikhail is the Angel of Providence and also the guardian of the Jews. Azra'il is the **Angel of Death.** Israfil is the Summoner to Resurrection.

In addition to these four archangels, there are lesser angels whose tasks vary considerably. The **hafaza,** or protector angels, guard humans against the **jinn** (demons) and other spirits. Also, when a human dies, Muslims believe that two special angels named **Munkir and Nakir** come to the dead in the tomb to ask questions concerning faith and doctrine. The evil are shown pictures of the hellfire they will endure in the hereafter, and the pious are given a glimpse of the eternal paradise that will be their deserving reward. There are also angels who are sent from

AN ISLAMIC GABRIEL IS DEPICTED IN "ABRAHAM'S SACRIFICE" FROM *THE ANTHOLOGY OF ISKANDAR* (CA. 1410, IRAN). (COURTESY ARAS)

heaven to fight alongside believers in earthly battles waged for the propagation of the faith. Some angels roam the world testifying to Allah about the presence of the faithful at prayer, Koran readings, and religious lectures. Angels are sent to protect the Ka'aba, the Black Stone that Muslims circumambulate during the *Hajj* or the *'Umra* (the off season pilgrimage). Lastly, angels hold up the throne of Allah, praising him eternally and asking continual forgiveness for the faithful.

Early Islamic thinkers postulated three orders of beings beyond God: angels, jinn, and humans. The jinn are a type of spirit created from fire who inhabit a subtly material intermediate realm between angels and humans. Like human beings, the jinn possess intelligence and free will and are thus capable of salvation. Angels, on the other hand, were created to always obey the will of Allah. This concept of angels immediately raises at least one question: If **Iblis,** the Muslim **Satan** or *Shaitaan* was originally an angel, how could he have disobeyed Allah's direct command to bow and worship Adam? Iblis refused to worship **Adam** on the grounds that he saw Adam as a lesser creature than himself. How could Adam, made from mere clay, be more worthy of worship than Iblis, a spiritually pure creation? Allah explained that the human had the potential to be even more deserving of worship as Adam and the sons and daughters of Adam would live their lives facing great temptations that were unknown to the angels in their spiritual form.

Some of the Sufi followers, who practice what is considered non-orthodox Islam, believe that Iblis loved Allah to such a great extent that he was willing to suffer eternal damnation as punishment for his disobedience to Allah's command. Within orthodox Islam, believers assert that Allah transformed Iblis into a jinn as punishment; another belief is that Iblis was always a jinn and just happened to be a resident of heaven at the time of his disobedience. The ultimate result of Iblis's direct disobedience to Allah's command was that he was banished from heaven forever. Iblis, renamed Shaitaan after his fall from grace, asked Allah to grant him permission to live until the Day of Judgment and to gather followers for the purpose of evil. The request was granted by Allah who is All-Knowing and All-Merciful.

In some areas of the world, angels, many with unusual names, play an important role in popular Islam. These practices may be rooted in the pre-Islamic religions of those areas. Angels also play an important role in some systems of Islamic mystical or speculative philosophy, most notably in the complex **angelology** of the Sufi thinker Suhrawardi. Some contemporary Islamic modernists dismiss the real existence of angels, viewing them symbolically as representing aspects of the human soul. However, for most devout Muslims, belief in angels remains an important part of one's faith.

—*Kathryn Sampson*

Sources:

Encyclopaedia of Islam. Vol 4. Leiden, Netherlands: E. J. Brill, 1978.

Glassé, Cyril. *The Concise Encyclopedia of Islam.* San Francisco: Harper San Francisco, 1989.

Strayer, Joseph R. *Dictionary of the Middle Ages.* Vol. 1. New York: Charles Scribner's Sons, 1982.

Israel

Israel (striver with God) is generally considered an angel of the order of **hayyoth,** a class of angels who surround God's throne. They are usually compared with the **cherubim** and the **seraphim.** According to *The Book of the Angel Raziel* Israel ranks sixth among the **throne angels.**

In the Alexandrian Gnostic *Prayer of Joseph,* the patriarch Jacob is an **archangel,** named Israel, who entered earthly life from a pre-existent state. Here, Israel is "an angel of God and a principal spirit," whereas further along Israel introduces himself as the archangel of the power of the Lord and the chief tribune among the sons of God. He also identifies himself as the angel **Uriel.**

Israel is also mentioned by the mystics of the geonic period (seventh–eleventh centuries), as a heavenly being whose function is to call the angels to sing God's praise. Israel is identified with the Logos by the philosopher Philo, whereas Louis Ginzberg, in *The Legends of the Jews,* calls him "Jacob's countenance in the throne of Glory."

Sources:

The Book of the Angel Raziel. (Credited to Eleazer of Worms). Warsaw, 1881.

Ginzberg, Louis. *The Legends of the Jews.* 7 vols. Philadelphia: Jewish Publication Society of America, 1954.

Odeberg, Hugo, ed., tr. *3 Enoch on The Hebrew Book of Enoch.* New York: Cambridge University Press, 1928.

Israfil

Although not mentioned in the Koran, Israfil, or Israfel (the Burning One) is one of the four **archangels** of **Islam,** along with **Mikhail, Djibril,** and **Izra'il.** Israfil is known particularly as the angel of Judgment Day, who blows his horn to awaken the dead. According to tradition, he is an extraordinarily tall angel, with his feet below the earth and his head reaching the pillars of God's throne. He is so saddened by the thought of hell that whenever he glances down to the infernal regions, which he is said to do six times a day, his tears would flood the earth if God did not prevent them from flowing.

Israfil is also an angel of music. He has four wings and a beautiful face. His body is covered with mouths that constantly praise God in a thousand different tongues. From his breath, God is said to create hundreds of thousands of other angels for the heavenly chorus.

Some traditions say that for three years before **Muhammad**'s first encounter with **Djibril** (who revealed the Koran), Israfil was the Prophet's disguised companion.

Sources:

Davidson, Gustav. *A Dictionary of Angels: Including the Fallen Angels.* 1967. Reprint. New York: Free Press, 1971.

Glassé, Cyril. *The Concise Encyclopedia of Islam*. San Francisco: Harper San
Francisco, 1989.
Ronner, John. *Know Your Angels: The Angel Almanac with Biographies of 100
Prominent Angels in Legend and Folklore, and Much More*. Murfreesboro,
Tenn.: Mamre Press, 1993.

Izra'il

Izra'il (Azrael) is the Muslim **angel of death** and one of the four
archangels of **Islam,** along with **Mikhail, Djibril,** and **Israfil.** There is
quite a bit of colorful folklore surrounding this figure. He is, for instance,
pictured as having gigantic proportions: one foot rests in either the fourth
or the seventh heaven, while the other is on the bridge between hell and
paradise. Also, if all the waters of the earth were to be poured upon his
head, not so much as a single drop would make it back to the earth.

Beginning life as a rather ordinary angel, his success (where other
angels failed) at bringing God a handful of earth from which to create
Adam earned his appointment as the angel of death. Some feel that
Izra'il has other angels who work beneath him, and that Izra'il himself
only comes for the souls of prophets. Izra'il keeps a roll of humanity, on
which the names of the damned are circled in black and the names of the
blessed, in light. When a person's day of death approaches, a leaf with
the person's name on it falls from the tree beneath God's throne. After
forty days have passed, Izra'il must sever the individual's soul from his
or her body.

Sources:

Davidson, Gustav. *A Dictionary of Angels: Including the Fallen Angels.* 1967.
Reprint. New York: Free Press, 1971.
Encyclopaedia of Islam. Vol 4. Leiden, Netherlands: E. J. Brill, 1978.
Glassé, Cyril. *The Concise Encyclopedia of Islam.* San Francisco: Harper San
Francisco, 1989.

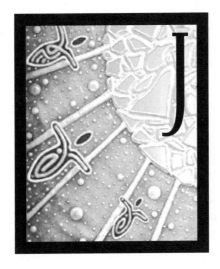

Be sure to send a lazy man for the angel of death.

—Jewish proverb

Jacob Wrestles with an Angel

The same biblical Jacob who dreamed of angels ascending and descending a ladder between heaven and earth also engaged in a famous wrestling match with an angel. Jacob's first encounter with angels occurred when he escaped his brother Esau's wrath after stealing Esau's blessing from their father, Isaac. The second encounter—in which he wrestled with the angel—occured many years later as Jacob was returning home. These angels, then, seemed to act as threshold guardians between the ordinary world of Jacob's parental home and the world of trials and adventures to which he journeyed.

In his wrestling match with the angel, Jacob seemed to be getting the upper hand until his opponent knocked Jacob's leg out of joint. Nevertheless, Jacob continued to cling to his opponent, demanding a blessing. This blessing, unlike the one he had obtained through deceit, was won through his persistence:

> And Jacob was left alone; and a man [an angel] wrestled with
> him until the breaking of the day. When the man [angel] saw
> that he did not prevail against Jacob, he touched the hollow
> of his thigh; and Jacob's thigh was put out of joint as he

wrestled with him. Then he said, "Let me go for the day is breaking." But Jacob said, "I will not let you go, unless you bless me." And he said to him, "What is your name?" And he said, "Jacob." Then he said, "Your name shall no more be called Jacob, but Israel, for you have striven with God and with men, and have prevailed." (Gen. 32:24–28)

Jacob called the place Peniel ("face of God"): "For I have seen God face to face, and my life is spared and not snatched away" (Gen. 32:30). Thus, as a consequence of this dream, Jacob received a new identity and a new status as the one who provided his people with a name—Israel.

This unusual story of hand-to-hand combat with an angel—variously identified as a man, an angel, a demon, or God himself—has naturally tended to puzzle commentators. If the attacker was indeed an angel, as the dominant line of interpretation suggests, one wonders why a man so blessed by God would be attacked by God's messenger. One explanation is that in some (nonextant) original version, the "angel" was a **jinn** or demigod. According to this line of interpretation, later priestly editors, in an effort to remove a seeming affront to strict monotheism, obscured the true identity of Jacob's assailant.

Whatever the original story might have signified, Jacob's nocturnal struggle has become a metaphor for struggling with a problem or a difficult decision during the hours when one should be resting. And this may not be that far removed from the tale's original meaning. After all, on the night of the wrestling match Jacob had sent his servants and family on ahead—as though he wanted to be left alone with his thoughts. The situation was precarious, because he could not predict how his estranged brother would receive him. Esau might even slay him. With such forebodings disturbing his sleep, perhaps Jacob awoke the next day feeling like he had been in a wrestling match all of the preceding night.

Sources:

Gnuse, Robert Karl. *The Dream Theophany of Samuel: Its Structure in Relation to Ancient Near Eastern Dreams and Its Theological Significance.* Lanham, Md.: University Press of America, 1984.

The Illustrated Bible Dictionary. Sydney, Australia: Hodder & Stoughton, 1980.

The Interpreter's One-Volume Commentary on the Bible. Nashville: Abingdon Press, 1971.

Jacob's Ladder

Jacob, third in the line of the patriarchs of Israel, (after **Abraham** and Isaac), had two remarkable encounters with angels. In the first, Jacob was on his way to Haran to take a wife from among the daughters of his uncle Laban. At the end of the first day's travel, he laid his head on a stone and slept:

> And he dreamed that there was a ladder set up on the earth, and the top of it reached to heaven. And behold, the angels of God were ascending and descending on it! And behold, the Lord stood above it and said, "I am the Lord, the God of Abraham your father and the God of Isaac; the land on which you lie I will give to you and your descendants; . . . I will not leave you until I have done that of which I have spoken to you." Then Jacob awoke from his sleep and said, "Surely the Lord is in this place and I did not know it." And he was afraid, and said, "how awesome is this place! This is none other than the house of God, and this is the gate of heaven." (Gen. 28:12–17)

JACOB'S VISION (1920s ILLUSTRATION).

This dream confirmed that Yahweh would honor the Abrahamic covenant with Jacob, even though Jacob had tricked his father, Isaac, into bestowing his blessing on him rather than on Jacob's brother, Esau.

Scholarly commentary on this verse asserts that the image of the ladder is more accurately rendered as a stairway or ramp. The image seems to allude to a **Mesopotamian** ziggurat (a temple built in a stepwise fashion). The gods contacted humanity at the top of the ziggurats, and the temple priests ascended and descended the tower in service to the divinities. Jacob's dream seems to apply this image to God and his ongoing interactions with humanity.

This dream emphasizes two characteristics of the Hebrew God. First, Yahweh is a sky god who resides in the celestial regions. Second, Yahweh is conceived of in regal fashion as a king from whose throne angels are dispatched on missions and to whose throne they return to report. For angels whose missions take them to the earth, the passageway from heaven leads them down the stairway Jacob saw in his dream.

The idea of a particular place where heaven and earth meet is a universal constant of the religious consciousness. Jacob, seemingly by accident, had stumbled upon such a sacred spot. He erected a stone marker to identify the place, which he named Beth-el, the "House of God."

From a folkloric perspective, talismans in the shape of miniature ladders were common in the ancient world and represented the means of ascent to heaven. The Mangors of Nepal still set up miniature ladders beside graves, and a ladder made of dough is traditionally placed next to coffins in some parts of Russia.

Sources:

Eliade, Mircea, ed. *Encyclopedia of Religion.* 16 vols. New York: Macmillan, 1987.

Gaster, Theodore. *Myth, Legend, and Custom in the Old Testament.* New York: Harper & Roe, 1969.

The Illustrated Bible Dictionary. Sydney, Australia. Hodder & Stoughton, 1980.

The Interpreter's One-Volume Commentary on the Bible. Nashville: Abingdon Press, 1971.

Jehoel (Jehuel)

Jehoel is regarded as mediator of the ineffable name, and one of the princes of the presence. He is also considered "the angel who holds the **Leviathan** in check," as well as chief of the order of **seraphim.** He is mentioned in *The Apocalypse of Abraham* as the heavenly choirmaster who accompanied **Abraham** on his visit to Paradise, revealing the course of history to him. It is also suggested that Jehoel constitutes an earlier name of **Metatron,** whereas the cabalistic *Berith Menuha* refers to him as the principal angel over fire.

Sources:

Davidson, Gustav. *A Dictionary of Angels Including the Fallen Angels.* New York: The Free Press, 1967.

Scholem, Gershom. *Jewish Gnosticism, Merkabah Mysticism, and Talmudic Tradition.* New York: The Jewish Theological Seminary, 1960.

Jinn

According to **Islam,** jinn (from which we get the term *genie*) are invisible spirits made of fire, who were created two thousand years before **Adam.** Islamic thinkers postulated three orders of beings beyond God: angels, jinn, and humanity. The angels, who were created out of light, are closest to God. The jinn, who are intermediate between angels and humanity, inhabit a subtly material or etheric realm. As do human beings, jinn possess intelligence and free will and are thus capable of being saved. For this reason, the Koran sometimes explicitly addresses itself to both humans and jinn. It is said that one night a group of jinn overheard the Prophet reciting the Koran and became believers. The spot where Muhammad later met with the jinn's leaders and accepted their allegiance is the site of the Mosque of the Jinn in Mecca.

Iblis, the Islamic **Satan,** was transformed from an angel into a jinn when he refused God's command that he worship Adam (who was created out of mere clay). Iblis and the other angels who shared his viewpoint were removed from their stations. Iblis and the jinn were exiled from Eden and subsequently became **demons.** (Also included among the outcasts were five of Iblis's sons.) Ejected from the presence of God, these former angels turned to trickery.

An example of a good jinn is the friendly "jinni" (genie) in the *Arabian Nights* who assists Alladin when he rubs his magic lamp. The jinn are also referred to as good spirits in *A Dictionary of Islam,* by Thomas P. Hughes. The entry titled "Genii" states, "The most noble and honorable among the angels are called the Ginn, because they are veiled from the eyes of the other angels on account of their superiority."

Sources:

Davidson, Gustav. *A Dictionary of Angels: Including the Fallen Angels.* 1967. Reprint. New York: Free Press, 1971.

Glassé, Cyril. *The Concise Encyclopedia of Islam.* San Francisco: Harper San Francisco, 1989.

Hughes. Thomas P. *A Dictionary of Islam.* Safat, Kuwait: Islamic Book Publ., 1979.

Ronner, John. *Know Your Angels: The Angel Almanac with Biographies of 100 Prominent Angels in Legend and Folklore, and Much More.* Murfreesboro, Tenn.: Mamre Press, 1993.

Joan of Arc

The French visionary Joan of Arc (ca. 1412–31), also known as the Maid of Orléans, is considered patron saint of France in Christian legend. She called herself Jeanne La Pucelle and used her claims to mystical experience and communion with angels to influence the course of French history in the fifteenth century, inspiring the French army to turn the tide of the Hundred Years' War.

She was a peasant who was born around 1412 in Domrémy-la-Pucelle, a village on the border between Lorraine and France. At age thirteen Joan began to hear a voice from God instructing her to go to the dauphin Charles, the uncrowned Valois king. She was convinced of hav-

JOAN OF ARC

ing been called to drive the English out of France. She eventually took a vow of virginity and prepared herself for the role of prophetic adviser to the king, a type of female mystic popular in the late medieval period.

Soon the voice became three voices, whom she later identified as the saints Catherine of Alexandria and Margaret of Antioch, both known for their heroic virginity, and the archangel **Michael,** protector of the French royal family. To Joan her messages were delivered by normal human beings, who now lived in heaven, except when they were with her. The archangel Michael, in particular, she described as a very gallant gentleman.

Joan established her authority by identifying herself with prophecies about a virgin who would save France and by accurately announcing a French defeat. The garrison captain of the town of Vaucouleurs, who could no longer ignore her, refused to endorse her mission to save France until she was exorcised. Although he was not fully assured, the captain gave her arms and an escort.

She cut her hair short, began wearing male clothing, and, with her companions, made her way through enemy territory, reaching the dauphin's court at Chinon in late February 1429. She claimed that she was sent by God and that she had been accompanied to the castle of Chinon by the archangel Michael and several other angels, some of whom had wings and crowns, and by Saint Catherine and Saint Margaret. Then she went up the steps of the castle to the room of the king, before whom, she declared, an angel bearing a crown did reverence.

Joan's strong belief that only she could save France impressed Charles and his court, though they too moved carefully, requiring an examination for heresy by theologians at Poitiers, who declared her a good Christian. In addition, a physical examination by three matrons certified that she was indeed a virgin. For a woman about to attempt the "miracle" of defeating the English, virginity added an aura of magical power. When Charles eventually allowed Joan to join the army marching to the relief of Orléans, her presence attracted several volunteers. During the battle she was wounded, thus becoming the hero of the day. Upon her suggestion, the army moved on, and by late July the dauphin was crowned King Charles VII at Reims, with Joan at his side.

When, driven by her voices and disobeying the king, her attack on Paris failed, she was captured in a skirmish outside Compiègne. She was accused of heresy and witchcraft by the English, who turned her over to a court of the Inquisition. The court refused to believe that the saints had visited her and maintained that Charles VII's coronation had been a "work of hell," because she had invoked evil spirits. The University of Paris affirmed that Joan was "a woman of **Belial, Satan,** and Behemoth."

She was tried on twelve charges of sorcery. Her trial in Rouen lasted from February 21 to May 28, 1431, and after weeks of unrelenting questioning and being threatened with death by fire, she finally denied her voices and agreed to wear women's clothes. When in prison she claimed that the archangel **Gabriel** had come to her and comforted her. She also claimed that she had asked the archangel Michael and her other voices if she would be burned, and they had told her to wait upon God and he would help her.

On May 31, 1431, Joan was declared a relapsed heretic and was burned at the stake. The executioner, greatly disturbed by her death, claimed her heart refused to burn and that it was found whole in the ashes. Throughout her ordeal, Charles VII, to whom she had delivered the crown of France, declined to come to her aid. In 1920 she was declared a saint and has since been a favorite subject of music and literature.

Sources:

Eliade, Mircea, ed. *Encyclopedia of Religion.* 16 vols. New York: Macmillan, 1987.

Guiley, Rosemary Ellen. *The Encyclopedia of Witches and Witchcraft.* New York: Facts on File, 1988.

Mercatante, Anthony S. *The Facts on File Encyclopedia of World Mythology and Legend.* New York: Facts on File, 1988.

Smith, John Holland. *Joan of Arc.* London: Sidwick & Jackson, 1973.

John the Baptist

John the Baptist—whom the Christian community identified as the prophesied **Elijah,** come to proclaim the imminent advent of the Messiah—is identified as an angel in several ways. All of the synoptic gospels (Matthew, Mark, and Luke), for example, portray John as the "messenger" (*angelos*) predicted in the Book of Malachi by citing Mal. 3:1 ("Behold, I send my messenger to prepare the way before me") in connection with their discussion of John's ministry.

Also, Elijah was transported directly into heaven, where tradition says that he was transformed into the angel **Sandalphon.** Hence if John was Elijah returned, he was also an embodiment of Sandalphon. Perhaps reflecting this angelic identification, or simply because he performed the role of messenger, John the Baptist was traditionally depicted as having wings by the Eastern Orthodox Church.

Sources:

Ferguson, Everett, ed. *Encyclopedia of Early Christianity.* New York: Garland, 1990.

The Illustrated Bible Dictionary. Sydney, Australia: Hodder & Stoughton, 1980.

Judaism

Angels in the traditional sense are prevalent in the great monotheisms: **Zoroastrianism,** Judaism, **Christianity,** and **Islam.** In these faiths, God is such an august and elevated personage that he does not usually involve himself in the day-to-day activities of the world. Instead, he has created a set of spiritual beings—the angels—who carry out his commands and deliver his messages.

Although most accounts of angel history consider Zoroastrianism to be the first religion to have true angels, attendant spiritual beings served Yahweh (God) from the very first biblical narratives, long before Persian religious ideas began to exercise an influence on Judaism. There is, however, some confusion in the earliest books of the Bible about the so-called **angel of the Lord.** In many passages that mention the angel of the Lord, it seems that God himself has appeared. Some scholars have hypothesized that in the original (nonextant) sources, Yahweh was the central actor, with no angel mentioned. According to this line of thinking, later scribes found it difficult to grasp that God himself would confront ordinary human beings face-to-face and thus altered the original stories so that God acted through an intermediary.

Angels are designated by different terms in Hebrew Scriptures. The most common term is *mal'akh,* "messenger," which is sometimes also used with reference to human messengers. (This term was the basis for the choice made by Greek translators—*angelos* means messenger in Greek—as well as the choice for Muslims—the Koranic term for angels is **mala'ika.**) In other places, the angels are called *elohim* (literally, "gods") or, more frequently, *bene'elohim* or *bene'elim* (sons of God). Finally, the Bible also refers to winged beings, such as the **seraphim** and the **cherubim,** which seem to have been adopted more or less directly from near-Eastern mythology.

The Hebrew Bible pictures angels as busy spiritual beings constantly coming and going as they carry out God's directives—as in **Jacob**'s vision of angels ascending and descending a ladder. In the first chapter of the Book of Job, the angels (referred to in Job as the "sons of God"), **Satan** among them, come together "to present themselves before the Lord" (1:6), reporting on what they have done and observed, at what appears to be a regular celestial gathering.

Beyond carrying messages to humanity, God sends his angels to protect or destroy. They also have the function of constantly offering him praise. Only in the last books of Hebrew Scriptures do angels begin to do more than simply worship God and carry out orders, as when the angel of the Lord in Zechariah intercedes with God on behalf of Israel (1:12–13).

Judaism

In Hebrew legend, "angels of pregnancy" are appointed by God to make the newborn male resemble his father to preclude the charge of adultery, which otherwise might be lodged against the mother.

Judaism

According to the Talmud, every Jew is assigned 11,000 guardian angels at birth.

As a general indication of the subsidiary role angels play in most of the Bible, Scripture mentions only two angels by name, **Michael** and **Gabriel.**

The final books of the Hebrew Bible, particularly Daniel, reflect the distinct influence of Persian **angelology.** As a result of several centuries of Persian control of the Middle East, Jews were brought into contact with Zoroastrian religious ideas. Of decisive significance in view of later developments in Judaism's sister religions, Christianity and Islam, was Zoroaster's doctrine of the ongoing struggle between good and evil—a dualistic world view that included war between good and evil angels. Earlier Hebrews had not postulated an evil counterdivinity or devil opposed to Yahweh. In Job, for example, Satan is a member of the heavenly court whose role appears to be that of a prosecuting attorney rather than an enemy of God.

To explain the origin of a devil in traditionally nondualistic Judaism, writers developed new stories, although they were never incorporated into canonical Scripture. These extrabiblical writings explain evil in terms of the revolt or disobedience of God's angels. In one story, Satan declared himself as great as God and led a rebellion of angels against the celestial order. Defeated, he and his followers were tossed out of heaven, and now they perpetually war against God by attempting to ruin the earth, God's creation. A lesser-known story, which is best preserved in the apocryphal **Book of Enoch,** tells how a group of angels lusted after mortal women and fell from grace after leaving their heavenly abode and copulating with them.

In addition to the notion of ongoing spiritual warfare between good and evil, Judaism also adopted the idea of a **final judgment** and resurrection of the dead at the end of time—a time when righteousness will finally triumph. This happy ending will be preceded by an all out war in which the angels of God will defeat Satan and his fallen angels once and for all. These notions particularly characterized the thought of the **Essenes,** a small Jewish sect whose surviving writings, the **Dead Sea Scrolls,** are characterized by an **apocalyptic** emphasis that prophesies a supernatural redemption at the hand of God and his angels, a view they share with the roughly contemporaneous writings of the **Apocrypha** and the Pseudepigrapha.

Israel was annexed by Rome during the first century B.C. Under Roman rule, various Jewish sects proliferated. The pious Pharisees, while believing in angels, did not particularly emphasize them. The Sadducees, a group of older landowners that included many priests, emphasized the authority of the first five books of Hebrew Scripture (the books of Moses) and are said to have rejected the notion of angels. The Essenes withdrew from mainstream Judaism in the mid-second century B.C. and established a monastery on the shores of the Dead Sea at Qumran, where they had a community until it was attacked and destroyed by Roman legions between A.D. 66 and 70.

Beyond the Hebrew Bible (the Christian Old Testament), there are several important bodies of Jewish religious literature in which notions about angels are further developed. The most important of these are contained in the **Talmud.** While attempting to tone down what they viewed as an unhealthy overemphasis on angels in the Apocrypha and the Pseudepigrapha, the talmudic rabbis simultaneously recognized such postbiblical revelations as the division between angels of peace and evil angels and the names of important angels other than Michael and Gabriel, such as **Uriel, Raphael,** and **Metatron.** The talmudic literature also adds much detailed speculation on the nature of angels without changing the fundamental notions that had been developed earlier. Much the same can be said about Jewish mystical speculations, such as those contained in the **Zohar.**

Today, particularly in Reform and Orthodox Judaism, the existence of angels as independent spiritual entities is generally discounted, rather they are viewed as symbolic or poetic or as embodying an earlier world-view no longer relevant. Even Orthodox Jews tend to interpret angels symbolically, without actually denying their ontological reality. Only the most traditional sects, such as the Hasidim, hold to a literal belief in angels.

Sources:

Eliade, Mircea, ed. *Encyclopedia of Religion.* 16 vols. New York: Macmillan, 1987.

Encyclopaedia Judaica. New York: Macmillan, 1971.

Margolies, Morris B. *A Gathering of Angels: Angels in Jewish Life and Literature.* New York: Ballantine, 1994.

Nielsen C., Niels Jr., et al. *Religions of the World.* New York: St. Martin's, 1983.

West, James King. *Introduction to the Old Testament.* New York: Macmillan, 1981.

Jung, Carl Gustav

Although the physical sciences have undermined belief in the concrete reality of heaven, hell, angels, and devils, the psychological discoveries of the last two centuries have given these entities new plausibility as psychic phenomena. Carl Jung, for instance, postulated the existence of a **collective unconscious** and discussed mythology and religion in terms of the "primordial images," or "archetypes," which every human being inherits. Born at Kesswil, Switzerland, Carl Gustav Jung (1875–1961) is considered the originator of analytical psychology. He studied medicine at the University of Basel, Switzerland, and took his M.D. in 1902 at the University of Zurich. Although he was a disciple of Sigmund Freud from 1907 to 1912, Jung's theories and methodology ultimately diverged.

Jung, whose thought was deeply influenced by his own Christian background and commitment to religious humanism, believed that religion represented a fundamental element of the psychotherapeutic process as well as of life, whereas Freud insisted upon an entirely scientific understanding of psychoanalysis. Jung had a much greater interest in religious symbolism than had Freud, and his interest apparently derived from the fact that in his clinical work he found the methods of Freud and of Alfred Adler, although they worked well with patients under thirty-five, were inadequate in dealing with the problems of patients over that age.

His paper on symbols of the libido, which appeared in 1913, marked Jung's break with Freudian theory, and the psychology that emerged focused on the division between conscious and unconscious, and on the vision of the personal unconscious as a branch on the tree of the collective unconscious. According to Jung, the human being could bring unconscious contents into consciousness through a process of individuation, or journey of the soul, called *Heilsweg*. Jung's analytical psychology emphasized the importance in this spiritual journey of archetypal symbols, which had a universal application in human life, as well as individual symbols, appearing in waking or dreaming life. He specified a method called active imagination in which the figures of the unconscious are seen as autonomous living entities of the psyche. Using this method it is possible to approach the archaic mentality from a position of conscious responsibility, acknowledging the unconscious and its personifications, such as demons, spirits, and angels, and seeking to find the appropriate way to respond to them.

After the break with Freud, Jung fell into a period of inner disorder during which he carried out a journey of exploration into his unconscious mind, and published very few works including *Psychology of the Unconscious,* and *VII Sermones ad Mortuos.* Among Jung's other significant works are *The Theory of Psychoanalysis* (1916), *Psychological Types* (1923), *Modern Man in Search of a Soul* (1933), *Psychology and Religion* (1938), *Psychology and Alchemy* (1953), *The Interpretation of Nature and the Psyche* (1955), *Archetypes and the Collective Unconscious* (1959), and *Memories, Dreams, Reflections* (1965).

Jung's focus was always on the psychological aspect of religion. He eschewed the discussion of the ontological questions that all highly developed religions pose, such as questions about the reality of the religious object beyond the psychological phenomenon. God is treated, therefore, simply as "a function of the unconscious, namely, the manifestation of a split-off sum of libido, which has activated the God-image."

Thus when Jung speaks of angels, it is always within the framework of his theory of the psyche. He sees **birds,** for example, as symbolizing spirits and angels. Angels also symbolize mythological births. He associates them with "the rebirth of the phoenix" and remarks: "Divine messengers frequently appear at these mythological births, as can be seen from the use we still make of god-parents." Presumably the stork who, according to an age-old legend, brings the newborn child from the sky, is an angelic messenger from God.

Jung also acknowledges the passage in Genesis (6:2) that relates "the sons of God saw the daughters of men, that they were fair; and they took them wives of all of which they chose." He asserts that the good and rational power ruling the world with wise laws is threatened by the chaotic, primitive force of passion. The libido, as a power transcending consciousness, is by nature demonic, being both God and the Devil. He also says that if evil was destroyed, everything, including God himself, would suffer a major loss. Moreover, he asserts that the human being can draw the gods down into the murk of passion, and that one abandons one's humanity by raising oneself up to the Divine.

Jung further acknowledges the Jewish legend according to which **Adam,** before he knew Eve, had a demon-wife named **Lilith.** Adam forced her to return to him using the help of three angels. Here the motif of the helpful bird is used again. Angels signify an upper, aerial, spiritual triad in conflict with the lower feminine power. For Jung angels are simply one part of an elaborate system of symbolism reflective of the labyrinthine odyssey of the human psyche, not literal spiritual beings existing independently of our perceiving minds.

—*Michela Zonta*

Sources:

Cavendish, Richard, ed. *Encyclopedia of The Unexplained. Magic, Occultism and Parapsychology.* London: Arkana Penguin, 1989.

Hostie, Raymond S. J. *Religion and the Psychology of Jung.* New York: Sheed & Ward, 1957.

Jung, Carl Gustav. *Psychological Types.* London: Routledge, 1933.

———. *Symbols of Transformation.* New York: Harper Torchbooks, 1956.

MacGregor, Geddes. *Angels. Ministers of Grace.* New York: Paragon House, 1988.

Kakabel

Kakabel (star of God), a powerful angel of folklore, is in charge of the stars and **constellations.** Considered by some to be a holy angel, and by others to be a fallen angel, Kakabel commands 365,000 lesser spirits. Kakabel teaches **astrology** to his surrogates.

Sources:

Ginzberg, Louis. *The Legends of the Jews.* 7 vols. Philadelphia: Jewish Publication Society of America, 1954.

Kemuel

According to Louis Ginzberg's *The Legends of the Jews,* Kemuel (assembly of God) is the angelic gatekeeper of heaven who tried to keep Moses from entering when he ascended to receive the Torah from God and take it back to Mount Sinai. Even though Kemuel had twelve thousand angels of destruction to do his bidding, Moses was able to destroy the gatekeeper for this attempted intervention.

Kemuel

Sources:

Davidson, Gustav. *A Dictionary of Angels: Including the Fallen Angels.* New York: Free Press, 1971.

Ginzberg, Louis. *The Legends of the Jews.* 7 vols. Philadelphia: The Jewish Publication Society of America, 1954.

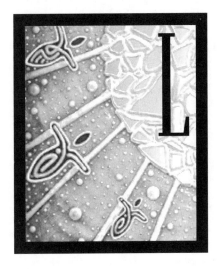

Music is well said to be

the speech of angels.

—Thomas Carlyle, Essays

Lahash

According to historian Louis Ginzberg in *The Legends of the Jews,* Lahash is the angel who, along with Zakun, tried to prevent a prayer by Moses from reaching God. Lahash and Zakun were helped by 184 myriad (1,840,000) spirits in this task but still failed. The punishment meted out to Lahash and Zakun for their interference was sixty lashes of fire.

Sources:

Davidson, Gustav. *A Dictionary of Angels: Including the Fallen Angels.* New York: Free Press, 1971.

Ginzberg, Louis. *The Legends of the Jews.* 7 vols. Philadelphia: Jewish Publication Society of America, 1954.

Lailah

Lailah is the angel of night in Jewish legend. She is in charge of conception and is appointed to guard spirits at their birth. As the story goes, Lailah carries sperm before God, who chooses what type of person will come from it and selects a preexisting soul to be sent to the embryo. An angel stands guard at the woman's womb to make sure the soul does not escape. Perhaps to help the soul for the nine months in the womb, the angel gives it a preview of its coming life, but just before birth the angel fillips the baby's nose and the child forgets its knowledge of the future. One legend states that Lailah fought for **Abraham** when he battled kings; others claim Lailah is a demonic angel.

Sources:

Davidson, Gustav. *A Dictionary of Angels: Including the Fallen Angels.* New York: Free Press, 1971.

Ginzberg, Louis. *The Legends of the Jews.* 7 vols. Philadelphia: Jewish Publication Society of America, 1954.

Margolies, Morris B. *A Gathering of Angels: Angels in Jewish Life and Literature.* New York: Ballantine, 1994.

Lakey, Andy

Artist and humanitarian Andy Lakey became a painter of angels following a miraculous **near-death experience** in 1986. Divinely inspired, Lakey, who had no prior knowledge of artwork or painting, believed he was given the insight into his purpose on earth. Subsequently he vowed to create 2,000 original angel paintings between the years 1990 and 2000.

Lakey's unique style involves a complex painting process that produces high levels of thickness on wood, which creates raised lines that are then washed with shimmering colors to create a highly luminous, intricately woven surface. This innovative style is called "Sensualism." Beyond the apparent visual quality, Lakey's work is especially designed to be tactily enjoyed, especially by those who are visually impaired.

All of Lakey's pieces, which are numbered, share a universal, spiritual quality. His angelic beings embody rounded, soft shapes that exist in fields of circular energy. Some have interpreted the orbs of light as suns, however the artist is loathe to specifically attribute a particular meaning. They could be suns or planets, says Lakey. Whatever the definitive interpretation it is clear that the message invoked is one of love, peace, and hope. This divine sense is summed up by Lakey who explains, "When I began painting, I could feel that the inspiration came from deep within my heart and soul, from the angels themselves. It's still the same today—I feel a power come out of me. It's as though I am tapping into the universe."

Along with the healing powers that his paintings offer to the world, Lakey also gives of himself through charitable contributions. Some of the charities he has benefitted are those that help the visually impaired, children, and battered women. Often those who acquire Lakey's paintings donate them to favorite charities. Among the more well-known of his clients are Peter Jennings, Ed Asner, Princess Margaret, and former president Jimmy Carter. Lakey's paintings may be seen on the walls of many hospitals, clinics, and centers for the blind. His paintings also hang in the Vatican, the Riverside Art Museum, in the homes of Ray Charles, Stevie Wonder, Gloria Estefan, Dudley Moore, and Prince Albert of Monaco, and in more than nineteen galleries throughout the United States.

Eileen Freeman, author of *Touched by Angels,* says of Andy Lakey's work, "His art enables me to feel the inherent power and energy of the angels, their single-mindedness and devotion, without mixing up irrelevant concepts like sex, race, age, culture, and all those other human characteristics we must get past in order to appreciate other representations of angels."

Sources:

Promotional material provided by Fran Clark & Co. Inc., Hunter, New York.

Shaw, Alexandra. "Andy Lakey: Come and Get a Glimpse of Heaven." *Manhattan Arts International* (Spring 1995) :5.

ANDY LAKEY AT WORK IN
HIS CALIFORNIA STUDIO.
(COURTESY FRANCES CLARK)

Language of Angels

Among the various religious traditions and during time periods in which angels have been regarded as significant celestial residents, there has often been speculation about the language angels use when speaking with one another. As one might anticipate, in traditional **Judaism** angels are said to speak Hebrew, in **Islam** they speak Arabic, and in medieval Catholicism it was speculated that angels spoke Latin.

Somewhat similar notions are found elsewhere. In southern Asia, for example, the primary script in which Sanskrit is written is called *devanagari,* which means city (*nagar*) of the gods or angels **(devas).**

Few passages in Scripture refer to the life of angels, although one passage does imply that angel are capable of communication. The Apostle Paul, in 1 Cor. 13:1, says, "I speak with the tongues of men and of angels." Theologians such as St. **Thomas Aquinas** did not interpret this to mean verbal communication, but rather speculated that angels communicated by means of wordless telepathic intuition, called "illumination."

Aquinas further postulated that among the orders of angels there is a distinct hierarchy of communication. Higher angels can enlighten lower angels, however the lower orders cannot reciprocate this enlightenment to their superiors. Lower angels can communication telepathically, but they convey only their wishes or desires. Also, according to the theologian, no angel can move the will of another. (See also **Swedenbörg, Emanuel**)

Sources:

Adler, Mortimer J. *The Angels and Us.* New York: Collier Books, 1982.
Ronner, John. *Know Your Angels: The Angel Almanac with Biographies of 100 Prominent Angels in Legend and Folklore, and Much More.* Murfreesboro, Tenn.: Mamre Press, 1993.
Wilson, Peter Lamborn. *Angels.* New York: Pantheon, 1980.

Leprechauns

Though *leprechaun* has become a general term for all Irish **fairies,** it originally seems to have been reserved for a particular species of *solitary fairies,* who are often depicted as cobblers. Leprechauns are known as tricksters who like to play pranks on humans and are fond of dance, whiskey, and Irish folk music. Some of the folklore associated with the leprechaun is well-known, such as the crock of gold at the end of the rainbow. Various methods, such as an unblinking stare, is supposed to give one power over leprechauns.

Sources:

Briggs, Katharine. *An Encyclopedia of Fairies*. New York: Pantheon, 1976.

McCoy, Edwin. *A Witch's Guide to Faery Folk*. St. Paul, Minn.: Llewellyn, 1994.

Leviathan

The word *leviathan* has come to mean any formidable or monstrous creature. The original Leviathan, however, was a biblical multiheaded sea monster defeated by Yahweh. Unfortunately, the biblical references are brief, as in the following passage:

"Thou didst divide the sea by thy might; thou didst break the heads of the dragons on the waters. Thou didst crush the heads of Leviathan, thou didst give him as food for the creatures of the wilderness (Ps. 74:13–14).

The lengthiest account of the confrontation between God and Leviathan can be found in chapter 41 of Job, though it is unclear how much of Yahweh's challenge to Job refers to an earlier tale and how much is extemporaneous. In any event, the Hebrew tale appears to derive from a Ugarit story in which Baal defeats a seven-headed sea monster with the aid of Mot. Furthermore, this story seems to be a variation of the well-known (to students of mythology) Babylonian myth of Marduk's defeat of the sea monster Tiamat.

Leviathan is also associated with Behemoth, another biblical sea monster. And, because of the association between the Devil and serpents, Leviathan is often identified with **Satan** or designated as one of Satan's demons.

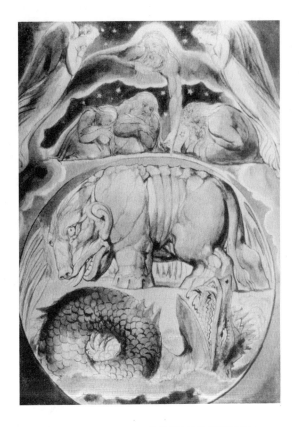

LEVIATHAN AND BEHEMOTH, FROM WILLIAM BLAKE'S ILLUSTRATIONS OF THE *BOOK OF JOB* (1825). (COURTESY ARAS)

Sources:

Davidson, Gustav. *A Dictionary of Angels: Including the Fallen Angels*. 1967. Reprint. New York: Free Press, 1971.

Sykes, Egerton. *Who's Who: Non-Classical Mythology*. New York: Oxford University Press, 1993.

Lilith

The Lilith of Jewish folklore appears to have originally been a **Mesopotamian** night demon with a penchant for destroying children. In

NAKED, WINGED DIVINITY BELIEVED TO BE THE GODDESS LILITH (TERRA-COTTA RELIEF, MESOPOTAMIA CA. 2000–1600 B.C.). (COURTESY ARAS)

the **Talmud** she was the first wife of **Adam** who refused to accept her subservient role. Adam rejected her, and God created Eve as a more obedient helpmate. Lilith is then said to have copulated with **Lucifer** and his demons, producing hundreds of *lilin,* female demons, who became the **succubi** of both Jewish and medieval Christian legend. Because she refused to accept a position subordinate to the first man, contemporary feminists have reinterpreted Lilith's story, identifying her as a strong-minded woman reacting against male oppression.

Sources:

Masello, Robert. *Fallen Angels . . . and Spirits of the Dark.* New York: Perigee, 1994.

Sykes, Egerton. *Who's Who: Non-Classical Mythology.* New York: Oxford University Press, 1993.

Lipika (Lords of Karma)

The Lipika are esoteric (**occult, theosophical**) angels of a very high order that inscribe all world events and personal experiences in the cosmic memory, referred to as the akashic records by occultists. *Lipika,* from the word *lipi* (writing), means, simply, the scribes. Although the name and basic concept derive ultimately from **Hindu** mythology, it has been among Theosophists that the notion of the Lipika has fully blossomed.

Helena Petrovna Blavatsky and other Theosophists have asserted that the occult notion of the Lipika is reflected in esoteric traditions about recording angels writing down a record of human deeds in the Book of Life.

Because everyone's karma is determined by the record of their deeds, the Lipika are also referred to as the Lords of Karma. Karma, the moral law of cause and effect, is often described as an impersonal principle—like the law of gravity—that ensures that every good or bad action is eventually rewarded or punished, either in the present lifetime or in a future incarnation. Certain religious thinkers have not been satisfied with the notion of an impersonal principle, however, and have postulated intelligent agents who regulate the operation of the law of karma. These are the Lipika, or the Lords of Karma, who, according to the Western esoteric tradition, adjust the effects of karma so that individual souls can learn from their mistakes and hence evolve spiritually and become better people.

Sources:

Drury, Nevill. *Dictionary of Mysticism and the Esoteric Traditions.* 2nd ed. Dorset, England: Prism, 1992.

Farthing, Geoffrey A. *Deity, Cosmos, & Man: An Outline of Esoteric Science.* San Diego: Point Loma Publications, 1993.

Southern Centre of Theosophy (Robe, South Australia). *Devas and Men: A Compilation of Theosophical Studies on the Angelic Kingdom.* 1977. Reprint. Adyar, Madras, India: Theosophical Publishing House, 1988.

Literature, Angels in

The angel has been an almost indispensable literary symbol for many poets and writers. In particular, one class of them, the Devil and his legions, has provided a vast source of inspiration. Of all Christian characters, **Satan** has appealed most strongly to the poets of all ages and languages, and it may be said that the Devil, from his minor place in the Holy Scriptures, has dominated most literary forms to the present day. Although writers such as Pedro Calderón, **John Milton,** Johann Goethe, and Lord Byron were fascinated by this character, the most distinguished poet to dedicate a considerable part of his body of work to the court of Satan was no doubt **Dante Alighieri.** At the core of Dante's *Divina Commedia* is Satan, who dwells in the apex of hell and a multitude of angels who reside in his Paradiso.

Belief in the Devil was traditionally accompanied by belief in witchcraft, widely considered a manifestation of diabolical activity, especially during the **Middle Ages.** Many allusions to good angels assisting in human warfare against demonic powers can be found in the secular literature of the period. An example appears in scene IV of **William Shakespeare**'s *Hamlet* when the young prince of Denmark, upon seeing his father's ghost, exclaims, "Angels and ministers of grace defend us!" Angels are again called upon in the final scene of *Hamlet* when Horatio, holding the dead prince, offers this farewell: "Good night, sweet prince, / And flights of angels sing thee to thy rest!"

Angels all but disappeared from literature with the passing of the Middle Ages, but one can witness their resurrection from the humanistic Renaissance, and their persistence from the sixteenth century down to the present day. However, Satan is not a character that dominates the literature of the Renaissance, in part due to the period's reaction against medieval thought.

One of the most significant post-medieval angelogogies can be found in the writings of **Emanuel Swedenbörg** (1688–1772), who devoted himself to studies arising out of what he claimed to be persistent communications from angels and other agencies in a spiritual world. He used the concept of angels to make the nature and vitalities of the spiritual world come alive to a society that had lost sight of the reality of the spiritual realm. According to Swedenbörg, angels are realities far superior to humankind, and are able to communicate wisdom because they are capable of receiving it. In his writings about the angelic world, he asserts that angelic writing is very different from human writing. They express affections with vowels, whereas with consonants they express the ideas springing from the affections. In angelic language a few words can express what it takes pages of human writing to say. He also asserts that angels have no personal power since they are only agents of God, and if an angel doubted the source of his power he would instantly become so weak that he could not resist a single evil spirit.

The works of Swedenbörg had a significant impact on the mystical poet **William Blake** (1757–1827). Angels literally abound in Blake's writings and drawings. Blake, who was probably more familiar with reincarnation and the karmic principal than most Englishmen of his day, regarded angels as the real forces behind the lives of mortal men and women. He was preoccupied with angels, both celestial and infernal, and the struggle between spirits of light and dark took on a vivid reality.

Other poets similarly regarded angels as very real forces and called upon them frequently in a number of literary works. Robert Browning, for example, in the poem *The Guardian Angel,* implores his angel to take charge of the creative process; Robert Burton, in *The Anatomy of Melancholy,* affirms the bit of folklore that each individual has a good and a bad angel; and Henry Wadsworth Longfellow often espoused on the language spoken by the angels.

The romantic poet Lord Byron was inspired to write this bit of whimsy: "The angels all were singing out of tune, / And hoarse from having little else to do, / Excepting to wind up the sun and moon, / Or curb a runaway young star or two."

In Victorian literature it was very common to find the use of angels as intermediaries between God and man. An example is a poem by Leigh Hunt called *Abou ben Adhem,* in which the main character wakens one night to find an angel writing in a book of gold the names of all those who love God.

The twentieth century found the German poet Ranier Maria Rilke embracing angels in his Duinesian Elegies, particularly in the first and second of them. According to Rilke, these celestial creatures represented the most sublime expression of beings who are able to ascend to God. He describes angels as:

> Successful first creatures, favorites of creation,
> high mountain ranges, dawn-reddened peaks
> of all creation, pollen of the flowering
> Godhead,
> junctures of light, avenues, stairways, thrones,
> spaces of essence, shields of ecstasy, storms
> of tumultuously enraptured emotion and
> suddenly, singly,
> mirrors which reconcentrate once again in their
> countenances their own outflowing beauty.

Angels also worked their way into longer literary works. Many stories about angels, Paradise, and divine intervention have been written by some of the major writers of this century and the turn of the last. Most of these stories are characterized by the intellectual skepticism and sense of spiritual dislocation typical of the modern Western point of view. However, the majority of great modern writers have been fascinated with the possibility that a moral order and intelligence lies hidden in the mysterious confusion around them.

G. B. Shaw (*Aerial Football: The New Game*), creates a chaotic Church of England Heaven where the playing fields of the Lord and of Eton can hardly be distinguished; John Steinbeck, in his *Saint Katy the Virgin,* canonizes an erstwhile, very bad pig; the hero of O'Henry's *The Cop and the Anthem* is arrested just at the moment he has resolved to go straight, and Mark Twain's good little boy comes to a loud, bad end in the *The Story of the Good Little Boy.*

In science fiction, Ray Bradbury's astronaut missionary asks what will constitute sin in other galaxies (*The Fire Balloons*) and Isaac Asimov in *The Last Trump* foresees some knotty problems when the Day of Resurrection arrives.

In other stories, E. M. Forster (*Mr. Andrews*) depicts a Christian and a Muslim unhappy with their respective Heavens; Edgar Allan Poe in *The Angel of the Odd* presents a hilarious angel in the shape of an angry cask with a thick German accent; in Gabriel Garcia Marquez's *A Very Old Man With Enormous Wings,* angels play the traditional role of messengers who bring, however, very contemporary messages. In Bernard Malamud's *Angel Levine,* a devout Jew is sent a young black angel who hangs out in Harlem until the Jew can overcome his racism.

Literature:

Number of books about angels

published last year: 150

The archetypical figure of the angel represented as the mysterious stranger who arrives to effect a change of heart is utilized by Robert Louis Stevenson (*Markheim*), and Philip Van Doren Stern (*The Greatest Gift*), while Arthur Machen's *The Bowmen* represents the genesis of all rumors and legends of the **Angels of Mons** in World War II.

Leo Tolstoy's (*The Three Hermits*) three ragged holy men cannot remember the words of the Lord's Prayer, but they can run on water in pursuit of the Bishop's ship. Franz Kafka, in his *The City Coat of Arms,* summing up his agnostic position, tells how humanity's plans to build a tower to heaven are put off from one generation to another until finally the idea becomes senseless.

Among other modern stories about angels and divine intervention are Oscar Wilde's *The Selfish Giant,* H. G. Wells's *The Man Who Could World Miracles,* Paul Gallico's *The Small Miracle,* Wilbur Daniel Steele's *The Man Who Saw Through Heaven,* and Flannery O'Connor's *Revelation.*

Sources:

Cacciari, Massimo. *The Necessary Angel.* Albany: State University of New York Press, 1994.

Chessman, Harriet Scott, ed. *Literary Angels.* New York: Fawcett Columbine, 1994.

Giovetti, Paola. *Angels: The Role of Celestial Guardians and Beings of Light.* York Beach, Maine: Samuel Weiser, 1993.

Grey, M. Cameron, ed. *Angels and Awakenings. Stories of the Miraculous by Great Modern Writers.* New York: Doubleday, 1980.

Rudwin, Maximilian. *The Devil in Legend and Literature.* Chicago: The Open Court Publishing Co., 1931.

Lucifer

The name Lucifer (Light Giver) refers to the planet Venus—the brightest object in the sky apart from the Sun and Moon—when appearing as the morning star. Lucifer has been erroneously equated with the fallen angel **Satan,** because of a misreading of a scriptural passage that applied to Nebuchadnezzar, king of Babylon, who in his glory and pomp had aspired to exalt himself to the level of God, as reported in Isaiah 14: "How art thou fallen from heaven, O Lucifer, son of the morning." Just as the brilliancy of Lucifer surpasses that of all other stars in the firmament, so the splendor of the king of Babylon surpassed that of all other Oriental monarchs.

The Babylonians and Assyrians personified the morning star as Belit and Istar, respectively. Others have speculated that the phrase "son of the morning" might refer to the crescent moon. Others argue for an identification with the planet Jupiter.

A WINGED, HORNED LUCIFER BEGINS HIS REIGN OVER THE SOULS OF THE DAMNED. ILLUSTRATION BY JOHN BAPTIST MEDINA FOR MILTON'S *PARADISE LOST*, (LONDON, 1688).

The Devil acquired the name Lucifer when the early Christian theologians Tertullian and St. Augustine identified him with the falling star in the passage from Isaiah. They made this association because the Devil was formerly a great **archangel** who rebelled against God and was tossed out of heaven. The legend of the rebellion and expulsion of Lucifer, as formulated by Jewish and Christian writers, describes Lucifer as the chief in the hierarchy of heaven, and as preeminent among all created beings in beauty, power, and wisdom. To this "anointed cherub" was apparently allotted power and dominion over the earth; and even after his fall and exclusion from his old domain, he still seems to retain some of his power and ancient title to sovereignty.

According to the writings of the rabbis and church fathers, his sin was pride, which was an act of complete egoism and pure malice, in that he loved himself to the exclusion of all else and without the excuse of ignorance, error, passion, or weakness of will. Other versions hold that his audacity went so far as to attempt to seat himself on the Great Throne.

In the medieval mysteries, Lucifer, as the governor of the heavens, is seated next to the Eternal. As soon as the Lord leaves his seat, Lucifer, swelling with pride, sits down on the throne of heaven. The indignant archangel **Michael** takes up arms against him and finally succeeds in driving him out of heaven down into the dark and dismal dwelling reserved for him for all eternity.

In heaven the archangel's name had been Lucifer; on earth it was Satan. The angels who joined his rebellion were also expelled from heaven and became the demons, of whom Lucifer is lord. Reference to Lucifer as the day-star occurs in **Ezekiel**'s prediction of the coming downfall of the king of Tyre. Here Lucifer is an angel, blazing with brilliant jewels, who was in Eden, the garden of God, walking up and down among the "stones of fire."

Lucifer may have been the hero of an earlier story in which the morning star tries to steal the role of the Sun but is defeated. This story is derived from the observation that the morning star is the last star proudly to defy the sunrise. It has also been suggested that the story is another version of the fall of **Adam** and his expulsion from Eden.

The name Lucifer was also applied to Satan by St. Jerome, writing in the fourth century, and other church fathers, in commenting on Luke 10:18: "I beheld Satan as lightning fall from heaven." The name Lucifer is applied by **Milton** to the demon of sinful pride in *Paradise Lost*. In Christopher Marlowe's play *Doctor Faustus* and in **Dante**'s *The Divine Comedy,* Lucifer is the king of hell.

Lucifer is the eponymous principal character of an epic poem by the seventeenth-century Dutch author Joost van den Vondel. He is the main character in the mystery play *The Tragedy of Man* (1861), by the Hungarian poet and dramatist Imre Madách. Lucifer is also the name used by **William Blake** in his illustrations to Dante's work. George Meredith refers to Prince Lucifer in his sonnet "Lucifer in Starlight," and Edmund Spenser describes him as "the brightest angel, even the Child of Light" in "An Hymne of Heavenly Love."

Sources:

Cavendish, Richard. *Man, Myth & Magic: The Illustrated Encyclopedia of Mythology, Religion and the Unknown.* New York: Marshall Cavendish, 1995.

Giovetti, Paola. *Angels: The Role of Celestial Guardians and Beings of Light.* Translated by Toby McCormick. York Beach, Maine: Samuel Weiser, 1993.

The Illustrated Bible Dictionary. Leicester, England: InterVarsity Press, 1980.

Rudwin, Maximilian. *The Devil in Legend and Literature.* Chicago: Open Court Publishing, 1931.

Lunar Mansions

Traditional cultures attributed great significance to the phases of the Moon, particularly to the waxing and waning cycles. Our seven-day week is derived from the ancient custom of further dividing up the lunar month according to new moon, first quarter, full moon, and last quarter. The lunar mansions represent a refinement of this tendency, subdividing the Moon's phases according to its day-to-day increase or decrease. With respect to traditional angel lore, the twenty-eight lunar mansions are associated with twenty-eight different angels.

For example, according to a seventeenth-century manuscript about magic in the British Museum, the fourth mansion (fourth day of the lunar cycle following the new moon) "destroys and hinders buildings, fountains, wells, gold mines . . ." (McLean, p. 127). One might thus anticipate that the angel ruling the fourth mansion would have some connections with these matters. According to a source cited in Gustav Davidson's *Dictionary of Angels,* the angel ruling the fourth mansion is Azariel, a Talmudic angel said to govern the waters of the earth. If we think in terms of the waters *under* the earth (as would a biblically informed scholar), it is easy to see how groundwater might "hinder" certain buildings, mines, and so forth.

To choose another example, the ninth mansion "destroys harvests and travellers and makes discord amongst men" (McLean, p. 128). The ruling angel of this mansion is Barbiel, an underworld angel and thus seemingly related to ninth-mansion matters.

Sources:

Davidson, Gustav. *A Dictionary of Angels: Including the Fallen Angels.* 1967. Reprint. New York: Free Press, 1971.

McLean, Adam, ed. *A Treatise on Angel Magic.* Grand Rapids, Mich.: Phanes Press, 1989.

Saints, and heroes who
die in battle, wise kings,
and hermits, were there
visible by thousands,
angels by thousands,
heavenly singers, like to
the sun in glory.

—Mahabharata,

ca. 800 B.C.

Magic, Invocations, and Prayers

Ceremonial magic and folklore traditions that utilize spells and talismans have long been called upon to supposedly tap the power of angels. For instance, the casting of circles for protection is an ancient practice that is used by magicians as a means of keeping at bay negative energies and entities. During the Western medieval period, for example, circles were drawn on the floor around the seriously ill and around newborns and their mothers to protect them from demonic forces.

A standard part of casting a circle involves invoking the directional powers. Traditionally, the four principal **archangels** were associated with the four **directions: Raphael** rules the East, **Michael** rules the South, **Gabriel** the West, and **Uriel** the North. When a magician casts a circle, the four angelic powers are invoked from each of the four directions. Invoking the directional energies may take place while the circle is being drawn, or as a separate step in the operation.

As the magician formally begins casting the circle he or she faces one of the cardinal directions (usually the East) at the perimeter of the circle, extends a ritual instrument (e.g., a wand or sword), and begins to draw an imaginary circle in the air while moving to the right. The magician continues slowly around the perimeter in a clockwise direction until reaching the starting point, thus completing and closing the circle. When the directional angels are invoked during this operation, the magician pauses at each of the cardinal points and invokes, in succession, the archangel of the East, the archangel of the South, the archangel of the West, and the archangel of the North. The invocation may be complex, or it may be something as simple as "May the archangel Raphael protect me from all evil approaching from the East" (substituting the other archangels and directions at the other cardinal points). At the end of the ceremony the casting process is reversed; each of the directional powers is banished as the magician moves counterclockwise.

Some conjurations sound more like prayers than magic, as in the "Conjurations of the Good Spirits" found in Gustav Davidson's *Dictionary of Angels:*

> O you glorious and benevolent angels, Urzla, Zlar, Larzod, Artal, who are the four angels of the East, I invoke you, adjure and call you forth to visible apparition. . . . (p. 357)

By way of contrast, Davidson also includes spells with less socially desirable ends, such as the "Death Incantation":

> I call thee, Evil Spirit, Cruel Spirit, Merciless Spirit; I call thee who sitiest in the cemetery and takest away healing from man. Go and place a knot in (N . . .'s) head, in his eyes, in his tongue, in his windpipe, and put poisonous water in his belly. If you do not go and put water in his belly, I shall send against you the evil angels Puziel, Guziel, Psdiel, Prsiel. . . . (p. 358)

This kind of magical angel lore is often dismissed by contemporary angel watchers who view angels as helping spirits who should not be manipulated. And, while perhaps still a living tradition to practitioners of ceremonial magic, it has all but disappeared at the level of popular folklore.

Sources:

Davidson, Gustav. *A Dictionary of Angels: Including the Fallen Angels.* 1967. New York: Free Press, 1971.
Cavendish, Richard. *The Black Arts.* New York: Capricorn Books, 1967.
Guiley, Rosemary Ellen. *The Encyclopedia of Witches and Witchcraft.* New York: Facts on File, 1989.

Mala'ika

Mala'ika is the Islamic term for angel. Like the Greek term **angelos,** *mala'ika* means "messenger," referring to one of the chief functions of angels—carrying messages between humans and God. Islamic thinkers postulated three orders of beings beyond God: angels, **jinn,** and humanity. The angels, who were created out of light, are closest to God. The jinn, who are intermediate between angels and humanity, inhabit a subtly material or etheric realm and were created out of fire. Finally, humanity was created out of clay.

Sources:
The Encyclopedia of Islam. Vol. 6. Leiden, Netherlands. E. J. Brill, 1978.
Glassé, Cyril. *The Concise Encyclopedia of Islam.* San Francisco: Harper San Francisco, 1989.

Malik

According to the Koran, Malik is the wicked angel who guards hell. He is aided by nineteen other angel guards (*sbires* or *zabayniya*). When the sinful residents of hell beg Malik for help, he tells them that they must stay in hell forever because they denied the truth when it was once showed to them. Malik makes life even worse for them by heating up the fires and making jokes.

The only relief comes for the Muslim sinners in hell, who can escape such treatment by reciting "Allah, the Compassionate, the Merciful." Malik knows that these true believers will one day be freed from hell by **Muhammad.**

Sources:
Davidson, Gustav. *A Dictionary of Angels: Including the Fallen Angels.* 1967. Reprint. New York: Free Press, 1971.
Glassé, Cyril. *The Concise Encyclopedia of Islam.* San Francisco: Harper San Francisco, 1989.
Ronner, John. *Know Your Angels: The Angel Almanac with Biographies of 100 Prominent Angels in Legend and Folklore, and Much More.* Murfreesboro, Tenn.: Mamre Press, 1993.

Mammon

In folklore, Mammon is a fallen angel, residing in hell as the Demon of Avarice who personifies greed and lust for money. In *Paradise Lost,* **John Milton** depicts Mammon as forever looking downward, at Heaven's golden pavement, rather than up at God. After the **War in Heaven,** when Mammon is relegated to hell, he is the one who finds underground precious metal that the demons use to build Pandemonium, their capital city.

In the *Dictionnaire Infernal* by De Plancy, Mammon is noted as hell's ambassador to England. He is equated with **Lucifer, Satan,** and Nebuchadnezzar. Gregory of Nyssa also interpreted Mammon to be a name for **Beelzebub.**

In the Bible, Mammon is quite hostile to God. The word *mammon* comes originally from Jesus' declaration in the Gospels: "No man can be a slave to two masters; he will hate one and love the other; he will be loyal to one and despise the other. You cannot serve both God and mammon [greed for worldly riches]" (Matt. 6:24; Luke 16:13).

Sources:

Davidson, Gustav. *A Dictionary of Angels: Including the Fallen Angels.* 1967. Reprint. New York: Free Press, 1971.

De Plancy, Collin. *Dictionnaire Infernal.* 4th ed. Bruxelles: Chez Tous Les Libraires, 1845.

Ronner, John. *Know Your Angels: The Angel Almanac with Biographies of 100 Prominent Angels in Legend and Folklore, and Much More.* Murfreesboro, Tenn.: Mamre Press, 1993.

Man Clothed in Linen

A "man clothed in linen" is referred to in Ezekiel chapters 9 and 10, and in Daniel 10 and 12. God appeared to the prophet **Ezekiel** to bring to his attention all of the abominations of the Israelites. In his anger, God told Ezekiel that he had appointed executioners to punish Jerusalem. According to Ezekiel,

> Then I saw six men approaching from the road that leads to the upper northern gate, each carrying a battle-axe, one man among them dressed in linen, with pen and ink at his waist; and they halted by the altar of bronze. (Ezek. 9:2)

God called to the man in linen with pen and ink at his side and told him to go through the city of Jerusalem and put a mark on the foreheads of those who groaned and lamented over the abominations practiced there. God then told the men with battle-axes to follow the man clothed in linen through the city and to kill all of the people—men, women and children—not so marked. The man clothed in linen returned to God and reported that he had done what was commanded.

The Lord said to the man dressed in linen,

> Come in between the circling wheels under the cherubim, and take a handful of the burning embers lying among the cherubim; then toss them over the city. (Ezek. 10:2)

A cherub took some fire and handed it to the man clothed in linen, who received it and went out.

According to Daniel, he was on the banks of the Tigris River when:

> I looked up and saw a man clothed in linen with a belt of gold from Ophir round his waist. His body gleamed like topaz, his face shone like lightning, his eyes flamed like torches, his arms and feet sparkled like a disc of bronze; and when he spoke his voice sounded like the voice of a multitude. (Dan. 10:5,6)

Daniel was not alone on the river, but he was the only one who saw this vision. He became weak and fell prostrate on the ground in a trance.

> Suddenly a hand grasped me and pulled me up on to my hands and knees. He said to me, "Daniel, man greatly beloved, attend to the words I am speaking to you and stand up where you are, for I am now sent to you." (Dan. 10:10,11)

Daniel stood up trembling. The "man," probably the angel **Gabriel,** told Daniel not to be afraid and said that Daniel's prayers had been heard and that he had come in answer to them. The angel said that he had been battling the angel prince of the kingdom of Persia and that **Michael,** the **guardian angel** of Israel, had come to his aid. The angel advised Daniel that he was there to explain the fate of his people in days to come.

While the angel spoke to Daniel, Daniel hung his head and was unable to speak. When the angel touched Daniel's lips his speech returned. The angel touched him again to restore his strength and told him not to be afraid, that all would be well with him, and to be strong. The angel proceeded to explain to Daniel historical events that would unfold in the following three and a half years in the kingdoms of Persia, Greece, and Egypt. These events would culminate in a time of great distress from which Daniel and his people would be delivered.

Linen was a ritually clean cloth worn by those in the immediate service of God, by priests in the temple, and by angels in heaven. It has been suggested that the man clothed in linen was not Gabriel at all, but the nameless **angel of peace.** He has also been associated with the heavenly scribe, identified as **Enoch.**

Sources:

Davidson, Gustav. *A Dictionary of Angels: Including the Fallen Angels.* New York: Free Press, 1967.

Gaster, Theodore. *Myth, Legend, and Custom in the Old Testament.* New York: Harper & Row, 1969.

The Illustrated Bible Dictionary. Sydney, Australia: Hodder & Stoughton, 1980.

MacGregor, Geddes. *Angels: Ministers of Grace*. New York: Paragon House, 1988.

Manna

Manna is the food of angels. During the biblical Exodus the Israelites feared that they had escaped Egypt only to starve to death in the wilderness. During the second month of their journey God promised Moses that his people would have bread in plenty.

> . . . in the morning a fall of dew lay all around [the camp]. When the dew was gone, there in the wilderness, fine flakes appeared, fine as hoar-frost on the ground. When the Israelites saw it, they said to one another, "What is that?," because they did not know what it was. Moses said to them, "That is the bread which the Lord has given you to eat." (Exod. 16:13–15)

Manna is Hebrew and means "What is this?" Biblical scholars say that a nourishing substance excreted by plant lice found on low tamarisk shrubs in the Sinai desert is similar to the description of manna found in the Bible. These excretions fall to the ground in the form in drops, and harden into grains that can be ground into flour and made into edible bread.

A further example of food from the angels can be found in First Kings, chapter 19. The story is of **Elijah**'s forty days in the wilderness, during which he was nourished by food and water delivered to him by an angel:

> He lay down under the bush and while he slept, an angel touched him and said, "Rise and eat." He looked, and there at his head was a cake baked on hot stones, and a pitcher of water. He ate and drank and lay down again. The angel of the Lord came again and touched him a second time, saying, "Rise and eat; the journey is too much for you." He rose and ate and drank and, sustained by this food, he went on for forty days and forty nights to Horeb, the mount of God.

Sources:

The Illustrated Bible Dictionary. Sydney, Australia: Hodder and Stoughton, 1980.

The New Catholic Encyclopedia. Vol. 9. Reprint. Washington, D.C.: Catholic University Press of America, 1981.

Wilson, Peter Lamborn. *Angels.* New York: Pantheon Books, 1980.

Mara

Mara is the Buddhist **Satan.** His name comes from a root meaning "to die." Although **Buddhism** has hell worlds, the real "hell" of Buddhism is the cycle of death and rebirth (reincarnation) in which human beings are bound, and the ultimate goal of Buddhism is liberation from this cycle. Mara's aim is not so much to draw people into hell, but rather to keep them in bondage to the cycle of reincarnation.

The best-known story involving Mara is the tale of his attempt to prevent the Buddha from achieving enlightenment. According to the legend, as the Buddha was on the brink of nirvana, Mara sent beautiful, tempting, heavenly women (Buddhist **apsaras**) to distract his attention. The Buddha was unmoved by passion, so Mara changed tact and tried frightening him with ferocious **demons.** The Buddha was still undisturbed, and Mara finally challenged his right to liberation. In response, the Buddha is said to have called the earth as his witness, whose response was so powerful that it frightened away Mara and his hordes. That very night, the Buddha achieved enlightenment.

Sources:

Conze, Edward. *Buddhist Thought in India.* 1962. Reprint. Ann Arbor: University of Michigan Press, 1967.

Ronner, John. *Know Your Angels: The Angel Almanac with Biographies of 100 Prominent Angels in Legend and Folklore, and Much More.* Murfreesboro, Tenn.: Mamre Press, 1993.

Mary

From her status as a lowly handmaiden in the early Christian community, Mary, the mother of Jesus, grew in popularity until by the early **Middle Ages** she surpassed her son as a subject for piety. As a compassionate intercessor between God and humanity, Mary played a role that in certain ways resembled that of angels. This link seems to have been at least partially responsible for her promotion to "queen of angels" by the ninth century. In her role as ruler of the angels, Mary is the source of the name of the city of Los Angeles (The Angels), whose Spanish founders named their new settlement Nuestra Senora, la Reina de los Angeles (Our Lady, the Queen of the Angels).

Mary has been countlessly depicted by artists throughout the centuries—often represented in the company of angels. The various Marionic legends, in particular, have served as popular themes.

The first legend, the Annunciation (**Gabriel**'s announcement to Mary that she would bear the Messiah), has been a particularly favored

THE NATIVITY IN JEAN MANSEL'S *LES FLEURES DES HISTOIRES* (CA. 1455–60). (COURTESY ARAS)

THE ANNUNCIATION (BENVENUTO DI GIOVANNI, SINALUNGA, SAN BERNARDINO, 1470). (COURTESY ARAS)

DETAIL OF THE *ASSUMPTION OF THE VIRGIN* BY TITIAN (FRARI CHURCH, VENICE, 1516–18). (COURTESY ARAS)

subject, and is one of the eleven scenes of the Bible collectively known as **The Acts of the Holy Angels.**

Information about the birth of Jesus Christ is reported to a certain extent only in the Gospels of Matthew and Luke. Luke interweaves the story of Jesus' birth with the account of the birth of **John the Baptist,** whose parents were Zechariah and Elizabeth (a cousin of Mary's). According to Luke, the angel Gabriel announced the birth of John to Zechariah even before conception took place. Since both he and his wife were very old, Zechariah was highly skeptical, and for this reason he was struck mute.

When Elizabeth was six months pregnant, the same angel visited Mary and announced that she too would give birth to a son by the **Holy Spirit.** The source of this material may have been the followers of John the Baptist, and if so, the annunciation originally came to Elizabeth rather than to Mary. This would explain how Elizabeth knows the name of Mary's child.

The heavenly actor again is Gabriel, and the appearance occurs in Nazareth, a town in Galilee. According to Luke (1:26–38):

> In the sixth month, God sent the angel Gabriel to Nazareth, a town in Galilee, to a virgin pledged to be married to a man named Joseph, a descendant of David. The virgin's name was Mary. The angel went to her and said, "Greetings, you who are highly favored! The Lord is with you." Mary was greatly troubled at his words and wondered what kind of greeting this might be. But the angel said to her, "Do not be afraid, Mary, you have found favor with God. You will be with child and give birth to a son, and you are to give him the name Jesus. He will be great and will be called the Son of the Most High. The Lord God will give him the throne of his father David, and he will reign over the house of Jacob forever; his kingdom will never end."

Some sources add the phrase "Blessed are you among women," which has contributed to the formulation of the "Ave Maria."

The mission of Gabriel is to announce to Mary that she will bear a son, whose name shall be Jesus, the Greek form of the ancient Semitic name Joshua, meaning "the Lord is salvation." When the angel breaks into song, the main theme surrounds the messianic role of the promised child, who will inherit the kingdom of David, and will fulfill the Jewish hope of the reestablishment of the Davidic reign, the resulting kingdom being eternal.

In earlier depictions, Mary is usually the submissive recipient of Gabriel's tidings. After the fourteenth century, however, Mary equals the stature of her angelic host. Gabriel, who traditionally is pictured holding a scepter, instead holds a lily, which becomes the symbol for Mary's purity, or a scroll bearing her good news.

Later in Luke Mary and Joseph travel to Bethlehem to pay the tax decreed by Caesar Augustus. The journey to Bethlehem is an ancient motif dating back to the early Church. The throne of the Roman emperor Maximilian in Ravenna depicts an obviously pregnant Mary seated on a donkey being led by an angel.

The second Marionic Legend surrounds the Nativity of Christ. While in Bethlehem Mary gives birth, and because she and Joseph can find "no room in the inn" she wraps Jesus in swaddling clothes and lays him in a manger. The Nativity of Christ is one of the oldest themes in the New Testament, as is the Adoration of the Magi:

> And there were in the same country shepherds abiding in the field, keeping watch over their flock by night. And, lo, the angel of the Lord came upon them, and the glory of the Lord shone round about them: and they were sore afraid. And the angel said unto them, "Fear not: for, behold, I bring you good tidings of great joy, which shall be to all people. For unto you is born this day in the city of David a Saviour, which is Christ the Lord." And suddenly there was with the angel a multitude of the heavenly host praising God. . . . (Luke 2:8–13)

This legend has been represented in mosaics in Bethlehem's Church of the Nativity (fourth century). The Virgin, sitting or reclining on a mattress, Joseph sitting, and Jesus in the cradle were joined after the sixth century by shepherds and magi bearing gifts. The scene was depicted in Byzantine churches because the Nativity of Christ is one of the major feast days of the Eastern Church. From the fourteenth century on, the Adoration of the Child became the most sacred representation in the West. In this representation, the Virgin kneels before the child, and there are often adoring angels hovering above the scene, or like the Virgin, kneeling before him.

The third Marionic Legend is the Dormition and Funeral of the Blessed Virgin. The various episodes of the dormition (death resembling sleep) of Mary are inspired by apocryphal accounts. In *Legends of the Madonna* (1903) Anna Brownell Jameson recounts an oriental legend in which Michael has cut off the hands of a "wicked" Jewish high priest who has attempted to overturn the funeral bier of the deceased Mary; at the intercession of St. Peter, however, the hands of the "audacious Jew" were reattached to his arms.

Attending angels are found in sacred art depicting the dormition of Mary. The annunciation of her death is made by Gabriel, or more often by **Michael** the **psychopomp** in his role as angel of the final reckoning and the weigher of souls. *Legends of the Madonna* contains a sketch by Fra Filippo Lippi showing Michael kneeling and offering a taper to Mary as he announces her approaching death. The earliest preserved monument to Mary's annunciation, a fresco in S. Mario de Gradellis, shows a rare instance in which Christ appears to his aged mother, who is stretched out in bed. The Apostles appear in large-scale compositions of the tenth century and later. They are positioned on clouds singly or in small groups and are usually escorted by angels. (This scene is rarely found in Western art.)

The Death of Our Lady or the Dormition is a major theme in Byzantine iconography, found in all churches celebrating the Great Feasts. The event is also depicted on artifacts. On tenth-century carvings Mary is shown reclining and surrounded by the apostles, with Peter censing her. Christ stands behind her, holding aloft her soul in the form of a doll swaddled in white, as one or two angels descend from heaven to receive her.

The fourth Marionic Legend, which includes the Resurrection and Assumption (the taking of the Virgin to heaven), is rarely treated in early art. The scene of the disciples finding her tomb empty on the third day does not commonly appear until the twelfth or thirteenth century in Western art. As Mary rises from the tomb she is assisted by angels.

The Assumption is a the more commonly held, and the most widely depicted of the latter two legends. A beatific Mary is usually depicted rising to heaven on a cloud borne by a multitude of angels. This scene is countlessly represented throughout Italian art in particular.

Sources:

Ferguson, Everett, ed. *Encyclopedia of Early Christianity.* Vol. 846 of the Garland Reference Library of the Humanities. New York: Garland, 1990.

Laymon, Charles M. *The Interpreter's One-Volume Commentary on the Bible.* New York: Abingdon Press, 1971.

The New Catholic Encyclopedia. Vol. 1. Reprint. Washington, D.C.: Catholic University Press of America, 1981.

Tyson, Joseph B. *The New Testament and Early Christianity.* New York: Macmillan Publishing, 1984.

Mastema

Mastema (Hebrew, "animosity"), also spelled Mansemat, is "the father of all evil, yet subservient to God," according to the **Book of**

Jubilees of the Old Testament **Apocrypha,** wherein Mastema is described as the Angel of Adversity. Elsewhere, Mastema is referred to as the Accusing Angel.

Mastema works for God by tempting mankind and serving as an executioner. He commands many **demons,** evil spirits born of the dead bodies of giants that were the offspring of fallen angels and mortal earth women. According to one legend, after the Flood, God intended to comply with Noah's request to lock away all of the evil spirits underground. Mastema was able to convince God it would be wise to allow some of the demons to continue their work, as sinful mortals still needed to be kept in line and have their faith tested at times. God agreed to allow one-tenth of the demons to carry on their work under Mastema's supervision.

There are other references to Mastema, as in Exod. 4:24, where he tries to kill Moses. It is also said that Mastema assisted the Egyptian wizards against Moses and Aaron when these Israelites presented themselves before the pharaoh to display their talent at feats of magic.

Sources:

Davidson, Gustav. *A Dictionary of Angels: Including the Fallen Angels.* 1967. Reprint. New York: Free Press, 1971.

Godwin, Malcolm. *Angels: An Endangered Species.* New York: Simon and Schuster, 1990.

Ronner, John. *Know Your Angels: The Angel Almanac with Biographies of 100 Prominent Angels in Legend and Folklore, and Much More.* Murfreesboro, Tenn.: Mamre Press, 1993.

Melchisedek

Melchisedek (the god Zedek is my king) is also known as Melchizedec, and Melch-Zadok. **Dionysius the Areopagite** referred to Melchisedek as the hierarch most beloved of God, whereas pseudo-Tertullian mentions him as a celestial virtue of great grace whose function in heaven is like the one Christ has on earth.

King of righteousness, Melchisedek is also mentioned in the Old and New Testaments, where he is the fabled priest-king of Salem (the ancient name of Jerusalem) and the one to whom **Abraham** gave tithes. The meeting of Abraham and Melchisedec is represented in a woodcut in the great Cologne Bible (1478–80), in Rubens's painting titled *The Meeting of Abraham and Melchizedek,* and in a painting by the fifteenth-century Dutch artist Dierick Bouts.

Melchisedek is called an angel of the order of **virtues** in Epiphanius's *Adversus Heareses,* whereas in Phoenician mythology, where he is called Sydik, he is regarded as the father of the seven **elohim** or angels of the divine presence. Melchisedek is called Zorokothera in the Gnostic *Book of the Great Logos*. According to Hippolytus, Melchisedec was a power greater than Christ.

In occult lore Melchisedek represents the **Holy Spirit,** whereas in the Book of Mormon, he is the prince of peace, his symbol being a chalice and a loaf of bread. In R. H. Charles's edition of 2 Enoch, Melchisedek is mentioned as the supernatural offspring of Noah's brother Nir. Nir was preserved in infancy by Michael and became, after the Flood, a great high priest, the "Word of God," and king of Salem. Melchisedek is also identified as Shem, one of Noah's sons, as in *Midrash Tehillim,* which also contains the legend of Melchisedec's feeding the beasts in Noah's ark.

Sources:

Charles, R. H. *The Book of the Secrets of Enoch.* Oxford: Clarendon, 1896.
Encyclopaedia Judaica. New York: Macmillan, 1971.
Margolies, Morris B. *A Gathering of Angels: Angels in Jewish Life and Literature.* New York: Ballantine, 1994.

Mephistopheles

The name Mephistopheles etymologically means "he who loves not the light," in contrast with **Lucifer** (light bearer). The name originated during the Renaissance from a combination of Greek, Latin, and possibly Hebrew elements, which explains the existence of variants of the name, such as Mephisto, Mephistophilus (in **Shakespeare**'s *Merry Wives of Windsor*), Mephist, and Mephisto.

The most well-known account of Mephistopheles can be found in the story of Faustus, who sold his soul to the Devil. The mythical story, which originated during medieval times, drew upon the life of a philosopher who decided to make a living by casting horoscopes and predicting the future. In the following decades the story was transformed into the legend of a philosopher who abandoned philosophy and joined league with the Devil to devote himself to practicing magic. Mephistopheles agrees to teach the doctor the Devil's knowledge and powers in exchange for Faust's soul.

The legend of Faust became a major topic of artistic inspiration in poetry and music following the creation of *Doctor Faustus* by Christopher Marlowe (1564–93). The trend reached its zenith with the 1831 publication of *Faust: Eine Tragodie* by Johann Wolfgang von Goethe (1749–1832), and continued to inspire nineteenth-century literature on the Devil.

Goethe's Faust, upon the termination of twenty-five years of devilish practice, repents and is saved. Faust's Devil was also somewhat metamorphosed from the medieval role of enemy in a dueling contest with Christ or with a saint or a virgin; the contest of the Devil in the eighteenth century became internalized, the battle taking place within oneself. This "new" devil was to a certain degree sympathetic to the human condition, and rather introspective. The Devil's introspection and humanization became a pattern in the sixteenth and seventeenth centuries and can be found reflected in some of the characters in Shakespeare's tragedies.

Ultimately, Goethe's Devil did not remain exclusively Christian: he became a more complex, multifaceted, and ambiguous character representing not only evil against good, but also the oppositions of matter against spirit and chaos versus order.

Although later operas have been produced that depict the Faust story, Goethe's Mephistopheles remains the most powerful interpretation of the character.

—*Isotta Poggi*

Sources:

Davidson, Gustav. *A Dictionary of Angels Including the Fallen Angels.* 1967. Reprint. New York: The Free Press, 1971.

Masello, Robert. *Fallen Angels . . . and Spirits of the Dark.* New York: Perigee, 1994.

Rudwin, Maximilian. *The Devil in Legend and Literature.* Chicago: Open Court Publishing, 1931.

Merkabah Rider

A Merkabah Rider was an ancient Jewish mystic who fasted and prayed to reach an ecstatic trance. While in the trance state, he sent his soul upward through the heavenly halls in an attempt to reach the Throne of Glory that is supported by the chariot of Merkivah. The objective of the Merkabah Rider was to join himself with the Universal Soul. During this journey, the Rider was constantly plagued by **demons.** The Merkabah Rider used prayer, magical talismans, incantations, and asceticism to enlist the aid of the angels, who would protect him throughout his journey and ultimately defeat his antagonists.

Sources:

Margolies, Morris B. *A Gathering of Angels: Angels in Jewish Life and Literature.* New York: Ballantine, 1994.

Schwartz, Howard. *Gabriel's Palace: Jewish Mystical Tales.* New York: Oxford University Press, 1993.

Mesopotamia

Mesopotamia was the ancient civilization that occupied the Tigris and Euphrates river valley up until the fourth century B.C. After Alexander the Great's conquest, the area became part of the Greek cultural sphere. Later, the area passed into Islamic control.

Mesopotamians, like many of the other traditional peoples of the world, imagined the universe as a three-tiered cosmos of heaven, earth, and underworld, with heaven reserved for deities. Because the Mesopotamian religious tradition placed its gods in the sky, it was natural that the divinities should come to be depicted with **wings,** the means by which birds and other creatures lift themselves above the earth. In **Greek** and Roman mythology, winged demigods were frequently messengers between the gods and humanity. The Greeks appear to have taken this iconographic convention directly from the Mesopotamians. Western representations of angels with wings were derived, in turn, from Greek and Roman traditions.

Sources:

Black, Jeremy, and Anthony Green. *Gods, Demons and Symbols of Ancient Mesopotamia: An Illustrated Dictionary.* Austin: University of Texas Press, 1992.

Cirlot, J. E. *A Dictionary of Symbols.* New York: Philosophical Library, 1971.

Dalley, Stephanie. *Myths from Mesopotamia.* New York: Oxford University Press, 1989.

Metaphysics and Angels

There are two distinct branches of the contemporary revival of interest in angels, one associated with traditional religious denominations and the other with the occult/metaphysical subculture frequently referred to as the **New Age** movement. Partly because of the vagueness of the term *New Age,* and partly because the term has acquired negative connotations, members of this alternative spiritual subculture prefer to refer to themselves and their subculture by other names. One of these terms is *metaphysical,* although it has been applied so loosely that it has become as vague as *New Age.*

The term *metaphysical* originates from the arrangement of Aristotle's works, in which Aristotle's speculations about the ultimate nature of reality were placed *after* (Greek, *meta*) his writings on physics—hence, *metaphysics.* Throughout the history of Western philosophy, metaphysics has been concerned with the aspect of a thinker's philosophical system that deals with ultimate reality. For medieval religious philosophers, these reflections often included speculations about angels. As a distant echo of these speculations, contemporary metaphysical discussions sometimes refer to the medieval question, How many angels can dance on the head of a pin? (The correct answer is an infinite number, because angels do not occupy space.)

In contrast to reductionistic philosophers who declared that everything was material, as well as in contrast to dualistic philosophers who argued for the existence of mind and matter, a number of important thinkers—most notably George Berkeley (1685–1753) and Georg Hegel (1770–1831)—declared that the ultimate nature of reality was mind or spirit. The physical world appears real but, like the landscape of dreams, is actually a manifestation of our collective thoughts. This school of metaphysics is traditionally referred to as idealism (a confusing term because of other connotations with the word *idealism*). Other, more popular thinkers such as **Emanuel Swedenbörg** and Andrew Jackson Davis were (correctly or incorrectly) identified as idealists, which caused the notion of angels to become associated with idealism.

One should also note that certain schools of South Asian philosophy, such as Advaita Vedanta, advocate a position that, while not the same as Western idealism, similarly denies the reality of physical world as we experience it in our normal, everyday state of consciousness. Through the translation of Asian philosophical texts, these schools of thought were becoming known to the West, and were sometimes referred to in discussions of philosophical idealism. South Asian thought systems also contributed the notion of karma to this admixture of ideas—a notion of cause and effect that could be interpreted to imply that the person in question was ultimately responsible for everything that she or he experienced. South Asian religion would also be the source for the term **deva,** which became the standard Theosophical term for angel.

The basic thrust of these strands of philosophical theorizing was picked up by the popular nineteenth-century healing movement referred to as mind cure. The mind cure movement eventually generated a number of different denominational bodies, most notably Christian Science, but also Unity, Science of Mind, and related New Thought churches. While few thinkers in the mind cure movement delved into the intricacies of Western philosophy, they knew enough to be able to refer intelligently to philosophical idealism in their explanation of why the mind cure worked: If everything is simply thoughts in manifestation, then obviously illness is no more than a wrong-headed idea. Hence, replacing a sick idea with a healthy idea should effect a cure. It is this connection with philosophical idealism that led the various religious bodies arising out of the mind cure movement to be referred to as *metaphysical* churches.

Members of these New Thought denominations often participate in the same general subculture as non-mind cure organizations, such as **Spiritualism** and Theosophy. The association of these diverse religious bodies with less formal expressions of the same kinds of spirituality constitute what has been referred to as the "occult-metaphysical" subculture, or the occult-metaphysical tradition. It was this subculture that gave birth to the New Age movement. However, because of the negative connotations that have accrued both to "new age" and "occult," metaphysical came to be adopted as a general term to refer to the entire subculture. Thus, for instance, bookstores that cater to members of this tradition of alternative spirituality are often called "metaphysical bookstores."

In summary, to clarify a murky term, one should distinguish at least three meanings of the term metaphysical as it applies to angels: (1) philosophizing about ultimate reality, (2) the mind cure movement, especially as represented by New Thought denominations, and (3) the metaphysical-occult/New Age subculture. While angels are associated with all three meanings of the term, the contemporary revival of interest in angelic beings is particularly "metaphysical" in the third sense.

Sources:

Lewis, James R., and J. Gordon Melton, eds. *Perspectives on the New Age.* Albany: State University of New York Press, 1992.

Melton, J. Gordon, Jerome Clark, and Aidan Kelly. *New Age Encyclopedia.* Detroit, Mich.: Gale Research, 1990.

Metatron

Metatron is one of the most important angels in the Western tradition. According to Johann Eisenmenger, Metatron represents the supreme **angel of death,** to whom God daily gives orders as to which souls will be taken that day. Metatron transmits these orders to his subordinates **Gabriel** and **Sammael.**

He is further believed to be in charge of the sustenance of the world. In the **Talmud** and Targum, Metatron is the link between God and humanity. Among various missions and deeds attributed to Metatron is the staying of **Abraham**'s hand at the point of sacrificing Isaac, although this mission has also been imputed to **Michael, Zadkiel,** Tadhiel, and, of course, to the **angel of the Lord.**

Metatron is thought to reside in the seventh heaven, and, with the possible exception of Anafiel, is the tallest angel in heaven. The **Zohar** computes his size as "equal to the breadth of the whole world," which in rabbinic lore was the size of **Adam** before he sinned.

Metatron is generally recognized as the heavenly scribe who records everything that happens in the ethereal archives. In the tale of the marriage of God and Earth, told in the *Alphabet of Ben Sira,* God demands from Earth the "loan" of Adam for one thousand years. Upon agreement to the loan, God writes out a formal receipt, which is on deposit "to this day" in the archives of Metatron.

Metatron is the first—and also the last—of the ten **archangels** of the Briatic world. In terms of seniority, he is actually the youngest angel in the heavenly host. He has been variously given the role of king of angels, prince of the divine face or presence, chancellor of heaven, angel of the covenant, chief of the ministering angels, and the lesser YHWH (the tetragrammaton, or Yahweh).

The meaning of the name Metatron is unclear. Rabbi Eleazar of Worms (Germany), an influential Hasidic leader and writer in the late twelfth and early thirteen centuries, thought it derived from the Latin *metator* (a guide or measurer). Hugo Odeberg asserts that the name Metatron originated in Jewish circles and "should be regarded as a pure Jewish invention, viz., a metonym for the term "little YHWH."" Odeberg also interprets the name as "one who occupies the throne next to the divine throne." According to Jewish historian Gershom Scholem, on the basis of *The Apocalypse of Abraham* the name might be a "vox mystica" for Yahoel (God).

According to one legend, Metatron was once the patriarch **Enoch,** who, when chosen by God to be the writer of truth, was transformed into a fiery angel with thirty-six wings and countless eyes. Most Talmudic authorities, however, do not identify Enoch with Metatron. The Tanhuna Genesis claims he was originally the archangel Michael.

Metatron has also been identified as **Satan;** as the dark angel who wrestled with **Jacob** at Peniel (Genesis 32); as the watchman (Isaiah 21); as the Logos; as **Uriel;** as the evil Sammael; as an angel of liberation; and as the Shekinah (the female principle of God in the world).

According to the Cabala, Metatron is the angel who led the children of Israel through the wilderness after the Exodus, whereas in occult writings he is depicted as the twin brother or half-brother of the angel **Sandalphon.** Metatron has also been identified as Isaiah's suffering servant, the Messiah of Christian theology, and has been credited with the authorship of Ps. 37:25, according to Talmud Yebamoth 16b. The Zohar speaks of Metatron as Moses' rod "from one side of which comes life and from the other, death."

In Jewish lore Metatron is the angel who caused another angel to announce, before the Flood, that God would destroy the world, whereas, according to Talmud Abodah Zarah 3b, Metatron is the teacher of prematurely dead children in Paradise.

—*Michela Zonta*

Sources:

Davidson, Gustav. *A Dictionary of Angels Including the Fallen Angels.* Reprint. 1967. New York: The Free Press, 1971.

Liebes. Yehuda. *Studies in the Zohar.* Trans. from the Hebrew by Arnold Schwartz, Stephanie Nakache, and Penina Peli. Albany, N.Y.: State University of New York Press, 1993.

MacGregor, Geddes. *Angels: Ministers of Grace.* New York: Paragon House Publishers, 1988.

Prophet, Elizabeth Clare. *Forbidden Mysteries of Enoch: Fallen Angels and the Origens of Evil.* Livingston, Mont.: Summit University Press, 1983.

Wilson, Peter Lamborn. *Angels.* New York: Pantheon Books, 1980.

Michael

Michael ranks as the greatest angel in all three of the major monotheisms, **Judaism, Christianity,** and **Islam.** His name, meaning "who is as God," derives originally from the Chaldeans (Mesopotamians), by whom he was worshiped as a deity. In Islam he is called **Mikhail.** He is traditionally considered to be chief of the order of **virtues;** chief of **archangels;** prince of the presence; angel of repentance, righteousness, mercy, and sanctification; and ruler of the fourth heaven, conqueror of **Satan.**

He is credited by Midrash Rabba as the author of the whole of Psalm 85, and in one account he is claimed to have wiped out, single-handedly and overnight, 185,000 men from the army of the Assyrian king Sennacherib, who was threatening Jerusalem in 701 B.C. In addition, he has been identified as the angel who stayed the hand of **Abraham** when the latter was on the point of sacrificing his son Isaac. In Rev. 20:1 it is claimed that Michael is the one who will descend from heaven with "the

Michael

In 1950 Michael was officially declared the patron of policemen by Pope Pius XII.

key of the abyss and a great chain in his hand" and bind the Satanic dragon for a thousand years.

In volume 2 of *The Legends of the Jews* (p. 303), Louis Ginzberg asserts that "the fire that Moses saw in the burning bush had the appearance of Michael, who had descended from Heaven as the forerunner of the Shekinah." According to a commentary on Gen. 18:1–10 contained in Talmud Berakot 35, Michael is recognized by Sarah as one of three "men" who were entertained unawares by Abraham. Michael is said to have assisted four other great angels—**Gabriel, Uriel, Raphael,** and **Metatron**—in the burial of Moses and to have disputed with Satan for possession of the body. Michael has often been equated with the **Holy Spirit,** the Logos, God, and Metatron in mystic and occult literature, and in Baruch III, Michael "holds the keys of the kingdom of Heaven."

In ancient Persian lore, he was called Beshter, "one who provides sustenance for humankind." This would make him analogous to Metatron. It is also said that the tears shed by Michael over the sins of the faithful formed the **cherubim.** Michael is invoked as St. Michael by Christians, and he is also known as the angel of the Last Judgment. He has been considered the "weigher of souls" since the tribes of Israel were in captivity in Egypt, where religious tradition held that there was a weigher of hearts of the deceased named Anubis. This dog- or jackal-headed deity was identified with the most important star in the Egyptian sky, Sirius, the Dog Star. In Persia the star was known as Tistar, the Chief, and the earlier Akkadian term was Kasista, the Prince.

In the **Middle Ages** Michael was regarded as the **psychopomp,** the conductor of souls to the otherworld. Because the church was anxious to attract the old pagan worshipers of Roman Gaul, who remained faithful to the god Mercury, they assimilated Michael with that underworld god. Chapels dedicated to Michael appeared over the ruins of earlier temples, and the many "Michael's Mounts" to be found throughout Europe attest to the power of the ancient archetype of the mound of the dead.

Prince of the host of the Lord;
Standard Bearer; Mighty Seraph;

DETAIL OF THE DYING MAN BEFORE HIS JUDGE. THE ARCHANGEL MICHAEL FULFILLS
ONE OF HIS MANY ROLES AS PSYCHOPOMP. HE IS PICTURED HERE IN STRUGGLE FOR
THE POSSESSION OF THE MAN'S SOUL, HURLING AGAINST THE DEVIL WITH
UPLIFTED SWORD. FROM THE *GRANDES HEURES DE ROHAN* ILLUMINATED BY THE
ROHAN MASTER (FL. 1418–40). (COURTESY ARAS)

One of the Seven that stand before the Throne;
Dauntless Challenger whose cry ran through the vaults
    of heaven: "Who is like to God!"
Guardian of God's chosen race,
Glorious Champion of the Church of Christ under the
New Law;
Triumphant Defender of the Women and her Child;
Vanquisher of the Dragon and Chainer of his strength;
Leader of souls into the holy light.

Father Husslein, S.J.

Michael, like Gabriel, is one of the most commonly pictured angels in visual art and is depicted most often as winged and with unsheathed sword, the warrior of God and slayer of the Dragon. Although in the Renaissance period he is represented with a wide variety of features, he is always young, strong, and handsome, usually wearing a splendid coat of mail and equipped with sword, shield, and spear, all shining bright, ready for battle. He is often seen in combat with Satan, who in this context is frequently represented as a serpent or dragon. Sometimes he is wearing a jeweled crown. His wings are generally conspicuous and very grand, and he usually holds in his hand the scales of justice. In Muslim lore Michael's wings are said to be "the color of green emerald," and he is covered with "saffron hairs, each of them containing a million faces and mouths and as many tongues which, in a million dialects, implore the pardon of Allah."

Among the recently discovered **Dead Sea Scrolls** there is one entitled The War of Sons of Light Against the Sons of Darkness, where Michael is called "the prince of light" and wars against the angels of darkness, the latter under the command of the demon **Belial.** In *The Legends of the Jews,* Ginzberg regards Michael as the forerunner of the Shechinah, as well as the angel who brought Asenath from Palestine as a wife for Joseph, and as the one who saved Daniel's companions from the fiery furnace. Michael, who is also regarded as the intermediary between Mordecai and Esther, and as the destroyer of Babylon, is said to have informed the fallen angels of the Deluge. When he wept, his tears changed into precious stones.

Longfellow, in *The Golden Legend* (1851), pictures Michael as the spirit of the planet Mercury, bringing the gift of patience. Michael figures prominently in secular writings, including those of **Dante** and **Milton,** and in contemporary fiction he serves as archdeacon to Bishop Brougha in Robert Nathan's *The Bishop's Wife*. Michael is called "leader of God's host" in Yeats's poem "The Rose of Peace." In 1950 Pope Pius XII declared Michael to be the patron of policemen, and it is foretold in Daniel that when the world is once again in real trouble Michael will reappear. Some religious scholars claim that this century is the one in which he will reveal himself once again.

Michael has also been a popular figure within the contemporary **New Age/metaphysical** subculture. Even prior to the current wave of angelic faddishness, Michael was invoked for protection by metaphysical practitioners and **channeled** by New Agers.

Sources:

Ginzberg, Louis. *The Legends of the Jews.* 7 vols. Philadelphia: Jewish Publication Society of America, 1954.

Godwin, Malcolm. *Angels: An Endangered Species.* New York: Simon and Schuster, 1990.

Longfellow, Henry Wadsworth. *Poetical Works.* 6 vols. Boston: Houghton, 1904.

MacGregor, Geddes. *Angels: Ministers of Grace.* New York: Paragon House, 1988.

Wilson, Peter Lamborn. *Angels.* New York: Pantheon Books, 1980.

Michelangelo

Michelagniolo di Lodovico Buonarroti Simoni, best known as Michelangelo (1475–1564), was born at Caprese, Italy, a Florentine dependency where his father was governor. His mother died when he was six. At ten he joined the Grammar School of Francesco da Urbino, and three years later he joined the *bottega* of Domenico Ghirlandajo as pupil and helper. He left after a year to study the collections of Lorenzo the Magnificent, head of the house of Medici, in whose palace he was taken to live.

In 1494 Michelangelo left Florence for Venice and Bologna, where he lived over a year. The following year he returned to Florence, where a new government had been formed under the influence of Savonarola. In 1496 he left for Rome to seek his fortune. When he returned to Florence in 1501 he executed the famous marble *David* for the Opera del Duomo. This marble and the cartoon of the *Battle of Cascina* or the *Bathers,* a composition of life-size nudes for the proposed fresco in the Sala del Consiglio, Palazzo Vecchio, are the most celebrated work of this period.

In 1508 Michelangelo was ordered to Rome by Pope Julius II to paint the vault and the higher parts of the side walls in the Sistine Chapel. Prophets, sibyls, nudes, and scenes from Genesis are represented on the vault, whereas other topics of the Old Testament, including the ancestors of Christ, are depicted on the lunettes and sprandels.

In 1534, at the age of fifty-nine, he left Florence finally for Rome, where he spent the remaining thirty years of his life. There he painted *The Last Judgment,* covering the whole wall above the altar of the Sistine Chapel, from 1536 to 1542. The Julius tomb for Pope Julius II, now in San Pietro in Vincoli, was executed in 1542. From 1542 to 1550 he painted the twin frescoes of the Paoline Chapel in the Vatican, and thereafter he devoted himself principally to architecture. Appointed in 1547, he remained architect-in-chief of St. Peter's until his death.

The *Pietà* of the cathedral in Florence was carved between 1545 and 1555, and it is likely that the Rondanini *Pietà* (Rondanini Palace, Rome) was begun in 1555. Upon his death in 1564, Michelangelo's body was taken to Florence, where a very elaborate funeral took place at San Lorenzo in July. He was buried at Santa Croce, in the parish where his family had long lived.

Angels are depicted in a number of Michelangelo's works, such as the paintings on the ceiling of the Sistine Chapel. In the panel *The Creation of Sun, Moon, Earth, and the Herbs,* God is shown, on the right, borne up by **cherubs,** creating the Sun and the Moon; on the left, as he flies away, he creates Earth and the herbs. As God creates the Sun and the Moon, he is seen in flowing lilac robes, the Sun by his right hand and the Moon by his left. There is a beautiful little cherub on his right who looks up at him.

The panel *Creation of Adam* is considered Michelangelo's greatest achievement. God, pictured as an old man, is again shown on the right of the panel, borne up by cherubs. He looks at **Adam,** his arm held out toward him, his hand almost touching Adam's. There is one cherub of particular beauty supporting God's left arm who looks with large, beautiful eyes at Adam.

Another exquisite angel is depicted in the *Temptation and Expulsion.* On the left of the panel Adam and Eve are shown being tempted by the serpent, and on the right they are driven from the Garden into the wilderness by an angel. The angel is seen high up in the picture just to the right of the serpent, driving Adam and Eve into the desert with a staff.

In another panel a captivating little cherub behind Isaiah's right shoulder has delightfully absurd curly hair and a most charming face. In a scene depicting Daniel, another cherub supports a large book. In the panel representing Libica two cherubs talking to each other about her actions bring a human touch to the painting. Charming little cherubs stand in pairs at either side of all sibyls and prophets represented in the paintings of the chapel, each pair reproduced in reverse on the opposite side of the prophet or sibyl.

The picture *The Last Judgment* in the Sistine Chapel is among the most famous in the world. It is divided into four belts, the top one of which contains angels and cherubs holding the emblems of the Passion of Christ. Angels are also depicted in the third belt, which has in the center seven massive cherubs sounding the last trump to waken the dead; between the trumpeters are two angels, each with an open book in his hand, from which everyone reads his past life while rising to the Judgment. On the left side of the same belt the souls arise to the Judgment, and saints and angels assist them in their upward path, some offering a hand, one a rosary.

The angel figures are nude, masculine in appearance, and are not winged. In fact the angels are not discernible from the human figures. Michelangelo chose this type of visual to show the close association that angels have with man.

In a marble group by Michelangelo in a chapel of the Vatican there are no angels, but there are engravings of another *Pietà* in which the Vir-

DETAIL OF THE *CREATION OF ADAM*, SISTINE CHAPEL, ROME (EARLY SIXTEENTH CENTURY). NOTE THE CHERUB PEERING OVER THE LEFT ARM OF GOD. (COURTESY ARAS)

SAINTS AND ANGELS LIFT
AND HELP HUMAN SOULS
ALONG THE PATH TO
JUDGMENT IN THIS DETAIL
FROM *THE LAST JUDGMENT*,
SISTINE CHAPEL, ROME
(EARLY SIXTEENTH
CENTURY). (COURTESY
LEONARD DAY)

gin sits at the foot of the cross, her eyes raised and her arms extended toward heaven, while two angels support the Christ, seated lower down and leaning against the knees of the Virgin. According to Michelangelo's custom, these angels have no wings, but their expression is such that it would be impossible to mistake them for earthly children.

Michelangelo's nudes of angels and men have not always been received with favor and acclaim among the church hierarchy. Inquisition Pope Paul IV, for example, called the completed Sistine Chapel a "stew of nudes" and wanted it destroyed. During the memorable reign of Pius V in 1564, the Council of Trent censured the work and ordered that it be "corrected." As Michelangelo had died the previous year, other artists were commissioned to paint drapery upon some of the figures. These touchups and cover-ups lasted well into the eighteenth century. Restoration of the Sistine Chapel began in earnest in the late 1970s and many of the cover-ups were painstakingly removed. With final restoration now complete, the true beauty of this creation can be enjoyed.

—Michela Zonta and Leonard Day

Sources:

de la Croix, Horst, and Richard G. Tansey. *Art Through the Ages.* 6th ed. New York: Harcourt Brace Jovanovich, 1975.

Stokes, Adrian. *Michelangelo: A Study in the Nature of Art.* New York: Philosophical Library, 1956.

Whitehouse, J. Howard, and Colin Rocke. *The Master: A Study of Michelangelo.* London: Oxford University Press, 1934.

Middle Ages

Medieval Christian thinking on **angelology** moved in two directions. The first was characterized by fascination with the personalities of specific angelic figures, both good and bad. Such writings as the **Book of Enoch,** the Testament of Abraham, and the Apocalypse of Elijah describe the functions of the angels **Uriel, Raguel, Sariel,** Jeremiel, and others, who serve alongside **Gabriel, Michael,** and **Raphael.** Christian noncanonical writings, especially the Nag Hammadi texts, continue and elaborate upon this trend. The vivid angelic traditions of the pseudepigrapha were popular in the medieval Christian world and were preserved in Greek and Latin hagiographical manuscripts.

The second tradition of medieval angelology was primarily a philosophical one in which speculation about the corporeality and hierarchy of angels was fundamental. The notion of the incorporeality of the angels, so prominent in later medieval scholasticism, was not generally accepted until the sixth century. The idea that angels have a spiritual, but not a fleshly, body is found in the writings of **Origen** and Augustine and seems to have been widely held in the patristic period.

THIS EARLY RENAISSANCE ENGRAVING EMPHASIZES THE OVERWHELMING POWER
OF DEATH PREVALENT DURING THIS PERIOD. THE ANGEL, POSITIONED IN THE ROLE
OF AN ANGEL OF DEATH, HOLDS UP AN HOURGLASS, WHICH HAS RUN OUT.
(COURTESY ARAS)

It was only with the early sixth-century writings of the mystical theologian **Dionysius the Areopagite,** who flourished about the year 500, that Christian angelology took on its classical form. In the ninth century Dionysius's *The Celestial Hierarchy* was translated into Latin by Hilduin of Saint-Denis and again by John Scotus Erigena. The latter translation, corrected by Anastasius the Librarian in 875, became a standard reference work in the High Middle Ages.

The Dionysian scheme bears a curious resemblance to the Gnostic order of angels criticized by the second-century saint Irenaeus; both systems may reflect Persian angelology passed on through the biblical and rabbinic literature of postexilic Judaism. The Jewish philosophical tradition from Philo to Maimonides included elaborate theories about angels that influenced both Christian and Muslim authors. In turn, the differing angelologies of the Muslim philosophers Avicenna and Averroës left their marks on medieval Jewish and Christian philosophies of angels.

John Scotus Erigena (CA. 810–CA. 877), who treated angels in the second tradition of medieval angelology in his principal work, *On the Division of Nature,* paved the way for development of the notion of angels as incorporeal beings and separate intelligences. In the twelfth century Peter Lombard set forth a Dionysian theory of the nature of angels that was commented on by Scholastic theologians of the following centuries, including Albertus Magnus, Bonaventure, **Thomas Aquinas,** and John Duns Scotus. All of these authors agreed on a basic definition of angels as spiritual beings, but they showed some differences of opinion on the question of their corporeality. These opinions are most sharply opposed in the writings of Thomas Aquinas and Duns Scotus.

Thomas Aquinas (1225–74) devoted fourteen books of the *Summa Theologica* to the nature and powers of angels. He held that angels have form but not matter and are therefore eternal and incorruptible. Angels are able to assume bodies, which take up space, so only one angel can be in a particular place at a certain time. In contrast, Duns Scotus (ca. 1264–1308), the last of the great medieval Scholastics, asserted that angels consist of both form and a noncorporeal matter particular to them alone, which makes it possible for more than one angel to occupy the same place at the same time. The ensuing debates over these positions may have given rise to the early modern legend that the Scholastics argued over such questions as how many angels can dance on the head of a pin.

Sources:

Bemrose, Stephen. *Dante's Angelic Intelligences: Their Importance in the Cosmos and in Pre-Christian Religion.* Rome: Edizioni di Storia e Letteratura, 1983.

Middle Ages

By the Middle Ages the exact count of angels peaked at 301,655,722.

MacGregor, Geddes. *Angels: Ministers of Grace*. New York: Paragon House, 1988.

Strayer, Joseph R., ed. *Dictionary of the Middle Ages*. 13 vols. New York: Scribner, 1982–89.

Mikhail

Islam shares certain angels with **Judaism** and **Christianity,** including **Michael** and **Gabriel.** Whereas Gabriel, whose Arabic name is **Djibril,** is easily the most important angel in all three religions, Michael (in Arabic, *Mikhail*) is far less significant for Muslims than he is for Jews and Christians. He is mentioned only once in the Koran (2:92).

According to tradition, Mikhail lives in the seventh heaven, has wings of an emerald color, and has hairs of saffron. Each hair has a million faces with mouths that speak in a million dialects, all imploring the pardon of God. A steadfast friend of humankind, Mikhail has not laughed once since hell was created.

Mikhail and Djibril were said to be the first angels to obey God's order to worship **Adam,** a command to which **Iblis,** the Muslim **Satan,** objected. As a warrior angel, Mikhail came to the aid of the faithful at the Battle of Badr. He is also mentioned as one of the angels who opened up **Muhammad**'s chest prior to "The Night Journey," the famous vision in which the prophet journeys into the heavens.

Sources:

Arberry, A. J. *The Koran Interpreted.* 1955. Reprint. New York: Macmillan, 1969.

The Encyclopedia of Islam. Vol. 7. Leiden, Netherlands: E. J. Brill, 1978.

Glassé, Cyril. *The Concise Encyclopedia of Islam.* Dan Francisco: Harper San Francisco, 1989.

Millennialism

The term *millenarian* or *millennialist* is applied to people who believe in the coming of a golden age—an age of light, truth, and love—usually by supernatural means, and whose religious life is saturated by this expectation. Although the term originated in the Christian tradition (referring to the paradisiacal thousand-year period of Christ's rule—the millennium—in which, according to Revelation 20, history and the world as we know it will terminate), by extension other, non-Christian religious movements that are characterized by such an expectation are also referred to as millenarian.

Norman Cohn, in his classic study *The Pursuit of the Millennium*, outlines five traits that characterize the way in which millennialist movements picture the collective salvation of humanity. The fifth and final characteristic he ascribes to millenarians is the belief that this collective salvation will be accomplished by or with the help of supernatural agents. In traditional **Christianity,** these supernatural agents are angels. Millennialist views of the end of time often include an **apocalyptic** scenario in which the old world is destroyed in order to make way for the new. At a spiritual level, this destruction usually involves battles between angelic and demonic forces, as in the Book of Revelation.

Sources:

Cohn, Norman. *The Pursuit of the Millennium.* New York: Oxford University Press, 1970.

Eliade, Mircea, ed. *Encyclopedia of Religion.* 16 vols. New York: Macmillan, 1987.

Lanternari, Vittorio. *The Religions of the Oppressed: A Study of Modern Messianic Cults.* New York: Mentor, 1956.

Morris, Henry M. *The Revelation Record: A Scientific and Devotional Commentary on the Book of Revelation.* Wheaton, Ill.: Tyndale House, 1983.

Milton, John

Angels are at the very center of John Milton's (1608—74) cosmic scenario, dwelling in organized ranks in the Empyrean, the highest heaven, a boundless region of light and freedom. Using the old Ptolemaic astronomy, Milton was able to build a magnificent literary atlas of comparative maps, showing the arrangements before and after the fall of the angels.

The oldest son of a London scrivener, John Milton was born in London on December 9, 1608. As a boy, he was very studious and was supplied with the best teachers by his father. He entered Christ's College, Cambridge, where he developed a deep interest in classical literature. Among his favorite poets were the Italians, through whom he improved his knowledge of medieval romance. Besides classical literature, the source of Milton's poetic inspiration was the biblical Christianity of Puritan England.

Milton left the University in 1632 without taking orders and spent the next six years of his life at Horton, where he pursued his studies in classical literature, history, mathematics, and music, with occasional visits to London. His earliest Italian verses were inspired by his love for a young Italian girl, whose first name, Emilia, is the only thing known about her. In this period he also developed his knowledge of English poetry from Chaucer to **Shakespeare,** Jonson, and the later Elizabethans, who considerably influenced all the poems written during these years.

In 1638, he went abroad. In Paris he met Hugo Grotius, whose *Adamus Exul* was one of the sources of *Paradise Lost.* He spent two months in Florence, then proceeded to Rome and Naples. He made his way back to England via Venice and Geneva. Once in England, he became involved in a long course of controversy, ecclesiastical and political, which determined the choice of themes, the doctrinal framework, and the spirit of *Paradise Lost, Paradise Regained,* and *Samson Agonistes.*

From 1649 to 1659, he served as Latin secretary to the council of state. In 1653, his wife died, and in 1656, he married Catharine Woodcock, whose early death in 1658 inspired the most touching of his sonnets. His marriage to Elizabeth Minshull in 1663 was an arrangement of convenience. The only English poems Milton wrote during these years were some sonnets on public events or persons and private incidents in Italian form.

In 1658 he resumed *Paradise Lost.* It was then composed to dictation, corrected, and completed by 1665—finally published in 1667. It was followed in 1670 by *Paradise Regained,* an epic on the "brief model" of the Book of Job, and by *Samson Agonistes. Paradise Lost,* like Dante's *Divine Comedy,* is primarily a didactic exposition of Milton's theological creed. His concept of God, Christ, and the angels and devils is the same as the one presented in *On Christian Doctrine,* which contains Milton's disdainful opinion of conventional dogmatisms about questions for which no sure answer is possible. *Paradise Lost* can be considered a restatement in poetic form of the doctrines that will finally justify God and indict man, whereas *Paradise Regained* constitutes Milton's ideal of Christian virtues such as obedience and temperance and the scorn of worldly glory.

Paradise Lost has many points in common with *Christian Doctrine.* In both, for instance, Milton says that angels are spirits and sons of God; that they see God dimly and are around his throne praising him; that seven in particular are before the throne; that both the good angels and the fallen ones are in a kind of order; that the fallen angels can do nothing without God's permission; and that the elect angels are impassible, although they do not look into the secrets of God (and in *Paradise Lost* God must instruct even **Michael** before he can know the future).

In Book 1 of *Christian Doctrine,* Milton finds that good angels are ministering agents around the throne of God, and that their principal office is praising God and presiding over particular areas. Sometimes they are divine messengers, but, although they have remarkable intelligence, they are not omniscient. In both *Christian Doctrine* and *Paradise Lost,* Milton asserts, against the majority of Protestant opinion, that by the name Michael the Bible signifies not Christ but the first of the angels; against a majority of all denominations, he alleges that the angels were created long before the world; and against almost everybody, he envisions hell as a local place outside the universe, with elect angels standing by their own strength, not by compulsive grace.

In *Paradise Lost,* however, Milton presents some ideas not found in *Christian Doctrine,* including some views that he could not have derived directly from the Bible, although they had wide acceptance among those who believed in angels: devils can suffer physical pain and in a sense are always in hell; devils are the deities of heathendom; God created men to repopulate heaven after the fall of angels; Satan tempted Eve from the mouth of the possessed snake; and angels, good or evil, know the world by intuition rather than by discourse and can control the humors in humans' bodies to produce dreams and visions.

In *Paradise Lost,* Milton also rejects the ancient view that fallen angels were corrupted by the beauty of women. He argues that the sons of God (the angels) were never involved with women, because the love they knew was not libidinous. He also, does not commit himself on the three principal angelological controversies between Protestants and Catholics—worship of angels, guardian angels, and the Dionysian orders—although his personal views were probably Protestant.

THE EMPYREAN AS PICTURED BY GUSTAVE DORÉ IN AN ILLUSTRATION FOR MILTON'S *PARADISE LOST* (1866).

Milton's angelic messengers are not merely epic machinery, but rather characters and agents in the justification of God's ways to men via the exploration of the causes and effects of the Fall. Milton never expressly denies the archangelic order, and he seems to use the other eight terms that **Dionysius** used for orders. Although he mentions **Beelzebub,** Zephon, Ithuriel, **Zophiel,** and Usiel only as **cherubim, Abdiel** only as **seraph,** and Nisroch only as **principality,** he names **Raphael** once as seraph and again as **virtue.** To the rest of the great spirits—**Satan,** Gabriel, **Uriel,** Michael—he applies only the general term *angel* or the special title **archangel.**

Raphael and Michael, along with Gabriel and Uriel, are the four angels ministering before the presence of God. Etymologically, Raphael means "medicine of God" or "God has healed," and Michael means "godlike" or "strength of God" or "who is as God." Traditionally, Raphael is also the angel of prayer, love, joy, and light and the guardian of the Tree of Life in the Garden of Eden; he is also the angel of science and knowledge, the preceptor angel. Michael is the angel of repentance, righteousness, mercy, and sanctification; he is the deliverer of the faithful, the angel of the final reckoning and the weigher of souls, the benevolent angel of death, and the mighty warrior of God.

In *Paradise Lost,* Milton names only Satan, Uriel, Raphael, and Michael as archangels. The three good angels of the list all have special worldly missions—Uriel to be the regent of the Sun, and the others to convey God's messages to Adam—but plainly they rank in heaven as archangels aside from these missions. Milton speaks repeatedly of the angels as pure spirits, intelligential substances, and the like. In *Christian Doctrine,* Milton says that a spirit does not have flesh and bones. Plainly, the angels of *Paradise Lost* are without flesh and bones, although this is not to say that they are simple forms.

Milton's concept of the composition of angels in *Paradise Lost* seems to suit the Puritan view of the angel as in some sense possessing a body, but one that is almost spirit. He thus follows an ancient tradition common to the great Alexandrian school of Christian philosophy, according to which the universe is full of incarnate spirits that are corporeal although not densely corporeal. They are seen only by clairvoyant eyes. In accordance with that ancient tradition, Milton's angels really do eat and excrete, although not in our crass way. They are not disembodied spirits; rather, their embodiment is so much finer than ours that they might seem to us to be so.

—*Michela Zonta*

Sources:

Hastings, James, ed. *Encyclopedia of Religion and Ethics.* Edinburgh: T. & T. Clark, 1930.

MacGregor, Geddes. *Angels: Ministers of Grace.* New York: Paragon House, 1988.

Swain, Kathleen M. *Before and After the Fall: Contrasting Modes in Paradise Lost.* Amherst: University of Massachusetts Press, 1986.

West, Robert H. *Milton and the Angels.* Athens: University of Georgia Press, 1955.

Ministering Angels

Ministering angels is a term subject to various interpretations. Some Talmudists judge ministering angels to constitute the highest order in the celestial hierarchy, the "hosts of the Lord." Others consider the ministering angels to be numerous and to belong to an inferior order. Some consider ministering angels to be angels who give help, service, care or aid, or fill wants or needs, especially those who serve as nurses. When still others speak of ministering angels, they mean angels who are sent forth from the court of God to carry out his commands.

The Talmud reports that ministering angels roasted meat and cooled wine for **Adam** when he was in the Garden of Eden. These angels would seem to fit into a category of servants. Angels are described as God's servants in Job 4:18, "Behold, he put no trust in his servants; and his angels he charged with folly." In Rev. 22:8, John, having heard and seen the prophecies described in Revelation, fell in worship at the feet of the angel who had shown them to him. The angel told John that he should not be worshipped, as he was just a servant of God as John himself was.

In addition to serving God, angels also serve the human race, as noted in Heb. 1:14, "Are not all angels spirits in the divine service, sent to serve for the sake of those who are to inherit salvation?"

Possibly the most well known ministering angel is depicted in the twelfth chapter of the Book of **Tobit,** when the angel **Raphael** accompanies Tobit's son Tobias on his journey to Media from Nineveh. Upon his return, Raphael instructs Tobias to apply fish gall to the eyes of his father, who is blind. Tobit's eyesight is restored. [And Raphael said:] "God sent me to heal you. . . . As for me, when I was with you I was not acting on my own will, but by the will of God" (Tobit 12:14–18).

According to Jewish tradition, God brought down from his highest heaven seventy ministering angels, led by Michael, the greatest of all angels, to teach languages to Noah's seventy descendants.

Sources:

Encyclopaedia Judaica. New York: Macmillan, 1971.
Giovetti, Paola. *Angels: The Role of Celestial Guardians and Beings of Light.* Translated by Toby McCormick. York Beach, Maine: Samuel Weiser, 1993.
New Catholic Encyclopedia. Vol. 1. Washington, D.C.: Catholic University of America, 1981.

Mithra

According to Vedic cosmology, Mithra is one of the shining gods, analogous to Judean-Christian angels. Mithra is mentioned in King's *The Gnostic and Their Remains,* where he is equated with **Metatron.** He is also present in Persian theology, where he is regarded as one of the twenty-eight *izeds,* or spirits, surrounding the great god Ahura-Mazda. Further, he is considered the counterpart of the archangel **Michael,** patron of Israel and chief of the heavenly hosts—the Sun-warrior, with ten thousand eyes.

Sources:

Davidson, Gustav. *A Dictionary of Angels Including the Fallen Angels.* New York: The Free Press, 1967.

Wilson, Peter Lamborn. *Angels.* New York: Pantheon Books, 1980.

Months (Angels of the)

The notion of a twelvefold division of the year derives from the lunar cycle (the orbital cycle of the Moon around the Earth), which the Moon completes twelve times per year. The lunar derivation is evident even in the word *month,* which derives from *moon.* The connection between the months and angels comes from the medieval tendency to associate almost everything with angels. Just as angels were said to **rule** the astrological signs and the **hours** of the day, there were twelve angels who ruled the months. The traditional correlations are as follows:

Month	*Angel*
January	Gabriel (or Cambiel)
February	Barchiel
March	Malahidael (or Machidiel)
April	Asmodel
May	Ambriel
June	Muriel
July	Verchiel
August	Hamaliel
September	Zuriel (or Uriel)
October	Barbiel
November	Advachiel (or Adnachiel)
December	Hanael

Today the connection between the nature of the given angel and the characteristics of the corresponding month seems tenuous or nonexistent. Although originally there must have been a logic for these traditional assignments, it has been lost in the intervening centuries.

Sources:

Cirlot, J. E. *A Dictionary of Symbols.* 1971. Reprint. New York: Dorset Press, 1991.

Davidson, Gustav. *A Dictionary of Angels: Including the Fallen Angels.* 1967. Reprint. New York: Free Press, 1971.

Mormonism, Angels in

The Mormons, more properly referred to as the Church of Jesus Christ of Latter-day Saints (LDS), hold beliefs about angels that are somewhat at variance from mainstream **angelology.** Although acknowledging the authority of the **Bible,** and thus sharing the tradition of biblical angels with other Christian denominations, the Mormons accept certain other, postbiblical documents as supplementing and expanding the biblical revelation. In particular, the Book of Mormon, the Doctrine and Covenants, and the Pearl of Great Price contain extensive discussions of angels.

Rather than viewing angels as a separate order of creation, the Mormon tradition regards the angels who visit the earth as persons. In the words of the Doctrine and Covenants (D&C), "There are no angels who minister to this earth but those who do belong or have belonged to it" (D&C 130:5). Different kinds of beings at different levels of development can play the messenger role that is the defining characteristic of angels. Any righteous person in the spirit world may serve as an angel, but particularly those who were "translated" (i.e., left the earth while still in their bodies, as did **Elijah**).

Mormons also distinguish between disembodied spirits serving as angels and angels that appear as "resurrected personages, having bodies of flesh and bones" (D&C 129:1). These resurrected angels have been particularly important in the history of Mormonism. For instance, **Moroni,** the angel who revealed the Book of Mormon, was a resurrected angel. The LDS tradition also teaches that other such embodied angels restored the Aaronic priesthood and the Melchizedek priesthood. Having a body is essential, because only embodied beings can lay hands on mortals during the passing of authority for priesthoods.

Disembodied angels can, however, convey knowledge, comfort, and assurances from God to mortals. God himself is sometimes referred to as an angel, in that he is called a messenger, as in "messenger of salvation" (D&C 93:8). Mormonism also accepts the idea of an original **War in Heaven,** during which **Satan** and his followers were cast out of heaven. These rebels are often referred to as fallen angels.

As for the idea of **guardian angels**—in the sense of each person having an assigned angel throughout life—many Mormons accept the notion, although it does not constitute part of the official teaching of the church. According to the *Encyclopedia of Mormonism,* "The term guardian angel may best be viewed as a figure of speech that has to do with God's protecting care and direction or, in special instances, with an angel dispatched to earth in fulfillment of God's purposes" (p. 42).

Sources:

Ludlow, Daniel H. *Encyclopedia of Mormonism*. Vol. 1. New York: Macmillan, 1992.

McConkie, Oscar W. *Angels*. Salt Lake City, Utah: 1975.

Ronner, John. *Know Your Angels: The Angel Almanac with Biographies of 100 Prominent Angels in Legend and Folklore, and Much More*. Murfreesboro, Tenn.: Mamre Press, 1993.

Moroni

Moroni is the Mormon Angel of God, son of "Mormon, the last great leader of the Nephites." Moroni (late fourth to early fifth centuries) is considered the last prophet and is the author of the final book in the Book of Mormon, which contains the plates of Nephi that cover a thousand years of Mormon history. When, ca. A.D. 421, Moroni finished his last entry, he buried it to be discovered by future generations.

Between the years 1823 and 1829, Moroni returned to earth as a resurrected messenger of God, and appeared at least twenty times to, among others, Mormon church founder Joseph Smith. These visits eventually led Smith to find the hidden golden plates of the Nephite records in the hill Cumorah in what is now Ontario County, New York. Moroni continued to appear to Smith and instructed him in his calling as prophet and counselor.

Moroni is usually depicted blowing a trumpet in reference to the prophecy of John in the Book of Revelation:

> And I saw another angel fly in the midst of heaven, having the everlasting gospel to preach unto them that dwell on the earth, and to every nation, and kindred, and tongue, and people, saying with a loud voice, Fear God, and give glory to him; for the hour of his judgment is come; and worship him that made heaven, and earth, and the sea, and the fountains of waters. (Rev. 14:6–7)

The symbol of Moroni appears on Church of Jesus Christ of Latter-day Saints (LDS) temple spires, graces the Book of Mormon, and is the official emblem on grave markers of American Mormon servicemen.

Sources:

Davidson, Gustav. *A Dictionary of Angels: Including the Fallen Angels*. 1967. Reprint. New York: Free Press, 1971.

Ludlow, Daniel H. *Encyclopedia of Mormonism*. Vol. 1. New York: Macmillan, 1992.

Peterson, H. Donl. *Moroni: Ancient Prophet, Modern Messenger*. Bountiful, Utah, 1983.

Movies, Angels in the

Angels, perhaps due to their fantastical and ethereal nature, have been the subject of numerous popular movies. Filmmakers revel in the opportunity to portray heaven and, in particular, what the residents of heaven look like and what they do. It is through this cinematic interpretation that the common view of heaven has become so entrenched in popular belief. Cinema heaven is approached through the golden gates guarded by St. Peter, and is usually misty and filled with clouds. Angels are typically white-robed, strum harps, are winged, and wear halos.

However, when angels leave their celestial abode, often they are stripped of their heavenly encumbrances and take on Hollywood's favorite role of guardian (which holds with the job traditionally assigned by theologians to this lowest ranking **choir**). These cinema guardians usually assume human form, one that is easily recognizable and identifiable to their human charges.

A classic example can be found in *The Bishop's Wife* (1947), in which Cary Grant is cast as the angel Dudley, sent to the aid of an absent-minded young Episcopalian bishop, played by David Niven. The assured Grant brings a relaxed quality to Dudley, and produces a calming effect among his troubled earthly charges. We, in the audience, are drawn to Grant in much the same way as the bishop, his wife, his family, and friends are. He soothes us with his calming tones and mesmerizes with his beatific features. It is impossible not to believe that Dudley is, indeed, heaven sent.

In the 1956 *Forever Darling,* a similarly handsome guardian angel appears to Susan Bewell, played by Lucille Ball, a screwball socialite convinced that she is losing her mind. Susan asks her playboy father, "Guardian angels don't have wings do they?" Her father answers, "Guardian angels aren't like angels from Heaven. They can look like ordinary men."

The urbane James Mason is cast as Susan's guide, who assures her that he is, in fact, her guardian angel. "If you are what you say you are," questions Susan, "why do you look like James Mason?" To which Mason replies, "I look the way you want me to look." (Mason would again take on the role of heavenly messenger in the 1978 film *Heaven Can Wait.*)

An angel not quite of the same gracious ilk appears in *It's a Wonderful Life* (1946), possibly one of the most watched films of all time. Frank Capra poignantly tells the story of George Bailey, a man of high moral fiber who rediscovers his own worth. In this movie, Henry Travers is cast as the bulbous-nosed, very droll angel second-class **Clarence** who gives the disturbed hero the gift of reliving events as they might have been had he never been born. Clarence may not possess the debonair qualities of Grant and Mason, but he has the faith of a child, and is probably the most recognized and best loved of all cinematic angels.

In myriad other Hollywood films, angels come to the aid of their charges for a variety of reasons. In *Here Comes Mr. Jordan* (1941), one of the most delightful feature films of the 1940s, the inhabitants of heaven are forced to admit their fallibility and set about to remedy their mistake. Joe Pendleton, played by Robert Montgomery, is a boxer called to meet his maker before his time. Thus, heavenly messenger Mr. Jordan must accompany him back to earth, where they search among those about to die for a suitable replacement body.

In 1950 *For Heaven's Sake* cast Clifton Webb as tart heavenly messenger Charles and the more benign Edmund Gwenn as his angelic sidekick Arthur. They are sent to earth to help the prospective parents of a child angel, referred to as Item, who has been waiting seven years to be born. For most of the film Webb assumes the role of a wealthy Texas rancher and clomps around Gary Cooper fashion. He is confronted by earthly temptations—women, drinking, gambling—and succumbs to several of them, although in Hollywood style, he is forgiven by his superiors, when alls well that ends well and Item is finally born.

Angels in the Outfield (1951) is unique in that it is a combination of sports enthusiasm and religious faith. Angels in this case, come to the aid of an entire baseball team, the Pittsburgh Pirates, as they rise from the bottom of the National League to win the pennant. This miracle comes about as a result of an unseen heavenly voice who visits Guffy, the Pirate's acerbic manager, played by Paul Douglas. If Guffy reforms his unsavory ways, promises the angel, Heavenly Choir Nine will assist his losing team to victory. "You play ball with me and I'll play ball with you," the angel bargains.

In 1970 director Jan Kadar put to film a short story by Bernard Malamud called *The Angel Levine*. This allegorical film again makes use of the guardian angel theme, but with a twist. Zero Mostel, as Morris Mishkin, is a world-weary, cynical Orthodox Jew, convinced that the world is against him. In answer to his constant complaints, God sends a divine intermediary in the guise of a dapper black man played by Henry Belafonte. The angel introduces himself as Alexander Levine, a Jewish angel on heavenly probation, and explains that his task is to convince Morris that he is legitimate.

The most recognized angel film of the seventies is the 1978 infectious comic fantasy *Heaven Can Wait* (a remake of *Here Comes Mr. Jor-*

CARY GRANT, DAVID NIVEN, AND LORETTA YOUNG IN
THE BISHOP'S WIFE. (RKO; COURTESY THE KOBAL COLLECTION)

LUCILLE BALL EXPLAINS TO HUSBAND DESI ARNAZ THAT JAMES MASON IS HER
GUARDIAN ANGEL IN *FOREVER DARLING.* (MGM; COURTESY THE KOBAL COLLECTION)

dan). This time Joe Pendleton is an aging quarterback for the Rams, played by Warren Beatty. However the cornerstone of the plot remains the same—Joe is accidentally snatched by heaven before his time. Joe insists that he is not ready to die and is eventually deposited into the recently murdered, unathletic body of millionaire Leo Farnsworth, who is working with the farcical coach Max Corkle to get in shape for an upcoming Super Bowl game. All the while the bewilderment of Farnsworth's wife and her scheming lover, who thought they'd killed Farnsworth the first time, add to the fun.

Among the most recent movies to make use of angelic themes is *The Kid with the Broken Halo* (1982), in which a young black angel (Gary Coleman) and his reluctant elder descend to earth and save three diversely ethnic souls.

In *The Heavenly Kid* (1985), macho Bobby Fontana is the ultimate loser in a drag race, and as his car tumbles over a cliff and explodes, he finds himself on a subway going nowhere. He is approached by a very earthy angel named Rafferty, played by Richard Mulligan. "I was expecting something different," says Bobby, "Angels and harps and that kind of stuff." "Oh no," Rafferty explains, "That's in uptown. This is midtown. Sort of a way station . . . temporary." Rafferty further explains that until Bobby takes on, and successfully completes, an assignment on earth he will ride the subway forever. Bobby is saved from this Hollywood purgatory by coming to the aid of Lenny, a young boy so dissatisfied with his life that he attempts suicide.

Date with an Angel, made in 1987 is a rather lackluster film about an angel who is sent to earth to interrupt the unpromising life of a young musician played by Michael E. Knight. There are some rather interesting points to note, however. The angelic being sent to the musician is female and when she descends to earth she cannot speak, implying that angels do not communicate in the same way as humans. Further, the angel falls in love with her heavenly charge, and unlike Dudley in *The Bishop's Wife,* chooses, and is allowed to remain on earth. When she metaphorically hangs up her wings, she literally is able to communicate, for she becomes of this world.

A darker film made in 1988 is *The Seventh Sign,* directed by Carl Schultz. This apocalyptic story revolves around an expectant mother, played by Demi Moore, whose unborn child is the key to the fate of the world. It seems that heaven is full and the soul of her child, if it dies, will unlock the seventh, and final seal that heralds the endtime. Jurgen Prochnow is cast as the mysterious angelic presence sent to earth to keep the biblical prophesy at bay.

On the European scene, the best contemporary interpretation of the fall of angels on earth is without doubt Wim Wenders's black and white masterpiece *Wings of Desire* (1987), which proposes that redemption occurs with a descent into physicality. Ganz, one of a pair of angels visiting Berlin, decides he wants to be human after falling in love with a circus performer. Wenders's angels, who have perceptual access to everyone's subconscious, are perfect humanists whose center of operations is the Berlin public library, and whose chief function is to calm savaged emotions and save despairing lives. Wender continues his saga in the film's sequel, *Far Away, So Close,* made in 1993.

Sources:

Kolker, Robert Phillip, and Peter Beicken. *The Films of Wim Wenders: Cinema as Vision and Desire.* Cambridge: Cambridge University Press, 1993.

Parish, James Robert. *Ghosts and Angels in Hollywood Films: Plots, Critiques, Casts and Credits for 264 Theatrical and Made-for-Television Releases.* Jefferson, N.C.: McFarland, 1994.

Walker, John, ed. *Halliwell's Film Guide.* New York: HarperCollins, 1994.

HARRY BELAFONTE IS THE ANGEL TO ZERO MOSTEL'S MORRIS MISKIN IN *THE ANGEL LEVINE.* (UNITED ARTISTS; COURTESY THE KOBAL COLLECTION)

Muhammad

Muhammad, the Prophet of **Islam,** was born into the Hashim family of the powerful tribe of Quraysh in the city of Mecca around A.D. 570. His father and his mother died when he was a young child, and he was placed under the care of his uncle, Abu Talib. Muhammad was known to be sincere and honest even before his call to prophethood, his title at this time being "Al-Amin," the faithful one.

At the age of twenty-five Muhammad accepted the marriage offer of a wealthy widow Khadija, fifteen years his senior. Muhammad had been under her employment, conducting caravan trade for her into Syria. The marriage was a happy one and resulted in two sons, who died in infancy, and four daughters.

During this period, Muhammad, perhaps influenced by the monotheism of the Christians and Jews in Syria and Mecca, was bothered by the paganism and idolatry of the Meccan society. It became his custom to spend a part of each year in retreat outside of Mecca in a cave on Mt. Hira fasting and meditating. At the age of forty, Muhammad believed that he received a message from God through the angel **Gabriel.**

Belief in the revelation given to Muhammad by the angel Gabriel (**Djibril** in Arabic) is a fundamental tenet of **Islam.** According to Muslims, Muhammad is the last of a long line of prophets. In orthodox Islam, Muhammad is regarded as the Seal of the Prophets, meaning that God's ongoing revelatory activity through the angels was finally completed in the revelation of the Koran through him.

One of the earliest and most credible of the biographers of Muhammad, Ibn Ishaq, described the encounter as a fearful one. The angel came to Muhammad in his sleep and commanded him to read, holding before him a brocaded cloth upon which was some writing. When Muhammad responded in confusion, the angel attempted to strangle him with the cloth until Muhammad felt close to death. The angel repeated the same procedure three times and finally announced: "Read! Thy Lord is the most beneficent, who taught by the pen, taught that which they knew not unto men" [96:3-5] (106).

At first Muhammad thought himself crazy or possessed by **jinn,** but after his wife Khadija and her Christian cousin Waraqah heard of his experience, they assured him that his source of revelation was the same as that of Moses. It seemed to them that the God of **Judaism** and **Christianity** was planning to use Muhammad as a prophet to teach his people in Arabia.

A silence of about three years followed this initial revelation during which Muhammad fell into a state of depression, feeling that he had been forsaken by God. However, the angel resumed relaying messages, and Muhammad began in earnest to preach about the new faith which he called Islam (submission). He felt that he was sent to teach his people about the one sovereign God whom Muhammad referred to as Allah. His first converts were his wife Khadija, his adopted son Zaid, and his close companion Abu Bakr.

Most of Muhammad's few early followers were insignificant members of society. The majority of Meccans opposed Muhammad as he challenged their belief in idols, gods, and goddesses. Perhaps even more importantly, Muhammad threatened to usurp the power they held in controlling the city of Mecca, which was a profitable center for pilgrimage and trade. Even though Muhammad and his small group of followers were under the protection of Abu Talib, Muhammad's uncle, a well respected man of the community, they experienced verbal assaults and minor aggression on behalf of their newfound faith.

In 619 Muhammad lost his faithful wife Khadija and his uncle Abu Talib who, despite the fealty he had generously offered to his nephew, died an unbeliever. Conflicts intensified between the early Muslims and the Meccan aristocrats, and Muhammad realized that he would need to leave the city soon. At about this time, prior to his leaving Mecca, Muhammad claimed that the angel Gabriel took him on a journey from Mecca to Jerusalem and from there through the seven heavens where he visited with the major previous prophets. He ultimately was admitted into the presence of God. Jerusalem is one of the three most holy places on earth for Muslims because of this journey, which is referred to by Muslims as *Leilat al-Isra'* (The Night Journey).

The news of this incredible mystical experience created even more animosity between the believers and the leaders of Mecca. Even some of the new converts began to express doubt in Muhammad.

Fortunately, the neighboring village of Yathrib, later called Medina (short for *Medinat an-Nabi* or The City of the Prophet), offered protection to the Prophet and his followers on September 24, A.D. 622. Muslims refer to this year as the *Hijra* (migration) and date their calendars from this time. Muhammad was welcomed to Medina as an arbiter between opposing parties. More importantly, the pagan Medinans converted to Islam under Muhammad's exhortation.

However, he was not able to persuade the three Jewish clans who lived in Medina to embrace his message as they refused to accept the discrepancies that existed between the Koran and their sacred Scriptures.

Muhammad

According to the Koran two angels are assigned to every person, one to record his good deeds, the other his evil.

Initially, Muhammad attempted to make concessions to the Jews in order to find their favor. He had prescribed that his followers pray in the direction of Jerusalem as did the Jews; he also commanded that the Jewish Day of Atonement to be a Muslim holy day of fasting. Not receiving the approval of the Jews, Muhammad changed his policy toward them with the support of Koranic revelations. Muslims were thus ordered to pray toward Mecca; the time of fasting was extended to include the entire month of Ramadan (the ninth lunar month in the Arabic calendar); **Abraham** (versus Moses) became the central figure in the history of Islam; and Koranic pronouncements against Jews became more severe.

Another task for Muhammad, in addition to tribal unification, was that of securing financial support for the believers who had sacrificed to follow the Prophet. Many became involved in raiding commercial Meccan caravans. The Prophet received revelations granting permission for the believers to fight, affirming the necessity of warfare to promote the welfare of the believers.

The prospect of gaining booty from the enemy boosted the Muslim morale, and for the ensuing expeditions Muhammad was able to engage a significantly larger number of warriors. In March 624 at Badr, the believers met up with about 950 Meccans intent on inflicting a serious blow to the Prophet and his followers. Because of Muhammad's superior military strategy and the zeal of his forces, the Muslims were able to overpower their enemies. The victory at Badr was interpreted as a sign of Allah's vindication of Muhammad's prophethood. Muhammad's prestige increased greatly. During this period Muhammad began the long series of multiple marriages that further strengthened his position as head of the community.

After their defeat, the Meccans realized that they needed to crush Muhammad's power once and for all. In 627 a great Arab confederacy gathered to wage battle against the believers. The Muslims dug a trench about the city of Medina and prepared for the worse. Due to unsuccessful attempts to cross the trench, poor weather conditions as well as Muhammad's secret negotiations with several influential tribes, the besiegers lost their determination and began to withdraw. This easy victory gave Muhammad further confidence. Significant numbers of conversions were made at this time.

In January 630 Muhammad, with an army of ten thousand men, entered Mecca with virtually no resistance. He removed the idols from the Ka'aba, the pagan place of worship, pardoned all prominent Meccan leaders and gave them generous rewards for their surrender. Muhammad thus won their respect and admiration. After Mecca's surrender, many other Arab tribes in the region followed suit. Christians and Jews were permitted to continue to practice their faiths but were required to pay tributes and taxes.

In March of 632 Muhammad led the Islamic pilgrimage to Mecca and delivered his farewell address to tens of thousands of his followers. Three months later at the age of sixty-three, he died a peaceful death.

The greatest twentieth-century Muslim thinker of India Muhammad Iqbal (d. 1938) summed up the feelings of Muslims for Muhammad in this way: "Love of the Prophet runs like blood in the veins of this community" (Schimmel, p. 239). The reports of Muhammad's sayings (*Hadith*) and actions (*Sunna*) were tirelessly collected by future generations after the Prophet's death. The Hadith and the Sunna, although not regarded as equal to the Koran, are viewed as the recordings of Muhammad's inspired words and actions. The Hadith provide Muslims with the details of every aspect of Muslim life and practice. Annemarie Schimmel, a prominent scholar at Harvard University, observes that the prophetic tradition serves to unify the Islamic culture. Whether a Muslim be from Morocco or Indonesia, "[he] knows how to behave when entering a house, which formulas of greeting to employ, what to avoid in good company, how to eat, and how to travel. For centuries Muslim children have been brought up in these ways" (p. 55).

The prophetic tradition has not only influenced every detail of the life of the individual believer, but it has also been the foundation of Islamic law and social government. Despite Muhammad's importance in Islam, it must be remembered that his position in Islamic theology is not comparable to that of Christ in Christian theology. The ultimate foundation of Islam is the Koran, perceived by Muslims to be the uncreated and eternal work of Allah.

—*Kathryn Sampson*

Sources:

Andrae, Tor. *Mohammed: The Man and His Faith*. Rev. ed. New York: Harper & Row, 1955.

Encyclopaedia of Islam. Vol 6. Leiden, Netherlands: E. J. Brill, 1978.

Glassé, Cyril. *The Concise Encyclopedia of Islam*. San Francisco: Harper San Francisco, 1989.

Ibn Ishaq. *Sirat Rasul Allah, (The Life of Muhammad)*. Translated by A. Guillaume. New York: Oxford University Press, 1980.

Iqbal, Muhammad. *Javidnama*. Translated by Arthur John Arberry as *Javidnama*. London: George Allen & Unwin, 1966. Translated by Shaikh Mahmud Ahmad as *The Pilgrims of Eternity*. Lahore: Institute of Islamic Culture, 1961.

Schimmel, Annemarie. *And Mohammed is His Prophet*. Chapel Hill: The University of North Carolina Press, 1985.

Munkir and Nakir

Munkir and Nakir are two blue-eyed black angels found in Muslim tradition. Their special job is to examine the souls of the recently deceased to determine if they are worthy of a place in paradise. The angels ask the deceased "who is **Muhammad**?" The believers will have the correct answer that Muhammad is Allah's messenger. They will then be left in peace until Resurrection Day. Those who fail the test—the sinners and infidels—are subjected to torture until the Day of Resurrection.

Sources:

Davidson, Gustav. *A Dictionary of Angels: Including the Fallen Angels.* New York: Free Press, 1971.

Encyclopaedia of Islam. Vol 6. Leiden, Netherlands: E. J. Brill, 1978.

Ronner, John. *Know Your Angels: The Angel Almanac with Biographies of 100 Prominent Angels in Legend and Folklore, and Much More.* Murfreesboro, Tenn.: Mamre, 1993.

Muses

According to Greek mythology, the nine Muses, personifications of artistic and literary inspiration, had **wings** and, although not explicitly angels or messengers of the gods, conveyed inspiration (a seemingly divine quality) to mortals. The daughters of the Titan Mnemosyne (Memory) and Zeus, only three Muses are recorded in the earliest tales: Mneme (also Memory), Melete (Practice), and Aoede (Song). Elsewhere they bear the names of the first lyre's first three strings: Nete (Bottom), Mese (Middle), and Hypates (Top).

The mythographer Hesiod named nine Muses, and various later authors assigned them to diverse arts: Calliope (epic poetry), Clio (history), Euterpe (flute playing), Terpsichore (lyric poetry or dance), Erato (lyric poetry or song), Melpomene (tragedy), Thalia (comedy), Polyhmnia (mime), and Urania (astronomy). The Muses were said to be led by Apollo, who danced with them at Olympian festivals. The few myths in which the Muses figure usually involve mortals who boast that they are more skilled at the arts than the Muses. The Muses ultimately defeat the braggart, and punish the offending mortal.

Sources:

Grant, Michael, and John Hazel. *Who's Who in Classical Mythology.* New York: Oxford University Press, 1993.

Tripp, Edward. *The Meridian Handbook of Classical Mythology.* New York: New American Library, 1970.

Music, Angels in

Angels have often been represented singing or playing harps, trumpets, or lutes. It is not usually difficult to recognize angels in the visual arts, even when they lack wings, but it is sometimes difficult to detect them in music, unless a direct allusion is provided by the words.

Although angel voices abound in Christmas hymns and carols, such as "Hark the Herald Angels Sing," for the most part historical knowledge is essential in order to recognize angels in music (independent of lyrics). This issue is discussed in some musicological literature, although more often in connection with bad angels than with good ones. Evil often seems to be more compelling than good, making the Devil seem more interesting than God.

Reinhold Hammerstein, for example, in his *Diabolus in Musica* a German study of the iconography of medieval music, focuses on bad angels. One of the basic ways of alluding to them musically is through the use of what he calls *pervertierte instrumente*. One "perverts" an instrument to produce, for instance, a horrible cacophony. When this is set beside a beautifully harmonious musical sequence, the contrast, along with minimal verbal help either from the title or from an advance interpretation in the published program, forms a pointer.

In Robert Schumann's *Faust* (first performed in 1862) it is possible to detect an evil angel taunting Gretschen in church. Then, in the epilogue, after she is transported to heaven, we can hear choirs of the good angels singing. Krzysztof Penderecki, in his *Dies Irae* (1978) seeks to present a hideous vision of hell on earth in which **Satan** and his hosts have descended to show us the nature of their terrible evil power. We can hear the lamentations of the damned and the vicious shrieks of their masters. In medieval mythology the Devil was supposed to leave an indescribably hideous stench behind him. In Penderecki's music one can almost smell his stench rising through the lamentations in this foretaste of hell.

In Gustav Mahler's Fourth Symphony (1892, rev. 1901–10)), a soprano angel sings, in an almost childlike way, a celebration of celestial joy. Mahler also uses angel motifs in his second and third symphonies. Frederic Massenet, in *Le Jongleur de Notre-Dame* (1902), presents moving musical imagery of good angels carrying to heaven the soul of a humble and devout man who is a juggler by trade and has offered his juggling, all that he has, to God. In Franz Liszt's *Dante Symphony* (1855–56), we can hear the angelic voices in the ninth heaven, to which Beatrice has guided Dante in the twenty-seventh canto of the *Paradiso*, after he has heard St. Peter bitterly rebuking his successors in the apos-

Music

There are 1,387 popular songs in existence that contain the word angel; 865 with devil; 1,907 with heaven; 648 with hell; and 88 with Satan.

WINGED MAN PLAYING A LUTE BY ALBRECHT DÜRER (1497).

after he has heard St. Peter bitterly rebuking his successors in the apostolic chair for avarice and power mania.

We know to expect circling angels ecstatically singing the praises of God. Very different is the Dance of Satan and his hosts in *Job* (1927–30), by Ralph Vaughan Williams, who, although working in an Anglican context, was of a mystical temper. His music may perhaps be better described as religious rather than as belonging to the Anglican—or indeed any—choral church tradition.

Giuseppe Verdi, in *Giovanna d'Arco* (1845), uses a somewhat mischievous method to express the contrast between good and bad angels. Joan is confronted by a group of each kind. The bad ones sing what is really a variation of a Neapolitan bordello song, while the good ones sing church music. That is a comparatively simple device for a composer to use to bring home the distinction. As musical drama Verdi's device is successful. The contrasting imagery of the bordello and the church colorfully expresses one symbol of the warfare between **Lucifer** and **Michael,** between the Devil and God.

In Sergei Prokofiev's Third Symphony (1928) the angel who brings music to the girl is neither good nor bad; at any rate she does not seem to belong to one category or the other. Nevertheless, the entity is plainly supernatural. By contrast, Wagner's *Der Engel* is a song about an angel engaged in the specific task of guiding him; it is thus a close cousin of the guardian angel concept, set to music.

Sources:

Hammerstein, Reinhold. *Diabolus in Musica: Studien zur Ikonographie der Musik in Mittelalter.* München: Francke, 1974.

MacGregor, Geddes. *Angels: Ministers of Grace.* New York: Paragon House, 1988.

Ronner, John. *Know Your Angels: The Angel Almanac with Biographies of 100 Prominent Angels in Legend and Folklore, and Much More.* Murfreesboro, Tenn.: Mamre Press, 1993.

Wilson, Peter Lamborn. *Angels.* New York: Pantheon Books, 1980.

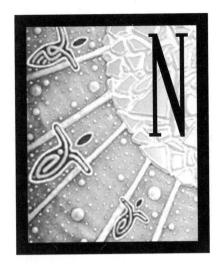

The Nature of Angels

Because we attribute characteristics to humans, it is not uncommon to often apply these same qualities (albeit it the better qualities of man) to angels. And because angels are believed to exemplify these attributes in their purest forms, it is natural for humans to strive to measure up. For example, a popular quote from Thomas Traherne in the seventeenth century is "How like an angel came I down!" In modern times, we often hear remarked, "she's an angel" or "what an angel."

Loyalty is one of these commonly assigned characteristics. Angels are thought to be truly loyal because they are not subject to their own changing agendas. Angels are wholly devoted to God and their loyalty to him is unquestioned. An example of human fealty as compared to pure angel loyalty can be found in the Old Testament. The young David was a soldier with the Philistine army under the leadership of Achish when it was going to attack an Israelite encampment. The Philistine soldiers mistrusted David as a Jew and refused to fight side by side with him, fearing that he would turn traitor. Achish told David that he found no fault with him, but that the other soldiers refused to go into battle with David in their ranks. He was therefore told to go home. David protested, asking why he should not be allowed to fight this battle for Achish as he had for the past year. "Achish answered David, 'I agree that you have been as true to me as an angel of God, but the Philistine commanders insist that you shall not fight alongside them'" (1 Sam. 29:9). Achish expressed his belief in David's loyalty by comparing it to that of an angel.

Infallible discernment is another quality of angels. Angels are separate from the human race and are not subject to its confusions, particularly when it comes to right and wrong. The wise woman of Tekoah flattered King David by comparing his discernment to that of an angel in order to secure the return of the young man Absalom to Jerusalem. She said, "I thought too that the words of my lord the king would be a comfort to me; for your majesty is like the angel of God and can decide between right and wrong" (2 Sam. 14:17).

Wisdom was another angelic quality that the wise woman of Tekoah recognized in King David when he asked her if she came at the behest of Joab. The woman admitted that this was so and said, "Your majesty is as wise as the angel of God and knows all that goes on in the land" (2 Sam. 14:20). Angels traditionally have knowledge of every occurrence on earth. This absolute knowledge together with the absolute discernment that angels possess and the doing of God's will as their sole purpose would indeed make angels wise.

Good judgment is another quality of angels to which man can aspire and that King David was recognized as possessing in angelic proportions. Mephibosheth's loyalty to King David was challenged by his own servant. Mephibosheth said to King David, "Your majesty is like the angel of God; you must do what you think right."

Sources:

Adler, Mortimer J. *The Angels and Us*. New York: Macmillan, 1982.
Freeman, Eileen Elias. "How Like an Angel!" *AngelWatch* (August 1993).
MacGregor, Geddes. *Angels. Ministers of Grace*. New York: Paragon House, 1988.

Near-Death Experience

Estimated number of Americans who say they survived near-death experiences in 1994 because of an angel: 50,000

Near-Death Experience

Dr. Raymond A. Moody, in his well-known book *Life After Life*, writes that the most common element in the accounts of near-death experiences he has studied is the encounter with a light of unearthly brilliance. He writes, "Despite the light's unusual manifestation, however, not one person has expressed any doubt whatsoever that it was a being, a being of light. . . . The love and the warmth which emanate from this being to the dying person are utterly beyond words, and he feels completely surrounded by it and taken up in it, completely at ease and accepted in the presence of this being." Moody says the being of light is seen differently depending upon the person's religious beliefs or background and training. Some see this being as Christ, others as an angel.

Dannion Brinkley, modern author of the book *Saved by the Light,* a story of his own near-death experiences, writes of his out-of-body journey toward a brilliant light when he died after being struck by lightning. Brinkley writes, "I looked to my right and could see a silver form appearing like a silhouette through the mist. As it approached I began to feel a deep sense of love that encompassed all of the meanings of the word. It was as though I were seeing a lover, a mother, a best friend, multiplied a thousandfold. As the Being of Light came closer, these feelings of love intensified until they became almost too pleasurable to withstand."

Interestingly enough, angels are more often noted in the near-death experiences of children than in those of adults. In an interview published in *Angels: The Mysterious Messengers,* Melvin Morse notes that whereas angels were reported in only ten to twenty percent of adult near-death experience veterans, children brought back from death reported encounters with angels between sixty and seventy percent of the time. In the same interview, Morse observed, "It's almost as if children have some sort of special relationship with angels, and you hear these kinds of angel experiences coming again and again and again" (p. 223). This is even the case among children with no religious training. Morse also notes that, in comparison with children, adults who survive *life-threatening* situations—situations that are not technically near-death experiences—more frequently report experiences that are regarded as encounters with **guardian angels.**

Sources:

Brinkley, Dannion, with Paul Perry. *Saved by the Light: The True Story of a Man Who Died Twice and the Profound Revelations He Received.* New York: Villard Books, 1994.

Hauck, Rex, ed. *Angels: The Mysterious Messengers.* New York: Ballantine, 1994.

Moody, Raymond A., Jr. *Life After Life: The Investigation of a Phenomenon, Survival of Bodily Death.* New York: Bantam, 1976.

Morse, Melvin. *Closer to the Light: Learning from the Near-Death Experiences of Children.* New York: Ivy Books, 1990.

Nephilim

The biblical term *Nephilim,* which in Hebrew means "the fallen ones" or "those who fell," refers to the offspring of the **sons of God** (traditionally interpreted as angels) and mortal women mentioned in Gen. 6:1–4. A fuller account is preserved in the apocryphal **Book of Enoch,**

"THESE [THE NEPHILIM] WERE THE MIGHTY MEN THAT WERE OF OLD, THE MEN OF RENOWN" (GEN. 6:4). ILLUSTRATION FOR DANTE'S *DIVINE COMEDY* BY GUSTAVE DORÉ (1861–68).

which recounts how a group of angels left heaven to mate with women and taught humanity such heinous skills as the art of war. The chief distinguishing characteristic of the Nephilim was their gigantic size. These giants are mentioned a number of times in both the Scriptures and the noncanonical books. There is a particularly vivid image in the book of Numbers, at a point where the wandering Israelites come upon a land occupied by giants. The Hebrew scouts give the following report:

> [A]ll the people that we saw in it are men of great stature. And there we saw the Nephilim (the sons of Anak, who come from the Nephilim); and we seemed to ourselves like grasshoppers, and so we seemed to them. (Num. 13:33)

Other groups of exceptionally tall people who appear to have been descendants of the Nephilim, such as the Anakim and the Rephaim, are mentioned in the books of Deuteronomy (2:11; 2:20; 3:11; 3:13) and Joshua (12:4; 13:12; 15:8; 17:15; 18:16).

There were still descendants of the Nephilim during King David's time. Four enormous members of the Philistine army are mentioned in 2 Samuel and in parallel verses in 1 Chronicles. These passages observe that at least one of these four men had six fingers on each hand and six toes on each foot, traits that may have marked the entire race. The author of 2 Samuel also notes that "these four were descended from the giants in Gath" (21:22)—which was the homeland of Goliath, the most famous giant in the Bible.

There are other allusions to the descendants of the Nephilim in the apocryphal books of Judith (16:6), Sirach (16:7), Baruch (3:26–28), and the Wisdom of Solomon (14:6).

Sources:

Davidson, Gustav. *A Dictionary of Angels: Including the Fallen Angels.* 1967. Reprint. New York: Free Press, 1971.

Freeman, Eileen. "The Angels Who Fell From Grace." *AngelWatch* 3 (October 1994): 5.

Godwin, Malcolm. *Angels: An Endangered Species.* New York: Simon and Schuster, 1990.

Prophet, Elizabeth Clare. *Forbidden Mysteries of Enoch: Fallen Angels and the Origins of Evil.* Rev. ed. Livingston, Mont.: Summit University Press, 1992.

Nergal

Nergal was the **Mesopotamian** Mars, a god associated with war and death. He was apparently adopted as a **guardian spirit** by the Chaldeans, one of the groups of people who ruled the Mesopotamian area in later centuries. His marriage to Ereshkigal, queen of the underworld, caused him to be identified as king of the underworld in later syncretistic religions, such as certain strands of **Gnosticism.** In certain reference books (e.g., Gustav Davidson's *Dictionary of Angels*), he is mistakenly identified as one of the great winged centaurs of ancient Mesopotamia, which explains his association with angels in some writers' minds. Also, in at least a few **occult** books, Nergal is identified as chief of the "secret police" in the infernal regions, thus causing him to be associated with fallen angels.

Sources:

Davidson, Gustav. *A Dictionary of Angels: Including the Fallen Angels.* 1967. Reprint. New York: Free Press, 1971.

Ronner, John. *Know Your Angels: The Angel Almanac with Biographies of 100 Prominent Angels in Legend and Folklore, and Much More.* Murfreesboro, Tenn.: Mamre Press, 1993.

New Age, Angels in the

The New Age can be viewed as a revivalist movement within a pre-existing **metaphysical-occult** community. As such, the New Age can be compared with **Christian** revivals, particularly with such phenomena as the early Pentecostal movement (i.e., a movement that simultaneously revived and altered a segment of Protestant Christianity). Comparable to the influence of Pentecostalism on Christianity, the New Age had an impact on some but not all segments of the occult community. Also like Pentecostalism, the New Age revival left a host of new organizations and denominations in its wake without substantially affecting the teachings of pre-existing organizations or denominations.

From another angle, the New Age can be viewed as a successor movement to the counterculture of the 1960s. As observers of the New Age vision have pointed out, a significant portion of New Agers are baby-boomers, people who two decades earlier were probably participating, at some level, in the phenomenon known as the counterculture. As the counterculture faded away in the early seventies, many former "hippies" found themselves embarking on a spiritual quest—one that, in many cases departed from the Judeo-Christian mainstream. Thus one of the possible ways to date the beginnings of the New Age movement is from the period of the rather sudden appearance of large numbers of unconventional spiritual seekers in the decade following the sixties.

As a movement without a set doctrine or without religious authorities to determine what new ideas should be admitted or excluded in the new age belief system, the New Age subculture has otherwise shown a remarkable permeability with respect to new notions. Without letting go of its basic world view, various particular ideas, practices, and so forth come and go as so many fads. Thus in the 1970s New Age, for example, the focus was on Asian spiritual teachers and on such traditional disciplines as yoga, meditation and tai chi. By the late 1980s when the mass media began to pay attention to the movement, these earlier interests were outshadowed by such phenomena as **channeling** and crystals. To outside observers, channeling and crystals seemed to be quintessentially New Age, so that, when these fads began fading, it appeared to outsiders that the movement itself was on the wane.

In fact, however, what had occurred was that the ever-changing surface of the New Age subculture was merely shifting to other interests, such as neo-shamanism, "inner child" work, and angels. How quickly such interests come and go can be seen in the entry list in the *New Age Encyclopedia.* At the time that volume was winding up in late 1989/early 1990, angels were so far out of the picture that no entry specifically on angels was included. However, into the 1990s, the subculture is virtually saturated by angel books, angel jewelry, angel newsletters, and specialized **angel stores,** resulting in an angel cover story in the December 1993 issue of *Time* magazine.

The point of origin for the current New Age interest in angels seems to have been theosophical ideas about the **devas** (the occult term for angels), as mediated to the larger New Age subculture by the community of **Findhorn.** This community in northern Scotland came to the attention of the occult-metaphysical subculture in the late 1960s. The early Findhorn community focused around a highly successful vegetable garden in which, residents claimed, community members were engaged in a unique cooperative arrangement with agricultural devas—spiritual beings which theosophical writers have claimed work at the etheric level to build up forms on the physical plane. Thus the devas, whom Theosophists had long identified with the angels of Western religious traditions, entered the consciousness of the New Age, though it would be more than two decades before they became the focus of attention.

Others believe this resurgence in angel interest may be an ancient human yearning that is simply still evolving. It is said that early peoples invented their spirits to help explain all they saw in the natural world. In the **Middle Ages,** theologians and scholars read the holy books and then theorized about angels for the joy of thought. Writer **Sophy Burnham** embraces this theory in the modern age by writing, "It is the existential longing for surcease that makes us believe that something other must exist."

Burnham is not alone in her belief: as a statistical indication of increasing interest, a 1992 Gallup youth poll found that 76 percent of American teenagers believed in angels—up from 64 percent in 1978.

New Age

Percentage of Americans who believe in angels: 69%

How long angels will ride their current crest of popularity is difficult to predict. One anomalous indicator is that, unlike other New Age fads, the New Age shares its present angel craze with the conservative Christian subculture—an unprecedented parallelism which indicates that the interest in angels may be more durable than earlier topics. A more historically-informed glance at angelic matters indicates a high correlation between an interest in angels and millennial expectancy. If this correlation holds true in the present case, angels should be with us until at least the end of the millennium. In any event, like earlier foci of New Age consciousness, angelic interest may never completely disappear as a topic for books and lectures, even long after the fad peaks.

Sources:

Burnham, Sophy. *A Book of Angels: Reflections on Angels Past and Present and True Stories of How They Touch Our Lives.* New York: Ballantine, 1990.

Eliade, Mircea, ed. *Encyclopedia of Religion.* 16 vols. New York: Macmillan, 1987.

Ellwood, Robert S., and Harry B. Partin. *Religious and Spiritual Groups in Modern America.* Englewood Cliffs, N.J.: Prentice-Hall, 1988.

Lewis, James R., and J. Gordon Melton, eds. *Perspectives on the New Age.* Albany: State University of New York Press, 1992.

Melton, J. Gordon, Jerome Clark, and Aidan Kelly. *New Age Encyclopedia.* Detroit, Mich.: Gale Research, 1990.

Nike

Nike, the Greek goddess of victory (later viewed as equivalent to the Roman Victoria), was Heracles' escort to Mt. Olympus. She was usually represented with **wings,** holding a crown over the heads of victors. With no elaborate myth of her own, Nike was more the symbol or personification of a quality than a character in the **Greek** pantheon.

Sources:

Grant, Michael, and John Hazel. *Who's Who in Classical Mythology.* New York: Oxford University Press, 1993.

Tripp, Edward. *The Meridian Handbook of Classical Mythology.* New York: New American Library, 1970.

Nimrod

Nimrod was a hunter, the son of Cush, and, according to legend, the moving force behind the Tower of Babel. In the book of Genesis, he is mentioned briefly in chapter 10:

NIMROD. ILLUSTRATION FOR DANTE'S *DIVINE COMEDY* BY GUSTAVE DORÉ (1861–68).

Nimrod . . . was the first on earth to be a mighty man. He was a mighty hunter before the Lord; therefore it is said, "Like Nimrod a mighty hunter before the Lord." The beginning of his kingdom was Babel, Erech, and Accad. . . . (Gen. 10:8–10)

In Jewish legend, Nimrod was one of the **Nephilim**—the children of the angels who, according to Genesis 6, "saw that the daughters of men were fair and . . . took to wife such of them as they chose." Such a genealogy would make him the son of a fallen angel.

Sources:

Ginzberg, Louis. *The Legends of the Jews.* Philadelphia: The Jewish Publication Society of America, 1954.

Ronner, John. *Know Your Angels: The Angel Almanac with Biographies of 100 Prominent Angels in Legend and Folklore, and Much More.* Murfreesboro, Tenn.: Mamre Press, 1993.

Nuriel

Nuriel (Fire) is the angel of hailstorms, as reported in Jewish legend, and was encountered by Moses in the second heaven. Nuriel manifests in the form of an eagle issuing from the side of Hesed (Kindness). He is grouped with **Michael,** Shamshiel, Seraphiel, and other great angels and is characterized as a "spell-binding power."

The **Zohar** pictures Nuriel as the angel who governs Virgo. He is said to be three hundred parasangs (about 1,200 miles) tall, with a retinue of fifty myriads (500,000) of angels. His height is exceeded only by the **erelim,** the **watchers,** Af and Hemah, and by the tallest hierarch in heaven, known as **Metatron.** Nuriel is mentioned in **Gnostic** lore as one of seven subordinates to **Jehuel,** prince of fire. In the book *Hebrew Amulets,* Schrire reports that his name can be found engraved on oriental amulets.

Sources:

Davidson, Gustav. *A Dictionary of Angels: Including the Fallen Angels.* 1967. Reprint. New York: Free Press, 1971.

Schrire, T. *Hebrew Amulets.* London: Routledge & Kegan Paul, 1966.

Insofar as we conquer the demons who stir up war and disturb peace, we perform better service for our ruler than they who bear the sword.

—Origen, *Against Celsus*

Occult

The Western occult tradition is one of the primary sources of angel lore fueling the contemporary interest in angels. This tradition was mediated to the **New Age** subculture through various sources, most notably the **Findhorn** community in Scotland. In the same way in which New Age came to have negative associations after the wave of media attention it received in the late 1980s, the term *occult* acquired negative connotations after a similar wave of media coverage in the 1970s. Also, because *occult* encompasses a broad range of ideas and practices, it is difficult to adequately define and delimit this term. This difficulty is compounded by the negative connotations the word has acquired both inside and outside of the metaphysical/occult subculture. *Occultism* calls to mind images of robed figures conducting arcane rituals for less than socially desirable ends.

Occult comes from a root word meaning hidden, and originally denoted a body of esoteric beliefs and practices that were in some sense "hidden" from the average person (e.g., practices and knowledge that remain inaccessible until after an initiation). Alternatively, it refers to supernatural powers that are normally imperceptible and thus hidden from the ordinary person (e.g., magical and astrological forces).

As beings who are normally hidden from ordinary mortals, angels are "occult" in the most general sense of the word. Angels are also associated with the mystical system of the Cabala, which constitutes the starting point for various magical practices, particularly the tradition referred to as Ceremonial Magic (which is part of the more general Western occult tradition). When, however, one talks about "occult angels" or "the occult view of angels," one normally is refering to the angelic tradition expressed in modern **Theosophical** writings.

Sources:

Bletzer, June G. *The Donning International Encyclopedic Psychic Dictionary.* Norfolk, Va.: Donning, 1986.

Shepard, Leslie A., ed. *Encyclopedia of Occultism & Parapsychology.* Detroit, Mich.: Gale Research, 1991.

Origen

Origen (ca. 185–254), both the greatest biblical scholar and the most original mind of the patristic period, attributed to angels a subtle or ethereal body. He also believed that angels are capable of falling from their high estate. Most fathers of the church, however, repudiated this view of Origen's as heretical.

In his philosophical masterpiece, *De Principiis,* Origen affirms that angels derive their position or rank according to their merit, and further hypothesizes that angels are neither impeccable nor unredeemable. Origen also treats the notion of **guardian angels,** suggesting that we are both tempted by evil spirits and guided and guarded by good ones—specifically that one angel is assigned to everyone as his or her protector.

Sources:

Bemrose, Stephen. *Dante's Angelic Intelligences: Their Importance in the Cosmos and in Pre-Christian Religion.* Rome: Edizioni di Storia e Letteratura, 1983.

MacGregor, Geddes. *Angels: Ministers of Grace.* New York: Paragon House, 1988.

Occult

According to occultists, an angel-year is a period of time lasting either 145 years or 365 years.

Orisha

In their efforts to discover angelic beings in different religions, contemporary researchers studying angels sometimes mention **orishas,** spiritual beings found in traditional Yoruba (African) religion as well as in several Yoruba-influenced religions in the Americas, such as Santeria.

Like **Hinduism,** the basic Yoruba worldview is ultimately monistic, postulating a single divine energy behind the apparent diversity of the perceived world. However, also like the Hindus, the Yoruba are simultaneously polytheistic, postulating a pantheon of some four hundred or so gods, the orisha. The Yoruba believe that the orisha were once human beings who led notable lives and became gods at death. Orisha also refers to one's individual destiny or "soul" (specifically, one's spiritual double in the other world).

In the syncretistic religious systems of the Western Hemisphere—systems such as Santeria (Cuba) and Candomblé (Brazil), which mix the Yoruba tradition with Catholicism and other religious elements—orishas are retained as important demigods. Particularly in these later religions, the comparison between orishas and angels is particularly appropriate, given that Catholic saints and angels supplied important models for the role orishas played in these new religions. For example, among the Candomblé it is believed that each person receives two orishas (one male, one female) at birth, and that these Orishas play the role of **guardian angels** (Parisen, p. 243) for the newborn. This is clearly a reformulation of the Yoruba tradition in terms of Western religion.

Sources:

Eliade, Mircea, ed. *Encyclopedia of Religion.* 16 vols. New York: Macmillan, 1987.

Parisen, Maria. *Angels & Mortals: Their Co-Creative Power.* Wheaton, Ill.: Quest Books, 1990.

It must be recess in
heaven if St. Peter is
letting his angels out.

—Zora Neale Hurston,

Their Eyes Were

Watching God

Padre Pio

Padre Pio was an Italian Roman Catholic priest who suggested that people in need of spiritual help who could not come to him in person send their **guardian angels** instead. A great many people followed his suggestion; so many, in fact, that the Padre was sometimes kept awake all night in dealing with the angels. In addition to receiving guardian angels, Padre Pio often sent his own guardian angel to give comfort and aid to others.

As a young priest, Padre Pio went into ecstasies in which he conversed out loud with Jesus, **Mary,** his guardian angel, and St. Francis. In 1918 Pio received the stigmata, marks resembling the crucifixion wounds of Jesus. Padre Pio was extremely popular and worshippers frequently cut pieces of his habit to keep as relics. Almost 100,000 people attended his funeral in 1968. The story of Padre Pio's life is told in the book *Send Me Your Guardian Angel* by Fr. Allesio Parente.

Sources:
Parente, Fr. Allesio. *Send Me Your Guardian Angel.* San Giovanni Rotondo: Our Lady of Grace Capuchin Friary, 1984.

Patristic Angelology

It was impossible for the early Christian fathers to neglect angels, principally because of the many references to them in the **Bible,** which plainly implies their ontological reality. Thus, the early fathers of the church were forced to recognize angels as part of their theological enterprise. Being so close to the traditional polytheism of the Mediterranean world, they also had to explain to their pagan antagonists that neither angels nor saints were worshiped as divinities and that angels, though revered for their superior status in the hierarchy of being, their closeness to God, and their benevolence to humanity, were nonetheless creatures like ourselves.

Beyond these issues, however, the Christian authors of the first five centuries were far too concerned with disciplinary and dogmatic issues to give much attention to theories about angels, with the exception of the brilliant Alexandrian theologian **Origen.** Origen attributed to angels an ethereal body, an attribution that would later be disputed by **Thomas Aquinas.** He also took the position that angels are capable of falling from their high estate and asserted that they derive their position or rank according to their merit; they are neither impeccable nor unredeemable.

It was only with the early sixth-century writings of the mystical theologian **Dionysius the Areopagite,** who flourished about the year 500, that Christian angelology took on its classical form. Dionysius's chief work on angles, *The Celestial Hierarchy,* took on rather different interpretations in Eastern and Western Christianity. Byzantine authors, from Maximus the Confessor in the seventh century to Gregory Palamas and his opponents in the fourteenth century, adapted and used the Dionysian system as part of a mystical theology with roots in the writings of the Alexandrian and Cappadocian fathers.

In the Latin West, however, Dionysius's work stimulated theories concerning the nature of angels. The early medieval authors Gregory the Great and Bede the Venerable used his writings in essentially pastoral discussions of the role of angels. In the ninth century *The Celestial Hierarchy* was translated into Latin by Hilduin of Saint-Denis and again by John Scotus Erigena. The latter translation, corrected by Anastasius the Librarian in 875, became a standard reference work in the High Middle Ages.

Sources:

Bemrose, Stephen. *Dante's Angelic Intelligences: Their Importance in the Cosmos and in Pre-Christian Religion.* Rome: Edizioni di Storia e Letteratura, 1983.

MacGregor, Geddes. *Angels: Ministers of Grace*. New York: Paragon House, 1988.

Strayer, Joseph R., ed. *Dictionary of the Middle Ages*. 13 vols. New York: Scribner, 1982–89.

Peretti, Frank E.

Frank E. Peretti is an evangelical Christian novelist whose works—especially his best-selling *This Present Darkness* (1986) and *Piercing the Darkness* (1989)—feature "spiritual warfare" between Christian angels and fallen angels. The action in these novels moves back and forth between two interacting levels: While angels and devils cross swords in the spiritual realm, Peretti's human heroes and heroines do battle with New Agers, witches, psychologists, secular educationists, and other groups viewed by conservative Christians as being under demonic influence.

One of the keys necessary for understanding Peretti is the belief that the concentrated prayers of Christians provide power and protection for warrior angels. This "prayer energy" empowers God's angels to win their battles against supernatural **demons.** A decisive defeat of **Satan**'s legions in the spiritual realm disempowers Satan's earthly minions, which in turn leads to their defeat.

The climax of the confrontation in *This Present Darkness* provides us with a good example of how this "prayer power" is supposed to work. In the final scene of the battle, Tal, leader of the angelic host, crosses swords with Rafar, leader of the demonic forces. At the same time, the Remnant of God's human "prayer warriors" engaged in the earthly struggle are distracted by the dramatic damage inflicted by their crusade. This distraction interrupts the flow of "power" to Tal, and Rafar almost gets the better of him. At the last possible moment, these Christians feel impressed by the Lord to direct their prayer power against the demon:

[Event in spiritual realm:]

Tal could only back away from the fearsome onslaught of the demon prince, his one good hand still holding his sword up for defense. Rafar kept swinging and slashing, the sparks flying from the blades as they met. Tal's arm sank lower with each blow. "The Lord . . . rebuke you!" Tal found the breath to say again.

[Appropriate Christian "prayer" response, intuited by an elderly lady:]

Edith Duster was on her feet and ready to shout it to the heavens. "Rafar, you wicked prince of evil, in the name of Jesus we rebuke you!"

[Effect of "prayer energy" in spiritual realm:]

Rafar's blade zinged over Tal's head. It missed.

[Further "prayer" action in physical realm:]

"We bind you!" shouted the Remnant.

[Effect in spiritual realm:]

The big yellow eyes winced.

[Action in physical realm:]

"We cast you out!" Andy said.

[Effect in spiritual realm:]

There was a puff of sulfur, and Rafar bent over. Tal leaped to his feet.

[Action in physical realm:]

"We rebuke you, Rafar!" Edith shouted again.

[Effect in spiritual realm:]

Rafar screamed. Tal's blade had torn him open.

Although Christians have always believed in the power of prayer, the Darkness novels picture prayer as having a fantastic, magical efficacy against fallen angels.

Peretti is a gifted writer who is able to weave together believable stories of the everyday world with fantastic Dungeons-and-Dragons struggles between otherworldly angels and demons. The results of this skillful juxtaposition are novels with an eerie narrative landscape that evangelical scholar Irving Hexham has described as "sanctified Stephen King." Peretti's art has created an exciting narrative world replete with supernatural phenomena, psychic intuitions, quasi-magical powers, and sword-swinging warriors. A fascination with the **occult** is evident in Peretti's descriptions of demons:

He was like a high-strung little gargoyle, his hide a slimy, bottomless black, his body thin and spiderlike: half humanoid, half animal, totally demon. Two huge yellow cat-eyes bulged out of his face, darting to and fro, peering, searching. His breath came in short, sulfurous gasps, visible as glowing yellow vapor.

Even though Christians have traditionally believed in the guidance of the **Holy Spirit,** the picture Peretti draws of highly personal angels conveying guidance to the minds of God's saints makes Christian inspiration more lively and dramatic. Peretti also pictures angels as capable of materializing to help God's chosen, as in *This Present Darkness* when the angel Betsy materializes to give one of the heroines, Bernice Krueger, a short motorcycle ride. Once Bernice has reached her destination, Betsy evaporates like some figure out of an occult novel. As with many of the events that take place in the Darkness novels, such eerie encounters reflect the fascination with the supernatural and, more specifically, with angels that has come to characterize contemporary conservative Christianity.

Sources:

Hexham, Irving. "The Evangelical Response to the New Age." In James R. Lewis and J. Gordon Melton, eds. *Perspectives on the New Age.* Albany, N.Y.: State University of New York Press, 1992.

Peretti, Frank E. *This Present Darkness.* Westchester, Ill.: Crossway Books, 1986.

———. *Piercing the Darkness.* Westchester, Ill.: Crossway Books, 1989.

Pestilence Angel

The Pestilence Angel is referred to in the First Book of Chronicles, chapter 21 as the angel who delivered the pestilence upon Israel as punishment to King David for having conducted a census of Israel and Judah. According to tradition, it was **Satan** who incited David to count the people, and David ordered this be done against the urgings of his military commander Joab. God proceeded to punish Israel. David then admitted that he wrongly acted and prayed that God remove his guilt. God sent word to David that he could take his choice of three years of famine, three months of military losses, or three days of the Lord's own sword, bringing pestilence throughout the country. David decided that it would be better to suffer at the hands of the merciful God than at the hands of man. So the Lord sent a pestilence throughout Israel, killing 70,000 of David's people:

> And God sent an angel to Jerusalem to destroy it; but, as he was destroying it, the Lord saw and repented of the evil, and said to the destroying angel at the moment when he was standing beside the threshing-floor of Ornan the Jebusite, "Enough! Stay your hand." When David looked up and saw the angel of the Lord standing between earth and heaven, with his sword drawn in his hand and stretched out over Jerusalem, he and the elders, clothed in sackcloth, fell prostrate to the ground; and David said to God, "It was I who

gave the order to count the people. It was I who sinned, I, the shepherd, who did wrong. But these poor sheep, what have they done? O Lord my God, let thy hand fall upon me and upon my family, but check this plague on the people." The angel of the Lord, speaking through the lips of Gad, commanded David to go to the threshing-floor of Ornan the Jebusite and to set up there an altar to the Lord. David went up as Gad had bidden him in the Lord's name. Ornan's four sons who were with him hid themselves, but he was busy threshing his wheat when he turned and saw the angel. (1 Chron. 21:15–20)

Ornan offered to give his threshing floor to King David, but the King insisted on paying Ornan full price for it, so that the offering to the Lord should come directly from him. David built an altar on the threshing floor and made his offering to the Lord. "Then, at the Lord's command, the angel sheathed his sword" (1 Chron. 21:27).

Sources:

Ferguson, Everett, ed. *Encyclopedia of Early Christianity.* Vol. 846 of the Garland Reference Library of the Humanities. New York: Garland Publishing, 1990.

New Catholic Encyclopedia. Vol. 1. Washington, D.C.: Catholic University of America, 1981.

Peter and the Angel

The story of the apostle Peter's rescue by an angel in the Acts of the Apostles is exceptionally useful for understanding how angels were understood in the early Christian community. This tale originates in the persecution of the early church in Palestine. Herod the king (grandson of Herod the Great), appointed to his position by Rome, vigorously persecuted the church as part of an effort to please the religious establishment. He executed James, the brother of John, and imprisoned Peter with the intent of executing him as soon as the Feast of Unleavened Bread had passed. Aware of his impending fate, the community prayed for his deliverance:

Peter was kept in prison; but earnest prayer for him was made to God by the church. The very night when Herod was about to bring him out, Peter was sleeping between two soldiers, bound with two chains, and sentries before the door were guarding the prison; and behold an angel of the Lord appeared, and a light shone in the cell; and he struck Peter on the side and woke him, saying, "Get up quickly." (Acts 12:5–7)

THE ANGEL DELIVERING PETER FROM PRISON.

From this passage it is evident that the Christian God is a god who responds to prayer. This is consistent with the traditional Hebrew understanding of a regal divinity who sends angel "courtiers" out from the court of heaven to deliver his messages to his people and to otherwise carry out his will. Also consistent with tradition, the angel who appeared to Peter is a being of light, indicating the celestial, solar origin of such beings.

The angel directs Peter to dress and follow him out of prison. Peter, half asleep, thinks he is in a dream:

Peter and the angel leave the cell, and when they had passed the second guard, they came to the iron gate leading into the city. It opened to them of its own accord, and they went out and passed on through one street; and immediately the angel left him. (12:9)

The theme of God intervening in human affairs to rescue a captive is consistent with Judeo-Christian tradition, an echo of God's rescue of his people Israel from their captivity in Egypt, not to mention Babylon. It is also significant that the angel appears rather abruptly, accomplishes the task at hand, and then leaves as soon as the mission is complete. This mode of action tends to deemphasize the importance of the angel and gives the glory to God. In this instance, when later relating the story of his rescue to other believers, Peter described to them "how the Lord had brought him out of the prison" (12:17), thus focusing attention—and particularly the praise—on God rather than his agent. Although the angel directs Peter at each stage in the rescue, the angel does not force Peter to obey. On the whole, angels respect one's free will, directing but not compelling human actions.

After escaping, Peter found his way to the house of Mary, the mother of John, where the local Christian community was gathered:

And when he knocked at the door of the gateway, a maid named Rhoda came to answer. Recognizing Peter's voice, in her joy she did not open the gate but ran in and told that Peter was standing at the gate. They said to her, "You are mad." But she insisted that it was so. They said, "It is his angel!" But Peter continued knocking; and when they opened, they saw him and were amazed. (12:13–16)

The gathered believers apparently thought that Peter had been put to death and that the maid had seen his angel or spirit. The extreme surprise of the people indicates that God and his angels do not intervene in human affairs every time they are requested. Why God should manifest on some occasions and not others is a mystery.

Immediately following the story of Peter, in the same chapter of Acts, we read of another instance of an angel's direct intervention in human affairs:

On an appointed day Herod put on his royal robes, took his seat upon the throne, and made an oration to them. And the people shouted, "The voice of a god, and not of a man!" Immediately an angel of the Lord smote him, because he did not give God the glory; and he was eaten by worms and died. (12:21–23)

The contrast between Peter's rescue and Herod's death is instructive: Peter is rescued by an angel, but gives God the glory. Herod, on the other hand, is acclaimed a god, takes the glory for himself, and is slain by an angel as a result. What the author of Acts means by "immediately an angel of the Lord smote him" is unclear. According to an independent account, Josephus's *Antiquities of the Jews,* an owl appeared during Herod's speech, which was taken as a bad omen. Stricken in the abdomen with severe pain, Herod died within three days of the event. The assertion that an angel struck him imputes unseen spiritual action, that God must have taken vengeance against a persecutor of the church.

Sources:

Freeman, Eileen. "Peter and His Angel." *AngelWatch* 3, no. 6 (December/January 1995): 6–8.

The Illustrated Bible Dictionary. Sydney, Australia: Hodder & Stoughton, 1980.

The Interpreter's One-Volume Commentary on the Bible. Nashville: Abingdon Press, 1971.

Pixies (Pigsies or Piskies)

Pixies are a type of **fairy,** residing, according to tradition, in Cornwall, Devon, and Somerset. Pixies have many alternative names, including pisgies, pigsies, piskies, pechts, pechs, pickers, grigs, and dusters. They are said to be small and winged, with large heads, pointed ears and noses, and arched eyebrows. They wear hats made from the tops of toadstools or foxglove, and are attracted to gardens in bloom. They also love coming together for large gatherings—known in northern England as Pixie Fairs—at which they play and dance.

Like other inhabitants of the fairy realm, they have a mixed relationship with humanity. Pixies do not normally seek out human contact, but, when they take a liking to someone, they will help him or her in various ways, such as doing work around the house or farm. On the other hand, they enjoy playing pranks on people, being especially fond of misleading travellers. The latter habit has given rise to the expression "pixie-led," a state in which one goes around in circles and cannot seem to find one's way back to the beaten path. It was said that one could break the spell of being pixie-led by turning one's coat inside-out.

It has been speculated that the name pixie comes from *Pict,* referring to the aboriginal peoples of the British Isles. This idea would explain some pixie traits, such as their tendency to avoid people (i.e., avoid the dominant Celts) and their occasional working for people (i.e., for the Celtic farmers who would feed them). The Picts were also said to work in gold, silver, and bronze, and the metal dust generated by their work may be the prototype of pixie dust—the magical powder associated with Peter Pan's comrade, Tinker Bell.

Sources:

Briggs, Katharine. *An Encyclopedia of Fairies*. New York: Pantheon, 1976.

McCoy, Edwin. *A Witch's Guide to Faery Folk*. St. Paul, Minn.: Llewellyn, 1994.

Planets (Angels of the)

Planets (from Greek *planasthai,* "to wander") are the familiar celestial bodies orbiting the Sun. They were regarded as stars by the ancients, who referred to them as "wanderers" because, unlike the so-called fixed stars, they were always changing their positions with respect to the background of the celestial sphere. The Sun and Moon are also "wanderers" in this sense, and traditional astrology referred to them as "planets." In traditional astrology, astrological influences manifest themselves primarily through the planets.

Because angels and planets are both inhabitants of the celestial spheres, it is not a great leap to make connections between them. Hence, writers informed both by **astrology** and **angelology** developed various schemas correlating the two. The Muslim thinker al-Barceloni, for example, postulated the following:

Planet	Angel
Moon	Gabriel
Sun	Raphael
Mercury	Michael
Venus	Anael
Mars	Sammael
Jupiter	Zadkiel
Saturn	Kafziel

According to the **Gnostics,** the **archons** served as antithetical, evil archangels, and thus, also corresponded to the seven planets. Because archons were also related to the seven deadly sins, the identification is as follows:

Planet	Sin
Moon	Envy
Sun	Greed
Mercury	Falsehood
Venus	Lust
Mars	Wrath
Jupiter	Pride
Saturn	Sloth

In other correlations, the character of the angel and the nature of the planet (according to astrological tradition) occasionally correspond, but frequently the connection is tenuous. In a few places no similarity of meaning can be found, making it appear that traditional assignments were somewhat arbitrary. (See also **Days of the Week**)

Sources:

Davidson, Gustav. *A Dictionary of Angels: Including the Fallen Angels.* 1967. Reprint. New York: Free Press, 1971.

Powers

Credited as the first order of angels created by God, it is the job of the order of powers to protect the world from being taken over by demons. They reside in the region between the first and second heavens and patrol against "devilish infiltration." They protect our souls from evil and act as ministers of God who avenge evil in the world.

On a personal level, whenever a struggle between good and evil takes place, the powers are involved. According to Rom. 13:1, "The Soul is subject to the powers." Further, at death the powers guide our transition to the next life.

Camael is believed to be "chief" of this **choir,** the sixth in the **Dionysian** schema.

TOOME'S ENGRAVING OF A POWER, SIXTH IN THE DIONYSIAN HIERARCHY OF ANGELS.

Sources:

Davidson, Gustav. *A Dictionary of Angels: Including the Fallen Angels.* 1967. Reprint. New York: Free Press, 1971.

Godwin, Malcolm. *Angels: An Endangered Species.* New York: Simon and Schuster, 1990.

Mansfield, Richard. *Angels: An Introduction to the Angelic Hierarchy.* Encinitas, Calif.: Estuary Publications, 1994.

Principalities

The principalities are the legions of angels who protect religions. They are the seventh **choir** in the **Dionysian hierarchy,** immediately above **archangels.** The principalities provide strength to the tribes of Earth to pursue and endure their faith. In the Epistle to the Trallians, composed in the second century A.D., St. Ignatius the Martyr speaks of the "hierarchy of principalities." Dionysius stated that this choir "watched over the leaders of people." They are also reported to be the guardians over the nations of the world. The choice of this term as well as the term **powers** for choirs of God's angels is somewhat problematic in that the Letter to the Ephesians refers to the "hosts of wickedness in high places" against which Christians have to struggle as "principalities" and "powers" (Eph. 6:12).

Among those considered "chief" of the principalities are Nisrock, originally an Assyrian deity considered in occult writings to be the chief chef to the Demon Princes of Hell; and Anael, one of the seven angels of creation.

Sources:

Davidson, Gustav. *A Dictionary of Angels: Including the Fallen Angels.* 1967. Reprint. New York: Free Press, 1971.

Godwin, Malcolm. *Angels: An Endangered Species.* New York: Simon and Schuster, 1990.

Mansfield, Richard. *Angels: An Introduction to the Angelic Hierarchy.* Encinitas, Calif.: Estuary Publications, 1994.

Prophet, Elizabeth Clare

ELIZABETH CLARE PROPHET (COURTESY KALI PRODUCTIONS)

Elizabeth Clare Prophet is the author of *Forbidden Mysteries of Enoch: Fallen Angels and the Origins of Evil* (1983). *Forbidden Mysteries of Enoch* addresses the question of whether angels were ever transformed into flesh-and-blood beings in order to perform earthly deeds. The book presents the thesis that angels took on human bodies and mated with humans, thereby becoming fallen angels. The fallen angels were responsible for corrupting mankind, and, according to Prophet, their progeny are among people of all cultures, religions, and walks of life, carrying out their evil mission.

Elizabeth Clare Prophet was born Elizabeth Clare Wulf on April 8, 1940, in New Jersey. She was raised in a Christian Science household and was a spiritual seeker from a young age. She was a student at Boston University when she met Mark L. Prophet, who had formed an organization called the Summit Lighthouse in Washington, D.C. The two were married in the early 1960s. Summit Lighthouse evolved into the Church Universal and Triumphant, which is now based in Montana. Elizabeth Prophet took control of the organization when her husband died in 1973.

Beyond the Enoch material, Church Universal and Triumphant has many teachings on angels. One of the most popular residents of the C.U.T. pantheon is St. **Michael,** the protector angel. A number of important church decrees involve the angels in general and St. Michael in particular.

CHARON, WHO FERRIED THE SOULS OF THE DEAD TO HADES IN ANCIENT GREEK
MYTHOLOGY. ILLUSTRATION FOR DANTE'S *DIVINE COMEDY* BY GUSTAVE DORÉ
(1861–68).

Sources:

Melton, J. Gordon. *New Age Encyclopedia*. Detroit, Mich. Gale Research, 1990.
Prophet, Elizabeth Clare. *Forbidden Mysteries of Enoch: Fallen Angels and
the Origins of Evil*. Livingston, Mont.: Summit University Press, 1983

Psychopomps, Angels as

The notion that the soul of the deceased does not immediately find
itself in heaven or hell after leaving its body is found in many cultures
worldwide. Rather, the soul must make a transition to its proper realm.
This transition is often symbolized by **birds** that take the soul to heaven,
by a bridge that the departed must cross, or by a journey through a tunnel
or across a body of water. In many societies, a religious functionary such

as a priest or a shaman performs the role of psychopomp—one who guides the dead to the otherworld.

One of the more familiar psychopomps of antiquity was Charon, the ferryman from Greek mythology responsible for transporting the spirits of the departed across the river Styx and into the realm of the dead. In the Christian world, it was natural that angels should come to perform the function of psychopomps, a job with which **Michael** is particularly associated. The old gospel tune "Michael Row the Boat Ashore" is an allusion to his work as a psychopomp. As the imagery of boat rowing suggests, the **archangel** Michael is portrayed as a kind of Christian Charon, ferrying souls from earth to heaven.

In the contemporary period, veterans of **near-death experiences** often report encountering "a being of light" whom they often identify as an angel and who acts as a kind of psychopomp.

Sources:

Hauck, Rex, ed. *Angels: The Mysterious Messengers.* New York: Ballantine, 1994.

Moody, Raymond A. *Life After Life.* New York: Bantam, 1976.

Tripp, Edward. *The Meridian Handbook of Classical Mythology.* New York: New American Library, 1970.

Puck

The word *puck* originally denoted a type of **fairy** and was an alternative term for hobgoblin (a helpful **goblin**). Because of **Shakespeare,** however, the central character in *A Midsummer Night's Dream*—a mischievous fairy named Puck—is now most often associated with this word. Like certain other inhabitants of the fairy realm, Puck delighted in playing pranks on people. Although perpetually preoccupied with entertaining himself, he was, however, also capable of compassion for wronged human beings.

Sources:

Briggs, Katharine. *An Encyclopedia of Fairies.* New York: Pantheon, 1976.

McCoy, Edwin. *A Witch's Guide to Faery Folk.* St. Paul, Minn.: Llewellyn Publications, 1994.

Purgatory, Angels of

Purgatory in Catholic doctrine represents the door to salvation for those souls who repent before dying and are ultimately going to see the light of Paradise, but who do not merit immediate admission to heaven. The most powerful literary depiction of purgatory came from the pen of

THE CELESTIAL NAVIGATOR FROM DANTE'S *DIVINE COMEDY* AS ILLUSTRATED BY GUSTAVE DORÉ.

PURGATORY, THE SEVENTH CIRCLE, FROM DANTE'S *DIVINE COMEDY*, ILLUSTRATED BY GUSTAVE DORÉ.

Dante, who describes an imaginary trip with his guide, the poet Virgil, through the afterlife kingdoms of **Hell,** Purgatory, and Paradise in the early fourteenth century. Dante's Purgatory is geographically located in the middle of the ocean opposite Jerusalem. It is structured as a mountain around which seven cornices are built, each representing one of the seven deadly sins.

The angels are sent by order of God from Paradise to guide the repentants in their ascent toward salvation. Each encounter with the angels, like the entire journey of Dante, is rich with metaphors and allegories. The angels' colors, gestures, and objects (e.g., like the sword and the keys of the doorkeeper) always symbolize a virtue that leads to the achievement of salvation.

After a brief encounter with the angel-boatman, who is responsible for carrying the souls to Purgatory—a boat propelled only by the angel's wings—the two travelers are welcomed at the foothill of the Mountain by the angel-doorkeeper. The two travelers ascend three steps, which symbolically represent contrition, confession, and expiation. Then, before opening the gate, the angel-doorkeeper marks Dante's forehead with seven symbolic p's (representing the structure of Purgatory).

Two angels guard the lowest part of the Mountain, the antepurgatory, where souls start their process of expiation and purification before ascending to their designated cornices. In the antepurgatory appears for the last time the tempter serpent, which is killed by the two angels with their swords.

Dante goes through the process of purification by having removed, one by one, all of the p's from his forehead. They are removed by the angel guides at the entrance of the various cornices, who represent the special graces sent by God to sinners for purification (inspiration to eschew sin, and enlightenment, cooperation, and fervor to practice virtue).

The angels of purgatory have three functions: they perform a purification rite (removing one by one the deadly sins from the soul), they illuminate with their light; and they lead the soul in its ascent to perfection and beatitude (by pointing out the stairways to the next cornice). Each of those who guard the cornices symbolically represent the purgation of sin from their cornice or wears a color that represents a virtue.

After all the p's have been washed away, Dante is ready to ascend higher. Having completed the expiatory labor of climbing the Mountain, he can now reach the Angel Guardian of the Terrestrial Paradise who welcomes those souls who have expiated their sins and are prepared to bear the vision of Christ, after which they ascend to the higher heavens of Paradise.

—*Isotta Poggi*

Sources:

Bemrose, Stephen. *Dante's Angelic Intelligences. Their Importance in the Cosmos and in Pre-Christian Religion.* Roma: Edizioni di Storia e Letteratura, 1983.

New Catholic Encyclopedia. Vol. 1. Washington, D.C.: Catholic University of America, 1981.

Toynbee, Paget, *Dante Alighieri. His Life and Works.* New York, Harper and Row, 1965.

Raguel

The name Raguel (also Raguil or Rasuil, among other variant spellings) means "friend of God." According to the **Book of Enoch,** Raguel is an **archangel** charged with overseeing the good behavior of the other angels. He is also said to be an angel of Earth and a guardian of the second heaven, and is supposed to have brought Enoch to heaven.

In **Gnosticism,** Raguel is placed on the same level as Thelesis, another high-ranking angel. Despite his exalted position, for some unexplained reason Raguel was reprobated in 745 A.D. by the Roman church (along with some other high-level angels, including **Uriel**). At this time Pope Zachary described Raguel as a **demon** who "passed himself off as a saint."

Generally speaking, however, Raguel occupies a much more prestigious position, and in the Revelation of John the following account of Raguel in his place as assistant to God appears: "Then shall He send the angel Raguel, saying: Go and sound the trumpet for the angels of cold and snow and ice, and bring together every kind of wrath upon them that stand on the left."

Sources:

Davidson, Gustav. *A Dictionary of Angels: Including the Fallen Angels.* 1967. Reprint. New York: Free Press, 1971.

Godwin, Malcolm. *Angels: An Endangered Species.* New York: Simon and Schuster, 1990.

Layton, Bentley. *The Gnostic Scriptures.* Garden City, N.Y.: Doubleday, 1987.

Ronner, John. *Know Your Angels: The Angel Almanac with Biographies of 100 Prominent Angels in Legend and Folklore, and Much More.* Murfreesboro, Tenn.: Mamre Press, 1993.

Rahab

In the Talmud, Rahab is referred to as an angel of the sea (Baba Batra 74B). In Hebrew, he is also called *sar shel yam,* "prince of the primordial sea." These titles were bestowed on him as a result of his exploits during Creation, as described in ancient Jewish legend. The story relates that God was working on separating the upper and lower waters of the cosmos in order to have an area in which to place Earth. God needed assistance and commanded Rahab to swallow all of the world's water. Rahab foolishly refused and was put to death by God for his disobedience. Unfortunately, though, his corpse exuded an extremely foul odor, and no one on Earth could stand it. So God relocated Rahab's remains deep beneath the sea.

According to a later legend, however, Rahab somehow becomes active and once again causes trouble. On this occasion, Rahab attempts to stop Moses and his Hebrew slaves from escaping the pharaoh of Egypt at the time of the crossing of the Red Sea during the Exodus. Rahab is apprehended and once again destroyed by God for his wrongdoings.

One more legend tells how Rahab returned the Book of the Angel Raziel to **Adam** after it had been thrown into the sea by jealous angels. (This book is supposed to contain all knowledge and to have been given to Noah by **Raphael.**) Apparently, Rahab was capable of some helpful deeds, although he was generally known for wrongdoing. Indeed, another meaning of his name is "violence."

Sources:

Davidson, Gustav. *A Dictionary of Angels: Including the Fallen Angels.* 1967. Reprint. New York: Free Press, 1971.

Margolies, Morris B. *A Gathering of Angels: Angels in Jewish Life and Literature.* New York: Ballantine, 1994.

Ronner, John. *Know Your Angels: The Angel Almanac with Biographies of 100 Prominent Angels in Legend and Folklore, and Much More.* Murfreesboro, Tenn.: Mamre Press, 1993.

Ramiel

Chief of thunder, Ramiel has charge of the souls that come up for judgment on the last day, although in **Enoch**'s writings he is reported as both a holy angel and a fallen one. In *The Syriac Apocalypse of Baruch* Ramiel is regarded as the presider over true visions and is the angel who interprets Baruch's vision, in which Baruch appears as the angel who destroys Sennacherib's hosts.

Ramiel is also mentioned in **Milton**'s *Paradise Lost* as being overcome by **Abdiel** on the first day of fighting in heaven. He is regarded as evil, being on the side of **Satan.** It has been said that Milton coined the name Ramiel as well as Ithuriel, **Zophiel,** and Zephon, although these names have come to light in early **apocryphal,** apocalyptical, and Talmudic sources.

Sources:

Charles, R. H., ed. and trans. *The Syriac Apocalypse of Baruch.* London: Society for Promoting Christian Knowledge, 1918.

Terry, Milton S., trans. *The Sibylline Oracles.* Rev. ed. New York: AMS Press, 1973.

Raphael

Raphael is one of the few angels mentioned by name in biblical lore. The name Raphael, meaning "God has healed" or "the shining one who heals," is of Chaldean origin. He was originally called Labbiel; the Hebrew term *rapha* means "healer," "doctor," or "surgeon." He is ruler of the angels of healing. He is often associated with the image of a serpent.

Raphael first appears in the Book of **Tobit,** where he travels with Tobit's son in disguise until the journey's end. He shows Tobias, who has caught a huge fish, how to use each part of the creature, "the heart, the gall and the liver . . . these are necessary for useful medicines . . . and the gall is good for anointing the eyes, in which there is a white speck, and they shall be cured." At the end of the journey Raphael reveals himself as "one of the seven holy angels" that attend the throne of God.

He is "one of the four presences set over all the diseases and all the wounds of the children of men" (1 Enoch), as well as one of the **watchers.** In 1 Enoch, chapter 22, Raphael is a guide in the underworld. According to Cabalists, Raphael is, along with **Gabriel** and **Michael,** one of the three angels who visited **Abraham.** He is also credited with healing Abraham of the pain of circumcision, the patriarch having neglected to observe this rite earlier in life. In addition, Raphael is claimed to be the

THE ARCHANGEL RAPHAEL IS MOST OFTEN PORTRAYED ACCOMPANYING TOBIAS (STUDENT OF VERROCCHIO, CA. FIFTEENTH CENTURY). (COURTESY ARAS)

angel sent by God to cure **Jacob** of the injury to his thigh he received when he wrestled with his dark adversary at Peniel.

According to another legend, it was Raphael who, after the Flood, handed Noah a "medical book," which might have been the famous Sefer Raziel, the Book of the Angel **Raziel.** Besides being ruler of the angels of healing, Raphael is considered the regent of the Sun, chief of the order of **virtues,** governor of the south, guardian of the west, ruling prince of the second heaven, overseer of the evening winds, guardian of the Tree of Life in the Garden of Eden, one of the six angels of repentance, and an angel of prayer, love, joy, and light. He is also an angel of science and knowledge and the preceptor angel of Isaac.

Although Raphael is officially considered a virtue, he is said to have the six wings of a seraph; at the same time, he belongs to the **cherubim,** the **dominions,** and the **powers.** He is said to be the chummiest and funniest of all angels and is often pictured chatting merrily with mortal beings. According to the fifteenth-century German abbot, historian, and occultist Trithemius of Sponheim, Raphael is one of the seven angels of the **Apocalypse,** and is also numbered among the ten holy **sefiroth.** He is generally credited to be the angel who troubled the waters at the pool in ancient Bethesda.

According to the legend contained in Frederick Conybeare's "The Testament of Solomon," when Solomon prayed to God for help in building the temple, God answered with the gift of a magic ring delivered to the Hebrew king personally by Raphael. The ring had the power to subdue all demons, and Solomon was able to complete the temple with the "slave labor" of demons. An Ophite (Gnostic sect) diagram depicts Raphael as a terrestrial **daemon** with a beastlike form in the company of three other angels: Michael, **Suriel,** and Gabriel.

Raphael is often pictured with Tobias, the central character of the book of Tobit. He is especially solicitous of pilgrims and other wayfarers and so is often depicted as such himself, carrying a pilgrim's staff and shod with sandals. Sometimes he is shown with a water gourd or wallet slung from a strap over his shoulder. His demeanor is generally mild and kindly, that of a friendly man rather than a magnificent angel. Such masters as Botticini, Lorrain, Pollajuolo, Ghirlandaio, Titian, and **Rembrandt** have portayed Raphael variously as a winged saint supping with Adam and Eve, as the "sociable archangel," as a "six-winged seraph," and as one of the seven angels of the presence, to whom **Blake** made reference in his "Milton."

Sources:

Conybeare, Frederick G. "The Testament of Solomon." *Jewish Quarterly Review* 11 (1898): 1–45.

Davidson, Gustav. *A Dictionary of Angels: Including the Fallen Angels.* 1967. Reprint. New York: Free Press, 1971.

Godwin, Malcolm. *Angels: An Endangered Species.* New York: Simon and Schuster, 1990.

MacGregor, Geddes. *Angels: Ministers of Grace.* New York: Paragon House, 1988.

Wilson, Peter Lamborn. *Angels.* New York: Pantheon Books, 1980.

Raphael (Sanzio)

Raphael Sanzio (1483–1520) was born in Urbino, Italy. While still a child, according to Giorgio Vasari, he was placed by his father, over the objections of his mother, in the shop of Perugino, a master of the Italian High Renaissance. His mother died in 1491, when Raphael was only eight. His father died in 1494. Raphael's guardian then became his paternal uncle, Bartolomeo, a priest.

It is generally agreed that Raphael's association with Perugino began at about the turn of the century, when Perugino was engaged in Perugia decorating the hall of the Corporation of Bankers (the Collegio del Cambio). At this age Raphael would have been an assistant rather than a pupil.

Raphael's early paintings may be divided into altarpieces, made for Città di Castello and Perugia, and smaller works, both devotional and secular, many of them made for the court at Urbino. Raphael seems to have traveled a great deal during the first eight years of the new century; he is recorded in Urbino in 1504 and 1506 and twice in 1507. He kept in contact with the court, which flourished after some troubles in 1502 and 1503.

Raphael arrived in Florence soon after October 1504, where he made friends with some young artists, including Aristotile da Sangallo and Ridolfo Ghirlandaio, and studied the works of Masaccio, Leonardo da Vinci, and **Michelangelo.** He was then hired by Pope Julius II to decorate one of his rooms, known as the Stanza della Signatura, and later the Stanza d'Eliodoro. His decorations established Raphael as one of the

MISCHIEVOUS CHERUBS FROLIC IN RAPHAEL'S *THE NYMPH GALATEA* (VILLA FARNESINA, ROME, CA. 1514). (COURTESY ARAS)

leading artists in Rome. His reputation was enhanced even more by the prints, made after his designs, that began to appear during the same period.

Angels are depicted in a number of Raphael's paintings, such as the frescoes in the Vatican and his *Madonna di San Sisto,* which was painted for the high altar of the rebuilt church of St. Sixtus in Piacenza. Raphael's angels, especially in his later works, are sexless, spiritual, graceful, and, at the same time, the personification of intelligence and power. These characteristics are found in the illustration of the archangel **Michael,** as well as in the *Expulsion of Heliodorus from the Temple,* which is found in the Stanza della Signatura in the Vatican.

The representation of St. Michael conquering **Lucifer** was a commission from Lorenzo de' Medici, who presented it to Francis I. The subject was chosen by Raphael as a compliment to the sovereign, who was the grand master of the Order of St. Michael, the military patron saint of France. It was originally painted on wood, and in 1773 it was transferred to canvas and restored three years later. At the beginning of this century the restorations were removed.

The beautiful young angel hovers in the air and lightly touches with his foot the shoulder of the demon in vulgar human form, fiery in color, with horns and a serpent's tail. The expression of the angel is serious and majestic as he gazes down upon the writhing Satan, whose face is full of malignant hate. Michael grasps his lance with both hands, and his head, with its light and floating hair, is juxtaposed against the background of his brilliant wings; his armor is gold and silver, a sword hangs by his side, and an azure scarf floats from his shoulders.

Raphael's representation of angelic visitors to **Abraham** in the fourth arcade of the loggia of the Vatican is one of the best known and most beautiful pictures on this subject. Both light and color play a large part in Raphael's *Deliverance of St. Peter,* the radiant angel in which has been described as compounded of air and light, without mortal weight. Above the *Deliverance of St. Peter* are the ladder and angels appearing to **Jacob** in his famous dream. Here Jacob's face is turned toward the ladder, on which are six angels, and Jehovah appears above with outstretched arms and surrounded by glory.

Another significant painting is the *Coronation of the Virgin* in the Vatican Museum. In this two-part composition the coronation is painted on the upper register, and shown below are the apostles gathered around the empty tomb. The Virgin is surrounded by several angels, some of whom are represented with baby heads with little wings folded under the chin.

The *Disputa del Sacramento,* in the Stanza della Signatura in the Vatican, is an ambitious orchestration of nearly life-size figures in space that occupies most of the field of vision. In the golden sphere of the vault of heaven, angels, many only barely discernible, attend God.

Other significant representations of angels are contained in Raphael's *Virgin and Child with St. Raphael and St. Michael* and in the *Vision of Ezechiel,* both in Florence's Uffizi Museum.

Sources:

Clement, Clara Erskine. *Angels in Art.* Boston: L. C. Page, 1898.
Jones, Roger, and Nicholas Penny. *Raphael.* New Haven: Yale University Press, 1983.
Wilson, Peter Lamborn. *Angels.* New York: Pantheon Books, 1980.

Rashnu

According to the ancient Persian religion of **Zoroastrianism,** Rashnu is the angel who stands at the bridge to heaven and passes judgment on the worthiness of newly dead souls who wish to enter. Rashnu ponders for three days on how the person has spent his life on earth and uses golden scales to measure the merit of his soul. Those who are found to be worthy are helped across the bridge. Those who are not deemed virtuous, receive no help and find that the bridge becomes as narrow as a razor's edge. As they attempt to cross, they fall off the bridge to be tortured by devils.

Sources:

Cohn, Norman. *Cosmos, Chaos and the World to Come: The Ancient Roots of Apocalyptic Faith.* New Haven: Yale University Press, 1993.
Noss, John B. *Man's Religions.* Reprint. 1956. New York: Macmillan, 1969.

Raziel

Raziel has been referred to as "the secret of God" and the "angel of mysteries." The Cabala reports Raziel as the personification of Cochma, second of the ten holy **sefiroth.** He is also said to be the author of the Book of the Angel Raziel (although the true author has been commonly identified as either Isaac the Blind or Eleazer of Worms, both medieval writers).

According to the legend, Raziel gave this book to **Adam,** which was eventually stolen by envious angels and thrown into the ocean. Then God allegedly ordered Rahab, angel of the deep, to retrieve the book and return it to Adam. The book came into the possession of, first, **Enoch,** and then Noah, who is said to have learned from it how to build the ark. Later, King Solomon derived his knowledge of magic from it.

The famous thirteenth-century Cabalist Abraham ben Samuel Abulafia also wrote under the name Raziel.

In the Jewish philosopher Maimonides' *Mishna Thora* (1168), Raziel is pictured as the chief of the order of erelim, as well as the herald of the Deity and the preceptor angel of Adam.

Sources:

Davidson, Gustav. *A Dictionary of Angels: Including the Fallen Angels.* 1967. Reprint. New York: Free Press, 1971.

Ronner, John. *Know Your Angels: The Angel Almanac with Biographies of 100 Prominent Angels in Legend and Folklore, and Much More.* Murfreesboro, Tenn.: Mamre Press, 1993.

Schwarts, Howard. *Gabriel's Palace: Jewish Mystical Tales.* New York: Oxford University Press, 1993.

Rembrandt

One of the greatest masters of European art, Rembrandt Harmenszoon van Rijn (1606–69), whose paintings include several angelic scenes, was of Dutch Reformed heritage. He was born in the university city of Leiden, where he grew up in humble circumstances. In 1620 he enrolled at the University of Leiden, which he eventually left to begin his training as an artist. After a few years he went to Amsterdam, where he studied with the history painter Pieter Lastman. He returned to Leiden six months later to work as an independent artist, producing several paintings, prints, and drawings, as well as a number of self-portraits.

About 1632 he moved to Amsterdam, where in 1633 he received an important commission from Prince Frederick Henry of Orange for a series of paintings depicting the Passion of Christ. In 1634 he married Saskia van Uylenburgh, the daughter of a wealthy family, and in 1639 he purchased a large home, which is now the Rembrandthuis Museum. His wife died in 1642, shortly after the birth of their son Titus. During his later years Rembrandt had many financial difficulties, including a declaration of insolvency. Further, he chose to live in isolation from Dutch society, although he continued to receive important commissions until his death.

Rembrandt's angels can be described as poetical, unearthly apparitions. Among the most remarkable angelic scenes by Rembrandt is *The Angel and The Prophet Balaam* (Musée Cognacq-Jay, Paris), one of his earliest historical paintings. This painting is based on the story of how Balak, king of the Moabites, asked the prophet Balaam to curse the people of Israel and how God transformed this curse into a blessing. It shows Balaam, who does not perceive that an angel of the Lord stands in his way, striking his donkey, who will not move. In the biblical account the beast reproaches him and the angel rebukes him, and Balaam realizes that he must heed the voice of God and his messenger.

The various scenes from the story of **Raphael** and Tobias from the Book of **Tobit** (a book of Scripture included in the Roman Catholic canon of the Old Testament and in the Protestant Apocrypha) have been represented in the works of artists of all nations. Rembrandt also painted the parting of Tobias from his father and mother, as well as several other incidents in the story. *The Angel Departing From the Family of Tobias,* in the Louvre, is remarkable for its spirited action. (In the scriptural account Tobit, Tobias's father, sends his son to recover a sum of money to provide for his wife after his death. During his journey, the young Tobias, guided by an angel, catches a fish with whose liver he later restores his father's eyesight. Then he recovers the money and takes a wife, with whom he returns home.) The painting represents the moment when the four characters of the story realize that Tobias's guide is the angel Raphael, who, having fulfilled his mission, ascends toward heaven.

Another beautiful angel is depicted in the painting called *Presentation in the Temple* (1627–28, Hamburg Gallery) that features the prophetess Hannah and her son Samuel. The brilliant gold-yellow sculptured angel's head above the pews creates color accents and separates the group from the rest of the temple. The painting *Jacob Wrestling with the Angel* (1648–55, State Museums, Berlin-Dahlem) is based on the story of **Jacob,** who, having sent his family and possessions across the brook Jabbok, spends the whole night wrestling with a stranger who is later revealed to be an angel of the Lord. In this painting Rembrandt depicts the moment at which the angel, who shows no trace of physical exertion, dislocates Jacob's hip.

In his portrayal of the story of **Abraham** preparing to sacrifice his son Isaac, Rembrandt focuses on the moment the angel prevents consummation of the sacrifice. This powerful and realistic picture is in the Hermitage at St. Petersburg. Rembrandt's illustration of Jacob's dream in the Dulwich Gallery, Holland, shows a stream of dazzling light that forms a ladder, up and down which float mystic, radiant angels. One of the most famous of Rembrandt's early etchings, *The Angel Appearing to the Shepherds,* is considered a good example of his use of a natural occurrence to illustrate a supernatural event. Here he added a native Dutch element by transforming the shepherds into cowherds, who evince their own primal fear before the glowing angelic apparition.

JACOB WRESTLING WITH THE ANGEL FROM THE HOLY BIBLE, REMBRANDT EDITION
(STATE MUSEUMS, BERLIN).

Rembrandt

Sources:

Clark, Kenneth. *Rembrandt and the Italian Renaissance.* London: John Murray, 1966.

Clement, Clara Erskine. *Angels in Art.* Boston: L. C. Page, 1898.

Munz, Ludwig. *Rembrandt.* New York: Harry N. Abrams, 1984.

Where the bright seraphim in burning row / Their loud uplifted angel trumpets blow.

—John Milton, "At a Solemn Music," 1645

Salamanders

Salamanders (not to be confused with amphibians by the same name) are **fairy**-like creatures associated with the element fire. They are said to be "fiery" beings with the appearance of lizards and to reside deep in the earth and in fires. They are responsible for all fires, from the tiniest flame to the most dramatic volcanic eruption. In the **occult** tradition, fire is associated with activity and with inspiration, and fire **elementals** (including salamanders) are said to work with human beings to maintain their vitality, inspiration, and enthusiasm.

As the archetypal spirits of the fire element, salamanders are occupied with maintaining the heat of the Earth. In ceremonial **magic** salamanders are the fire elementals of the South, who are called upon to witness rituals. The task of the elementals, like that of the nature **devas,** is to build up forms in the natural world, thus providing an arena in which other beings, such as human souls, can evolve spiritually. Some occultists view elementals as soulless entities who simply disappear at death, but others see them as spirits who eventually evolve into devas (angels). Because they are associated with fire, salamanders are under the **rulership** of the archangel **Michael.**

Sources:

Andrews, Ted. *Enchantment of the Faerie Realm: Communicate with Nature Spirits & Elementals.* St. Paul, Minn.: Llewellyn Publications, 1993.

McCoy, Edwin. *A Witch's Guide to Faery Folk.* St. Paul, Minn.: Llewellyn Publications, 1994.

Sammael

Sammael (from *sam,* "poison," plus *el,* "angel") is considered both evil and good. He is known as the chief ruler of the fifth heaven, as "that great serpent with twelve wings that draws after him, in his fall, the solar system" (Revelation 12), as well as the **angel of death,** whom God sent to fetch the soul of Moses at the time of his death. Sammael is regarded in rabbinic literature as chief of the Satans and as the angel of death. In the *Secrets of Enoch,* he is the prince of demons and a magician.

In Talmud *Yalkut,* Sammael is Esau's **guardian angel,** and in *Sotah,* he is regarded as Edom's angelic prince guardian. He is equated with the serpent who tempted Eve and, by seducing her, is considered to be the father of Cain in the *Sayings of Rabbi Eliezer.* In the **Zohar** he is the dark angel who wrestles with **Jacob** at Peniel.

Sammael is cited in Arthur Waite's *The Holy Kabbalah,* as "the severity of God" and as the fifth archangel of the world of Briah, where he corresponds to the sefira Geburah. In Baruch, chapter 3, and in the Ascension of Isaiah, the names Sammael and **Satan** are used interchangeably. Sammael also has a literary presence; for instance, in Longfellow's lengthy poem *The Golden Legend,* he is mentioned as the angel of death.

Sources:

Davidson, Gustav. *A Dictionary of Angels: Including the Fallen Angels.* 1967. Reprint. New York: Free Press, 1971.

Ronner, John. *Know Your Angels: The Angel Almanac With Biographies of 100 Prominent Angels in Legend and Folklore, and Much More.* Murfreesboro, Tenn.: Mamre Press, 1993.

Waite, Arthur. *The Holy Kabbalah.* New Hyde Park, N.Y.: University Books, 1960.

Sandalphon

Sandalphon (also Sandolphon or Sandolfon) is an angelic prince (*sarim*) said to have originally been **Elijah,** the prophet of Israel. Apparently, Elijah turned into Sandalphon when he was transported to heaven in a burning chariot by a whirlwind, while still alive.

In rabbinic lore, Sandalphon is the twin brother of the angel **Meta-tron.** According to one legend, Metatron carries prayers through nine hundred heavens up to God; according to another, when the prayer is in Hebrew, Sandalphon joins with him in making a garland of such prayers of the faithful to adorn the head of the Lord.

Sandalphon is one of the tallest celestial creatures in heaven—it would be more than a five-hundred-year journey to travel from his toes to the top of his head—and Moses once referred to him as "the tall angel." Sandalphon is credited with being in charge of different heavens according to different sources: the fourth, according to Islamic tradition; the sixth, as asserted in the third chapter of the **Book of Enoch;** and the seventh, according to the **Zohar.** In any case, he battles persistently against the evil and formidable **Sammael** (Satan).

Other references to Sandalphon include the poem "Sandalphon" by Longfellow, in which he is called the Angel of Glory, Angel of Prayer; a Cabalistic account of his being able to decide the sex of a child in embryo; and an etymological description of his name as meaning "one who likes to wear sandals [soft shoes]" when he appears before the Almighty.

Sources:

Davidson, Gustav. *A Dictionary of Angels: Including the Fallen Angels.* 1967. Reprint. New York: Free Press, 1971.
Encyclopaedia of Islam. Vol 6. Leiden, Netherlands: E. J. Brill, 1978.
Ronner, John. *Know Your Angels: The Angel Almanac with Biographies of 100 Prominent Angels in Legend and Folklore, and Much More.* Murfreesboro, Tenn.: Mamre Press, 1993.

Sariel

Sariel (also known under several variant names, including Suriel, Zerachiel, and Saraqel) is one of the original seven **archangels,** according to the **Book of Enoch.** His name means "God's command," and he is responsible for the lot of the angels that violate God's sacred ordinances. Although Sariel usually appears as a holy angel, he is sometimes mentioned as one who has fallen from the grace of the Lord. According to Malcolm Godwin (*Angels: An Endangered Species*), he has even been known as the **angel of death,** especially given his role as the angel sent to fetch the soul of Moses on Mount Sinai.

Sariel is considered a prince of the presence, like **Metatron,** as well as an angel of healing, like **Raphael.** He is called Sariel the trumpeter and Sariel the angel of death in the *Falasha Anthology.* Sariel is said to have inspired Moses toward knowledge and to have instructed Rabbi Ishmael ben Elisha in the laws of hygiene, as reported in Talmud Berachoth 51a.

Sariel's name appears in **Gnostic** amulets, and he is listed as one of the seven angels in the Ophitic Hebdomad system of primordial powers (Origen, Contra Celsum 6, 30). It is also reported that when Sariel is invoked, he manifests in the form of an ox. According to the Cabala, Sariel is one of the seven angels that rule Earth.

Sariel is associated with the skies and is in charge of the **zodiac** sign Aries (the Ram); he also instructs others on the course of the Moon. (This was once considered to be secret knowledge that was not to be shared.) According to Davidson, in occult lore Sariel is one of the nine angels of the summer equinox and is effective as an amulet against the evil eye. Sariel also appears in the recently unearthed **Dead Sea Scrolls** as a name on the shields of the "third Tower," also known as "the Sons of Light." (There were a total of four "towers"—each a separate group of soldiers).

Sources:

Davidson, Gustav. *A Dictionary of Angels: Including the Fallen Angels.* 1967. Reprint. New York: Free Press, 1971.

Godwin, Malcolm. *Angels: An Endangered Species.* New York: Simon and Schuster, 1990.

Leslau, Wolf, trans. *Falasha Anthology.* New Haven: Yale University Press, 1951.

Ronner, John. *Know Your Angels: The Angel Almanac with Biographies of 100 Prominent Angels in Legend and Folklore, and Much More.* Murfreesboro, Tenn.: Mamre Press, 1993.

Satan

Satan's name is commonly believed to have originated from the term *satan,* which connotes the idea of opposition. The traditional account that Satan was originally an angel but led a revolt against God and ultimately was banished along with his followers from heaven can be found in the **apocryphal,** noncanonical Hebrew, and apocalyptic books. This is the literature that inspired **John Milton**'s *Paradise Lost* in the seventeenth century.

Originally Satan represented more of an abstract entity than the personification of evil. When he appeared in the Hebrew Scriptures (the Old Testament), he represented an adversary, a divine agent who could assume either human or angelic features. Satan is in charge of testing humans' integrity (e.g., Job), although God has the authority to set limits to Satan's power to do evil.

It was in the New Testament that Satan became the Devil personified and was pictured as a **dragon** or a serpent. Still, while Satan's power was acknowledged, he was conceived as only part of creation: he could

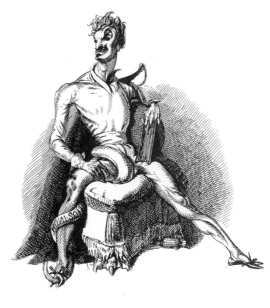

GUSTAVE DORÉ DEPICTS SATAN WITH BAT-LIKE WINGS AND CLOVEN HOOVES IN THE COMPANY OF WRITHING SNAKES. ILLUSTRATION FOR MILTON'S *PARADISE LOST*.

PROTOTYPE OF THE NINETEENTH-CENTURY ROMANTIC DEVIL. FROM *THE DEVIL WALK* BY THOMAS LANDSEER, LONDON, 1831.

not overwhelm God, and was under God's power. In fact, if his power could directly confront God's authority, the underlying principle of monotheism could not hold. In **Judaism** and **Christianity** there is no space for the dualistic opposition of good and evil. (Dualism in antiquity was developed within the Persian religion of **Zoroastrianism,** and in Manicheism and **Gnosticism.**)

In Christianity, Satan is pictured as the tempter, accuser, punisher, and the leader of the fallen angels, who with the advent of the kingdom of God will be ultimately defeated.

Islam shares with Christianity a number of concepts about Satan. He is found in the Koran, as *al-Shaytan* (the demon), and was conceived of as tempter. He is also associated with the lower human principles, the

Satan

Names for include Prince of Darkness,

Lucifer, Beelzebub, ha-Satan, Devil,

Metatron, "old dragon," Azazel,

Mastema, Beliel, Duma, Sier,

Salmael, Gadreel, The Angel of Rome,

Samael, Asmodeius, Mephistopheles,

and Oblis (also Old Horney, Lusty

Dick, The Gentleman, Monsignor,

Black Bogey, Old Nick, Old Scratch,

and the Old Lad Himself).

flesh, or the *nafs,* and has the power to lead humans astray by disguising his identity and inducing humans to do evil deeds.

In biblical literature, Satan and the serpent are often interchangeable, particularly in the apocalyptic literature. It was in the third century A.D., however, that the Christian philosopher **Origen** fully established the association between Satan and the snake. In the following centuries the snake was conceived as either the tool of Satan or his incarnation.

Satan, however, is not only the symbol of death and evil. In the folkloric Judeo-Christian and Islamic traditions, where he is typically depicted as the "horned one," he appears in association with fertility and sexuality cults, and in the practice of witchcraft. Satan was held responsible for the healing powers of witches practicing the Sabbath rituals for centuries throughout Europe.

The role of Satan in the world has provided inspiration in literature, poetry, art, and music throughout history. There are numerous accounts of imaginary trips to the underground kingdom of Satan, of pacts with the Devil, possessions, and exorcisms. In these stories the concept of Satan's role has evolved as a reflection of philosophical views of human conditions. While he has been blamed for the evil on earth that led to massacres and destructions, he has also been responsible for inspiring the highest artistic creativity.

—*Isotta Poggi*

Sources:
Davidson, Gustav. *A Dictionary of Angels Including the Fallen Angels.* Reprint. 1967. New York: The Free Press, 1967.
Masello, Robert. *Fallen Angels . . . and Spirits of the Dark.* New York: Perigee, 1994.
Rudwin, Maximilian. *The Devil in Legend and Literature.* Chicago: The Open Court Publishing Company, 1931.

Seasons (Angels of the)

The connection between the seasons and angels comes from the medieval tendency to associate almost everything with angels. In the same way in which angels were said to rule the **months** and rule the **hours** of the day, there were angels who ruled the seasons. Gustav Davidson, in an appendix to his *Dictionary of Angels,* reproduces an occult schema of angel/season associations that contains angels with unfamiliar names:

Spring

> *Governing angel:* Spugliguel (head of the sign of spring);
> *Serving angels:* Amatiel, Caracasa, Core, Commissoros

Summer

> *Governing angel:* Tubiel (head of the sign of summer); *Serving angels:* Gargatel, Gaviel, Tariel

Autumn

> *Governing angel:* Torquaret (head of the sign of autumn); *Serving angels:* Tarquam, Guabarel

Winter

> *Governing angel:* Attarib (head of the sign of winter); *Serving angels:* Amabael, Cetarari (Ctarari)

A more traditional schema is to associate each of the principal **archangels** with each of the seasons: **Raphael**/spring, **Uriel**/summer, **Michael**/fall, and **Gabriel**/winter.

Sources:

Steiner, Rudolf. *The Four Seasons and the Archangels.* Bristol, England: Rudolf Steiner Press, 1992.

Davidson, Gustav. *A Dictionary of Angels: Including the Fallen Angels.* 1967. Reprint. New York: Free Press, 1971.

Sefiroth

Sefiroth represent a divine emanation through which God manifested his existence during the creation of the universe. It is believed that God radiated from himself ten basic intelligences, each of which represented a trait or characteristic of himself. According to the Jewish mystical philosophy of the Cabala, these ten creative powers govern and shape the universe, both seen and unseen and may be compared with the Platonic powers or intelligences.

In the Cabala, there are ten holy sefiroth who issue from the right side of God, whereas the ten unholy ones issue from his left. It is believed that God uses the sefiroth as intermediaries in dealing with and controlling his lower Creation.

The sefiroth are generally identified as Kether, God's will and his thought; Hokhmah, God's plan for the universe; Binah, God's intelligence; Hesed, divine love; Gevurah, divine judgment; Rahamin, divine compassion (or Tiphereth, beauty, in some systems); Netsah, lasting endurance or eternity; Hod, divine majesty; Yesod, the base of every activity in God; and Shekinah, the presence of God.

In addition, the great sefiroth in the form of personalized angels are: **Metatron**, archangel of the *hayyoth hakodesh;* **Raziel**, archangel of the arelim or erelim; **Zadkiel**, archangel of the *hashmalim;* **Kamael,** archangel of the **seraphim; Michael,** archangel of the *shinanim;* Haniel, archangel of the *tarshishim;* **Raphael,** archangel of the *bene elohim;* and **Gabriel,** archangel of the *kerubim.*

According to the sixteenth-century commentator Isaac ha-Cohen of Soria, of the ten evil emanations, only seven were permitted to endure. Of these seven only five have been "authenticated," that is to say Ashmedai, Kafkefoni, Taninniver (blind dragon), **Sammael,** and Sammael's mate **Lilith** are recognized.

Sources:

Encyclopaedia Judaica. New York: Macmillan, 1971.

Margolies, Morris B. *A Gathering of Angels: Angels in Jewish Life and Literature.* New York: Ballantine, 1994.

Parisen, Maria. *Angels and Mortals: Their Co-Creative Power.* Wheaton, Ill.: Quest Books, 1990.

Semyaza

Semyaza (also Semjaza or Semiaza, among other variant spellings) was the leader of wicked fallen angels who led two hundred other angels to earth to mate with mortal women. According to the **Book of Enoch,** these angels also encouraged other sinful activities by teaching humans about such things as cosmetics, thus encouraging vanity, and weapons, thereby promoting battle.

The Book of Enoch goes on to describe how the mortal women with whom the angels mated gave birth to many giants who were so huge that they ate all the food on Earth, then went on to eating humans, and eventually started to eat one another. When earth was in complete anarchy, God sent the archangel **Michael** down from heaven to confine the corrupt angels in the valleys of Earth until doomsday. The giants that these angels fathered were destroyed, but their evil spirits went on wreaking havoc until they were wiped out by the great Flood.

According to Robert Graves in *Hebrew Myths,* Semyaza is now eternally residing in the sky in the form of the constellation Orion, hanging between heaven and Earth with his head hanging downward.

Sources:

Davidson, Gustav. *A Dictionary of Angels: Including the Fallen Angels.* 1967. Reprint. New York: Free Press, 1971.

Graves, Robert. *Hebrew Myths.* New York: Anchor, 1989.

Ronner, John. *Know Your Angels: The Angel Almanac with Biographies of 100 Prominent Angels in Legend and Folklore, and Much More.* Murfreesboro, Tenn.: Mamre Press, 1993.

Seraphim

The seraphim are the angels of love, light, and fire. They are the highest order of the **hierarchy** of **choirs** and serve God as caretakers of his throne. Seraphim express their love for God by constantly singing his praises. In Hebrew tradition the endless chant of the seraphim is known as the Trisagion—*Kadosh, Kadosh, Kadosh* (Holy, Holy, Holy is the Lord of Hosts, the whole earth is full of His Glory), which is considered a song of creation and celebration. Because they are the closest beings to God, they are also called "the burning ones," for they are aflame with their love.

The three choirs of the seraphim, the **cherubim,** and the **thrones,** according to the medieval mystic Jan van Ruysbroeck, never take part in human conflict but are with us when we are in peaceful contemplation of God and experience a constant love in our hearts. They also inspire humans to become inflamed with divine love.

While he was on the Isle of Patmos, St. John the Divine had visions that revealed the angels **Gabriel, Metatron, Kemuel,** and Nathanuel were among the seraphim.

Isaiah is the only one to speak of the seraphim in Hebrew Scriptures (the Old Testament), when he recounts his vision of the flaming angels above the Throne of God: "Each had six wings: two covered the face, two covered the feet and two were used for flying." Further mention of the seraphim may be considered in Num. 21:6 when reference is made to "fiery serpents." According to 2 Enoch (an **apocryphal** work) the seraphim have six wings and four heads and faces.

It is from the ranks of seraphim that **Lucifer** emerged. In fact, the Fallen Prince was considered the angel who outshone all others until his fall from Grace.

Sources:
Davidson, Gustav. *A Dictionary of Angels: Including the Fallen Angels.* 1967. Reprint. New York: Free Press, 1971.
Mansfield, Richard. *Angels: An Introduction to the Angelic Hierarchy.* Encinitas, Calif.: Estuary Publications, 1994.

Seven Heavens

Prior to the invention of the telescope and the Copernican revolution, it was generally believed that the earth was the stable center of the universe, around which the Sun, Moon, stars, and the five known planets revolved. Because the Sun, Moon, and planets moved along paths of their own, entirely independently of the stars, it was believed that they were

CRYSTALLINE HEAVEN BY
GUSTAVE DORÉ.

"stuck" on a series of concentric crystalline (i.e., transparent) spheres that revolved around the Earth between the stars and the Earth.

From this conception of the universe arose the idea of seven "levels of reality," corresponding to the seven celestial spheres. The ordinary level of humanity's experience was referred to as the "sublunar" realm, meaning that it is the level below the sphere of the moon. Another popular number was nine, which seems to have been derived by considering the Earth itself as well as the sphere composed of the fixed stars as constituting distinct levels. Given this view of reality, it was natural that the angels should be regarded as being arranged in a **hierarchy** of levels, hence **Dionysius**'s schema of nine choirs of angels.

In ancient Neoplatonism the various levels of reality were regarded as having been sequentially "emanated" by the formless Godhead from the realm of the fixed stars to the physical plane. The **Gnostics** introduced an interesting twist on this basic idea by asserting that the physical world was created by mistake and is a prison from which we should attempt to escape. Trapping human spirits in this world, the evil creator established **archons** (evil **archangels**) at each of the seven levels to prevent humans from escaping.

Traditionally, the seven heavens are as follows:

First heaven (Shamayim)

The lowest heaven, Shamayim borders the Earth and is ruled by **Gabriel.** It contains the clouds, the winds, the Upper Waters, and is home to the two hundred astronomer-angels who preside over the stars.

Second heaven (Raquia)

Raquia is ruled by the angel **Raphael,** and, according to Enoch, it is within this heaven that the fallen angels are imprisoned awaiting final judgment in complete darkness.

Third heaven (Sagun or Shehaquin)

According to Enoch, hell lies within the northern boundaries of the third heaven. Sagun is ruled by Anahel, and is the residence for **Izra'il,** the Islamic angel of death. It is here that the wicked are tortured by angels. In the southern regions, however, there exists a bountiful paradise, thought to be the Garden of Eden, where the souls of the righteous will come after death.

Fourth heaven (Zebhul or Machanon)

Ruled by **Michael,** the fourth heaven "is the site of the heavenly Jerusalem, the holy Temple and its Altar" (Godwin, p. 122). It is here, according to Enoch, that the Garden of Eden is actually housed, not in the third heaven.

Fifth heaven (Machon or Ma'on)

Machon is home to God, Aaron, and the avenging angels. The northern boundaries, said to be ruled by either **Sandalphon** or **Sammael,** is home to the fallen grigori (**watchers**). In the southern regions, on the other hand, reside the **ministering angels** who endlessly chant the praises of the Lord.

Sixth heaven (Zebul or Makhon)

The sixth heaven is ruled by Zebul at night and Sabath during the day. This stormy, snow-ridden dwelling is home to the seven phoenixes and the seven **cherubim** who sing the praises of God. A multitude of other angelic beings also reside here who study an array of subjects including astronomy, ecology, the seasons, and mankind.

Seventh heaven (Araboth)

The holiest of heavens, Araboth is ruled by **Cassiel,** and is home to God on his Divine Throne, along with the highest orders of angels—the **seraphim,** cherubim, and **thrones.**

Sources:
Godwin, Malcolm. *Angels: An Endangered Species.* New York: Simon and Schuster, 1990.
MacGregor, Geddes. *Angels: Ministers of Grace.* New York: Paragon House, 1988.
Robinson, James M. *The Nag Hammadi Library.* 1977. Reprint. New York: Harper & Row, 1981.
Turner, Alice K. *The History of Hell.* New York: Harcourt Brace, 1993.

Sex and Angels

Angels in medieval art are usually androgynous, and it is not until the Renaissance that women and children angels are depicted. Within Western Catholic theology, references to the virility of angels are extremely scarce, although biblical evidence of manly angels certainly exists. Examples are the **cherubim** with the flaming swords who guard the gates of Eden, as well as the angel with whom **Jacob** wrestles until daybreak.

The paucity of references to angelic virility might have derived from the early Christian wish to distinguish the angels from the pantheon of Greek gods, often criticized for endless fornications and for their crimes of rape. Later Christian authors scrupulously avoided references to masculinity among the angels, especially because demonology attributed masculine traits to those angels who had been expelled from heaven. They gradually removed from angels their masculine attributes.

Even though angels have sometimes been given a masculine role, some aspects of the masculine role have been clearly excluded from God's holy angels. Angels have been consistently assimilated to the functions of the human soul. For some authors the soul is simply another angelic form; for others the angel comprises only part of the functions of the human soul, those that concern intelligence and will.

Enjoyment, and not desire, is the design with respect to angels. Throughout Christian theology angels are granted the enjoyment that comes from seeing God face-to-face. This kind of enjoyment is promised to the soul that attains an angelic state, and, as far as a soul is concerned, this enjoyment is feminine. As a matter of fact, the soul that experiences this enjoyment is often referred to as "she." Not only is the soul a feminine noun taking a feminine pronoun, but the soul's capacity to become married to Christ places it in a distinctly feminine position in relation to God the Son. Making the soul feminine in many cases led to a sense of the maleness of angels or the maleness of God, although this maleness was not of the order of virility most often associated with pagan gods, demons, and genies.

The question of the angelic body and the **gender of angels** has fascinated many authors and has been the topic of significant philosophical and theological disputes since ancient times. Beginning around the fourth century A.D. with St. Gregory of Nazianzus and St. Gregory of Nyssa, extending through St. Augustine and **Dionysius the Areopagite,** and reaching an apotheosis in the thirteenth century with **Thomas Aquinas,** angels gained more and more importance, eventually constituting the vast majority of the inhabitants of the Heavenly City. For the most part, angels were not considered to be divided according to sex, since as invisible beings they were bodiless and thus not sexed.

From the time in which Philo of Alexandria commented in the first century A.D. on the text in Genesis 6:1–4 reporting that the sons of God—angels—took as wives the daughters of men—human women—it has been an article of faith that God's holy angels could not be accused of such acts, the agents of which could only be the fallen angels or fallen angelic humans. For Philo it was perfectly appropriate that good angels couple with something, namely, knowledge and virtue. Later, it appears, angels and the daughters of right reason became so thoroughly undivided that they did not need to couple.

Philo's idea that the angels who couple with the daughters of men in Genesis are actually devils was taken up by Augustine and also formed part of Aquinas's response to the question of the angelic body and angelic sexual function. By considering the **sons of God** in the Genesis account to be fallen angels, Augustine collapsed the distinction between humans and angels and set up a group of angelic humans whose corruption and fall derived from their attraction to female beauty. Augustine went on to speak of those angelic humans who did not fall and were not tempted by the daughters of men, asserting that these earthly angels procreated to produce citizens for the City of God. His angels were devoid of both sexual desire and the concerns of kinship, and he used the term *angels* to mean any servant or messenger of God, not necessarily a heavenly being. The Augustinian view seems to presuppose that angels are male and that there is no reason for there to be female angels, daughters of God.

Thomas Aquinas addresses the issue of the angelic body in the fifty-first question of the first part of the *Summa Theologica* (1266–73). He asserts that the angels assume bodies and that they have bodies naturally united to them, although they do not exercise functions of life in the bodies assumed. He then addresses the issue of the gender of angels, stating that the angels of God are of neither sex so long as they remain in heaven.

Sources:

Godwin, Malcolm. *Angels: An Endangered Species*. New York: Simon and Schuster, 1990.

MacGregor, Geddes. *Angels: Ministers of Grace*. New York: Paragon House, 1988.

Schneiderman, Stuart. *An Angel Passes: How the Sexes Became Undivided*. New York: New York University Press, 1988.

Shakespeare's Concept of Angels

The beloved English dramatist and poet William Shakespeare (1564–1616) incorporated his eschatological ideas, including those about angels, into his work, though one might argue that his biblical knowledge was used lightly. His plays seem rather to reflect the dramatist's pure joy in the theater, his passion for words, and his often tongue-in-check delight in an intimate acquaintance with human nature.

One modern writer, Roger L. Cox, argues differently. In his book *Between Earth and Heaven: Shakespeare, Dostoevsky, and the Meaning of Christian Tragedy* (1969), Cox maintains that Shakespeare was "indebted specifically to the New Testament, not to biblical commentators or religious reformers, and what [he] has borrowed is not merely random phrases or quotable verses, but the very fabric of biblical thought with its characteristic patterns of language and imagery."

"Shakespearean tragedy," writes Cox, "derives some of its principal motifs and conceptions from the letters of St. Paul."

Shakespeare's work does seem to reflect that heaven is conceived as God's kingdom above the clouds, reserved for the souls of the righteous, and that he held a belief in **Satan** or **Lucifer** and a hell where the damned were eternally tormented by fire. His view of good and evil angels forever whispering their exhortations and temptations at the shoulders of mortals was based on the teachings of the church in Shakespeare's time.

In an introduction to *Religion and Modern Literature: Essays in Theory and Criticism* (1975), editor G. B. Tennyson writes:

> One might argue that the Globe Playhouse is quite a long way from the church porch, that Shakespeare's dramas are works in which this world figures more prominently than the next, works in which human action plays a greater role than divine action. But much of this secularity is deceptive. . . . The stature of a Hamlet or a Lear is a function of the religious world-view that Shakespeare shared with his audience, for the Elizabethan plays are descendants of the medieval drama of religious inspiration.

Thus in Shakespeare angels are represented as the embodiment of Goodness, Perfection, and Beauty; as singers of sweet songs; as messengers; as guardians; as warriors for righteousness; and as compassionate and merciful beings, understanding of human nature. Shakespeare also frequently contrasts the good and evil angels, and often compares virtuous women to angels.

Angels as the Embodiment of Goodness, Perfection, and Beauty

In *Love's Labour's Lost,* angels represent Good to the simple-minded page Moth, but Shakespeare also uses the term to refer to a beautiful woman. Boyet, attendant to the princess of France, relates to her the details of a romantic plot, directed toward her by King Ferdinand, which he has overheard in the woods. Moth is given his instructions by the king and responds innocently: "For, 'quoth the king,' an angel shalt thou see, /

THE IMPISH PUCK FROM SHAKESPEARE'S *A MIDSUMMER NIGHT'S DREAM* BY ARTHUR HUGHES. (COURTESY ARAS)

Yet fear not thou, but speak audaciously." / The boy reply'd, "An angel is not evil; / I should have fear'd her had she been a devil" (5.2.105–8).

Angels are equated with Perfection in *Two Gentlemen of Verona.* Valentine admits he has been "an idle truant, / Omitting the sweet benefit of time / To clothe mine age with angel-like perfection" (2.4.66).

Angels again represent Perfection in *Henry VIII,* when the lord chancellor tells the archbishop of Canterbury and members of the council chamber, "we are all men / In our own natures frail, and capable / Of our flesh; few are angels . . ." (5.2.57).

In *The Tempest,* Prospero, the banished duke of Milan, equates angels with Beauty. Angry at his daughter Miranda's attraction to the shipwrecked Prince Ferdinand, Prospero compares the handsome youth to the deformed slave Caliban, offspring of a witch. He tells Miranda, "Thou think'st there are no more such shapes as he, / Having seen but him and Caliban: Foolish wench! / To the most of men this is a Caliban, / And they to him are angels" (1.2.481).

Angels as Sweet Singers

Shakespeare has a romp with the idea that angels are sweet singers in *A Midsummer Night's Dream.* After an attempt at playing a practical joke on his fellow craftsmen by donning the head of an ass, Bottom, the weaver, is left alone in the deep woods. To quell his fear, he begins bellowing a song about birds. Meanwhile, Titania, queen of the fairies, is sleeping nearby under a magic spell contrived by her husband, Oberon. While she slept he streaked her eyelids with the juice of a flower that would make her fall madly in love with the first thing she saw upon waking. When she hears Bottom's song the spell is activated. "What angel wakes me from my flowery bed?" she asks, and upon seeing the weaver, ass's head and all, she declares her love (3.1.132).

Angelic choirs are likened to the music of the spheres in *The Merchant of Venice.* As Lorenzo and his love Jessica enjoy a starry night, he tells her,

> Look how the floor of heaven
> Is thick inlaid with patines of bright gold;
> There's not the smallest orb which thou behold'st
> But in his motion like an angel sings,
> Still quiring to the young-ey'd cherubims:
> Such harmony is in immortal souls;
> But, whilst this muddy vesture of decay
> Doth grossly close it in, we cannot hear it.
>   (5.1.58–65)

Angels as Messengers

The concept of angels as messengers is the basis for a quote from young Arthur in the play *King John.* On learning that his trusted Hubert, chamberlain to the king, has sworn to put out the boy's eyes with hot irons, Arthur is stunned and says, "And if an angel should have come to me / And told me Hubert should put out mine eyes / I would not have believ'd him" (4.1.68–70).

In *Macbeth,* the lord Lennox asks for an angelic messenger as war looms: "Some holy angel / Fly to the court of England, and unfold / His message ere he come; that a swift blessing / May soon return to this our suffering county" (3.6.45).

Guardian Angels

A good example of the Shakespearean concept of **guardian angels** is found in *Henry VIII* when an old woman brings the king news of the birth of his daughter: "Now, good angels / Fly o'er thy royal head, and shade thy person / Under their blessed wings!" she greets King Henry (5.1.159–60).

In *Henry V,* the archbishop of Canterbury addresses the king with a similar salutation: "God and his angels guard your sacred throne, / And make you long become it! (1.2.7–8).

Angels are again portrayed as guardians in *Richard III.* After the ghost of Clarence wishes death upon King Richard, it turns to Henry, earl of Richmond, and bestows a blessing: "Good angels guard thy battle! live, and flourish!" (5.3.138). Earlier in the play, the ailing duchess of York bids Lady Anne, "Go thou to Richard, and good angels tend thee!" (4.1.93).

Guardian angels are called upon in *Hamlet* to bear the dead prince's soul to heaven. As Hamlet utters his final words and then is silent, Horatio breathes, "Goodnight, sweet prince, / And flights of angels sing thee to thy rest!" (5.2.371).

Angels as Warriors

Shakespeare often employs the biblical portrait of angels as powerful warriors for righteousness. In *Richard II,* King Richard attempts to reassure the duke of Aumerle of Richard's royal power, in spite of victories by Bolingbroke, the future King Henry IV. Richard compares himself to the Sun rising, plucking "the cloak of night" from the backs of the traitors. He tells Aumerle, "For every man that Bolingbroke hath press'd / To lift shrewd steel against our golden crown, / God for his Richard hath in heavenly pay / A glorious angel: then, if angels fight, / Weak man must fall; for heaven still guards the right" (3.2.59–63).

In *Richard III,* the ghost of Buckingham curses King Richard in his dream, then turns to the earl of Richmond, soon to be King Henry VII, who is also dreaming of Buckingham, and says, "But cheer thy heart, and be thou not dismay'd: / God and good angels fight on Richmond's side" (5.3.174–5).

In *Macbeth,* as Macbeth plans Duncan's assassination, he considers the life of the good king:

> Besides, this Duncan
> Hath borne this faculties so meek, hath been
> So clear in his great office, that his virtues
> Will plead like angels, trumpet-tongued, against
> The deep damnation of his taking-off:
> Striding the blast, or heaven's cherubin, hors'd
> Upon the sightless couriers of the air,
> Shall blow the horrid deed in every eye. . . .
> (1.7.16–24)

Good and Evil Angels

Shakespeare's treatment of the good and evil (or fallen) angels is directly in line with his religious beliefs. In *Measure for Measure,* Angelo is aware of good and evil at war within himself as he formulates a plan to obtain sweet Isabellas's sexual favors in exchange for her brother's life. He finds himself praying with "empty words" while his mind "anchors on Isabel." With heaven in his mouth and a "strong and swelling evil" in his heart, Angelo reflects on the power of his office, but realizes he is only human. "Let's write good angel on the devil's horn," he moans, "Tis not the devil's crest" (2.4.16).

In the general confusion of *The Comedy of Errors,* Dromio of Syracuse refers to an officer as "he that came behind you, sir, like an evil angel, and bid you forsake your liberty" (4.3.20–21).

In *Henry VIII,* Cardinal Wolsey bids farewell to his servant Cromwell, telling him, "I charge thee, fling away ambition: / By that sin fell the angels; how can man, then, / The image of his Maker, hope to win by it?" (3.2.441–3).

As Falstaff banters with the chief justice in *Henry IV,* the justice chides him for his misleading of young Prince John: "You follow the young prince up and down, like his ill angel" (1.2.186). Later, in a bar scene, Falstaff refers to his page, saying, "There is a good angel about him; but the devil outbids him too" (2.4.362).

In *Macbeth,* Malcolm tells McDuff, "That which you are my thoughts cannot transpose; / Angels are bright still, though the brightest fell" (4.3.21–22). Roger L. Cox, in *Between Earth and Heaven,* proposes that this line comes from Luke 10:18: "I saw Satan fall like lightning from heaven."

Merciful Angels

Shakespeare's work also shows he believed angels to be compassionate, merciful, and understanding of human nature, much like Christ. In *Measure for Measure,* Isabella, sister of Claudio, who is condemned to die for causing his betrothed Juliet to become pregnant, begs acting lord deputy Angelo for her brother's pardon. Angelo insists that Claudio is to be beheaded, and Isabella, soon to become a nun, exhorts, "—but man, proud man! / Dressed in a little brief authority,— / Most ignorant of what he's most assured, / His glassy essence—like an angry ape, / Plays such fantastic tricks before high heaven / As make the angels weep; who, with our spleens, / Would all themselves laugh mortal" (2.2.119–25).

In *Henry VIII,* the duke of Norfolk speaks well of Queen Katherine's love for her husband, comparing it with angelic love: "her that loves him with that excellence / That angels love good men with; even of her / That, when the greatest stroke of fortune falls, / Will bless the king . . ." (2.2.35–38).

In *Hamlet,* King Claudius is overcome with guilt about his brother's murder and calls upon the angels for mercy and understanding: "O limed soul, that, struggling to be free, / Art more engag'd! Help, angels! Make assay" (3.3.68–69).

Women as Angels

Comparison between virtuous women and angels is often couched in simile and metaphor in Shakespearean drama. In *Henry V,* as the king attempts to woo Katherine, he tells her, "An angel is like you, Kate, and you are like an angel" (5.2.110).

In *Troilus and Cressida,* it is the lady who makes the comparison: "Women are angels, wooing" (1.2.312), Cressida says.

Shakespeare's vision of angels is clear in Romeo and Juliet. As Romeo courts Juliet beneath her window in the Capulets' garden, she sighs, "Ah me!" Romeo responds:

She speaks:—
O, speak again, bright angel! for thou art
As glorious to this night, being o'er my head,
As is a winged messenger of heaven
Unto the white-upturned wondering eyes
Of mortals that fall back to gaze on him
When he bestrides the lazy-pacing clouds
And sails upon the bosom of the air.
(2.2.26–33)

Shakespeare's Concept of Angels

In *Hamlet,* the ghost of Hamlet's father reveals the truth about his own murder, and speaks of his widow as "my most seeming virtuous queen," now wed to King Claudius, the elder Hamlet's killer. He refers to her as "a radiant angel" (1.5.55).

The prince of Morocco in *The Merchant of Venice* believes be will win the fair Portia by choosing a casket of gold from among two others, one lead and one silver. Only by choosing the casket that contains her picture will he win her hand. He reasons: "They have in England / A coin that bears the figure of an angel / Stamped in gold; but that's insculp'd upon; / But here an angel in a golden bed / Lies all within" (2.7.55-58).

In spite of numerous references to women as angels, however, Shakespeare does provide a contrast to that notion. In *Love's Labour's Lost,* Don Adriano de Armado fumes, "Love is a familiar, love is a devil; there is no evil angel but love" (1.1.177–8). Nevertheless, he ends his tirade with the admission that **Cupid**'s "disgrace is to be called boy; but his glory is to subdue men." Armado declares that he is truly in love with the wench Jacquenetta. "Assist me, some extemporal god of rhyme, for I am sure I shall turn sonneteer . . ." (1.1.189-91), he closes.

Shakespeare's Sonnet 144 contains perhaps his most striking contrast to the idea that women are as angels:

> Two loves I have of comfort and despair,
> Which like two spirits do suggest me still;
> The better angel is a man right fair,
> The worser spirit a woman, colour'd ill.
> To win me soon to hell, my female evil
> Tempteth my better angel from my side,
> And would corrupt my saint to be a devil,
> Wooing his purity with her foul pride. . . .

—Ann Sheridan

Sources:

Clark, Cumberland. *Shakespeare and the Supernatural.* New York: Haskell House, 1931.

Cox, Roger L. *Between Earth and Heaven: Shakespeare, Dostoevsky, and the Meaning of Christian Tragedy.* New York: Holt, Rinehart and Winston, 1969.

Frye, Roland Mushat. *Shakespeare and Christian Doctrine.* Princeton, N.J.: Princeton University Press, 1963.

Geddes, MacGregor, *Angels, Ministers of Grace.* New York: Paragon House, 1988.

Morris, Harry. *Last Things In Shakespeare.* Tallahassee, Fla.: Florida State University Press, 1985.

Shakespeare, William. *The Complete Works of William Shakespeare.* New York: Avenel Books, 1975.

Tennyson, G. B., and Edward E. Ericson, Jr., eds. *Religion and Modern Literature: Essays in Theory and Criticism.* Grand Rapids, Mich.: William B. Eerdmans, 1975.

Shemhazai and Azazel

Judaism, Christianity, and **Islam** all have angel lore related to angelic lust for human beings. Although the basic idea of spirit beings or demons having sex with human beings is very ancient, Judeo-Christian speculation on such ideas grew out of two short, obscure verses in Genesis (6:2 and 6:4) about the "sons of God" taking to wife the "daughters of men." In these rather odd verses, "sons of God" is taken to indicate angels. The traditional interpretation of these passages is that these sons of God are fallen angels.

One of the Jewish tales flowing out of this theme is the story of Shemhazai (a variant spelling of **Semyaza**) and **Azazel,** a tale which was adopted in Islam as the story of **Harut and Marut.** According to the story, humanity's inability to avoid temptation and sin prompted God to consider destroying the world by flood. The angels Shemhazai and Azazel reminded God that the angels had warned him in advance about humankind. God responded by asserting that angels would have failed just as quickly, if not more so, if placed under the same conditions. In answer to God's challenge, Shemhazai and Azazel journeyed to earth to show that angels could do better.

Almost immediately, however, they were overcome by desire for an attractive woman, and begat horrible giants (later destroyed in the Flood). Shemhazai repented for his sin, and hung himself upside down in the sky, where he remains to this day as the constellation Orion. Azazel, however, refused to repent, and remains on the earth to this day, encouraging women to wear jewelry and cosmetics in their effort to lead mortal men into sin.

Sources:

Davidson, Gustav. *A Dictionary of Angels: Including the Fallen Angels.* 1967. Reprint. New York: Free Press, 1971.
Encyclopaedia of Islam. Vol 6. Leiden, Netherlands: E. J. Brill, 1978.
Ronner, John. *Know Your Angels: The Angel Almanac with Biographies of 100 Prominent Angels in Legend and Folklore, and Much More.* Murfreesboro, Tenn.: Mamre Press, 1993.

Sons of God

There are two competing stories of the origin of fallen angels. The most familiar one is that **Lucifer,** prince of angels, out of pride led a rebellion against God and was tossed out of heaven with his followers. This version of the story became the official view. An alternative narrative is that a group of angels lusted after mortal females and acquired their fallen state after they had left their heavenly abode and copulated with them. This alternative story, which at one time was widely known, eventually disappeared from popular folklore because it clashed with the official church position (or what became the official position by the late **Middle Ages**) that angels were beings of pure spirit and thus could not engage in sexual intercourse.

The latter version of the angelic fall story is laid out in the **Book of Enoch,** a book that was never incorporated into the canonical Scriptures. There is, however, what appears to be a brief allusion to the Enoch tale in Gen. 6:2–4, which states that the "sons of God" took the "daughters of men" as wives. "Sons of God" was taken to indicate angels, though this was later disputed by church theologians. Support for the view that "sons of God" refers to angels comes from the book of Job (1:6): "Now there was a day when the sons of God came to present themselves before the Lord, and Satan also came among them."

It would be difficult to determine who these "sons" might be if they were not angelic beings. Having lost the original context for interpreting Gen. 6:2–4, some contemporary writers have hypothesized that they were the alien occupants of flying saucers who performed genetic experiments on our distant ancestors, producing what became human beings.

Sources:

Davidson, Gustav. *A Dictionary of Angels: Including the Fallen Angels.* 1967. Reprint. New York: Free Press, 1971.

Godwin, Malcolm. *Angels: An Endangered Species.* New York: Simon and Schuster, 1990.

Prophet, Elizabeth Clare. *Forbidden Mysteries of Enoch: Fallen Angels and the Origins of Evil.* 1983. Reprint. Livingston, Mont.: Summit University Press, 1992.

Sophia

Although iconographically angels often appear feminine, they are traditionally regarded as being asexual or masculine. Sophia (sometimes referred to as Pistis Sophia), whose name in Greek means wisdom, is a marked exception to this convention. In both Greek and Hebrew, the word for wisdom is feminine, and in both the ancient Greek and Hebrew thoughtways wisdom was sometimes personified, as in the apocryphal book The Wisdom of Solomon:

With thee is wisdom, who knows thy works and was present when thou didst make the world, and who understands what is pleasing in thy sight and what is right according to thy commandments. Send her forth from the holy heavens, and from the throne of thy glory send her, that she may be with me and toil, and that I may learn what is pleaseing to thee.

(Wisd. of Sol. 9:9–10)

It is but a short step from this kind of language about wisdom personified to the conception of a divine being or demigod. In much later Cabalistic thought, the second **sefiroth** is feminine—Binah (Wisdom).

In the **Gnostic** movement of the early centuries of the Christian era, Sophia came to occupy a central role in the creation story. In the beginning, according to the Gnostics, there was only a highly refined spiritual realm, the *pleroma,* which was occupied by higher spiritual beings who were referred to as **aeons.** The precise number of aeons varied according to the particular writer, but in almost every scenario the lowest aeon was Sophia (Wisdom). Through either pride or an accident, Sophia gave birth to an evil being that in turn created the physical world, a prison in which the divine sparks that constitute the essence of human beings are trapped. The goal of humanity is to awaken to its divine heritage and return to its true home in the pleroma.

Sources:

Layton, Bentley. *The Gnostic Scriptures.* Garden City, N.Y.: Doubleday, 1987.

Robinson, James M. *The Nag Hammadi Library.* 1977. Reprint. New York: Harper & Row, 1981.

Wilson, Peter Lamborn. *Angels: Messengers of the Gods.* 1980. Reprint. London: Thames and Hudson, 1994.

Spiritualism

Spiritualism has several different meanings, but it usually refers to a religious movement originating in the mid-nineteenth century. This movement has always stressed survival after death and communication with the dead by means of psychic mediumship. Claiming to embody a "scientific" spirituality, Spiritualists reject many doctrines of traditional religions, such as eternal damnation.

Most known societies have believed in the possibility of communication with the spirit world. One of the key notions of mainstream Spiritualism is the idea of spirit guides—disembodied helper spirits who are often deceased relatives. These guides resemble traditional **guardian angels,** a specific category of angelic beings said to be assigned to watch over each person. Despite functional similarities, these two categories of beings (ghosts and angels) have traditionally been regarded as entirely distinct. Today, however, because many people who have undergone **near-death experiences** have reported seeing deceased loved ones on "the other side," the distinction between disembodied helper spirits and guardian angels has blurred for many.

Sources:

Cavendish, Richard, ed. *Encyclopedia of the Unexplained: Magic, Occultism and Parapsychology.* London: Arkana Penguin Books, 1989.

Doyle, Arthur Conan. *The History of Spiritualism.* New York: Arno Press, 1975.

Giovetti, Paola. *Angels: The Role of Celestial Guardians and Beings of Light.* Translated by Toby McCormick. York Beach, Maine: Samuel Weiser, 1993.

Sraosha

Sraosha is one of the amesha spentas, who are the Zoroastrian equivalents of the Judeo-Christian **archangels.** Sraosha set the world in motion and is also the angel who carries the soul away following death. According to one legend, Sraosha comes to Earth each night to chase the demon of violence and anger. In Manicheism, which combines Zoroastrian, Gnostic, Christian, and pagan elements, Sraosha is the "angel of obedience" who judges the dead.

Sources:

Cohn, Norman. *Cosmos, Chaos and the World to Come: The Ancient Roots of Apocalyptic Faith.* New Haven, Conn.: Yale University Press, 1993.

Noss, John B. *Man's Religions.* 4th ed. New York: Macmillan, 1969.

Stamps, Angels on

The 1995 issue of new 32-cent U.S. postage stamps with **cherubs** on them attests to the angel craze of the early 1990s. However, there have been literally thousands of stamps featuring angels, from countries as diverse as Korea, Saudi Arabia, and the former Soviet Union. The connection between angels and stamps appears to be that the principal function of traditional angels is to deliver messages—making their association with postage stamps a natural one. Because traditional iconography portrays angels with **wings,** there would appear to be an especially appropriate connection between angels and air mail. In fact, for many years Vatican City issued air mail stamps with classical paintings of the **archangels.**

Sources:

Freeman, Eileen. "Angels on Stamps—Bringing Messages." *AngelWatch.* November–December 1992.

Steiner, Rudolf

Rudolf Steiner (1861–1925), born in Kraljevic, Austro-Hungary, was the founder of a **theosophical** splinter group, the Anthroposophical Society. A brilliant scientist and philosopher, Steiner made original contributions in many fields. (He is perhaps best remembered as the founder of the Waldorf educational system.) He elaborated theosophical teachings about **devas** (angels) in one of the most complex systems of such beings in occult literature.

Steiner conceived of humankind as a microcosm within the macrocosm of universe, whose secrets could be revealed by exploring the Akashic records, a kind of library in the nonphysical realms. He claimed that much of what he taught came directly from these records. According to his interpretation of human evolution, humankind lost its original spiritual and supersensible capabilities in its descent to the "material plane." Steiner developed his own ideas of reincarnation and karma, according to which some spiritual beings (angelic), who exist in higher planes, interact continuously with human beings and encourage their advancement toward spiritual consciousness, while others (demonic), who are the personification of evil, wish people to remain anchored to a materialistic world.

Steiner took the traditional hierarchy of **choirs** originally laid out by the early sixth-century theologian **Dionysius the Areopagite** and adapted it to his theosophical schema. Traditionally, the angels are arranged into nine choirs, which are grouped in three hierarchies. Steiner redesignated them as follows:

Traditional	Anthroposophical
I. First hierarchy	
1. **Seraphim**	Spirits of love
2. **Cherubim**	Spirits of the harmonies
3. **Thrones**	Spirits of will
II. Second hierarchy	
4. **Dominations**	Spirits of wisdom
5. **Virtues**	Spirits of movement
6. **Powers**	Spirits of form
III. Third hierarchy	
7. **Principalities**	Spirits of personality or time
8. **Archangels**	Fire spirits
9. **Angels**	Sons of life or of twilight

In Steiner's scheme the work of the first hierarchy is difficult for ordinary humans to comprehend. The angelic beings at this level extend their very substance into the universe in order to provide the substratum for this ordered cosmos. Put another way, they are responsible for transforming spiritual light into the hard substance of this reality.

The second hierarchy is similarly involved in the creation of the cosmos, forming the substance provided by the first hierarchy into the recognizable patterns of our world. While none of these tasks are "angelic" in the traditional sense, they accord well with the theosophical tradition, which pictures the devas as being primarily concerned with the creation of forms.

In the third hierarchy, we finally find intelligences concerned with the development and awakening of humanity. Although not all angels work directly with human beings, there is an angel assigned to each person, the intelligence we traditionally call a **guardian angel.** Unlike the classical guardian angel, however, Steiner's angels are primarily concerned with the individual's spiritual growth, which may or may not involve "protection" in the usual sense. They attempt daily to guide us through our thoughts, moods, intuitions, and inspirations. Steiner taught that we can help our guardian angels perform their tasks by being aware of them and of their guidance.

One of Steiner's more interesting ideas involves the notion of angels who guide communities. Every institution from marriages to large professional associations has an indwelling angel uniting the consciousness of its members. The work of these group angels blends into the work of the archangels, whose job it is to guide a nation, a people, or a language, which in turn blends into the work of the principalities, who guide the development of humanity as a whole. Steiner also asserted that some angels have stepped out of the line of spiritual evolution to play roles as adversaries so that developing humanity would have obstacles to overcome. These fallen angels are either Ahrimanic (too dark) or Luciferic (too light).

Although work on the whole of humanity takes place at the level of the principalities, these intelligences draw upon the diverse qualities of seven specific archangels in their work to elevate humanity. According to Steiner, **Michael** took over from **Gabriel** in 1879 and will be the driving force for human development until the end of the second century of the next millennium. Michael's task during this cycle is to free humanity from the overmaterialistic culture that has been developing for centuries, and Steiner viewed his own mission as contributing to Michael's work.

Sources:

Berger, Arthur S., and Joyce Berger. *The Encyclopedia of Parapsychology and Psychical Research.* New York: Paragon House, 1991.

Parisen, Maria, ed. *Angels and Mortals: Their Co-Creative Power.* Wheaton, Ill.: Quest, 1990.

Steiner, Rudolf. *Spiritual Beings: In the Heavenly Bodies and in the Kingdoms of Nature.* 1961. Reprint. Hudson, N.Y.: Anthroposophic Press, 1992.

Swedenbörg,
Emanuel

Suffix Angels (Nominal Angels)

Suffix angels are angels created by ancient writers by simply adding one of two Hebrew endings, *-el* or *-irion,* to ordinary words. The root words for these nominal angels were often adopted from Hebrew. For instance, the author of the **Book of Enoch** took the word for hail—*barad* in Hebrew, added *-el,* and produced Baradel, the Angel of Hailstones. By the time of Pope Zachary, this tendency had so blossomed that there were angels for almost everything. As a consequence, a church council convened in the year 745 declared that only the three angels mentioned by name in the **Bible—Raphael, Gabriel,** and **Michael**—could be called upon by the faithful.

Sources:

Davidson, Gustav. *A Dictionary of Angels: Including the Fallen Angels.* 1967. Reprint. New York: Free Press, 1971.

Ronner, John. *Know Your Angels: The Angel Almanac with Biographies of 100 Prominent Angels in Legend and Folklore, and Much More.* Murfreesboro, Tenn.: Mamre Press, 1993.

Swedenbörg, Emanuel

Emanuel Swedenbörg (1688–1772) was a Swedish scientist and philosopher who, later in life, became famous for his visions of higher spiritual realms and for his supposed travels to these realms. He had little interest in religious matters until 1744, when at age fifty-six, he had a remarkable waking experience—he travelled to the spirit world and conversed with its inhabitants, who he called "angels." Then followed a whole series of visions and dreams in which he met, among others, Jesus, God, and some of the great figures of history.

Because of his many travels to extraterrestrial realms, he was able to dictate thorough descriptions of heaven, hell, and particularly, angels. He writes in *Heaven and Hell* (1859), "I have seen a thousand times that angels are human forms, or men, for I have conversed with them as man to man, sometimes with one alone, sometimes with many in company."

Swedenbörg was emphatic in his belief that the angelic form, in every respect, is human. He described angels has having faces, eyes, ears, breasts, arms, hands, and feet. He was quick to point out, however, that "angels cannot be seen by man with his bodily eyes, but only with the eyes of the spirit which is within him."

Swedenbörg further recounted specific features of the angelic realm. Angels wear garments and live in houses like humans, "but with a difference, that they are all the more perfect, because angels exist in a more perfect state." He suggested that the raiment of an angel is reflective of his or her level of intelligence, thus "the most intelligent have garments that glitter as with flame, and some are resplendent as with light; while the less intelligent have garments of clear or opaque white without splendor."

As wondrous as their garments seem, so, too, are the abodes of Swedenbörg's angels. He described palaces, "their upper parts . . . refulgent as if they were pure gold, and their lower parts as if they were precious stones."

Angels do communicate and possess a unique type of language and mode of writing. "Their writing has a literal sense and an inner spiritual sense, and it derives directly from their thought" (Giovetti, p. 113). According to Swedenbörg, "Angels can express in one word what man cannot do in a thousand; and besides this, there are comprised in one word of angelic language innumerable things, which cannot be expressed in the words of human language at all."

The tasks and roles of Swedenbörg's angels correspond in part to those commonly attributed to this celestial **choir.** Some are guardian beings who help mortal men as they pass in death from this world to the next; others take care of little children; protect the righteous on earth and guide them toward heaven; and some moderate the goings on in hell.

The devils in Swedenbörg's cosmos have the opposite task—that of tempting mankind toward evil. According to Swedenbörg, all beings, including angels, have the free will to choose what course they will follow. Angels, wrote Swedenbörg, were not created by God at the beginning of time, rather they evolved as human beings died and returned to the Original Source. Those who choose good will reside in a celestial realm, while those who choose infernal forces are destined for hell.

Sources:

Giovetti, Paola. *Angels: The Role of Celestial Guardians and Beings of Light.* Translated by Toby McCormick. York Beach, Maine: Samuel Weiser, 1993.

Swedenbörg, Emanuel. *Divine Providence.* New York: Swedenbörg Foundation, 1972. (Originally published 1764.)

———. *Heaven and Hell.* Boston: Swedenbörg Printing Bureau, 1907.

Sylphs

Sylphs are very small winged **fairies** associated with the element air. They are said to be light, almost transparent beings who are responsible for all movements of air, from the slightest breeze to the mightiest hurricane. In the **occult** tradition, air is traditionally associated with the mental body, and air **elementals** (sylphs) are said to work with human beings to inspire creativity, lofty thoughts, and intuition.

As the archetypal spirits of the air element, sylphs are occupied with maintaining the atmosphere of the planet. In ceremonial **magic,** the sylphs are the air elementals of the East, who are called upon to witness rituals. The task of the elementals, like that of the nature **devas,** is to build up forms in the natural world, thus providing an arena in which other beings, such as human souls, can evolve spiritually. Some occultists view elementals as soulless entities who simply disappear at death, but others see them as spirits who eventually evolve into devas (angels). Because of their association with air, the sylphs are under the **rulership** of the archangel **Raphael.**

Sources:

Andrews, Ted. *Enchantment of the Faerie Realm: Communicate with Nature Spirits & Elementals.* St. Paul, Minn.: Llewellyn Publications, 1993.

McCoy, Edwin. *A Witch's Guide to Faery Folk.* St. Paul, Minn.: Llewellyn Publications, 1994.

Talmud

The world's large religious traditions tend to have many different "layers" of religious literature, each composed at a different period. Within **Judaism,** there is an extensive body of literature composed around the time of the Roman occupation—the **Apocrypha** and the Pseudepigrapha—that did not become part of either the biblical canon or the larger body of authoritative writings. Part of the reason the Apocrypha and the Pseudepigrapha failed to become authoritative was that later rabbis believed the authors of these texts overemphasized the role and importance of angels so much that Judaism was on the verge of falling into the apostasy of polytheism.

This reaction was codified in the next important body of Jewish religious literature to emerge, the Talmud. The Talmud was composed and edited during the first five centuries of the Christian era. While attempting to tone down what they viewed as an unhealthy overemphasis on angels in the Apocrypha and the Pseudepigraha, the talmudic rabbis simultaneously recognized such postbiblical revelations as the division between angels of peace and evil angels and the names of important angels other than **Michael** and **Gabriel,** such as **Uriel, Raphael,** and

Metatron. The talmudic literature also adds much detailed speculation on the nature of angels without changing the fundamental notions that had been developed earlier.

As part of the effort to de-emphasize the importance of angels, some of the talmudic scholars asserted that God created a batch of angels every day who praised him during that day, destroyed the whole lot of them overnight, and then created a new batch the next day. Others proposed that there were both temporal and eternal angels. Despite this move to downplay angels, much significant angel lore was codified in the Talmud, for example, the following ideas:

> Angels walk upright, speak Hebrew, and are endowed with understanding; they can fly in the air, move from one end of the world to another, and foretell the future. . . . They have the shape of man, but consist half of fire and half of water. (*Encyclopaedia Judaica,* p. 968)

The Talmud also asserts that the angels are numberless and are divided into higher and lower orders. It recognizes four **archangels** familiar to Christianity—Gabriel, Michael, Raphael, and Uriel—and includes innumerable angels who **rule** specific functions, everything from prayers and anger to pregnancy and hail.

Sources:
Encyclopaedia Judaica. New York: Macmillan, 1971.
Margolies, Morris B. *A Gathering of Angels: Angels in Jewish Life and Literature.* New York: Ballantine, 1994.

Taylor, Terry Lynn

It was in 1985, while on hiatus from work on her master's degree in counseling, that Terry Lynn Taylor became seriously interested in angels. During a period of overwhelming stress she came across a quote by G. K. Chesterton, "Angels can fly because they take themselves lightly," which so piqued her interest that she became sensitive to the role angels play as spiritual helpers and guides. From then on her life began to change.

Taylor set out to find a book that would help her attract angels into her life. Not finding the book she was looking for, she decided to write her own. Since writing *Messengers of Light,* she has written three more angel books: *Guardians of Hope, Answers From the Angels,* and *Creating With the Angels.* She publishes a quarterly newsletter about angels, conducts classes and workshops to promote angel consciousness, and has a feature column in the magazine *Angel Times.*

Sources:

Taylor, Terry Lynn. *Answers From the Angels: A Book of Angel Letters.* Tiburon, Calif.: H. J. Kramer, 1993.

———. *Creating With the Angels: An Angel-Guided Journey Into Creativity.* Tiburon, Calif.: H. J. Kramer, 1993.

———. *Guardians of Hope: The Angels' Guide to Personal Growth.* Tiburon, Calif.: H. J. Kramer, 1992.

———. *Messengers of Light: The Angels' Guide to Spiritual Growth.* Tiburon, Calif.: H. J. Kramer, 1990.

Television, Angels on

Since television's inception, it is likely that every drama and situation comedy has had at least one episode that involved the appearance of an angel. While the actual storylines may vary, the general plot usually revolves around one of two ideas: how the lives of the characters in the program would have altered if a pivotal character had never existed (a la *It's a Wonderful Life*), or the granting of a wish to a person who is most deserving. The *It's a Wonderful Life* storyline is arguably the most used of its kind, appearing in one form or another at least once every holiday season.

Historically, angels on television appear as normal human beings, they are rarely portrayed with the traditional flowing white gowns and wings on their backs. The fact that other humans do not recognize them as angels is usually pivotal to the plot as the angel is often on Earth to help out a person in need.

During the golden age of television, much of the programming that went on the air was, to say the least, experimental. Television executives searched other mediums, such as film, theater, and radio, to find successful material that would easily cross over to video. Probably the first major appearance of angels on television during this period occurred in 1957 when Hallmark Hall of Fame presented the television adaptation of Mark Connelly's spiritual play, *The Green Pastures*. This production was experimental in two ways: first because angels appear as main characters, and second because it featured an all black cast. This highly acclaimed fable of life in heaven starred William Warfield as De Lawd, with Vinette Carroll and Hilda Haynes as angels, and retold biblical stories in black English vernacular.

One of the most popular television shows during the early 1960s was Rod Serling's *The Twilight Zone,* a series of weekly teleplays with offbeat, unusual, and often ironic themes. Due to the remarkable "fantasy" life associated with angels, Serling and other science-fiction writers made good use of this theme for a number of plots.

In the first season Serling produced an episode called "A Passage for Trumpet." The story surrounds a man named Joey Crown played by Jack Klugman. Certain that he'll never amount to anything, Joey decides to commit suicide only to be saved by the angel "Gabriel" who proceeds to show Joey what the world would be like without him, again following the *It's a Wonderful Life* story line.

The angel theme would show up twice more during *The Twilight Zone's* original five-season run. In 1962, Serling produced an episode entitled "Mr. Bevis." After losing his job, wrecking his car, and being evicted from his apartment, all in the same day, Bevis, played by Orson Bean, makes the acquaintance of guardian angel J. Hardy Hempstead who helps him put his life back together. Originally, Serling intended "Mr. Bevis" as a pilot for a series starring Burgess Meredith, wherein each week, the angel would get Bevis out of yet another scrape. However the pilot did not sell.

Although most of *The Twilight Zone* story lines were sober and sur-realistic, in 1962 Serling produced a light-hearted, humorous episode entitled "Cavender is Coming." The plot told the story of an angel assigned to make a clumsy woman's life better. Comedienne Carol Burnett starred as the main character, and veteran comic actor Jessie White (best known as the original Maytag repairman) portrayed the angel.

While angels have appeared on television programs since the golden age, programs featuring an angel as the main character have been rare. In 1976, *Good Heavens,* a light-hearted situation comedy, appeared on ABC television. The original pilot of the short-lived series, entitled "Everything Money Can't Buy," cast Jose Ferrer as the only regularly featured character—an angel in a three-piece pinstripe suit and white fedora. However, the series was recast, and Carl Reiner served as the angel during the show's one-season run. Each episode dealt with Reiner bestowing a wish (always non-monetary) upon a different human (played by various guest stars).

In an unsuccessful television pilot from 1982, *The Kid With the Broken Halo,* Gary Coleman portrayed a young angel who tries to earn his wings by helping three desperate families with the assistance of senior angel, Robert Guillaume.

By far the most popular attempt at a television series featuring an angel as the main character was *Highway to Heaven,* which ran on NBC from 1984 to 1988. The dramatic series starred Michael Landon (who also served as the show's producer) as Jonathan Smith, an angel on pro-bation whose mission on Earth is to bring love and understanding to humans who are in some sort of trouble. Assuming the guise of a travel-

MICHAEL LANDON STARRED IN THE 1980s HIT *HIGHWAY TO HEAVEN*. THIS EPISODE
TITLED "A SPECIAL KIND OF LOVE" ALSO FEATURED PAUL WALKER (LEFT) AND BRAD
SMITH (RIGHT). (NBC-TV; COURTESY THE KOBAL COLLECTION)

ing laborer, Jonathan is often aided by his human companion Mark Gordon (played by Victor French), an ex-police officer who had been saved by Jonathan. The emotion packed storylines made the show a success. However, there was room for humor, such as the episode entitled "I Was a Middle-Aged Werewolf," in which Landon parodies a character he portrayed in the 1957 horror movie, *I Was a Teenage Werewolf.*

Along this same theme, CBS aired the short-lived television drama series *Touched by an Angel* in 1995. This distaff version of *Highway to Heaven,* starred Roma Downey as an acerbic, independent angel whose mission is to protect children who are fated for greatness but are not meeting their promise. She takes her orders from Della Reese, a messenger on high.

Another unsuccessful series with an angel theme produced in 1995 was *Heaven Help Us.* The plot line followed a young couple named Doug and Lexy Monroe played respectively by John Schneider and Melinda Clark. The Monroe's were killed in a plane crash while on their honeymoon. They awoke on the thirteenth floor of a hotel (because of superstition, hotels do not usually have a thirteenth floor), where they met their guiding angel, Mr. Shepherd played by Ricardo Montalban. Mr. Shepherd informs the Monroe's that, though they had never done anything particularly bad in their lives, they had never done anything particularly good either and as a result must now perform a series of good deeds. The plot of the first show focused on the Monroe's attempts to reunite Lexy's parents.

Television has also aired a number of made-for-television movies with angels involved in the storyline. *The Littlest Angel,* produced in 1969, starred Johnny Whitaker in a musical about a shepherd boy who dies falling off of a cliff and then struggles to become an angel. He learns a lesson in giving and eventually earns his wings with the help of fellow angels played by Fred Gwynne, E. G. Marshal, Cab Calloway, and Tony Randall.

In 1977, a remake of *It's a Wonderful Life* called *It Happened One Christmas* first appeared on television. In this version, the main character played by Jimmy Stewart in the movie was portrayed by Marlo Thomas with Cloris Leachman as the angel.

One of the most memorable made-for-television movies was *Human Feelings* (1978). This movie starred Billy Crystal as Miles Gordon and a frustrated angel/clerk to God, portrayed by Nancy Walker (known to all of the angels as Mrs. G). In a takeoff of the biblical tale of Sodom and Gomorrah, God threatens to destroy Las Vegas in seven days unless six righteous people can be found among its population. Miles takes on the task, disguised as a mortal. The movie also starred Pamela

Sue Martin, Jack Carter, Pat Morita, and Jack Fiedler (who made an angelic appearance in *The Twilight Zone* episode, "Cavender is Coming." The NBC movie has been rerun a number of times.

The burgeoning interest in angels in the 1990s has created a resurgence of television shows exploring this topic. The subject of angels on television has not, however, been limited to television dramas and situation comedies or made-for-television movies, indeed many times angels have served as the topic for daytime talk shows, prime time news magazine shows and public service shows. Among such programs were "Angels: Mysterious Messengers," an NBC special hosted by Patty Duke, which aired in 1994, and "In Search of Angels," a PBS special hosted by Debra Winger also from 1994.

—*Dana A. Hansen and Matthew F. Merta*

Sources:

Brooks, Tim, and Earle Marsh. *The Complete Directory to Prime Time Network TV Shows, 1946 to the Present.* New York: Ballantine, 1992.

Gianakos, Larry James. *Television Drama Series Programming: A Comprehensive Chronicle, 1959–1975.* Metuchen, N.J.: Scarecrow Press, 1978.

Marill, Alvin H. *Movies Made for Television: The Telefeature and the Mini-Series, 1964–1986.* New York: Zoetrope, 1987.

Shulman, Arthur, and Roger Youman. *How Sweet It Was, Television: A Pictorial Commentary on Its Golden Age.* New York: Bonanza Books, 1969.

Terrace, Vincent. *Fifty Years of Television: A Guide to Series and Pilots, 1937–1988.* New York: Cornwall Books, 1991.

Zicree, Mark. *The Twilight Zone Companion.* New York: Bantam Books, 1982.

Thanatos

The Greek god Thanatos (Death) was the son of Nyx (Night) and brother of **Hypnos** (Sleep). Thanatos met mortals when their allotted time ran out and carried them off to Hades (the underworld). As a messenger of the gods, Thanatos was pictured with **wings.** Hated even by the other Olympians, he functioned as the Greek **angel of death.**

Sources:

Grant, Michael, and John Hazel. *Who's Who in Classical Mythology.* New York: Oxford University Press, 1993.

Tripp, Edward. *The Meridian Handbook of Classical Mythology.* New York: New American Library, 1970.

Theosophy

The **Metaphysical/New Age** subculture, which is the principal locus of contemporary angel interest, grew out of several different nineteenth-century movements, including Theosophy. Although Theosophy embodies more than one set of ideas, in contemporary usage it refers to the particular synthesis of ideas from the philosophical systems of China and India and the works of the **Gnostics,** the Neoplatonists, and the Cabalists, manifested in the Theosophical Society, founded in New York in 1875 by Helena Blavatsky.

Theosophy postulates a complex view of the universe within which humanity's origins, evolution, and ultimate destiny are delineated. The visible world arises from the ultimate, immutable Source, an immaterial reality of which, as in Hindu philosophy, the universe is the manifestation and from which it is guided. The process of cosmic manifestation is characterized by two phases, the first being *involution,* during which a multitude of spiritual units emerge from the Source and, after becoming more and more involved in matter, finally achieve self-consciousness in the physical world. During the second phase, *evolution,* the human *monads* (souls) develop their inner potentials, free themselves from matter, and return to the Source with an increased consciousness.

The eternal human spirit attains mastery through cycles of reincarnation, in accordance with karma, the moral law of cause and effect. In each incarnation new experiences are attained, leading to the development of the soul to a degree that is proportionate to the use that is made of each experience. According to Theosophy, a long series of reincarnations is required for the soul to achieve its supreme aim.

Like the ancient Gnostics, whom they view as predecessors, Theosophists populate the cosmos with innumerable spiritual entities. A significant class of these entities are what Theosophists call the **devas,** a Sanskrit term for the demigods of **Hinduism** and **Buddhism.** Within Theosophy, devas are roughly equivalent to angels, although devas have many more functions than do traditional angels. In particular, devas oversee natural forces and are responsible for building up forms on inner planes as well as on the physical plane.

Some strands of Theosophy view devas as human souls who have, through the process of reincarnation, evolved into higher spiritual beings. Other strands, such as the Theosophy of Alice Bailey's Arcane School, place the devas on a separate evolutionary path. In particular, Bailey sees devas as evolving from elemental spirits and **fairies,** rather than from human forms.

Devas became part of the metaphysical subculture in the early seventies when the **Findhorn** community was being featured in New Age periodicals. The early community focused around a highly successful vegetable garden in which community members were engaged in a unique

Theosophy

Estimated number of people worldwide who claim they are angels in human form: 100,000

cooperative arrangement with agricultural devas (understood in theosophical terms). Thus the devas, who had long been identified with the angels of Western religious traditions, entered the consciousness of the New Age.

Sources:

Eliade, Mircea, ed. *Encyclopedia of Religion.* 16 vols. New York: Macmillan, 1987.

Hastings, James, ed. *Encyclopedia of Religion and Ethics.* Edinburgh: T. & T. Clark, 1980.

Shepard, Leslie A., ed. *Encyclopedia of Occultism & Parapsychology.* 3d ed. Detroit, Mich.: Gale Research, 1991.

Thomas Aquinas

St. Thomas Aquinas, Catholic theologian and philosopher, was born in Roccasecca, Italy, in 1224. Educated by the Benedectines of Monte Cassino, he earned a master in arts degree at the University of Naples before entering the Order of Dominicans in 1244. He then studied philosophy and theology in Paris and Cologne. In 1252 he was sent to the University of Paris for advanced study in theology and taught until 1259, when he went back to Italy to spend ten years teaching at various Dominician monasteries. Illness forced him to leave teaching, and after a five-year illness, Aquinas died in 1274.

Aquinas, whose eclectic philosophy, including his musings on angels, is principally a rethinking of Aristotelianism within the framework of **Christianity** (plus significant influences from earlier Christian philosophers), produced his writings during his twenty years as an active teacher. Besides a variety of recorded disputations and commentaries (*On Being and Essence, De Anima, On Physics, On Interpretation, Posterior Analytics, Ethics, Metaphysics, Politics* and the unfinished expositions of Aristotle's *De Caelo, De Generatione,* and *Metheora*), his works primarily consist of theological and philosophical treatises written in Latin, such as the short treatise *Principles of Nature,* in which he discusses several philosophical subjects, from the distinction between essence and existence to the Aristotelian dependence of abstracted universals on individual material things; the *Summa contra gentiles,* four books in which he argues against nonbelievers and heretics; *Against the Errors of the Greeks,* in which he expresses his opinion about the doctrinal points disputed by Greek and Latin Christians; and the unfinished *Summa Theologica,* a three-part treatise on sacred doctrine that contains the principles of Thomistic theology.

The element providing the *Summa Theologica* with conceptual unity consists of the Dionysian circle, implying the going forth of all things from God and the return of all things to God. Part 1 includes questions and treatises about creation, angels, humanity, and divine government. The two sections of the second part are about virtues, vices, law, and grace, and the questions contained in the third part consider Christ and his sacraments as indispensable means to salvation.

Aquinas thoroughly treated the subject of angels, providing an influential **angelology** for his age. Based on the assumption that humans cannot be the highest beings in the created order, Aquinas's angelology posits a race of superior beings with capacities far beyond our own.

Even without an evolutionary understanding of the universe, he perceived why angels are necessary in a natural hierarchy. He asserted that angels are the next step beyond humanity in the order of beings. He argued that since intellect is above sense, there must be some creatures who are incorporeal and therefore comprehensible by the intellect alone.

He thus assigned to angels an incorporeal nature, departing from earlier philosophers who had asserted that angels were constituted from a subtle material substance. Aquinas's work does refer to Aristotle, according to whom nothing is moved except a body and so it might well be argued that Aquinas believed an angel must be in some way a corporeal substance. However, he also quoted the psalmist in Ps. 104:4, who affirms that God "maketh his angels spirits." He defended the view that angels do not belong to a species as do humans, but each is a separate substance and its own species. He also held that angels are incorruptible. In spite of their incorporeal nature, angels can sometimes assume bodies, since the scriptural account of **Abraham**'s entertaining angels makes this plain.

During Aquinas's time, it was generally recognized by the Church that angels are impeccable. Their state of perfection was believed to be such that they did not stand in any danger of sinning as men and women do. Aquinas held that **Lucifer,** like all the angels, was created in a state of grace. Nevertheless, he impiously exercised the free will with which all angels are endowed. Otherwise he could not have sinned, since, according to Aquinas, angels achieve everlasting bliss the instant they do one meritorious act, and thereafter they are so close to God that it is impossible for them to turn away from him. Hence, the angels who did not rebel can never sin.

Aquinas also accepted the concept of the **guardian angel** and held that only angels of the lowest rank are appointed to this office.

Sources:

Edward, Paul, ed. *The Encyclopedia of Philosophy*. New York: Macmillan, 1967.

MacGregor, Geddes. *Angels: Ministers of Grace*. New York: Paragon House, 1988.

Magill, Frank N., ed. *Masterpieces of World Philosophy*. New York: Harper-Collins, 1990.

Maritan, Jacques. *The Sin of the Angel: An Essay on a Reinterpretation of Some Thomistic Positions*. Westminster, Md.: Newman Press, 1959.

Thoughtforms

In **occult** and **metaphysical** writings, it is often asserted that "thoughts are things." The Western occult tradition views the cosmos as a multitude of levels or "planes" of reality. The physical level that constitutes the world of our ordinary experience is the densest and "lowest" plane of this hierarchy. The other levels are normally invisible to human perception.

The so-called mental plane, which is several levels above the physical, consists of a highly refined spirit/matter/energy substance. When we think, and particularly when we hold a concentrated thought, we create, even if only temporarily, a mental "object" that takes on an existence outside our mind. These mental creations, emerging out of mental plane substance, are *thoughtforms*. The effective agents constructing and maintaining such forms are **devas** (angels).

In the occult view, thoughtforms become subtle but nevertheless powerful agents that, at least potentially, affect events on the physical level. For instance, if one persistently visualizes a certain desired state of affairs, thoughtforms are created that exert a subtle, "magnetic" influence in that direction, similar to creative visualization.

Sources:

Bailey, Alice A. *Ponder on This: A Compilation*. New York: Lucis Publishing, 1971.

Bloom, William. *Devas, Fairies and Angels: A Modern Approach*. Glastonbury, England: Gothic Image Publications, 1986.

Threshold Guardians

A basic characteristic of religious consciousness is distinguishing between sacred and secular space. Ceremonial sites such as temples have traditionally been set aside as special places to approach the gods, venerated spots where the business of everyday life is not allowed to intrude. As part of the traditional pattern of constructing sacred space, certain spirits or demigods are imagined as standing at the threshold—at the doorway of the temple or at the gateway to the ceremonial grounds—turning away unfriendly spirits and otherwise protecting the place.

GOTHIC ARCHANGEL DOOR
BY BRUNELLESCHI
(FIFTEENTH CENTURY).

The ancient Assyrian **cherubim** are examples of such threshold guardians. Assyrian art depicts the cherubim as spiritual beings having large, winged bodies of sphinxes, eagles, or other animals, with faces of lions or human beings. They were positioned at the entrances of temples and palaces as threshold guardians. Relying upon the Assyrian model, the Bible relates that God placed cherubim at the gates of Eden to prevent **Adam** and Eve from returning:

> He drove out the man; and at the east of the garden of Eden
> he placed the cherubim, and a flaming sword which turned
> every way, to guard the way to the tree of life. (Gen. 3:24)

In this passage and others (e.g., Exod. 25:18–22, in which the cherubim are carved on the Ark of the Covenant), these angels are clearly performing the guardian function they served in ancient Assyria.

In later Christian thinking, it was natural to conceive of angels as the guardians of churches. A common motif was to carve a representation of **Michael,** the warrior **archangel** most associated with soldiering, into the doorway. In **Gnostic** thought, the **archons** of the various levels of the cosmos served as threshold guardians. Part of the knowledge imparted to Gnostic initiates was the passwords needed to pass through each archonic threshold.

Sources:

Davidson, Gustav. *A Dictionary of Angels: Including the Fallen Angels.* 1967. Reprint. New York: Free Press, 1971.
Layton, Bentley. *The Gnostic Scriptures.* Garden City, N.Y.: Doubleday, 1987.
Mansfield, Richard. *Angels: An Introduction to the Angelic Hierarchy.* Encinitas, Calif.: Estuary Publications, 1994.

Thrones

The thrones, known as "the many eyed ones," are third in the **Dionysian hierarchy** of angels. They are angels of justice and it is their job to carry out God's decisions. It is to the thrones that Dionysius refers when he states that, "God brings his justice to bear upon us."

The thrones are possibly the most oddly represented of the choirs in that they are described as fiery wheels. Undoubtedly this description is based on accounts from the prophet **Ezekiel,** who around the year 580 B.C. described a windstorm with a thunderhead that was glowing in the northern sky. Humanlike winged creatures with four heads and faces darted with lightning speed across the heavens. He recounts that they were carried on four wheels whose rims were "covered with eyes . . . their construction being as it were a wheel within a wheel." They were in constant motion "like the noise of great waters . . . and above their heads [was] the likeness of a throne. . . ." These angels are believed to be deployed like charioteers around the throne of God (Ezek. 1:13–19).

Similar accounts are presented by **Elijah** who was taken to heaven in a whirlwind and by **Enoch** who describes these angels as "of the fiery coals."

Raphael is thought to be ruler of this realm, which exists either in the third or fourth heaven. According to Jewish legend, the Hebrew patriarchs automatically become members of this order of angels upon reaching heaven.

Sources:

Davidson, Gustav. *A Dictionary of Angels: Including the Fallen Angels.* 1967. Reprint. New York: Free Press, 1971.

Godwin, Malcolm. *Angels: An Endangered Species.* New York: Simon and Schuster, 1990.

Mansfield, Richard. *Angels: An Introduction to the Angelic Hierarchy.* Encinitas, Calif.: Estuary Publications, 1994.

Tobit

The various scenes from the story of **Raphael** and Tobias in the Book of Tobit (a book of Scripture included in the Roman Catholic canon of the Old Testament and in the Protestant Apocrypha) have been represented in the works of artists of all nations, including several notable paintings by **Rembrandt.** In the story of Tobit, Tobias's father sends his son to recover a sum of money to provide for his wife after his death. During his journey, the young Tobias, guided by an angel, catches a fish with whose liver he later restores his father's eyesight. With the help of the angel, who is disguised as a mortal man, he recovers the money, then takes a wife, with whom he returns home. It is not until the end of the adventure that Raphael reveals his angelic character and, having fulfilled his mission, returns to heaven.

Sources:

Ronner, John. *Know Your Angels: The Angel Almanac with Biographies of 100 Prominent Angels in Legend and Folklore, and Much More.* Murfreesboro, Tenn.: Mamre Press, 1993.

Wilson, Peter Lamborn. *Angels.* New York: Pantheon Books, 1980.

Traffic Angels

The term "traffic angels" refers to the numerous accounts of motorists who are mysteriously helped by **guardian angels.** Such inexplicable manifestations include voices that tell a driver to stop or change lanes, help for stranded motorists that comes out of nowhere, vehicles physically moved out of harm's way, and vehicles that avoid crashes. The following are two examples.

Padre Pio's biographer, Fr. Allesio Parente, reported that the priest's guardian angel once drove one of Parente's friends for three hours in a car while the man was asleep at the wheel. In 1980, an elderly widow was driving when a large car towing a boat suddenly darted into her path. She froze in fear and saw her car heading toward a seemingly unavoidable collision. At that point, her late husband, who had been dead for three months, materialized in the car, steered the vehicle into a ditch and then disappeared.

Sources:

Georgian, Linda. *Your Guardian Angels*. New York: Simon & Schuster, 1994.

Giovetti, Paola. *Angels: The Role of Celestial Guardians and Being of Light*. Translated by Toby McCormick. York Beach, Maine: Samuel Weiser, 1993.

Trolls

Trolls are a type of large, grotesque **fairy,** originating in Germany and Scandinavia. They are stupid, hairy creatures who hate human beings and other classes of fairies. They are said to enjoy throwing rocks at people and animals, and are prone to inexplicably long bouts of laughter. Traditional folklore portrays them as unpleasant, but not demonic. In most familiar troll tales, these beings guard bridges or some other throughway, and harass passers by.

Sources:

McCoy, Edwin. *A Witch's Guide to Faery Folk*. St. Paul, Minn.: Llewellyn, 1994.

Twain, Mark

Samuel Langhorne Clemens, better known as Mark Twain, frequently used biblical images in his work, and was particularly fascinated with the figure of **Satan.** He was born at Florida, Missouri, on November 30, 1835. In 1839 his family moved to Hannibal, where in 1847 he worked as a printer on the *Journal and Gazette* following his father's death. He left Hannibal for St. Louis in 1853, and in 1856 he moved to Cincinnati. In 1862 he published "The Petrified Man"; in 1863 "The Empire City Massacre"; and "Those Blasted Children" in 1864.

He married Olivia Langdon in 1870; in the same year his son Langdon Clemens was prematurely born. The following year he published *Mark Twain's Autobiography and First Romance* and moved to Hartford,

Connecticut. *Old Times on the Mississippi* appeared in the *Atlantic Monthly* in 1875, and *The Adventures of Tom Sawyer* was published in 1876. In the following years he published *A True Story and the Recent Carnival of Crime* (1877), *A Tramp Abroad* (1880), *Adventures of Huckleberry Finn* (1885), and *A Connecticut Yankee in King Arthur's Court* (1889).

In 1891 he closed his home in Hartford and moved to Europe with his family, where in 1896 his favorite child, Susy, died. He returned to America in 1900. *Extracts from Adam's Diary* was published in 1904, *Eve's Diary* followed in 1906, and *Extract from Captain Stormfield's Visit to Heaven* appeared in 1909. Shortly afterward, Twain died (April 21, 1910) and was buried at Elmira, New York.

It has often been recognized that Twain was more influenced by the Bible than by any other book and that he drew upon it for ideas, subjects, and imagery. His choice of biblical subjects was dictated by his own background, since he had lived in a community where many people revered the Bible as the Word of God.

Among his favorite biblical characters, besides **Adam,** was **Satan,** with whom he had long been fascinated, although he had managed to keep him out of the diaries of Adam and Eve. Prior to writing "That Day in Eden," Twain had done several pieces in which Satan figured prominently. Among them is the 1897 "Letters to Satan"; the 1904 "Sold to Satan," in which he plays Faust, having determined to sell his soul; and "A Humane Word from Satan" which appeared in 1905.

Twain also showed an interest in Satan's relatives. In 1898 he recorded in his notebook an idea for a story about "Little Satan, Jr.," which became one of the versions of "The Mysterious Stranger." In the published version, however, it is not Satan's *son* but his nephew who bears the name Satan. "That Day in Eden," which relates how Adam and Eve came to eat the apple and thus to bring moral sense and death into the world, is supposed to have been written by Satan on the day of the Fall. Most of the diary consists of a dialogue between Satan and Eve as the former tries to explain the words God had used.

In "Letters from the Earth," written in 1909, Satan is banished from heaven and visits Earth to see how the human experiment is coming along. Satan writes a series of letters to his friends, the angels **Michael** and **Gabriel,** describing the foolishness of humanity and discussing in considerable detail the book man values most, the Bible. As Satan narrates the story of the Fall, he makes the point that God was insane to expect Adam and Eve to obey a command they could not understand. Besides Satan, other angels mentioned in Twain's works include the old-headed angel named Sandy McWilliams, found in "Captain Stormfield's Visit to Heaven."

Sources:

Chessman, Harriet Scott, ed. *Literary Angels.*. New York: Fawcett Columbine, 1994.

Ensor, Allison. *Mark Twain & The Bible*. Lexington: University of Kentucky Press, 1969.

Long, E. Hudson. *Mark Twain Handbook*. New York: Handrick House, 1957.

Rudwin, Maximilian. *The Devil in Legend and Literature*. Chicago: Open Court Publishing, 1931.

Twenty-Eight Angels, Inc.

Twenty-Eight Angels, Inc. (TEA) was founded by artist and angelologist Karyn Martin-Kuri to provide balanced information on the subject of angels to individuals and the media. In 1992 TEA established the first angel information hotline (1-800-28ANGELS), which fosters a connection with people interested in angels all over the world. Martin-Kuri sponsored the First and Second American Conferences on Angels in 1992 and 1993, and, in 1994, the First International Conference on Angels and Art in Florence, Italy. A series of events have been scheduled for 1996 in conjunction with the release of two books by K. Martin-Kuri, both published by Ballantine: *The Angels Are Calling: A Message for the Millennium* and the autobiography of the the founder of Twenty-Eight Angels entitled *Living with Angels,* which will feature her artwork.

TEA has released a *Course on Angels,* a ten-level workbook for individuals and groups to learn to work with angels. The organization also offers tapes and booklets on heavenly topics. In addition to her work with TEA, Martin-Kuri is a featured writer of *Angel Times* magazine and contributes to other journals and periodicals in the United States and Europe. She is a popular speaker who tours throughout the United States and abroad explaining the current phenomenon of angelic interaction. She is also gifted with the ability to assist individuals privately to improve their relationship to the angelic world. Karyn Martin-Kuri can be reached at Twenty-Eight Angels, Inc., P.O. Box 116, Free Union, VA, 22940; Phone 1-800-28ANGELS. (See also **Contemporary Angel Artists**)

UFOs and Angels

Whereas traditional societies have viewed every aspect of the world as sacred, the Judeo-Christian-Islamic family of religions divested much of the natural world of religious meaning, leaving the sky as the locus of sacrality. The Supreme Deity resides in a celestial abode according to Judeo-Christian Scripture, from reference in the Exodus passage about how "the Lord looked *down* on the Egyptian army" (14:24) to Jesus' mention of God as "Our Father who art in *Heaven*" (emphases added). Angels, too, have traditionally been viewed as celestial beings if only by virtue of their **wings.**

Decades ago the psychiatrist **Carl Jung** noted religious themes in UFO discourse and dubbed flying saucers "technological angels" (i.e., angels for an age that can no longer believe in the supernatural but can believe in fantastic technological achievements). UFOs or flying saucers have been invested with religious significance almost from the time they became a public phenomenon in the 1950s. This religious dimension of flying saucers is often expressed unconsciously through certain themes in UFO literature. Of these, the celestial origin of the "space brothers" is the most obvious theme. Often stories of encounters with space beings fea-

RUTH NORMAN (1900–93), WHO WENT BY THE NAME URIEL, WAS CO-FOUNDER OF
THE UNARIUS ACADEMY OF SCIENCE. IN THIS PHOTO, SHE IS SEATED IN FRONT OF
A REPRESENTATION OF THE LANDING OF THE SPACE BROTHERS, WHICH UNARIUS
ANTICIPATES WILL OCCUR IN 2001. (COURTESY MICHAEL GRECCO)

ture messages (e.g., warnings) to earthlings from advanced extraterrestrial civilizations. In this message bearing role, they perform the central defining function of angels. Particularly in the fifties, when nuclear war seemed imminent, it was sometimes thought that the space brothers might intervene in human history to save us from our own self-destructive tendencies. In this redemptive activity, they were again playing a role traditionally reserved for angels.

Since the 1950s, an entirely different concern has arisen to supplant the redemptive theme in ufological literature, namely, the abduction theme. Beginning rather modestly, stories by individuals who claimed to have been abducted by aliens grew steadily until the publication of Whitley Strieber's *Communion* in 1987. This fantastic, novelized account of abduction by aliens caused interest in the phenomenon to explode.

By the early 1990s more books on the abduction phenomenon were being published than books on all other ufological topics combined. These narratives almost always feature emotionless aliens subjecting abductees to some kind of painful operation. In these stories, extraterrestrials play the role of fallen angels. Thus, if the earlier space brothers were technological angels, the kidnapping type of more recent decades are technological devils.

Another persistent topic in ufological literature has been the theme that the human race is the product of genetic experimentation by aliens millennia ago with an earlier race of humanoid monkeys. This "ancient astronauts" view sometimes includes a sexual theme, namely, that the aliens sexually abused our ancestors, or even that the extraterrestrials (fallen angels) mated with earth women to produce a superior race. As evidence for this peculiar view, advocates sometimes cite the Genesis verses about the **Nephilim:**

> The Nephilim were on the earth in those days, and also afterward, when the sons of God came in to the daughters of men, and they bore children to them. These were the mighty men that were of old, men of renown. (Gen. 6:4)

These "sons of God," according to this line of interpretation, are the aliens who—by means of genetic manipulation or sexual insemination—produced the Nephilim, a superior terrestrial race.

Sources:

Godwin, Malcolm. *Angels: An Endangered Species*. New York: Simon and Schuster, 1990.

Lewis, James R., ed. *The Gods Have Landed: New Religions from Other Worlds*. Albany, N.Y.: State University of New York Press, 1995.

Prophet, Elizabeth Clare. *Forbidden Mysteries of Enoch: Fallen Angels and the Origins of Evil*. Rev. ed. Livingston, Mont.: Summit University Press, 1992.

Thompson, Keith. *Angels and Aliens: UFOs and the Mythic Imagination*. Reading, Mass.: Addison-Wesley, 1991.

Undines

Undines are a type of **fairy** associated with the element water. They reside in oceans and other bodies of water and are said to appear in the form of sea horses with human faces. Larger and more developed undines are said to form the basis for the legends of mermaids and mermen. Water is traditionally associated with emotions and sensuality, and in **occult** sources the undines are said to work with human beings through their "astral body" to help develop sensitivity and emotions.

As the archetypal spirits of the water element, undines are occupied with maintaining all of the earth's bodies of water. In ceremonial **magic,** the undines are the water **elementals** of the West, who are called upon to witness rituals. The task of the elementals, like that of the nature **devas,** is to build up forms in the natural world, thus providing an arena in which other beings, such as human souls, can evolve spiritually. Some occultists view elementals as soulless entities who simply disappear at death, but others see them as spirits who eventually evolve into devas (angels). Because of their association with water, the undines are under the **rulership** of the archangel **Gabriel.**

Sources:

Andrews, Ted. *Enchantment of the Faerie Realm: Communicate with Nature Spirits & Elementals*. St. Paul, Minn.: Llewellyn Publications, 1993.

McCoy, Edwin. *A Witch's Guide to Faery Folk*. St. Paul, Minn.: Llewellyn, 1994.

Uriel

Uriel, whose name means "fire of God," is one of the leading angels in noncanonical lore. He is identified variously as a **seraph, cherub,** regent of the sun, flame of God, angel of the presence, presider over Tartarus (hell), archangel of salvation, and, in later Scriptures, as Phanuel, "face of God." The name Uriel may be derived from Uriah the prophet. In **apocryphal** and **occult** works Uriel has been equated with **Nuriel,** Uryan, Jeremiel, Vretil, **Sariel,** Puruel, Phanuel, **Jehoel,** and **Israfil.**

He is often identified as the cherub who "stands at the Gate of Eden with a fiery sword," or as the angel who "watches over thunder and terror"

(1 Enoch). In the *Apocalypse of St. Peter* he appears as the Angel of Repentance, who is graphically represented as being as pitiless as any demon. In the *Book of Adam and Eve* Uriel is regarded as the spirit (i.e., one of the cherubs) of the third chapter of Genesis. He has also been identified as one of the angels who helped bury **Adam** and Abel in Paradise, as well as the dark angel who wrestled with **Jacob** at Peniel. Other sources depict him as the destroyer of the hosts of Sennacherib, as well as the messenger sent by God to Noah to warn him of the impending Deluge.

According to Louis Ginzberg, Uriel represents "the prince of lights." In addition, Uriel is said to have disclosed the mysteries of the heavenly arcana to Ezra, interpreted prophecies, and led **Abraham** out of Ur. He is considered one of the four angels of the presence in later Judaism. He is also the angel of September and may be invoked ritually by those born in that month.

It is asserted that the divine discipline of alchemy was brought down to earth by Uriel, and that Uriel gave the Cabala to man, although this key to the mystical interpretation of Scripture is also said to have been the gift of **Metatron.** Uriel is described by **Milton** as "regent of the sun" and the "sharpest sighted spirit of all in Heaven," and Dryden, in *The State of Innocence,* depicts Uriel as descending from heaven in a chariot drawn by white horses. Uriel was reprobated at a church council in Rome in A.D. 745, but now he is St. Uriel, and his symbol is an open hand holding a flame.

He is identified with the "benign angel" who attacked Moses for neglecting to observe the covenantal rite of circumcision with regard to his son Gershom, although the same role is identified with **Gabriel** in the **Zohar** I, 93b, which reports that Gabriel "came down in a flame of fire, having the appearance of a burning serpent," with the express purpose of destroying Moses "because of his sin."

Uriel is also alleged to be the Angel of Vengeance pictured by Prud'hon in *Divine Vengeance and Justice,* located in the Louvre. Among the **archangels,** however, the least widely represented in art is Uriel. As the interpreter of prophecies, he is usually depicted carrying a book or a papyrus scroll.

AN INCIDENT FROM MILTON'S *PARADISE LOST* INVOLVING THE ANGEL URIEL. ILLUSTRATION BY GUSTAVE DORÉ (1866).

In *Milton's Ontology, Cosmogony and Physics* (1957), Walter Curry writes that Uriel "seems to be largely a pious but not too perceptive physicist with inclinations towards atomistic philosophy." Uriel is described in the second book of the Sibylline Oracles as one of the "immortal angels of the Undying God," who on the Day of Judgment:

> will break the monstrous bars framed of unyielding and unbroken adamant of the brazen gates of Hades, and cast them down straightway, and bring forth to judgement all the sorrowful forms, yea, of the ghosts of the ancient Titans and of the giants, an all whom the flood overtook . . . and all these shall he bring to the judgement seat . . . and set before God's seat.

During the incident when Jacob wrestles with a dark angel there is a mysterious merging of the two beings, and Uriel says, "I have come down to earth to make my dwelling among men, and I am called Jacob by name." A number of the patriarchs supposedly became angels, such as **Enoch,** who was transformed into Metatron. Uriel's transformation, however, is the first recorded instance of an angel becoming a man.

Uriel

Uriel is known as the sharpest-eyed of the archangels.

Sources:

Curry, Walter Clyde. *Milton's Ontology, Cosmogony, and Physics.* Lexington, Kent.: University of Kentucky Press, 1957.

Davidson, Gustav. *A Dictionary of Angels Including the Fallen Angels.* 1967. Reprint. New York: Free Press.

Ginzberg, Louis. *The Legends of the Jews.* Philadelphia: The Jewish Publication Society of America, 1954.

Godwin, Malcolm. *Angels: An Endangered Species.* New York: Simon and Schuster, 1990.

MacGregor, Geddes. *Angels: Ministers of Grace.* New York: Paragon House, 1988.

West, Robert H. *Milton and the Angels.* Athens: University of Georgia Press, 1955.

Urim

Friedrich Klopstock, in his poetic drama *The Messiah (Der Messias),* identifies Urim as a **cherub.** This use of Urim as the name of an angel is unusual. The name means "illumination" and is used in the Bible to denote a household idol. It is usually adopted in association with the term *tummin,* "perfection," referring to oracles for ascertaining the will of God. This association derives from the Babylonian-Chaldean (**Mesopotamian**) "tablets of destiny," which were believed to possess the virtue of casting the fate of men.

It is also believed that the urim and tummin engraved on Aaron's breastplate represented the insignia of his office of high priest. According to Talmud *Yoma,* the urim and tummin are among the five holy things found in the First Temple and absent from the Second Temple. They are also cited in the **Zohar,** as well as in **Milton**'s *Paradise Regained III,* as "those oraculous gems / On Aaron's breast."

Sources:

Davidson, Gustav. *A Dictionary of Angels: Including the Fallen Angels.* 1967. Reprint. New York: Free Press, 1971.

Klopstock, Friedrich Gottlieb. *The Messiah.* Reprint. 1795. Boston: John West & Co., 1811.

Usiel

Usiel (Strength of God) is generally considered a fallen angel and among those who wedded human wives and begat giants. He is also listed as the fifth of the ten unholy **sefiroth.** According to the *Book of the Angel Raziel,* Usiel is among the seven angels before the throne of God, and among the nine set over the four winds. A conjuration of Usiel and an accounting of his adjunct princes are found in *The Key to Faust's Three-fold Harrowing of Hell.* **Milton** regards Usiel as an "unfallen" angel, belonging to the order of **virtues,** as well as one of **Gabriel**'s lieutenants during **Satan**'s rebellion.

Sources:

Davidson, Gustav. *A Dictionary of Angels: Including the Fallen Angels.* 1967. Reprint. New York: Free Press, 1971.

"The Book of the Angel Raziel". MS. 3826, Sloane Collection British Museum, London. Cited in Davidson, p. 365.

Valkyries

The valkyries were female warrior angels of Norse (Viking) legend who flew on horseback over the battlefield, choosing which warriors were to be slain and then carrying them back to Valhalla, the Norse paradise. The flash of their armor was said to be the cause of the northern lights (aurora borealis). During their movement from this world to the next, the valkyries crossed over a rainbow bridge connecting heaven and earth.

Prior to their role as angels of death, the valkyries of older Norse mythology originally may have been priestesses of Freyja, queen of heaven. They were subordinate to the Norns (the Norse Fates) and originally may have been their assistants. The Norn Skuld (the Fate of Necessity) often rode with the valkyries.

Sources:

Ronner, John. *Know Your Angels: The Angel Almanac with Biographies of 100 Prominent Angels in Legend and Folklore, and Much More.* Murfreesboro, Tenn.: Mamre Press, 1993.

Sykes, Egerton. *Who's Who: Non-Classical Mythology.* New York: Oxford University Press, 1993.

ONE OF THE VALKYRIE,
WINGED NORSE
WARRIOR GODDESSES.
(COURTESY ARAS)

Victor

Victor is the angel who appeared to St. Patrick and convinced him to return to Ireland to convert the Irish to Christianity. When Britain was part of the Roman Empire, sixteen-year-old Patrick had been kidnapped from his family home in Britain and taken to Ireland as a slave to be a swineherd. He was eventually guided by a supernatural voice who gave Patrick directions to the south of Ireland, where he got on a ship and sailed to France and freedom. Near the end of the Roman Empire the angel Victor appeared to Patrick and requested that he return to Ireland for the purpose of converting the pagan land to Christianity.

Sources:

Davidson, Gustav. *A Dictionary of Angels: Including the Fallen Angels.* 1967. Reprint. New York: Free Press, 1971.
New Catholic Encyclopedia. Vol. 1. Washington, D.C.: Catholic University of America, 1981.

Virtues

The virtues, known as "The Brilliant or Shining Ones," are the angels of miracles, encouragement, and blessings who become involved wherever people are struggling with their faith. David is said to have received encouragement from virtues to do battle against Goliath. The virtues are also the angels from whom **Abraham** drew his strength when God asked him to sacrifice his only son, Isaac. The principal duties of these angels are to work miracles on Earth. They are allowed to intervene with respect to the physical laws of the earth, but they are also responsible for supporting these laws. Valor is brought forth to humankind, as is the virtue of grace, by this **choir,** the fifth in the **Dionysian** scheme.

Sources:

Davidson, Gustav. *A Dictionary of Angels: Including the Fallen Angels.* 1967. Reprint. New York: Free Press, 1971.
Mansfield, Richard. *Angels: An Introduction to the Angelic Hierarchy.* Encinitas, Calif.: Estuary Publications, 1994.

Vohu Manah

Vohu Manah (Good Mind or Good Thought) is the principal Zoroastrian **archangel,** and revealed the truths of **Zoroastrianism** to Zoroaster, the founder of the religious tradition. The religion of Zoroaster is best known for its dualism. The god of light and the upper world, Ohrmazd or Ahura Mazda (Wise Lord), and his angels are locked in a cosmic struggle with the god of darkness and the lower world, Angra Mainyu or Ahriman (Evil Spirit), and his demons.

The principal Zoroastrian angels are the **holy immortals** (the amesha spentas or ameshaspands). These beings are named after qualities valued by Zoroastrians. Vohu Manah is the firstborn of Ahura Mazda and chief of the holy immortals. At the age of thirty, Zoroaster had a vision of Vohu Manah, who appeared to the prophet in a form nine times larger than an ordinary person. After questioning Zoroaster, Vohu Manah led his spirit into the heaven of Ahura Mazda, who was holding court with his angels. God then instructed the prophet in the principles of the true religion.

Sources:

Cohn, Norman. *Cosmos, Chaos and the World to Come: The Ancient Roots of Apocalyptic Faith.* New Haven, Conn.: Yale University Press, 1993.

Eliade, Mircea. *A History of Religious Ideas.* Vol. 1. Chicago: University of Chicago Press, 1978.

Noss, John B. *Man's Religions.* 4th ed. New York: Macmillan, 1969.

War in Heaven

The earliest account of rebelling angels is contained in the apocryphal *Book of the Secrets of Enoch*. According to Christian legend, there was a great battle fought at the beginning of time between good angels, who supported God, and the rebel angels, who supported **Satan**'s attempt to take God's place. It is believed that this tremendous battle took placed on the second day of Creation.

God created all angels with the free will to choose between good and evil. Further, it was believed, that for some he strengthened with the Grace to pursue good, while the other faction, equally strong, had the greater leaning toward lesser pursuits. When this group sinned, a war broke out, with the archangel **Michael** at the helm of the good angels and **Lucifer** as leader of the legions of darkness. The Mont St. Michel on the Norman coast is the eternal monument to the victorious leader of the hosts of heaven in the war against the rebel angel.

When Lucifer left heaven, it was said that he took with him one-third of the celestial residents. A few church fathers, however, believed that not all of the followers of Lucifer were thrown with their rebel chief into hell, rather a number of them were left on Earth in order to tempt

"THE FALL OF THE REBEL ANGELS" FROM MILTON'S *PARADISE LOST*. ILLUSTRATION BY GUSTAVE DORÉ.

man. It has been suggested that these angels maintained a neutral position in the rivalry, and that God gave them the opportunity to choose Earth as their home.

According to **Origen,** there were also some "doubtful angels" who were uncertain whether or not to take the side of God or Lucifer. It was from these hesitant and irresolute creatures that humans are thought to have originated.

In literature, the most significant story about the War in Heaven can be found in **John Milton**'s multi-volume *Paradise Lost,* in which an arrogant Satan leads rebelling angels against the faithful who defend the Mount of God in heaven. When he is thrown out of heaven, Satan eventually corrupts the first humans as revenge.

Sources:

Giovetti, Paola. *Angels: The Role of Celestial Guardians and Beings of Light.* Translated by Toby McCormick. York Beach, Maine: Samuel Weiser, 1993.
Godwin, Malcolm. *Angels: An Endangered Species.* New York: Simon and Schuster, 1990.
Rudwin, Maximilian. *The Devil in Legend and Literature.* Chicago: Open Court Publishing, 1931.

Watchers (Grigori)

According to Jewish legend, the grigori (watchers) are a superior order of angels whose proper place is either the third or the fifth heaven. They are said to look like human beings (except much larger), never sleep, and are forever silent. While there are both good and bad grigori, most extant lore revolves around the evil watchers who fell from grace after copulating with human women.

The story of the grigori is detailed in several scriptural apocalyptic books. Chief among these are the **Book of Enoch** and the **Book of Jubilees.** A fragment of this tale was incorporated into a brief passage in the book of Genesis (6:2), where it states that the "sons of God saw that the daughters of men were fair and they took to wife such of them as they chose." Traditionally, "sons of God" was taken to indicate angels, although later churchmen rejected the idea that angels could have intercourse with human beings.

As outlined in Gustave Davidson's *Dictionary of Angels* individual watchers were responsible for certain activities on earth:

1. Armaros: taught men the resolving of enchantments
2. Araquiel (Arakiel): taught men the signs of the earth
3. Azazel: taught men to make knives, swords, and shields, and to devise ornaments and cosmetics
4. Baraqijal (Baraqel): taught men astrology
5. Ezequeel (Ezekeel): taught men the knowledge of the clouds

6. Gadreel: introduced weapons of war
7. Kokabel (Kawkabel): taught the science of constellations
8. Penemue: instructed mankind in writing and taught children the "bitter and sweet, and the secrets of wisdom"
9. Sariel: taught men the course of the moon
10. Semjaza: taught men enchantments, root-cutting, etc.
11. Shamshiel: taught men the signs of the sun

Sources:

Baskin, Wade. *Dictionary of Satanism*. New York: Philosophical Library, 1962.

Davidson, Gustav. *A Dictionary of Angels: Including the Fallen Angels*. 1967. Reprint. New York: Free Press, 1971.

Ronner, John. *Know Your Angels: The Angel Almanac with Biographies of 100 Prominent Angels in Legend and Folklore, and Much More*. Murfreesboro, Tenn.: Mamre Press, 1993.

Wilson, Peter Lamborn. *Angels*. New York: Pantheon Books, 1980.

Wings

Wings, which are the most distinctive angelic symbol, are emblematic of spirit, power, and swiftness. The portrayal of angels with wings was common throughout the entire **Middle Ages,** a reflection of the accepted Christian idea of angels as winged beings. (Scripture, however, says nothing about angels having wings.) The earliest winged angels in Christendom appear during the rule of Constantine, the first Christian emperor of Rome. The first representations of winged angels bear a striking resemblance to **Nike,** Greek goddess of victory, who undoubtedly provided a model for Christian artists.

The figure of the winged angel evolved during the fourth century, soon crystallizing into a formula and remaining common until the sixth century, after which it came into its own again in Carolingian art and the Romanesque art of Italy and southern France. It was foreign to Gothic art, although it became common again in Italy during the thirteenth through fifteenth centuries.

Seraphim and **cherubim** are usually represented as disembodied heads with one, two, or three pairs of wings, symbolizing purity of spirit informed by love and intelligence. The head is an emblem of the soul, love, and knowledge, whereas the wings have the conventional significance already mentioned. This is a very ancient way of representing the two highest orders of angels, whose faces are very human, thoughtful, and mature in the earliest instances, gradually becoming more childlike in order to express innocence. They later degenerated into small infant heads with little wings folded under the chin.

Wings

An angel weighing a human 200 pounds would need a wing span of between 36 and 120 feet.

The bodies of the angels of Orcagna, in the Campo Santo at Pisa, end in delicate wings instead of legs. Other depictions have wings fade into a cloudy vapor, or burst into flames, as in one of **Raphael**'s frescoes in the Vatican, where the hair, wings, and limbs of cherubs end in glowing flames. Wings were used not only by Christian artists but also by the artists of ancient Egypt, Babylon, Nineveh, and Etruria as symbols of might, majesty, and divine beauty.

Why bird wings should have been taken to represent the spirit is not difficult to understand. To the ancients, birds must have been viewed as marvelous creatures—animals who could shake themselves loose from the earth and float aloft in the invisible medium of the air, an environment much like that of the spirit world. It is but a short step from seeing winged animals as travelers of the air to imagining winged angels as travelers of the spirit realm.

—*Michela Zonta*

Sources:

Berefelt, Gunnar. *A Study on the Winged Angel: The Origin of a Motif.* Stockholm: Almqvist Wiksell, 1968.

Clement, Clara Erskine. *Angels in Art.* Boston: L. C. Page, 1898.

THE PANTHEONS OF EARLY CULTURES WERE USUALLY WINGED, AS EXEMPLIFIED BY NISROCH, THE EAGLE-HEADED ASSYRIAN GOD.

Wisdom Literature

Post-biblical, or wisdom literature, usually depicts angels as independent beings, who are distinguishable by name and distinctive trait. An interest in the nature and individual character of the angels developed with the belief that the mysteries related to the end of days and man's future could be discovered only through the intermediary of angels. This was the main assumption of wisdom literature, which viewed revelation as corroboration of the validity of existing doctrines, rather than the point of departure for the acquisition of knowledge.

The Jews, who had become familiar with many of the old Babylonian myths through the wisdom of the Chaldeans, sought to ascribe many of the old Babylonian tales about gods and heroes to the world of angels in order to avoid contradiction with the monotheistic character of Judaism. Thus, various sources ascribe the wisdom of **Enoch, Abraham,** and Noah to their intimate knowledge of the world of angels and their communication with it. Pagan magic and demonology, as well as pagan literature, where angels usually appear in the company of pagan gods, also had a considerable influence on Jewish doctrine of angels.

Jewish doctrine of angels was not evenly embraced among the various cultures of the Jewish people, but rather was secretly acquired by a narrow circle of the specially initiated, such as, for example, the secret societies of the Essenes, among whom it found its widest distribution, and the Qumran sect.

Post-biblical literature divided angels into several classes that provided particular services. For instance, in the book of Daniel (8:16; 9:21), the angel **Gabriel** is defined as an interpreter of Daniel's vision. Similarly, other angels appear as interpreters of symbolic visions in later apocalyptic writings.

The **archangels,** a group of seven angels who head the world of angels, are also mentioned in various sources, where they are generally described as dwelling in the proximity of God and in charge of tasks of special significance for world history. Another group of four angels, designated as "the angels of the Presence," are mentioned in Enoch, in the Book of Adam and Eve, and in rabbinic literature, as having the important role in the punishment of the fallen angels.

Fallen angels, in particular, are frequently mentioned in post-biblical literature. The earliest report of fallen angels can be found in the Book of Enoch. Their story also appears in the Book of Jubilees, where fallen angels are said to have descended to earth to instruct mankind how to order society, but when they arrived on earth they were seduced by the daughters of men. However, there are several other versions of the legend of the fallen angels, such as those contained in Talmudic sources.

Among other groups of angels mentioned in post-biblical literature are the seventy "princes of the people" appointed over each of the seventy peoples of earth; the "guardian angels," who seem to have been a religious concept common to the entire Semitic world, and whose function is to be on guard before God at all times and to supervise the actions of man.

According to post-biblical literature, the major function of angels is to offer praise to God, although their function as intermediaries between God and man is also important. Some sources mention the angels' role as intercessor, pleading for man before God. Good angels also appear in opposition to evil angels who act as prosecutors before the throne of God. In *Sefer ha-Razim,* angels are used for purposes of magic, and the names of the angels, when coupled with those of Greek gods and magic phrases are considered efficacious for incantations.

Many sources stress the imperfect nature of angels, who are not regarded as omniscient, but rather as incapable of answering questions put to them. No unbridgeable gulf is supposed to exist between the material world and the world of angels, and it is believed, as mentioned in the Book of Enoch, that some righteous men could be transformed into angels. Israel, known as Jacob, is declared to be "the archangel of the power of the Lord" (Origen, Commentary to John, 11, 84, 15), and the people of Israel as a whole, are regarded as being equal to angels and, consequently, under the protection of God himself (Jub. 15:27ff.).

Sources:

Encyclopaedia Judaica. Jerusalem: The MacMillan Company, 1971.

The Illustrated Bible Dictionary. Sydney, Australia: Hodder and Stoughton, 1980.

The Interpreter's One-Volume Commentary on the Bible. New York: Abingdon Press, 1971.

Wormwood

Wormwood (meaning "bitterness") is an angel described in Rev. 8:10–11. This account of the end of the world tells how John of Patmos first had visions of the impending disaster. To begin with, God is seated on his throne in heaven holding a scroll kept closed with seven seals that no one can open except for a seven-eyed, seven-horned lamb (Christ). With each opening of a seal some cataclysmic event occurs on the earth.

First there is the release of the Four Horsemen of the Apocalypse: War, Famine, Death, and Civil Conflict. This is followed by martyrs calling out for justice, then an earthquake on Earth while the Sun turns black and the Moon red. When the seventh and last seal is opened, Wormwood appears: ". . . a great star fell from heaven, blazing like a torch, and it fell on a third of the rivers and on the fountains of water. The name of the star is Wormwood." On Earth Wormwood causes the death of many mortals by poisoning the rivers and waters.

Wormwood is also referred to in a work of fiction by C. S. Lewis entitled *The Screwtape Letters.* The letters are addressed to Wormwood, who is the nephew of Screwtape (an important official in His Satanic Majesty's "Lowerarchy"). Wormwood himself is characterized by Lewis as "a sort of junior devil on earth."

Sources:

Davidson, Gustav. *A Dictionary of Angels: Including the Fallen Angels.* 1967. Reprint. New York: Free Press, 1971.

Lewis, C. S. *The Screwtape Letters.* Reprint. New York: Bantam Books, 1995.

Ronner, John. *Know Your Angels: The Angel Almanac with Biographies of 100 Prominent Angels in Legend and Folklore, and Much More.* Murfreesboro, Tenn.: Mamre Press, 1993.

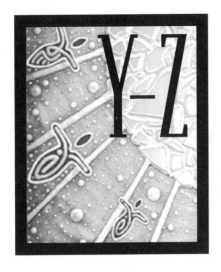

An angel collects all the prayers offered in the synagogues, weaves them into garlands, and puts them on God's head.

—Zohar

Yazatas

The prophet Zoroaster was the reformer who transformed Persian polytheism into the first monotheism. Although little is known about the old Persian polytheism, apparently some of the old gods were demoted and retained as angels in Zoroaster's synthesis.

The struggle between good and evil occupies center stage in the Zoroastrian worldview. The god of light and the upper world, Ohrmazd or Ahura Mazda (Wide Lord), and his angels are locked in a cosmic struggle with the god of darkness and the lower world, Angra Mainyu or Ahriman (Evil Spirit), and his demons.

The oldest angels in the Zoroastrian system are the six (sometimes seven) **holy immortals,** often identified as **archangels.** The holy immortals play an important role in the foundation of the faith, revealing the true religion to Zoroaster in a series of visions. As Zoroastrianism developed, the number of celestial beings multiplied, leading some observers to remark that the old polytheistic system had unwittingly been revived in the later stages of this religious tradition.

At some point, a new class of angel, the yazatas ("worshipful ones"), emerged. They became so important that they seemed to eclipse Ahura Mazda himself. Chief among the yazatas was Mithra, the god/angel of light and truth, the mediator between earth and heaven, as well as the preserver and judge of this world. Other new angels, some of them transparently former gods of the old **Indo-European** pantheon, were Haoma, angel of the sacred intoxicant: Vata (or Vayu), who rules the winds, and Verethragna, the Persian equivalent of the Indian god Indra.

Sources:

Cohn, Norman. *Cosmos, Chaos and the World to Come: The Ancient Roots of Apocalyptic Faith.* New Haven, Conn.: Yale University Press, 1993.

Eliade, Mircea, ed. *A History of Religious Ideas.* Vol. 1. Chicago: University of Chicago Press, 1978.

Noss, John B. *Man's Religions.* 4th ed. New York: Macmillan, 1969.

Zadkiel

The name Zadkiel (also Tzadkiel or Zidekiel, among other variant spellings) means "the righteousness of God." Zadkiel is an angel with several different identities, depending on the reference source. In *A Theological Discourse of Angels,* by Benjamin Camfield, Zadkiel is the angel of Jupiter, because he is ruler of the sign of the zodiac of that planet. According to the **Zohar** (Numbers 154A), Zadkiel is one of two chieftains who assist **Michael** when the **archangel** goes into battle. Zadkiel is also said to be a co-chief of the order of shinanim (along with **Gabriel**) and one of the nine rulers of heaven, as well as one the seven archangels presiding next to God. In rabbinic works, Zadkiel is "the angel of benevolence, mercy, memory, and chief of the order of **dominions**" (Davidson, p. 324). But perhaps the most common identity of Zadkiel is the one presented in the Bible, where he prevents **Abraham** from sacrificing his young son Isaac to God.

Sources:

Davidson, Gustav. *A Dictionary of Angels: Including the Fallen Angels.* 1967. Reprint. New York: Free Press, 1971.

Ronner, John. *Know Your Angels: The Angel Almanac with Biographies of 100 Prominent Angels in Legend and Folklore, and Much More.* Murfreesboro, Tenn.: Mamre Press, 1993.

Zagzagel

Zagzagel is the angel of the burning bush who figured prominently in the life of Moses. Moses "led the flock along the side of the wilderness and came to Horeb, the mountain of God. There the angel of the Lord appeared to him in the flame of a burning bush" (Exod. 3:1,2). Zagzagel was Moses' tutor and was one of the three angels who accompanied the soul of Moses to heaven. Zagzagel is also a teacher of angels who speaks seventy languages. He is the chief guard of the fourth heaven, although he is said to reside in the seventh heaven, the abode of God.

Sources:

Ausubel, Nathan, ed. *A Treasury of Jewish Folklore.* New York: Crown Publishers, 1948.

Davidson, Gustav. *A Dictionary of Angels: Including the Fallen Angels.* 1967. Reprint. New York: Free Press, 1971.

Zodiac (Angels of the)

The zodiac (literally, "circle of animals," from the Greek *zoion,* living being, figure), is the name given to the imaginary circular zone of the heavens in which the Sun, Moon, and planets have their orbits. Because the orbits of the planets in the solar system all lie within approximately the same geometric plane, from any position within the system all of the heavenly bodies appear to move across the face of the same set of constellations. The zodiac is divided into twelve astrological signs associated with the twelve constellations—Aries, Taurus, Gemini, Cancer, Leo, Virgo, Libra, Scorpio, Sagittarius, Capricorn, Aquarius, and Pisces.

The notion of the zodiac is very ancient, with roots in the early citied cultures of **Mesopotamia.** The first twelve-sign zodiacs were named after the gods of these cultures. The Greeks adopted astrology from the Babylonians, and the Romans, in turn, adopted it from the Greeks. These peoples renamed the signs of the Babylonian zodiac in terms of their own mythologies, which is why the familiar zodiac of the contemporary West bears names from Mediterranean mythology. The notion of a twelve-fold division derives from the lunar cycle (the orbital cycle of the Moon around the Earth), which the Moon completes twelve times per year.

Because various gods have traditionally been associated with the signs of the zodiac, it seems natural to suggest a possible correlation between angels and the zodiac. The connection is also a natural one to make because angels and astrological signs are both located primarily in the celestial realm. It was thus almost inevitable that angels came to be associated with the zodiac. The traditional correlations are as follows:

Sign	Angel
Aries	Malahidael or Machidiel
Taurus	Asmodel

ANGELS OF TIME. NOTE HOURGLASS AT BOTTOM AND CONSTELLATIONS IN CEILING.
(SIR WALTER CRANE COLLECTION, MILAN) (COURTESY ARAS)

Gemini	Ambriel
Cancer	Muriel
Leo	Verchiel
Virgo	Hamaliel
Libra	Zuriel or Uriel
Scorpio	Barbiel
Sagittarius	Advachiel or Adnachiel
Capricorn	Hanael
Aquarius	Cambiel or Gabriel
Pisces	Barchiel

Many Judaic beliefs about astrology and angels were derived from Chaldean and **Egyptian** sources. The names of many of the angels were manufactured from the nature of their assignments in an almost atavistic regression to a pagan pantheon that assigned gods and goddesses for almost every natural force. The number of these became so vast in the **apocryphal** and pseudepigraphal literature that the rabbis believed they posed a threat to Judaic monothesism and so condemned all of the writing in this genre. Because such writings were suppressed, little information regarding the nature of these angels survives today.

Sources:

Cirlot, J. E. *A Dictionary of Symbols*. 1971. Reprint. New York: Dorset Press, 1991.

Davidson, Gustav. *A Dictionary of Angels: Including the Fallen Angels*. 1967. Reprint. New York: Free Press, 1971.

Margolies, Morris B. *A Gathering of Angels: Angels in Jewish Life and Literature*. New York: Ballantine, 1994.

Zohar

The Zohar, or *Sefer ha-zohar,* meaning "The Book of Splendor," is considered the central work in Jewish mysticism, as well as the most influential work of the Cabala. Its compilation is attributed to Shim'on bar Yoh'ai, although its true author is Mosheh de Leon (1240–1305), a Castilian cabalist who wrote it during the last third of the thirteenth century. The Zohar joined the Bible and Talmud in the triad of the most sacred books of Judaism.

The Zohar was written mostly in Aramaic and presents an elaborate mystical system that considerably influenced the later evolution of Jewish mysticism through its mythical conceptions on cabalistic theosophy. Mosheh de Leon wrote the main part of the Zohar, which circulated in manuscript and was published in 1558 in Mantua and Cremona, whereas the rest was written by a later anonymous cabalist early in the fourteenth century. The latter part differs from the first both in style and in its cabalistic concepts.

The Zohar presents five central myths: the myth of the cosmogonical process, the initial evolvement of the ten **sefiroth** from the eternal Godhead; the myth of the dynamic interrelationship within the realm of the Divine emanations; the sexual symbolic myth of the relationship between the masculine and feminine elements in the Divine world, the latter represented by the Shekinah; the myth of the struggle between the holy Divine realm on the right and the evil system on the left; the messianic myth and the apocalyptic description of the redemption.

Jewish mysticism has given considerable consideration to angels, grouping them into categories such as angels of severe judgment and angels of mercy, as well as evil and ministering angels. Like other mystical texts, the Zohar assigns specific heavenly roles to angels and arranges them into various **hierarchies:** these angels, representing spiritual powers of the finest and ethereal substance, may assume human form or may appear as spirits when they execute their missions on earth. Furthermore, according to the Zohar, the good angels came into being on the first day of Creation and enjoy eternal life, whereas the others, who rebelled against God and were consumed by fire, were created on the second day of Creation. The angels live in the seven heavenly halls, the *heikhalot,* and a special hall is set aside for a certain type of angel that mourns the destruction of the Temple.

According to the Zohar, every human comes into the world with a good angel and a bad one, and when he dies, he is met by angels of peace or destruction depending upon his deeds on earth. Angels know the future of mankind, which is made known in heaven by a herald. In addition, every day angels are sent to Earth with special missions: some serve the human body, whereas others serve the soul. According to the Zohar the first encounter between the angels and man took place when the mysterious Book of Heaven was handed to **Adam** through **Raziel, Hadraniel, and Raphael.**

—Michela Zonta

Sources:

Eliade, Mircea, ed. *Encyclopedia of Religion.* New York: Macmillan, 1987.
Encyclopaedia Judaica. Jerusalem: The Macmillan Company, 1971.
Liebes, Yehuda. *Studies in the Zohar.* Translated from the Hebrew by Arnold Schwartz, Stephanie Nakache, and Penina Peli. Albany, N.Y.: State University of New York Press, 1993.
Wigoder, Geoffrey, ed. *The Encyclopedia of Judaism.* New York: Macmillan Publishers, 1989.

Zophiel

Zophiel (God's Spy) is a spirit invoked in the prayer of the Master of the Art in Solomonic conjuration rites. He is also one of **Michael**'s two chieftains. **Milton** mentions Zophiel in *Paradise Lost* as the one informing the heavenly hosts of a further attack by the rebel crew, whereas in Friedrich Klopstock's *The Messiah* he represents "the herald of hell." The American poet Maria Del Occidente chose Zophiel as one of the main characters of her book-length poem *Zophiel,* inspired by the story contained in the apocryphal Book of Tobit. In this poem, Zophiel is a fallen angel but retains traces of his original virtue and beauty.

Sources:

Davidson, Gustav. *A Dictionary of Angels: Including the Fallen Angels.* New York: Free Press, 1967.

Klopstock, Friedrich Gottlieb. *The Messiah.* 1795. Reprint. Boston: John West & Co., 1811.

Zoroastrianism

In the history of religions, Zoroastrianism has been an unusually efficacious faith, exercising an influence on the doctrines of other religions disproportionate to the size of its following. The notion of angels as agents of God (rather than as demigods) is but one of Zoroastrianism's legacy to **Judaism, Christianity,** and **Islam.**

Zoroastrianism was founded in ancient Persia (modern-day Iran) in about 1000 B.C. (some sources say much earlier, others around 600 B.C.) by the prophet Zoroaster. It was the official religion of the area until Alexander the Great's conquest, after which it was later restored. In the seventh century A.D., Islamic invaders took over the area, and Zoroastrianism disappeared from the land of its birth. A relatively small body of Zoroastrians, who are called Parsees in the subcontinent, survive in contemporary India, many in the Bombay area.

The religion of Zoroaster is best known for its dualism. The god of light and the upper world, Ohrmazd or Ahura Mazda (Wise Lord), and his angels are locked in a cosmic struggle with the god of darkness and the lower world, Angra Mainyu or Ahriman (Evil Spirit), and his demons. Unlike Christianity, in which the outcome of the war between God and the Devil has already been decided, Zoroastrianism portrays the struggle as more or less evenly matched (although many strands of the tradition would assert that Ahura Mazda's triumph is inevitable). Individual human beings are urged to align themselves with the forces of light, and are judged according to whether their good or evil deeds predominate.

Eventually there will be a final battle between good and evil, after which there will be a general judgment in which everyone will be put through an ordeal of fire (a river of molten metal), in which good individuals will have their dross burned away and evil people will be consumed. The souls of the blessed will be resurrected in renewed physical bodies.

Many of the components of this vision of the end times—a final battle between good and evil, judgment of the wicked, resurrection of the dead, and so on—were adopted by Jewish apocalyptic thinkers. From texts composed by these apocalypticists, such notions were adopted into Christianity and Islam.

For reasons that are unclear, angels are often associated with religions and religious movements that place a special stress on such events expected to take place at the end of time (referred to as the *eschaton* in Greek, from which we get the word *eschatology*).

It appears that Zoroaster set out to reform the preexisting religion of Persia rather than to create a new religion. It is also clear that he preached the centrality of one god, Ahura Mazda. The other divinities of the earlier pantheon were reduced to the status of mere agents of the supreme deity—that is, to angels. Also, some of the gods of the original **Indo-European** pantheon were transformed into **demons,** although this transformation may have resulted from factors completely independent of the reforming activities of Zoroaster.

Chief among the Zoroastrian angels are the **holy immortals** (the *amesha spentas* or *ameshaspands*). These beings are named after qualities valued by Zoroastrians, such as Vohu Manah (Good Thought or Good Sense) and Armaiti (Piety or Harmony). In a certain sense, the amesha spentas are the **archangels** of the Zoroastrian religious system. Corresponding to these archangels of light are agents of the evil Ahriman, such as Druj (the Lie).

As Zoroastrianism developed, the number of celestial beings multiplied, leading some observers to remark that the old polytheistic system had unwittingly been revived in the later stages of this religious tradition. At some point, a new class of angel, the **yazatas,** emerged. They became so important that they seemed to eclipse Ahura Mazda himself. Chief among the yazatas was **Mithra,** the god/angel of light.

Yet another group of angelic beings to emerge were the **fravashi.** They seem to have originally been spirits of the ancestors, but gradually developed into guardian spirits, both of human beings and of celestial beings. Somewhat like the notion of Plato's ideal forms, the fravashi is the immortal part of the human being that remains in heaven even when the individual is incarnate on the earth.

Sources:

Cohn, Norman. *Cosmos, Chaos and the World to Come: The Ancient Roots of Apocalyptic Faith.* New Haven, Conn.: Yale University Press, 1993.

Eliade, Mircea, ed. *A History of Religious Ideas.* Vol. 1. Chicago: University of Chicago Press, 1978.

Noss, John B. *Man's Religions.* 4th ed. New York: Macmillan, 1969.

Appendices
& Master Index

Angel Bibliography

The angel bibliography is by no means a comprehensive listing of angel titles. Given the number of new works published each year, we would require a separate volume to fully enumerate. Rather, the bibliography is meant as a launching pad to steer you to representative works divided by topics of interest such as fiction, instructional titles, and scholarly works.

Angelic Encounters

Anderson, Joan Wester. *An Angel to Watch Over Me: True Stories of Children's Encounters with Angels*. New York: Ballantine, 1994.

——. *Where Angels Walk, True Stories of Heavenly Visitors*. New York: Ballantine, 1992.

——. *Where Miracles Happen, True Stories of Heavenly Encounters*. Brooklyn, New York: Brett Books, 1994.

Fearheiley, Don. *Angels Among Us*. New York: Avon, 1993.

Freeman, Eileen Elias. *Touched by Angels: True Cases of Close Encounters of the Celestial Kind*. New York: Warner Books, 1993.

Goldman, Karen. *Angel Encounters: Real Stories of Angelic Intervention*. New York: Simon & Schuster, 1995.

Guiley, Rosemary. *Angels of Mercy*. New York: Pocket, 1994.

Moolenburgh, H. C. *A Handbook of Angels*. Woodstock, N.Y.: Beekman, forthcoming.

——. *Meetings with Angels: A Hundred & One Real-Life Encounters*. Middlebury, Vt.: Atrium, 1993.

Pruitt, James. *Angels Beside You*. New York: Avon, 1994.

Smith, Robert C. *In the Presence of Angels*. Virginia Beach, Virg.: A.R.E. Press, 1993.

Tyler, Kelsey. *There's an Angel on Your Shoulder: Angel Encounters in Everyday Life*. New York, N.Y.: Berkley Publishing, 1994.

Webber, Marylinn Carlson, and William D. Webber. *A Rustle of Angels: Stories About Angels in Real-Life and Scripture*. Grand Rapids, Mich.: Zondervan, 1994.

Angels and Art

Berefelt, Gunnar. *A Study on the Winged Angel: The Origin of a Motif.* Stockholm: Almquist and Wiksell, 1968.

Brigidi, Stephen. *Angels of Pompeii.* New York: Ballantine, 1992.

Cacciari, Massimo. *The Necessary Angel.* Albany: State University of New York Press, 1994.

Jiménez, José. *El àngel caìdo. La imagen artìstica del àngel en el mundo contemporàneo.* Barcelona: Editorial Anagrama, 1982.

Long, Valentine. *The Angels in Religion and Art.* Chicago: Franciscan Herald, 1970.

Children's Fiction

Anderson, Rachel. *Little Angel, Bonjour.* New York: Oxford University Press, 1989.

———. *Little Angel Comes to Stay.* New York: Oxford University Press, 1987.

Bartone, Elisa. *The Angel Who Forgot.* New York: Simon & Schuster, 1992.

Boone, Debby. *The Snow Angel.* Eugene, Oreg.: Harvest House, 1991.

Burgess, Melvin. *An Angel for May.* New York: Simon & Schuster, 1995.

Carney, Mary L. *Angel in My Backpack.* Ann Arbor, Mich.: Zondervan, 1987.

Delton, Judy. *Back Yard Angel.* Boston: Houghton Mifflin, 1983.

Hall, Lynn. *Dagmar Schultz and the Angel Edna.* New York: Macmillan Children's Book Group, 1989.

Manushkin, Fran. *Rachel, Meet Your Angel!* New York: Puffin Books, 1995.

Marzollo, Jean. *The Snow Angel.* New York: Scholastic, 1995.

Rodriguez, Anita. *Jamal & the Angel.* New York: Crown Books for Young Readers, 1992.

Skocz, Anita J. *Crystal Star Angel.* Mahwah, N.J.: Paulist Press, 1994.

Fiction

Beverley, Jo. *Emily and the Dark Angel.* New York: Walker & Co., 1991.

Burnham, Sophy. *The President's Angel: A Novel.* New York: Ballantine, 1993.

Cummings, Pat. *C.L.O.U.D.S.* New York: Lothrop, Lee & Shepard Books, 1986.

Macomber, Debbie. *The Trouble With Angels.* New York: HarperPaperbacks, 1994.

Peretti, Frank E. *Piercing the Darkness.* Westchester, Ill.: Crossway Books, 1989.

———. *This Present Darkness.* Westchester, Ill.: Crossway Books, 1986.

Rosenberg, Nancy Taylor. *California Angel.* New York: Dutton, 1995.

Zelazny, Roger. *A Farce to Be Reckoned With.* New York: Bantam Books, 1995.

Inspirational

Café, Sonia, and Neidi Inneco. *Meditating with the Angels.* York Beach, Maine: Samuel Weiser, 1994.

Connell, Janice T. *Angel Power*. New York: Ballantine, 1995.

Crockett, Arthur. *Angels of the Lord: Calling Upon Your Guardian Angel for Guidance and Protection*. Antioch, Ill.: Global Communications, 1993.

Daniel, Alma, Timothy Wyllie, and Andrew Ramer. *Ask Your Angels*. New York: Ballantine, 1992.

Drahos, Mary. *Angels of God, Our Guardians Dear*. Ann Arbor, Mich.: Servant, 1995.

Freeman, Elaine Elias. *The Angel's Little Instruction Book: Learning from God's Heavenly Messengers*. New York: Warner Books, 1994.

Graham, Billy. *Angels: God's Secret Agents*. 1975. Reprint. Dallas: Word Publishing, 1994.

Keith, Juanita O. *The Angels Proclaim Radiant Living*. Des Moines: Archer Creative Press, 1995.

Kinnaman, Gary. *Angels: Dark and Light*. Ann Arbor, Mich.: Servant Publications, 1994.

Malz, Betty. *Angels Watching Over Me*. Grand Rapids, Mich.: Chosen Books, 1986.

Melashenko, E. Lonnie. *In the Presence of Angels: A Collection of Inspiring, True Angel Stories*. Boise, Idaho: Pacific Press, 1995.

Price, John Randolph. *The Angels Within Us*. New York: Fawcett Columbine, 1993.

Saint Michael and the Angels. Compiled from Approved Sources. Rockford, Ill.: TAN Books, 1983.

Spangler, Ann. *An Angel a Day*. Grand Rapids, Mich.: Zondervan, 1994.

Instructional

Freeman, Eileen Elias. *Angelic Healing: Working with Your Angels to Heal Your Life*. New York: Warner Books, 1994.

Georgian, Linda. *Your Guardian Angels: Use the Power of Angelic Messengers to Enrich and Empower Your Life*. New York: Simon & Schuster, 1994.

Goldman, Karen. *The Angel Book: A Handbook for Aspiring Angels*. New York: Simon & Schuster, 1992.

———. *Angel Voices: The Advanced Handbook for Aspirant Angels*. New York: Simon & Schuster, 1993.

Howard, Jane. *Commune With the Angels: A Heavenly Handbook*. Virginia Beach: A.R.E. Press, 1992.

Keller, Thomas, and Deborah Taylor. *Angels: The Lifting of the Veil*. Norfolk, Virg.: Hampton Roads, forthcoming.

Reynolds, Dana. *Be an Angel*. New York: Simon & Schuster Trade, 1994.

Sharp, Sally. *100 Ways to Attract Angels*. Minneapolis, Minn.: Trust Publishing, 1994.

Taylor, Terry Lynn. *Creating With the Angels: An Angel-Guided Journey Into Creativity*. Tiburon, Calif.: H. J. Kramer, 1993.

———. *Guardians of Hope: The Angels' Guide to Personal Growth*. Tiburon, Calif.: H. J. Kramer, 1992.

———. *Messengers of Light: The Angels' Guide to Spiritual Growth*. Tiburon, Calif.: H. J. Kramer, 1990.

Taylor, Terry Lynn, and Mary Beth Crain. *Angel Wisdom—365 Meditations and Insights from the Heavens.* San Francisco West: HarperCollins, 1995.

Popular Works

Burnham, Sophy. *Angel Letters.* New York: Ballantine, 1991.

——. *A Book of Angels: Reflections on Angels Past and Present and True Stories of How They Touch Our Lives.* New York: Ballantine, 1990.

Chessman, Harriet Scott, ed. *Literary Angels.* New York: Fawcett Columbine, 1994.

Church, F. Forrester. *Entertaining Angels: A Guide to Heaven for Atheists & True Believers.* San Francisco: Harper & Row, 1987.

Davidson, Gustav. *A Dictionary of Angels: Including the Fallen Angels.* 1967. Reprint. New York: Free Press, 1971.

Giovetti, Paola. *Angels: The Role of Celestial Guardians and Beings of Light.* Translated by Toby McCormick. York Beach, Maine: Samuel Weiser, 1993.

Godwin, Malcolm. *Angels: An Endangered Species.* New York: Simon & Schuster, 1990.

Grey, M. Cameron, ed. *Angels and Awakenings. Stories of the Miraculous by Great Modern Writers.* New York: Doubleday, 1980.

Hauch, Rex, ed. *Angels: The Mysterious Messengers.* New York: Ballantine, 1994.

Humann, Harvey. *The Many Faces of Angels.* Marina del Rey, Calif.: DeVorss, 1987.

MacGregor, Geddes. *Angels: Ministers of Grace.* New York: Paragon House, 1988.

Masello, Robert. *Fallen Angels . . . and Spirits of the Dark.* New York: Perigee, 1994.

Miller, Margaret. *How Like an Angel.* New York: International Polygonics, 1982.

Norman, Marty. *One Hundred and One Uses for A Dead Angel.* New York: Ingram, 1995.

Parish, James Robert. *Ghosts and Angels in Hollywood Films.* Jefferson, N.C.: McFarland & Co., 1994.

Price, Hope. *Angels.* New York: Avon Books, 1993.

Pruitt, James. *The Complete Angel: Angels Through the Ages—All You Need to Know.* New York: Avon Books, 1995.

Rhodes, Ron. *Angels Among Us: Separating Truth From Fiction.* Eugene, Oreg.: Harvest House, 1994.

Ronner, John. E. *Do You Have a Guardian Angel? and Other Questions Answered About Angels.* Mamre Press, 1985.

——. *Know Your Angels: The Angel Almanac with Biographies of 100 Prominent Angels in Legend and Folklore, and Much More.* Murfreesboro, Tenn.: Mamre Press, 1993.

Taylor, Terry Lynn. *Answers From the Angels: A Book of Angel Letters.* Tiburon, Calif.: H. J. Kramer, 1993.

Wilson, Peter Lamborn. *Angels.* New York: Pantheon Books, 1980.

Scholarly Works

Adler, Mortimer J. *The Angels and Us.* New York: Macmillan, 1982.

Avens, Robert. *The New Gnosis: Heidegger, Hillman and Angels.* Dallas: Spring Publishing, 1984.

Bamberger, Bernard J. *Fallen Angels.* Philadelphia: Jewish Publication Society of America, 1952.

Dionysius the Areopagite. *The Celestial Hierarchies.* Godalmins, Surrey, UK: The Shrine of Wisdom, 1949.

———. *The Mystical Theology and the Celestial Hierarchies.* Godalmins, Surrey, UK: The Shrine of Wisdom, 1949.

Margolies, Morris B. *A Gathering of Angels: Angels in Jewish Life and Literature.* New York: Ballantine, 1994.

Maritan, Jacques. *The Sin of the Angel: An Essay on a Reinterpretation of Some Thomistic Positions.* Westminster, Md.: Newman Press, 1959.

McDannell, Colleen, and Bernhard Lang. *Heaven: A History.* 1988. Reprint. New York: Vintage, 1990.

Parisien, Maria. *Angels & Mortals: Their Co-Creative Power.* Wheaton, Ill.: Quest, 1990.

Prophet, Elizabeth Clare. *Forbidden Mysteries of Enoch: Fallen Angels and the Origins of Evil.* Livingston, Mont.: Summit University Press, 1983.

Schneiderman, Stuart. *An Angel Passes. How the Sexes Became Undivided.* New York: New York University Press, 1988.

Steiner, Rudolf. *Spiritual Beings: In the Heavenly Bodies and in the Kingdoms of Nature.* 1961. Reprint. Hudson, N.Y.: Anthroposophic Press, 1992.

Swedenbörg, Emanuel. *Divine Providence.* New York: Swedenbörg Foundation, 1972. (Originally published 1764.)

———. *Heaven and Hell.* Boston: Swedenbörg Printing Bureau, 1907.

Thomas Aquinas. *On Spiritual Creatures.* Translated from the Latin with an introduction by Mary C. Fitzpatrick in collaboration with John J. Wellmuth. Milwaukee, Wis.: Marquette University Press, 1949.

Angel Filmography

This section contains listings for films that have angels as their primary focus. We have specifically excluded films where the primary characters are ghosts or other spiritual beings, who, while they seem to serve a somewhat angelic role, truly function as spirits proper. An example of a film you *won't* find is *Topper,* where Cary Grant and Constance Bennett star as the Kirbys, a pair of socialite *ghosts* who return to earth.

Almost an Angel

A thief (Hogan) killed in a car accident is given the chance to redeem himself by returning to Earth as a good samaritan angel.

(1990) **Cast:** Paul Hogan, Elias Koteas, Linda Kozlowski, Charlton Heston, Joe Dallesandro **Dir:** John Cornell

Always

A romantic tale about a daredevil firefighting pilot (Dreyfuss) who is killed saving his best friend. An angel (Hepburn) assigns him his first mission in the afterlife—guardian angel to an inexperienced pilot who steals his girlfriend's heart. Remake of *A Guy Named Joe.*

(1989) **Cast:** Holly Hunter, Richard Dreyfuss, John Goodman, Audrey Hepburn, Brad Johnson, Marg Helgenberger, Keith David,

Roberts Blossom, Jerry Belson **Dir:** Steven Spielberg

The Angel Levine

An elderly Jewish tailor (Mostel) complains to God about his miserable life and is taken by surprise when a black Jewish angel (Belafonte) is the answer to his prayers. From a story by Bernard Malamud.

(1970) **Cast:** Zero Mostel, Harry Belafonte, Ida Kaminska, Milo O'Shea, Eli Wallach, Anne Jackson, Gloria Foster **Dir:** Jan Kadar

Angel on My Shoulder

A dead gangster (Muni) strikes a bargain with the devil for leniency. Remade as a TV movie in 1980 starring Peter Strauss.

(1946) **Cast:** Paul Muni, Claude Rains, Anne Baxter, Erskine

Sanford, Hardie Albright **Dir:**
Archie Mayo

The Angel Who Pawned Her Harp

An angel (Cilento) manages to right a few wrongs after entering the life of a pawnshop broker (Aylmer) in Islington, England.

(1954 Great Britain) **Cast:** Felix Aylmer, Diane Cilento, Robert Eddison **Dir:** Alan Bromly

Angels: The Mysterious Messengers

Television documentary that presents the personal stories of people who claim guardian angels aid them in times of need. Narrated by Patty Duke. (1994)

Angels in the Outfield

The Pittsburgh Pirates baseball team gets a little celestial help in their race for the pennant.

(1951) **Cast:** Paul Douglas, Janet Leigh, Keenan Wynn, Donna Corcoran, Lewis Stone, Spring Byington, Bruce (Herman Brix) Bennett, Marvin Kaplan, Ellen Corby, Jeff Richards **Dir:** Clarence Brown

Angels in the Outfield

A lowly baseball team begins a winning streak with the help of some heavenly guidance. Remake of the 1951 movie by the same name.

(1994) **Cast:** Danny Glover, Tony Danza, Christopher Lloyd, Holly Goldberg Sloan, Ben Johnson, Joseph Gordon, Jay O. Sanders **Dir:** William Dear

The Bishop's Wife

An angel with the unlikely name of Dudley (Grant) descends to Earth during the Christmas season to aid Henry Brougham (Niven), a bishop who, in his all-consuming desire to build a new cathedral, is losing track of his family and of his vocation.

(1947) **Cast:** Cary Grant, Loretta Young, David Niven, Monty Woolley, Elsa Lanchester, James Gleason, Glady Cooper, Regis Toomey **Dir:** Henry Koster

Charley and the Angel

A compassionate but impatient angel (Morgan) teaches a dying man (MacMurray) kindness and humility so that he can part on good terms with his family.

(1973) **Cast:** Fred MacMurray, Cloris Leachman, Harry Morgan, Kurt Russell, Vincent Van Patten, Kathleen Cody **Dir:** Vincent McEveety

Clarence

The inept but benevolent angel from *It's a Wonderful Life* risks his wings to save a suicidal young woman.

(1991) **Cast:** Robert Carradine, Kate Trotter **Dir:** Eric Till

Date with an Angel

A romantic comedy about an aspiring musician (Knight) who rescues a beautiful angel (Beart) out of a swimming pool during his bachelor party, then begins to question his upcoming marriage to a cosmetic mogul's daughter.

(1987) **Cast:** Emmanuelle Beart, Michael E. Knight, Phoebe Cates, David Dukes, Bibi Besch **Dir:** Tom McLoughlin

Defending Your Life

A yuppie advertising executive (Brooks) dies in a car accident and is sent to Judgment City where he is given nine days to "defend his life."

(1991) **Cast:** Meryl Streep, Rip Torn, Lee Grant, Albert Brooks, Buck Henry, George Wallace **Dir:** Albert Brooks

Der Himmel Über Berlin (Wings of Desire)

Two angels, Cassiel and Damiel, travel through Berlin observing mankind, listening in on their thoughts, and assisting them when necessary. Damiel grows tired of the angelic life, falls in love with a trapeze artist, and reenters the world as a human.

(1988 Germany) **Cast:** Bruno Ganz, Peter Falk, Solveig Dommartin, Otto Sander, Curt Bois **Dir:** Wim Wenders

For Heaven's Sake

Two angels (Webb and Gwenn) are sent to Earth to speed along the arrival of a baby (named Item) and to save her prospective parents' marriage.

(1950) **Cast:** Clifton Webb, Joan Bennett, Robert Cummings, Edmund Gwenn, Joan Blondell **Dir:** George Seaton

Forever Darling

A chemist's wife (Ball) calls upon her guardian angel (Mason) to save her marriage when her husband (Arnaz) becomes too occupied with his job.

(1956) **Cast:** Lucille Ball, Desi Arnaz, James Mason, Louis Calhern, John Emery, John Hoyt, Natalie Schafer, Nancy Kulp **Dir:** Alexander Hall

A Guy Named Joe

An aviator (Johnson) is guided through battle and romantic troubles by an angel who is a deceased WWII pilot (Tracy). Remade in 1989 as *Always*.

(1944) **Cast:** Spencer Tracy, Irene Dunne, Van Johnson, Ward Bond, James Gleason, Esther Williams, Lionel Barrymore **Dir:** Victor Fleming

Heaven Can Wait

A football player (Beatty) is mistakenly taken to heaven before his time and returns to Earth to search for a suitable replacement body. Remake of the 1941 film *Here Comes Mr. Jordan*.

(1978) **Cast:** Warren Beatty, Jack Warden, Dyan Cannon, James Mason, Charles Grodin, Elaine May. **Dir:** Warren Beatty, Buck Henry

Heaven Only Knows

An angel (Cummings) comes to the aid of a soulless gambler (Donlevy) in the old West.

(1947) **Cast:** Robert Cummings, Brian Donlevy, Jorja Curtwright, Marjorie Reynolds, Bill Boodwin, John Litel, Stuart Erwin **Dir:** Albert S. Rogell

Heavenly Kid

A 1950s hot-rod crash victim is offered entrance into heaven, but the deal requires him to return to Earth to educate his nerdy son on how to be "cool" and worldly.

(1985) **Cast:** Lewis Smith, Jason Gedrick, Richard Mulligan **Dir:** Cary Medoway

Here Comes Mr. Jordan

A young prizefighter (Montgomery) is accidentally killed in a plane crash due to a bureaucratic mix-up in heaven and, in a heavenly attempt to rectify the situation, is returned to Earth as a soon-to-be millionaire. Remade as the 1978 film *Heaven Can Wait*.

(1941) **Cast:** Robert Montgomery, Claude Rains, James Gleason, Evelyn Keyes, Edward Everett, Sydney Buchman. **Dir:** Alexander Hall

The Horn Blows at Midnight

A band trumpeter (Benny) dreams he is Athanael, an archangel who is to blow the note bringing the end of the world at midnight of the Last Day.

(1945) **Cast:** Jack Benny, Alexis Smith, Dolores Morgan, Allyn Joslyn, Reginald Gardiner, Guy Kibbee, John Alexander, Margaret Dumont, John Dumont **Dir:** Raoul Walsh

Human Feelings

An angel (Crystal) is given the ultimatum to drive sin from Las Vegas or God will destroy the city.

(1978) **Cast:** Billy Crystal, Nancy Walker, Pamela Sue Martin, Pat Morita, Jack Carter **Dir:** Ernest Pintoff

I Married an Angel

Rodgers and Hart musical about a beautiful angel who lures a playboy away from his usual business. This is the last Jeanette MacDonald/Nelson Eddy film.

(1942) **Cast:** Jeanette MacDonald, Nelson Eddy, Binnie Barnes, Edward Everett Horton, Reginald Owen, Mona Maris, Janis Carter, Inez Cooper, Douglass Dumbrille **Dir:** Woodbridge S. Van Dyke

In Search of Angels

The history, meaning, and allure of angels and angelic images from classical art to motion pictures is provided in this PBS documentary. Narrated by Debra Winger. (1994)

In Weiter Ferne, So Nah! (Faraway, So Close!)

Cassiel, the angel from Wenders's *Wings of Desire,* also decides to become human, but unlike Damiel, fails to find happiness. Raphaela, a fellow angel, and Emit Flesti, a demon, vie for his soul.

(1993 Germany) **Cast:** Otto Sander, Peter Falk, Horst Buchholz, Nastassia Kinski, Bruno Ganz, Solveig Dommartin, Ruediger Volger, Lou Reed, Willem Dafoe **Dir:** Wim Wenders

It Came Upon a Midnight Clear

A deceased New York policeman (Rooney) is blessed with a heavenly miracle to keep a Christmas promise to his grandson.

(1984) **Cast:** Mickey Rooney, Scott Grimes, George Gaynes, Annie Potts, Lloyd Nolan, Barrie Youngfellow **Dir:** Peter Hunt

It Happened One Christmas

Remake of *It's a Wonderful Life* featuring Marlo Thomas in the role popularized by Jimmy Stewart.

(1977) **Cast:** Marlo Thomas, Wayne Rogers, Orson Welles, Cloris Leachman, Barney Martin **Dir:** Donald Wrye

It's a Wonderful Life

A despondent George Bailey (Stewart) is saved from committing suicide by Clarence (Travers), an angel who has yet to earn his wings. Clarence helps Bailey realize what a wonderful life he has really had by showing him the world as it would be had he never existed. An American classic.

(1946) **Cast:** James Stewart, Donna Reed, Henry Travers, Thomas Mitchell, Lionel Barrymore, Samuel S. Hinds, Frank Faylen,

Gloria Grahame, H. B. Warner, Ellen Corby **Dir:** Frank Capra

The Kid with a Broken Halo

Gary Coleman plays an inexperienced angel who must assist three desperate families in order to earn his wings.

(1982) **Cast:** Gary Coleman, Robert Guillaume, June Allyson, Mason Adams, Ray Walston, John Pleshette, Kim Fields, Georg Stanford Brown, Telma Hopkins **Dir:** Leslie Martinson

The Littlest Angel

A musical fantasy about a shepherd boy who has trouble leaving his earthly life behind and accepting the transition to a heavenly existence.

(1969) **Cast:** Johnny Whitaker, Fred Gwynne, E. G. Marshall, James Coco, Cab Calloway, Connie Stevens, Tony Randall **Dir:** Joe Layton

La Merveilleuse Visite (The Marvelous Visit)

An angel, rescued by a priest after falling from the sky, causes problems when he wanders into a nearby village.

(1974 France) **Cast:** Gilles Kohler, Deborah Berger, Jean-Pierre Castaldi, Marcel Carne **Dir:** Deborah Berger

Made in Heaven

Two souls (Hutton, McGillis) who meet in heaven must rely on their love as they search to find each other when reborn on Earth.

(1987) **Cast:** Timothy Hutton, Kelly McGillis, Maureen Stapleton, Mare Winningham, Ann Wedgeworth, Don Murray, Amanda Plummer, Ellen Barkin, Timothy Daly **Dir:** Alan Rudolph

Mr. Destiny

A comedy inspired by *It's A Wonderful Life*. A junior executive haunted by failure encounters a bartender-angel who gives him the chance to relive his life.

(1990) **Cast:** James Belushi, Linda Hamilton, Michael Caine, Jon Lovitz, Hart Bochner, Rene Russo **Dir:** James Orr

One Magic Christmas

Harry Dean Stanton plays a guardian angel who descends to Earth to restore a woman's (Steenburgen) faith in time for the holidays.

(1985) **Cast:** Mary Steenburgen, Harry Dean Stanton, Gary Basaraba, Arthur Hill, Elisabeth Harnois, Robbie Magwood **Dir:** Phillip Borsos

That's the Spirit

In this fantasy musical, a widowed actress (Ryan) is comforted by her deceased husband who returns to Earth as an angel.

(1945) **Cast:** Peggy Ryan, Jack Oakie, June Vincent, Gene Lockhart, Arthur Treacher, Irene Ryan, Buster Keaton **Dir:** Charles Lamont

Two of a Kind

A bank robber and a crooked teller (Travolta, Newton John) are the center of a bet made between God and the angels. If these individuals cannot redeem themselves, the angels lose the bet and God is permitted to destroy Earth.

(1983) **Cast:** John Travolta, Olivia Newton John, Charles Durning, Beatrice Straight, Scatman Crothers, Oliver Reed **Dir:** John Herzfeld

Waiting for the Light

During the Cuban missile crisis, an angel makes his home in a small-town diner that was recently taken over by a woman (MacLaine) and the townspeople flock to see him.

(1990) **Cast:** Shirley MacLaine, Teri Garr, Vincent Schiavell, John Bedford Lloyd **Dir:** Christopher Monger

Angel Resources

This section contains listings for
- music and video services
- organizations
- publications
- religious groups
- retail and/or mail order services
- World Wide Web (internet) home pages

that may be of interest to people looking for more information on angels. It is arranged alphabetically; the retail and mail order section is further arranged by state and country.

Music/Video

ASTROMUSIC
P.O. Box 118
New York, NY 10033
Includes such offerings as *Music of the Angels, Music of the Angels II, Heavenly Relationships,* and *Angelic Meditations.*

DELORES DEVINE
P.O. Box 4323
Winter Park, FL 32793
Angel-inspired music tapes with prayer for healing. Send SASE for information.

ENLIGHTENED SPIRIT PRODUCTIONS
P.O. Box 170145

St. Louis, MO 63117
Marge Myers is a composer who has created a tape of her angelic music, *A Hug Around the Heart.* Write for info or call (314) 961-3660.

HELIOS MUSIC
Box 374
Mt. Shasta, CA 96067
Phone: (916) 926-5997

LIGHTWORKS AUDIO & VIDEO
P.O. Box 661593AT
Los Angeles, CA 90066
Includes such offerings as the video *Opening to Angels: Being Receptive to the Angelic Realm in Your Daily Life.* Send $1.00 for catalog.

Andy Lakey Art Studio

40485 Murrieta Hot Springs #D

Murrieta, CA 92563

(909) 695-4130

SOUND Rx

P.O. Box 2644, Dept. AT
San Anselmo, CA 94979-2644
Features the music of Steven
Halpern including *Gifts of the
Angels*. Phone: 1-800-909-0707

SOUND AND SPIRIT

P.O. Box 461347
Los Angeles, CA 90046
Music of Randall Leonard
including *Angels in the Rain*.
Write for information or call (213)
876-5381.

Organizations

**ANGEL COLLECTORS CLUB OF
AMERICA**

16342 W. 54th St.
Golden, CO 80403
A large club for collectors with
local chapters, round robins, a
biannual convention, a newsletter,
and roster; dues $12.

ANGELS OF THE WORLD

2232 McKinley Ave.
St. Albans, WV 25177
Smaller general interest club with
round robins, a convention (held in
alternate years to the ACCA
convention), and club newsletter.

**THE ANGELWATCH™
FOUNDATION, INC.**

P.O. Box 1397
Mountainside, NJ 07092
Publishes *AngelWatch* ™, a
bimonthly newsletter, magazine,
and resource guide on angels.
Subscriptions are $16 in the U.S.,
$20 U.S. in Canada, and $25 U.S.
elsewhere (for airmail delivery).

BE AN ANGEL DAY

Angelic Alliance
P.O. Box 95
Upperco, MD 21155

Sponsors the annual "Be an Angel
Day." Phone: (410) 833-6912

HALOS

Program sponsored by Denny
Dahlmann, owner of the retail
store Angel Treasures. HALOS is
an acronym for Helping Angel
Lovers Own Stores.

TAPESTRY

P.O. Box 3032
Wasquoit, MA 02536
Sponsors an annual conference on
angels and other activities.

TWENTY-EIGHT ANGELS, INC.

P.O. Box 116
Free Union, VA 22940
Provides balanced information on
the subject of angels; maintains
the original angel information line,
1-800-28 ANGEL.

Publications

ANGEL NEWS

519 W. Plantation Blvd.
Lake Mary, FL 32746
Angel crafts, poems, stories,
drawings, potpourri, and much
more in this quarterly publication.
Contact Daphne Baumbach.

ANGEL TIMES

4360 Chamblee-Dunwoody Rd.
Atlanta, GA 30341
First full-color magazine devoted
to angels; published bimonthly.
Phone: (404) 986-9787

ANGELIC THOUGHTS

42 Pearwood Rd.
Rochester, NY 14624
Write to Audrey Yantz for
information on subscribing.

ANGELS WORLDWIDE NEWSLETTER

Box 54112
Longsdale West PO
North Vancouver, BC V7M 3L5
  CANADA

Religious Groups

ANGEL WALK

P.O. Box 1027
Riverton, WY 82501
  Nondenominational, religious-metaphysical center. Phone: (307) 856-7365

EVERYDAY ANGELS

5739 Lover's Lane
Shreveport, LA 71105
  A grassroots prayer initiative to honor, empower, and bless those who are seeking to make a spiritual/creative difference on Earth. Phone: (318) 869-1947

FIRST CHURCH OF THE ANGELS

P.O. Box 4713
Carmel, CA 93921
  Church that focuses on angelic healing.

OPUS SANCTORUM ANGELORUM

Marian Center
134 Golden Gate Ave.
San Francisco, CA 94102
  Catholic organization.

PHILANGELI (FRIENDS OF THE ANGEL)

1115 E. Euclid St.
Arlington Hts., IL 60004
  Catholic organization.

QUESTHAVEN

P.O. Box 20560
Escondido, CA 92029
  Sponsors religious retreats and workshops emphasizing angels. Flower Newhouse organization.

Retail and/or Mail Order

ALABAMA

A WING & A PRAYER

2000 Riverchase Galleria
Birmingham, AL 35244
  Retail store. Phone: (205) 985-3569

ARKANSAS

NORTH COUNTRY FRAMING-N-BOUTIQUE

P.O. Box 2708
Kenai, AR 99611
  Retail angel store that includes icons, scents, and florals. Phone: (907) 262-7777

ARIZONA

ANGELS ART & CRYSTALS

3006 W. Hwy. 89A
Sedona, AZ 86339
  Retail store. Phone: (602) 282-7089

DESERT THISTLE HERBS

7227 E. Shea
Scottsdale, AZ 85260
  Retail store with unusual angels.

CALIFORNIA

ANGEL ART STUDIO

310 Olive St., Ste. L.
Santa Barbara, CA 93101
  Mail order catalog featuring plaster, prints, T-shirts, etc.

ANGEL AWARENESS

4349 Elkhorn Blvd. #234
Sacramento, CA 95842
  Mail order catalog offering such items as books, tapes, stickers, and T-shirts; catalog $1.00.

ANGEL BABIES
25422 Trabuco Rd., Ste. 105-149
Lake Forest, CA 92630
> Large mail order catalog. Phone: (714) 855-4209

ANGEL DE LAS FLORES
318 N. Santa Cruz Ave.
Los Gatos, CA 95030
> Retail store specializing in angels. Phone: (408) 354-3375

ANGEL PRESENCE
16783 Bernardo Center Dr., Ste. B
San Diego, CA 92128
> Retail store affiliated with Angel Treasures in Royal Oak, MI. Phone: (619) 674-4411

ANGEL PRODUCTIONS
2219 Desert Creek
Simi Valley, CA 93063
> Offers a wide variety of angel related products, including tapes and music boxes.

ANGEL STAR
16190 Monterey Rd.
Morgan Hill, CA 95037
> Angel-inspired stickers, cards, pins, and signs; wholesale only.

ANGELIC GLASS C/O TRIDENT
19430 E. San Jose Ave.
City of Industry, CA 91748
> Manufacturers of etched glass angel items including bookends, plaques, and candlesticks; wholesale only. Contact Dada Kastaniuk at (909) 594-9235.

THE ANGELS RAINBOW
P.O. Box 1514
Summerland, CA 93067
> Mail order angelic prosperity products.

ANGELS BY THE SEA
75 Mt. Hermon Rd., #C
Scotts Valley, CA 95066
> Retail store. Phone: (408) 439-0696

ANGELS & TREASURES
2100 Arden Way #155
Sacramento, CA 95825
> Retail store affiliated with Angel Treasures in Royal Oak, MI. Phone: (916) 564-4256

ARK ANGELS
116 Main St.
Tiburon, CA 94939
> Retail shop and mail order. Send SASE for mail order list. Phone: (415) 535-9077

THE ART CENTER ANGEL BOUTIQUE
315 Chestnut
Mt. Shasta, CA
> Retail store. (916) 926-2297

CHEERFUL CHERUB
P.O. Box 26302
San Diego, CA 92196
> Unusual catalog offers items including Catholic-style angels and rubber stamps.

COSMA DONNA'S HEAVEN ON EARTH
1050 E. Walnut St.
Pasadena, CA 91106
> Retail store. Phone: (818) 585-1569

CRYSTAL ANGEL
740 El Camino Real
Belmont, CA 94002
> Retail store. Phone: (415) 592-9539

FLORAL IMPACT
P.O. Box 5510
Santa Monica, CA 90405
> Line of cherubs, including picture frames and boxes.

THE FOOL'S JOURNEY—MARIE HADDAD
1900 Vallejo, #201
San Francisco, CA 94123

Angel T-shirts, sweats, and baby rompers.

THE GARDEN ANGEL SHOP

1330 Jackson Gate Rd.
Jackson, CA 95642
 Small angel gift shop tucked inside the Gate House Inn, a bed and breakfast. Phone: (209) 223-3500

A GATHERING OF ANGELS

Paradise, CA (916) 877-8804
Chico, CA (916) 893-5055
 Retail store, 2 locations.

KINDRED SPIRITS, LTD.

561 N. Joan St.
La Habra, CA 90631
 Phone: (310) 697-2505

MARILYNN'S ANGELS

275 Celeste Dr.
Riverside, CA 92507
 Angels from weather vanes to night lights; retail and oldest angel mail order business; send $1.00 for catalog.

PREBLE STUDIOS

P.O. Box 22682
San Francisco, CA 94122
 Angel tote bags and T-shirts. Send SASE for information.

RED ROSE DISTRIBUTING

P.O. Box 1859
Burlingame, CA 94011
 Unusual angel items; wholesale division. Phone: 1-800-451-5683 for wholesale catalog.

ST. ANDREWS ABBEY CERAMICS

Valyermo, CA 93563
 Ceramic angels made by the monks of St. Andrews. Phone: (805) 944-1047

SWEET MEDICINE STUDIOS

P.O. Box 724
Desert Hot Springs, CA 92240

Stationery, cards, and T-shirts adapted from the angels of Edward Burne-Jones. Send $1.00 for mail order flyer.

TARA'S ANGELS

31781 Camino Capistrano
San Juan Capistrano, CA 92675
 Retail store; hosts discussion groups. Phone: 714-248-8822

WINGS BOOKSTORE

226 N. Mt. Shasta Blvd.
Mt. Shasta, CA 96067
 Retail store. Phone: (916) 926-3040

WINGS'N THINGS

P.O. Box 873
Rancho Cucamonga, CA 91729
 Mail order catalog.

COLORADO

ANGEL STATION

835 Main Ave.
Durango, CO 81301
 Retail store. Phone: (303) 382-0244

ANGELS FOR ALL SEASONS

3100 S. Sheridan Blvd.
Denver, CO 80227
 Retail store. Phone: 1-800-290-9941

A LITTLE BIT OF HEAVEN ON EARTH

534 Main St.
Durango, CO 81301
 Retail store. Phone: (303) 259-0954

CONNECTICUT

ANGEL FARE

84 Main St.
Torrington, CT 06790
 Retail store.

DISTRICT OF COLUMBIA

HEAVEN ON EARTH

P.O. Box 40335
Washington, D.C. 20016
Children's angel dolls; retail and wholesale. Owner donates at least 10% of pre-tax profits to children's charities. Phone: 1-800-351-ANGEL

FLORIDA

AMAZING GRACE

335 W. Venice Ave.
Venice, FL 34285
Retail angel store.

ANGEL GARDENS

Rt. 3, Box 114
Gainesville, FL 32606
Angel store offering angel fountains, plants, and statuary. Phone: (904) 462-7722

ANGEL KISSED CHOCOLATE

P.O. Box 17561
Plantation, FL 33318
Heavenly confections.

ANGELIC ENTERPRISES/ALL ABOUT ANGELS

P.O. Box 548
Destin, FL 32540
Mail order personalized guardian angels and audio books; send $1.00 for catalog. Phone: (904) 654-7705

BELIEVE IN ANGELS

45 Edinburgh Dr.
Palm Beach Gardens, FL 33418
Angel bumper stickers.

BUFFALOFLOWERS

1125 Summerwood Cir.
Wellington, FL 33414
Soft-sculpture angels, kitchen angels, christening angels made from natural materials.

GEORGIA

THE ANGEL CONNECTION

124 Powers Ferry Rd.
Ste. E.
Marietta, GA 30067
Mail order catalog; $4.50 refundable with $10 order.

HEAVENLY HOSTS

P.O. Box 86
Snellville, GA 30278
Handcrafted angels by mail order in ceramic, glass, and fabric; send $1.00 for color catalog.

ILLINOIS

ANGEL KISSES OF ST. CHARLES

504 E. Main
St. Charles, IL 60174
Retail store with wide variety of angels.

GUARDIAN ANGEL SHOP

1018 Byron
Chicago, IL 60613
Retail store. Phone: (312) 549-6804

IOWA

GREAT AMERICAN ANGEL COMPANY

P.O. Box 721
Bettendorf, IA 52722
Mail order angel dolls; write for catalog.

KANSAS

ANGEL ON MY SHOULDER

7011 W. Central, Ste. 132
Wichita, KS 67212
Retail store. Phone: (316) 942-0088

LOUISIANA

MY GUARDIAN ANGEL

P.O. Box 13897
New Orleans, LA 70185
    Angel cards. Send SASE for flyer.

MARYLAND

ANGELIC BOOKSTORE

111 Central Ave.
Gaithersburg, MD 20876
    Retail store. Phone: (301) 840-
    0207

ANGELS EXPRESS

P.O. Box 8094
Gaithersburg, MD 20898
    Angelic mail order. Phone: (301)
    216-2638

EAST COAST ANGELS

P.O. Box 1103
Stevensville, MD 21666
    Ceramic angels trimmed in 18K
    fired gold, angel fabric baby
    bonnets and bibs. Send $1.00 for
    color flyer.

HEAVENS TO BETSY

Bankers Galleria
8098 Main St.
Ellicott City, MD 21043
    Retail store.

MASSACHUSETTS

ANGELICA

7 Central St.
Salem, MA 01970
    Retail store. Phone: (508) 745-9355

ANGELS LOFT

Rte. 18
N. Bedford St.
E. Bridgewater, MA 02333
    Retail store. Phone: (808) 378-8333

APT

76 Laurel St.
Fitchburg, MA 01420
    Angel T-shirts, wholesale and
    retail. Phone: 1-800-221-7757

CHERUBS

1 Deerfield Ave.
Shelburn Falls, MA 01370
    Retail store. Phone: (413) 625-
    2545

NECESSARY ANGEL

37 Harvard
Brookline, MA 02146
    Retail store. Phone: (617) 277-
    2114

MICHIGAN

THE ANGEL COLLECTION

33335 Grand River Ave.
Farmington, MI 48336
    Victorian angels and cherubs;
    retail store and mail order. Write
    for flyer.

ANGEL PEACE

115 NE Timber Creek Rd.
Lee's Summit, MI 64064
    Retail store.

ANGEL TREASURES

1727 Plymouth Rd.
Ann Arbor, MI 48105
    Retail store affiliated with Angel
    Treasures in Royal Oak, MI.
    Phone: (313) 213-0905

ANGEL TREASURES

1861 W. Grand River
Okemos, MI 48864
    Retail store affiliated with Angel
    Treasures in Royal Oak, MI.
    Phone: (517) 347-0004

ANGEL TREASURES

401 N. Main
Royal Oak, MI 78067

Retail store. Phone: (810) 548-5799

ANGEL TREASURES OF ROCHESTER

425 Walnut St.
Rochester, MI 48307
  Retail store affiliated with Angel Treasures in Royal Oak, MI. Phone: (810) 650-4944

THE ANGELS ARBOR

29558 Walnut St.
Flat Rock, MI 48134
  Retail store.

MINNESOTA

PRESENTS OF ANGELS, LTD.

4404 France Ave. S.
Edina, MN 55410
  Retail store. Phone: (612) 926-8008

MISSOURI

THE ANGEL LADY

216 S. Spring St.
Independence, MO 64050
  Retail store. Phone: (816) 252-5300

NEW HAMPSHIRE

CHRISTMAS COUNTRY ANGELS

Rt. 108
Plaistow, NH 03865
  Write for catalog.

NEW JERSEY

ANGEL WINGS

P.O. Box 430
Hope, NJ 07844
  Angel potpourri. Write for wholesale information.

ANGELS AND ROSES

34 Sycamore Ave.
Bridgewater, NJ 08807
  Mail order hand-made angel dolls in ceramic and straw, plus angel prints, cards, and stationery; send $1.00 for catalog.

HEAVENLY HALOS

P.O. Box 391
Hackettstown, NJ 07840
  Hand-crafted angel dolls for special occasions.

LITTLE ANGELS

1275 Bloomfield Ave.
Bldg. I, Door 7
Fairfield, NJ 07004
  Retail store and wholesale business featuring Victorian angels with potpourri and fragrance; catalog available. Phone: (201) 808-6908

THE LITTLEST ANGEL

921 Landis Ave.
Vineland, NJ 08360
  Retail store. Phone: (609) 691-9588

NEW YORK

ANGEL ALLEY

6010 Drott Dr.
Syracuse, NY 13057
  Angel items including dolls. Send SASE for illustrated flyer.

EVERYTHING ANGELS

P.O. Box 467
New York, NY 10028-0004
  Mail order catalog. Send $2.00 for catalog, refundable with order. Call for retail store locations. Phone: 1-800-99-ANGEL

HEARTS DESIRE

103 Bronx Dr.
Cheektowaga, NY 14227-3268

Hand-painted angels on T-shirts and sweats. Phone: (716) 656-1220

Retail store and permanent angel gallery; includes a large number of angel-related tapes for people who are visually impaired.

NORTH CAROLINA

INNER SPACES

403 W. Weaver St.
Carrboro, NC 27510
    Retail store.

OHIO

MY FAVORITE THINGS

501 N. High St.
Lancaster, OH 43130
    Angel boutique.

OKLAHOMA

THE ANGEL'S ATTIC

4 E. Main
Broadway Sq.
Shawnee, OK 74801
    Retail store.

ANGELS & THINGS

8236 E. 71 St.
Tulsa, OK 74133
    Write to Penny Baker for more information.

OREGON

ALL ABOUT ANGELS

10767 Butte St. NE
Butteville, OR 97002
    Retail store.

ANGELIC WONDERS

1310 G Center Dr.
Medford, OR 97501
    Retail store. Phone: (503) 772-1643

ANGELS & US

3257 SE Hawthorne Blvd.
Portland, OR 97214

PENNSYLVANIA

ANGEL, MY ANGEL

549 S. Main St.
Shrewsbury, PA 17361
    Retail store. Phone: (717) 235-7057

ANGELS LANDING

347 Butterfly Lane
Hermitage, PA 16148
    Small retail store. Phone: (412) 342-4942

HEAVENLY SCENTS

5827 Stony Hill Rd.
New Hope, PA 18938
    Cherubs and angels; retail and wholesale.

JEANMARIE'S ANGELS

RD 4, Box 64LE
Saylorsburg, PA 18353
    Hand-made angels; retail and wholesale.

TENNESSEE

CARROT-TOP & CO.

1710 Jackson Sq. Dr.
Hixson, TN 37343
    Angel gifts by mail order.

MAMRE PRESS

107-AFS. 2nd Ave.
Murfreesboro, TN 37130
    Angel books; send SASE for catalog.

TEXAS

CELESTIAL ANGELS

Hulen Mall
4800 S. Hulen St.

Ft. Worth, TX 76132
Retail store. Phone: (817) 294-5444

HEAVENLY TREASURES

5100 Beltline Rd. #248
Village On The Parkway
Dallas, TX 75240
Retail store. Phone: (214) 980-2645

IMAGES TO CHERISH

P.O. Box 59484
Dallas, TX 75229
Mail order angel catalog. Phone: 800-352-9939

SPECIAL SIGNATURES

11334 Earlywood Dr.
Dallas, TX 75218
Hand-painted cards, postcards, and original books of angel poetry and legends.

TIN ANGEL

1402 5th St.
Seabrook, TX 77586
Retail store. Phone: (713) 474-7978

VISUAL ENVIRONMENTS

1818 W. 36th St.
Austin, TX 78731
T-shirts, sweats, and personalized collages. Write for mail order catalog. Phone: (512) 482-0160

THE WHISTLING ANGEL

2420 Live Oak
San Angelo, TX 76901
Hand-crafted angels, stamps, etc.

UTAH

GUARDIAN ANGELS

Box 391 Trolly Sq.
Salt Lake City, UT 84102
Retail store; send $1.50 for catalog.

VERMONT

CREATIVE GIFTS

54 Horizon View Dr.
Colchester, VT 05446
Country-style heirloom angels.

VIRGINIA

AMONG THE ANGELS

402 Laskin Rd.
Virginia Beach, VA 23451
Retail store. Phone: (804) 491-3382

ANGELS GALLERY & GIFTS

14109 St. Germain Dr.
Centreville, VA 22020
Retail store; or write to P.O. Box 221281, Chantilly, VA 22021 for mail order catalog.

SOMETHING ANGELIC WITHIN™

1212 1/2 W. Cary
Richmond, VA 23220
Angel T-shirts, plus unique rubber stamps; send $1.00 for catalog.

UNLIMITED ANGELS

1900 Esquire Rd.
Richmond, VA 23235
Retail store. Phone: (804) 272-8893

CANADA

ANGEL TREASURES

5905 Franklin Ave.
Niagara Falls, Ontario CANADA
Retail store affiliated with Angel Treasures in Royal Oak, MI.
Phone: (905) 374-6188

ANGEL TREASURES

46 King St.
St. Jacobs, Ont. N0B 2N0 CANADA
Retail store affiliated with Angel Treasures in Royal Oak, MI.

ANGELS ONLY . . . AND FRIENDS

20439 Douglas Crescent
Langley BC Z3A 4B6 CANADA
   Retail store. Phone: (604) 534-
   2244

MEXICO

**CON ANGEL: DECORACIÓN Y
   REGALOS**

San Jerónimo 410 Col. Tlaltenango
Cuernavaca, Morelos 62170 MEXICO
   Retail store. Phone: 73-13-22-08

*World Wide Web (Internet)
Home Pages*

ANGELS ON THE NET

   Maintained by Karen Knowles and
   Mark Lufkin, "helping to bring the
   world closer to the angelic
   kingdom." URL:
   http://www.magicnet.net/~netangel

**THE FOOL'S JOURNEY—MARIE
   HADDAD**

1900 Vallejo, #201
San Francisco, CA 94123
   T-shirts and wearable art boutique.
   E-mail: tfj@namaste.com; URL:
   http://www.namaste.com/tfj/tfj.html

JUST WINGIN' IT

P.O. Box 7065
Riverside, CA 92513-7065
   Angel and New Age catalog.
   E-mail: jwi@jwi.com; URL:
   http://www.jwi.com/~jwi

ODE TO THE ANGELS MARKETING

P.O. Box 1041
Pt. Roberts, WA 98281-1041
   Angel boutique. E-mail:
   angels@islandnet.com; URL:
   http://www.islandnet.com/~angels/

SUN ANGELS INNOVATIONS

   Products, services (including
   interactive numerology readings)
   as well as links to related angel
   resources on the internet. URL:
   http://www.sun-angel.com/

Index

Ashanti, 12, 13
Asian philosophy, 272
Asimov, Isaac, 251
Asmodel, 292, 421
Asmodeus, **59**
Ass of Balaam, 65–66, *67*, 347–48
Assumption of Mary, *265*, 267
Assumption of the Virgin (Titian), *264*
Assyrian guard, 90, *90*, 216, 392–93
Astaroth, **59–60**
Astral body, 198
Astrology, **60–61**, *61*
    dance of hours in, 212–13
    and days of week, 122–25, *125*
    planets in, 331
The Astronomy (Cochin the Younger),
    61
Asuras, **62**, 220
Atar, as angel of fire, 21
Attarib, 357
Attila the Hun, invades Rome, 68
Atuniel, as angel of fire, 21
Augustine, St., 93
    on angels, 95
    on Devil, 253–54
    on sons of God, 363
Aureole (halo, nimbus), 56, 196–98,
    197, 216, 217
Aurora borealis (northern lights), 407
Authors. *See also* Literature, angels in
    evangelical, **150–51**
Autumn, 357
Averroës, 285
Avicenna, 285
Azariel, 255
Azazel, **62–63**, 413
    and Shemhazai, 371

B

ba, 141
Baal, 70
Babylon, Jews relocated to, 153
Babylonians, 216
    influence of on Judaism, 415–16
Badagars, 68
Badr, battle of, 68, 302
    Mikhail and, 286
Bailey

Alice, 388
George, 98–100
Zuzu, 100
Balaam, 65–66, *67*
    in art of Rembrandt, 347–48
Balak, 65
Ball, Lucille, 295, *297*
Bamberger, Bernard J., 138–39
Bambuti, 13
Baradel, 377
Baraqijal (Baraqel), 413
Barbiel, 255, 292, 423
al-Barceloni, schema of planets and
    associated angels, 332
Barchiel, 292, 423
Baroque architecture, 47–48
Battle of Heaven, 96. *See also* War in
    Heaven
Battlefield
    angels on, **66–70**
    angels of Mons, 33–34
Bean, Orson, 384
Beatrice, of Dante's *Divine Comedy*,
    117, 118
Beatty, Warren, 298
Beatus of Liebana, *36*
Beauty, angels as, 365
Bede the Venerable, 324
Bedr, battle of. *See* Badr, battle of
Beelzebub, **70**
Belafonte, Henry, 296, *299*
Beliar, **70–71**
Belief in angels, resurgence in, 315–16
Beliel, **71**
Belphegor, **71–72**
bene'elim, 235
Bene elohim, 72, 206, 235
Berkeley, George, 272
Bernini, Gianlorenzo, 48
Beshter, 276
Beth-el, 230
*Between Earth and Heaven:
    Shakespeare, Dostoevsky, and the
    Meaning of Christian Tragedy*
    (Cox), 364, 368
Bible. *See also* Hebrew Scriptures; New
    Testament
    angels in, **72–74**
    first angels mentioned in, 90
    guardian angels in, 189
    influence of on Mark Twain, 396

Francis Xavier, 68

Fravashi, **165,** 186, 426

Free will, of angels, 390, 411

Freeman, Eileen Elias, 36, **165–67,**
191–92, 201, 245

French, Victor, 386

Freyja, 407

Friday, 124

Furnace, angel of, 6, **22,** 170

Fylgja (fylgir), **167**

G

Gabriel, **169–73,** *171, 172,* 423. *See
also* Djibril
and Abraham, *222*
as angel of fire, 21
at Annunciation, 8, *8,* 95, 263–66,
264
in Catholic Church doctrine, 94
feast day of, 209
female character of, 169–70, 174
guards Israel, 139
in Islam, 135–36
and Joan of Arc, 234
in Joseph's dream, 103
as man clothed in linen, 261
Milton's view of, 289, 290
and Moses, 403
and Muhammad, 300
rulership of, 123, 135, 143, 213,
292, 332, 357, 360, 402
as sefiroth, 358
in Talmud, 381, 382
as television angel, 384
and Zechariah, 265

Gadreel, 414

Gandharvas, **173–74**

Ganz (movie angel), 299

Garcia Marquez, Gabriel, 251

Garden of Eden. *See also* Gates of Eden
Adam and Eve ejected from, 5, *6, 9*
cherubim as guards of, 90
guardians of, 393

Garden of Gethsemane, 74, *75*

Gargatel, 357

Garnier, Charles, 48

Gatekeepers of heaven
Hadraniel as, 195

Kemuel as, 241

Gates of Eden. *See also* Garden
of Eden
angel at, 402
cherubim at, 6, 9, 90, 393

Gaul, Goths invade, 68

Gaviel, 357

Gender of angels, **174,** 362
artistic representation of, 57, 58
Thomas Aquinas on, 363

Genesis, fall of angels in. *See* Sons of
God

Genii, 43–44, 230, 231
as guardian spirits, 113

Geonic mystics, 224

Georgian, Linda, 190

Gethsemane, garden of, 74, *75*

Gevurah, 357

Ghosts, vs. angels, **174–75**

Giants
in Book of Enoch, 146–47
Nephilim as, 313

Gibbor the Giant (Nimrod), 105

Ginzberg, Louis, 222, 243, 276, 278,
403

Giotto, *57,* 58, **175–78,** *177, 197*
representation of angels by, 176

Giovanna D'Arco (Verdi), 307

Giovanni, Benvenuto di, *264*

Glasson, Francis, 71

Glory of Angels, 56

Gnomes, 143, **178–79**

Gnosis, 179

Gnostic Christianity, 128, 179

Gnosticism, **179**
Abraxas and, 4–5
aeons in, 11–12
archons in, 51–52
demiurge in, 128
Essenes and, 126
Hadraniel in, 195
Nergal in, 314
Raguel in, 339
schema of planets and associated
archons in, 332
seven heavens in, 360
Sophia in, 373
threshold guardians in, 393

The Gnostics and Their Remains (King),
291

Goblins, **180,** 336

H

ha-Cohen, Isaac, 358
Hadith (Traditions of the Prophet), 221, 303
Hadraniel, **195–96**
Hafaza, **196**, 221
Halo (nimbus; aureole), **196–98**, *197*
    in angel iconography, 56, 216, 217
HALOS (Helping Angel Lovers Own Stores) organization, 24
Ham, Mordecai, 180
Hamaliel, 292, 423
Hamlet (Shakespeare), 249, 367, 369, 370
Hammerstein, Reinhold, 305
Hamshalim, 206
Hanael, 292, 423
Haniel, 358
Haoma, 420
Harps, 305
    in angel iconography, 216
    and the music of heaven, **198–99**
Harut and Marut, **199–200**. *See also* Shemhazai and Azazel
Hashmalim, 357
Hasidim, angels in, 237
Hasmed, 35
Hauck, Rex, 311
Haughey, Karen M., **107**
Haurvatat, 210
Haynes, Hilda, 383
Hayward, Captain Cecil, 34
Hayyoth, **200**, 206
    Israel (angel) as, 223–24
Hayyoth hakodesh, 357
Healing, angelic, **201–2**
Heaven Can Wait (film), 296–98
Heaven and Hell (Swedenbörg), 377
Heaven Help Us (television series), 386
Heavenly bodies, to Greek philosophers, 185
The Heavenly Kid (film), 298
Heavenly scribe, 274
Heaven(s), *202,* **202–3**
    Dante's concept of, 119
    and Hell, *202,* 202–3
    Islamic, 211
    in movies, 295
    music of, 198–99
    seven, 359–61, 360

Shakespeare's concept of, 364, 366
    Swedenbörg's concept of, 378
    war in, **411–13,** *412*
    in Western religions, 76
Hebrew Myths (Graves), 358
Hebrew patriarchs, as thrones, 394
Hebrew prophets. *See* specific prophet, e.g., Elijah
Hebrew Scriptures. *See also* Old Testament
    angels in, 55, 73–74, *75,* 93, 235
    dragon in, 138
    eschatology in, 145
    Gabriel in, 169, 170
    Satan in, 354
    seraphim in, 359
    Yahweh vs. dragon in, 137–38
Hegel, Georg, 272
Heikhalot, 424
Heliodorus, punishment of, 7–8
Hell
    Christian concept of, 133
    Dante's concept of, 117–18, *118*
    heaven and, *202,* **202–3**
    Muslim sinners in, 259
    Shakespeare's concept of, 364
Hemah, 35
Hempstead, J. Hardy (television angel), 384
Henry IV (Shakespeare), 368
Henry V (Shakespeare), 367, 369
Henry VIII (Shakespeare), 365, 367, 368, 369
Herculaneum, winged figures at, 43
Here Comes Mr. Jordan (film), 296
Hermes (Mercury), 183, *203,* **203–4**
Herod, death of, 330–31
Heroes, origin of, 72. *See also* Nephilim
Hesed, 357
Hesiod, 304
Hexham, Irving, 326
Heywood, Thomas, 52
Hezekiah, 7
Hierarchy of angels, 55, 92, **204–6,** *205*
    angels (lowest choir) in, 33
    archangels in, 41, 95–96
    basis of in Ezekiel's vision, 153–54
    cherubim in, 89–90, *90, 91*
    Christian doctrine of, 96–97
    Dante's, 119

Index

Angels A to Z 469

M

O

P

S

in angel iconography, 216–17
and angels on stamps, 374
in Christian art, 56
of Cupid, 112
in early Christianity, 43
in Mesopotamian iconography, 271
of Michael, 278
as motif in architecture, 42, 43
Satan's (Dante), 118
Wings of Desire (film), 299
Winter, 357
Wisdom
of angels, 310
femininity of, 372–73
Wisdom of Solomon, 372–73
Wisdom (post-biblical) literature,
415–17
Wise woman of Tekoah, 310
Witchcraft, Satan and, 356
Witches, familiars of, 160, 218
Wizard of Oz, (film) 135
Women as angels, Shakespeare's
concept of, 369–70
The Work of the Holy Angels (Opus
Sanctorum Angelorum), 190
World War I, angels of Mons in, 33–34,
69
World War II, angel sightings during, 69
Wormwood, **417–18**
Wright, Elsie, 110–11
Writing
of angels, 378
automatic or inspired, 88

Y

Yahweh
in early Judaism, 235
in Gnostic Christianity, 128
lesser, 274
and Leviathan, 247
vs. dragon, 137–38
Yaldabaoth, in Gnosticism, 128, 179
Yama, 19
Yao, 13
Yazatas, 165, **419–20,** 426
Yesod, 357
Yoruba, orishas of, 13, 320–21
Young, Loretta, *297*

Your Guardian Angels (Georgian), 190
Yumboes, 83

Z

Zabayniya, 259
Zacharias, Gabriel appears to, 95
Zachary, Pope, 339, 377
Zadkiel (Tzadkiel, Zidekiel), 332, 357,
420
Zagzagel, **420–21**
Zakun, and Lahash, 243
Zebhul (or Machanon) (fourth heaven),
361
Zebul (or Makhon) (sixth heaven), 361
Zechariah, Gabriel and, 265
Zerachiel. *See* Sariel
Ziggurats, 229
Zodiac, angels of the, **421–23,** *422*
Zohar, **423–24**
angels in, 237
Gabriel in, 21, 403
Hadraniel in, 195
on Hayyoth, 200
hierarchy of angels in, 206
Metatron in, 274, 275
Nuriel in, 318
Sammael in, 352
Zadkiel in, 420
Zophiel, **425**
Zophiel (Del Occidente), 425
Zoroaster (Zarathustra), 419, 425
and archangels, 92–93
and Vohu Manah, 410
Zoroastrianism, 92–93, **425–27**
final judgment in, 160
fravashi in, 165
good vs. evil in, 149
influence of on Judaism, 63, 235,
236
Rashnu in, 346
Vohu Manah in, 409, 410
Zorokothera, 269
Zuriel, 292, 423